Between Byzantine Men

The presence and importance of same-sex desire between men in the Byzantine Empire has been understudied. While John Boswell and others tried to open a conversation about desire between Byzantine men decades ago, the field reverted to emphasis on prohibition and an inability to read the evidence of same-sex desire between men in the sources. *Between Byzantine Men: Desire, Homosociality, and Brotherhood in the Medieval Empire* challenges and transforms this situation by placing at center stage Byzantine men's desiring relations with one another.

This book foregrounds desire between men in and around the imperial court of the 900s. Analysis of Greek sources (many untranslated until now) and of material culture reveals a situation both more liberal than the medieval West and important for its rite of brother-making (*adelphopoiesis*), which was a precursor to today's same-sex marriage. This book transforms our understanding of Byzantine elite men's culture and is an important addition to the history of sex and desire between men.

Between Byzantine Men will appeal to scholars and general readers who are interested in Byzantine History, Society, and Culture, the History of Masculinity, and the History of Sexuality.

Mark Masterson is Associate Professor of Classics at Te Herenga Waka/ Victoria University of Wellington, New Zealand. He is the author of *Man to Man: Desire, Homosociality and Authority in Late-Roman Manhood* (2014), as well as a number of articles and book chapters on sexuality and masculinity. He is also one of editors of the collection, *Sex in Antiquity: Exploring Gender and Sexuality in the Ancient World* (2015).

Between Byzantine Men

Desire, Homosociality, and Brotherhood
in the Medieval Empire

Mark Masterson

LONDON AND NEW YORK

First published 2022
by Routledge
4 Park Square, Milton Park, Abingdon, Oxon OX14 4RN

and by Routledge
605 Third Avenue, New York, NY 10158

Routledge is an imprint of the Taylor & Francis Group, an informa business

© 2022 Mark Masterson

The right of Mark Masterson to be identified as author of this work has been asserted in accordance with sections 77 and 78 of the Copyright, Designs and Patents Act 1988.

All rights reserved. No part of this book may be reprinted or reproduced or utilised in any form or by any electronic, mechanical, or other means, now known or hereafter invented, including photocopying and recording, or in any information storage or retrieval system, without permission in writing from the publishers.

Trademark notice: Product or corporate names may be trademarks or registered trademarks, and are used only for identification and explanation without intent to infringe.

British Library Cataloguing-in-Publication Data
A catalogue record for this book is available from the British Library

Library of Congress Cataloging-in-Publication Data
A catalog record has been requested for this book

ISBN: 978-0-815-35382-9 (hbk)
ISBN: 978-1-032-28444-6 (pbk)
ISBN: 978-1-351-13523-8 (ebk)

DOI: 10.4324/9781351135238

Typeset in Times New Roman
by codeMantra

Contents

Acknowledgments vii
A Note on Translations viii
A Note on Transliteration of Greek (and Related Matters) viii
A Note on the End Notes viii
List of abbreviations ix

Introduction 1
Prelude: Letter 44 *of Nikephoros Ouranos 1*
What This Book Does and How It Does It 4
A Christian Empire 5
Letter 26 *of Nikephoros Ouranos 6*
A Comparison 9
Civil Law 11
Canon Law/Penitentials 12
Men in the Life of Mary the Younger *13*
Prospect 15

1 **Eroticism and Desire in Epistolography** 24
How to Read Byzantine Epistolography 25
Letters of Theodoros Daphnopates 26
   Letter 18 27
   Letter 17 30
Desire's Dreams and Visions in Letters of an Emperor
   and His Friend 38
   Dreams and Visions in the *Suda* 39
   A Letter from Constantine 41
   A Letter from Theodoros 46
Two Letters of Symeon the Logothete 49
Conclusion 53

vi   Contents

**2   Histories of Masculine Beauty and Desire: The Case of
     Emperor Basil I**   67
     Historiographies from the Mid-Tenth Century 68
     Narrative of the Rise of Basil I 69
     Summary of Things to Come 71
     Amorous Language 73
     Theophilitzes and Hetaireiai *74*
     The Emperor's Horse 77
     Grappling and a Naked Scourging 79
     Basilikinos/Basiliskianos: Handsome Competition 85
     Eagle and Ganymede 90
     Male Backsides and Romans 101
     Conclusion 107

3   Framing the Brotherhoods of Emperor Basil I   121
     Basil's Brotherhoods in the Historiographies 122
        Nicholas 122
        John 128
        Other Brothers 135
     Liturgies for the Adelphopoiesis *Ritual 135*
     *A Tenth-Century Prayer: "A Thing Flowery and Much-desired
        by Us, The Sweet Scent of Love" 139*
     *Framing "A Thing Flowery and Much-desired by Us, The
        Sweet Scent of Love" 146*
        Scripture 146
        Court Ceremonial and Epistolography 148
     Conclusion 153

   Appendix of Prayers   155

4   Revisiting the Bachelorhood of Emperor Basil II   169
     Introduction 169
     The State of the Question of Basil's Bachelorhood 170
     Symeon the New Theologian's Evidence 174
     Basil II as Symeon's Referent 178
     Conclusion 184

   Conclusion   193

   Works Cited   205
      Major Primary Sources 205
      Secondary Sources 206
   Index   217

Acknowledgments

It has not been easy working on this book since the world changed so much, but friends have helped.

I have thanks to offer to the following:
   Jonathan Else for being a lovely thing in my life that I did not expect to see again;
   Hugh Young, Tim Bish, and Lars Anderson for being vitally interested and supportive;
   Alex Drummond and Lynn Peace have been there for me too;
   Richard Arnold, Dougal McNeill, and Yiyan Wang have made me smile often;
   A shout-out to the Enigma Café Staff for being so friendly while I typed this book into my computer;
   to Anne Else, whom I am so pleased to know;
   to Zdravko Lulich for his support.
   My scholar friends from around the world have likewise been supportive: Stephanie Cobb, Derek Krueger, Nancy Rabinowitz, Amy Richlin, Steven Smith, Shaun Tougher;
   On line, I have enjoyed the interest and banter of Ben Cartlidge, Rebecca Colesworthy, Stephen Guy-Bray, and Giacomo Sanfilippo.
   Frank Garrett ran an online seminar on Nietzsche throughout 2021 which was a wonderful diversion and I learned things.
   Christabel Marshall has been my research assistant and student for a number of years and is also a good friend. She helped me a number of times throughout the process of writing this book.
   I miss seeing my friend Barbara Gold in New York.
   I miss my friends in California: Gary Matus, Dan Sheehan, and, most of all, Park Neely;
   I miss Deborah Hollingsworth back in California, and we both miss Timothy Heartt (DM).
   I thank the Classics Programme and the School of Languages and Cultures at Victoria University of Wellington, New Zealand. I also especially wish to thank Lisa Lowe, Ida Li, and Lagi Aukusitino in the School

of Languages and Cultures, Gerry Keating at Image Services, and Tess Tuxford in the Research Office;

I also thank the Royal Society of New Zealand for the Marsden Grant which did so much to help this project along, and the Dumbarton Oaks Research Library for a Summer Fellowship in 2015 and also for being so welcoming when I was in the neighborhood again in 2018;

Lastly, I thank Michael Greenwood, Louis Nicholson-Pallett, and Assunta Petrone at the press for their help in getting this project across the line.

And Nelson.

A Note on Translations

Unless otherwise specified, all translations are my own.

A Note on Transliteration of Greek (and Related Matters)

As I most often have the words in Greek nearby that I am converting into the Latin alphabet, I have decided that it is unnecessary to use macrons and other such things, unless I am quoting someone's scholarship that is using them. This means, to take some examples, that an o in the Latin script can be omicron or omega, and an e can be either epsilon or eta. How this works will be clear enough and any confusion can be cleared up by the Greek that is almost invariably nearby.

If I am quoting a noun or adjective or a verb in isolation, the reader may anticipate that I am using the Nominative singular for the noun, the Nominative singular masculine for the adjective, and the first person singular present indicative for the verb. When I am quoting directly from a passage, I will quote/transliterate the form that appears there. Words will sometimes look different, as Greek is inflected.

Sometimes I use English translations of the names of works, e.g., *On Imperial Reigns*, while at other times the Latin titles, e.g., *Theophanes Continuatus*. I would be grateful for patience as the field as a whole has many customs and one ends up following the practice of the people whom one reads. A perfect solution here is elusive.

Lastly, if a name is common enough in English usage, e.g., Constantine or Basil, I have used the anglicization. If it is uncommon, then I have transliterated the Greek (and I tend to avoid Latinization of names). An exception: I opted to keep Paulos (and not Paul) as Nikephoros' correspondent because the Apostle Paul figures in comments that concern Paulos and Nikephoros. It seemed much easier that way. In any case: again a perfect solution is not to be found.

A Note on the End Notes

Notes are included in this book to provide references or add supplemental material of various kinds, e.g., the Greek texts, additional explanations, expansions. While the notes are not irrelevant, the argument of the book proceeds independently of them and curiosity is the reason to consult them.

Abbreviations

AB	=	*Analecta Bollandiana*
BMGS	=	*Byzantine and Modern Greek Studies*
ByzSt	=	*Byzantine Studies/Études byzantines*
CMH	=	*The Cambridge Medieval History*
DOCat	=	*Catalogue of the Byzantine and Early Mediaeval Antiquities in the Dumbarton Oaks Collection*
DOP	=	*Dumbarton Oaks Papers*
DOSeals	=	*Catalogue of Byzantine Seals at Dumbarton Oaks and in the Fogg Museum of Art*
FM	=	*Fontes Minores*
JDAI	=	*Jahrbuch des Deutschen Archäologischen Instituts*
JMedHist	=	*Journal of Medieval History*
JÖB	=	*Jahrbuch der Österreichischen Byzantinistik*
JWalt	=	*Journal of the Walters Art Gallery*
Lampe	=	Lampe and Liddell, *A Patristic Greek Lexicon*
LSJ	=	Liddell, Scott, Jones, and McKenzie, *A Greek–English Lexicon*
MUSJ	=	*Mélanges de l'Université Saint-Joseph, Beirut*
OCP	=	*Orientalia christiana periodica*
ODB	=	*Oxford Dictionary of Byzantium*
OHBS	=	*The Oxford Handbook of Byzantine Studies*
PG	=	*Patrologia Graeca*
SBMünch	=	*Sitzungsberichte der Bayerischen Akademie der Wissenschaften, Philosophisch-historische Klasse*
TLG	=	*Thesaurus Linguae Graecae*

Introduction

Prelude: *Letter 44* **of Nikephoros Ouranos**

This account of desire and sociability between men in the Byzantine Empire in the tenth and early eleventh centuries commences with a letter written circa 1000 by Nikephoros Ouranos: *Letter 44*. Nikephoros was a writer[1] and noted political figure in the long reign (976–1025) of Emperor Basil II. His career was spectacular.[2] After holding a number of offices, military, civil, and even lay religious, he was *doux* (military commander) of Antioch and "Master of the East,"[3] a to that time unparalleled title, in the first decade of the eleventh century.[4] Nikephoros held the highest degree of trust of the gloomy and untrusting Emperor Basil II.[5] Nikephoros apparently also was a eunuch.[6] *Letter 44* is one of five letters that Nikephoros wrote to Paulos *Krites*.[7] Paulos was *krites* ("judge") of the Hippodrome and the Armeniak theme,[8] and the testimony of a lead seal shows he was *protospatharios* (a dignity in the imperial hierarchy)[9] and *kourator* (administrator of imperial holdings) in addition.[10] Both of these men existed within close proximity to the emperor. Note the presence of desire in this communication from one man to another at a pinnacle of Byzantine society:

> To Paulos *Krites*:
> If you practice silence until now, schooling (*paideuon*/παιδεύων) or testing me, let it be enough for you of school (*paideias*/παιδείας) and test, whether I am liable to charges of many great faults against you, or even that no time before this moment has brought you satisfaction where I am concerned. Look, while being schooled (*paideuomenoi*/παιδευόμενοι) and not being worthy of a word from you, do I stop asking you about your affairs and worrying about them, or do I give in and get in there to dare to write first, so that, whether blamed on account of daring or accepted on account of affection, I may in any case get writing or a word (from you), whether longed for by me and lovable or even threatening and scolding? For this voice (of yours) is longed for by me, just as assaults and blows are by lovers (*erosi*/ἐρῶσι) from their beloveds (*eromenon*/ἐρωμένων). Or just as the river's flow is by those who thirst, the flow

DOI: 10.4324/9781351135238-1

that is, on the one hand, fearful, huge, and threatening to sweep away the one who approaches, but, nevertheless, is clear, cool, and sweetest. Therefore let it be thus for me, whether you praise me, accuse me, or take hands to me to treat me roughly, only may you write, providing things pleasant and sufficient to comfort me, and may you have your fill of game-playing (*paidias*/παιδιᾶς) or school (*paideias*/παιδείας).

(Nikephoros Ouranos, *Letter 44*)[11]

Wanting a letter from Paulos, Nikephoros depicts the epistolary silence he endures as punishment.[12] And, it's not fair, as he cares about Paulos' affairs. In any case, like a needy boyfriend who texts too much, he persists in writing, hoping for attention and abasing himself. Any word, even if it's negative, will do, for it would at least be attention. Referring to *eromenoi*/ἐρώμενοι (boy beloveds, known from classical Greece) and their lovers (*erontes*/ἐρῶντες), which is a synonym for the better known *erastai*/ἐρασταί, Nikephoros casts himself as the poorly treated lover to Paulos' physically abusive beloved. Nikephoros also compares Paulos to an enticing, yet perilous river. The letter concludes with a plea, again, for attention of any kind and for an end to the games and hard-hearted schooling Paulos puts Nikephoros through.

Desire is present in a number of ways in this letter. *Eromenoi* and *erontes* have already been noted. Both of these words call to mind the prominent Greek word for sexual desire: *eros*/ἔρως. There are mentions of affection (*philtron*/φίλτρον), and a voice that's longed for (*potheines*/ποθεινῆς) and desired (*eperastou*/ἐπεράστου), the latter again related to *eros*. Another set of words, those for school(ing) (*paideia*/παιδεία), to school (*paideuo*/παιδεύω), and game-playing (*paidia*/παιδιά), all have a discernible relation to the word *pais* (παῖς). *Pais* means boy, and it is a word sexualized in the context of this letter, since it is a *pais* who can be an *eromenos*, and therefore an object of sexual desire.

But it is not just the sexy and desirous vocabulary, recognizable to men of this educated milieu, that foregrounds same-sex desire in these words from one man to another, the dangerous and yet beautiful river that appears toward the end of the letter does so also:

...this voice (of yours) is longed for by me, just as assaults and blows are by lovers from their beloveds. Or just as the river's flow is by those who thirst, the flow that is, on the one hand, fearful, huge, and threatening to sweep away the one who approaches, but, nevertheless, is clear, cool, and sweetest.

That desired voice, whose effect Nikephoros compares to the impacts that can characterize raucous relations between beloveds and lovers, is like a physically imposing river that promises peril, while also being beautiful and welcoming. And as the sexy vocabulary noted above calls carnal things to the minds of educated writers and readers, Nikephoros' metaphorical great river does the same via intertextuality.[13]

Since this river is a great channel of water that both causes awe and yet attracts in the context of same-sex desire, it recalls and is intertextual with the famous sea of beauty from Plato's *Symposium*, a work known to the men of this milieu. In her description of the ladder of love, Diotima tells how the lover, who proceeds in the correct way, moves from desire for individual bodies to the more abstract beauties of institutions and eventually receives a transcendent vision of singular beauty. Diotima uses the metaphor of a "mighty sea":

> And [the idealized lover] looking now to mighty beauty and no longer like a slave, low and of little account, being servile and loving the beauty in one thing—the beauty of a boy or some man, or a particular institution—but turned to and gazing upon the mighty sea of beauty, he brings to birth the beautiful and magnificent words and conceptions in plentiful philosophy, until strengthened and made greater, he should thereupon gaze on a single beauty...
>
> (Plato, *Symposium* 210D)[14]

This moment of intertextuality with a well-known passage in the celebrated *Symposium* naturally comes to mind, as *Letter 44* has a number of the same things on its mind: same-sex desire, physicality, a great body of water. A reader of this passage from Plato may balk a little at this idealization from Golden-Age Greece. After all, the progress to the single abstract beauty is not an easy one as it commences with a physical lure: a boy or man. Is transcending equilibrium possible, if we are still on earth amid handsome bodies? Knowledge of this intertext suggests that Nikephoros, who speaks of assaults and rough handling, has not risen above this earthly plane. Still, a sea is not a river, and Nikephoros failing while Diotima limns a possible path to sublimation puts space between letter and Platonic dialogue. But the glamour of the *Symposium* means it is always a likely intertext and meaning happens, as here, through the later text diverging from the earlier. But the *Symposium* need not be the only intertext. It may be sharing the stage.

For example, in the tenth of Philostratus the Elder's *Letters* (third century CE), the narrator addresses a younger male beloved, who in the passage appears as a fetching shepherd, seems born of the sea like Aphrodite, and surpasses flowers in a meadow. Finally, when the narrator comes to a river, he thinks of the young man as an elementally beautiful river that surpasses the sea:

> If I come [to you] as some traveler on the road, you seem to me to mind your flock and sit, while charming the rocks. And if I come to the sea, the sea produces you, just as the deep did Aphrodite. And if to a meadow, you surpass the flowers themselves, although no such thing grows there, for if they are beautiful and graceful elsewise, they are but of one day.

And indeed, while being near a river, I do not know how it has vanished, but I form a mental image of you flowing beautiful (*kalon*/καλόν), great, and much greater than the sea.

(Philostratus the Elder, *Letter 10*)[15]

If anything, this is closer to the Nikephoros' letter than the glamorous Plato. In both Philostratus and Nikephoros desire, a river, and overwhelming feelings that threaten to swamp an attracted narrator appear, and both are letters too.[16]

In summation, *Letter 44* not only portrays the feelings Nikephoros has with words of same-sex desire, e.g., words related to *eros*, *pais*, and the others of affection and desire, it also calls the things of desire to mind through imagery to be found in earlier texts that are also concerned with same-sex desire. Indeed, *Letter 44*'s depictions of mental erotic obsession and (even violent) carnality bulk larger in the reader's perception in proportion to the level of the reader's education. The letter wears its connection to high levels of education on its sleeve, as it were: it tropes incessantly on *paideia* (school, education); the Greek is elevated; the language looks back to golden-age Greece; the imagery is extravagant and literary. It encourages the educated mind to ponder, discover, and admire. *Letter 44* documents a connection between these two men and suggests ways for Paulos (and us now) to envision Paulos' connection to Nikephoros.

What This Book Does and How It Does It

Documentation of same-sex desire in history is an important activity and is what is owed to truth. The foregoing analysis of *Letter 44* that centered desire was true to this goal. The analysis paid attention both to the surface of the letter and to things that may have come to mind on the basis of competencies Byzantine writers and readers possessed, and the result was a reparative reading of the letter. Reparative readings of historical sources favor happy affect and envision, speculatively, wholes from parts. These readings are also attuned to contingency and the unexpected. Regulation and disapproval are not as much a consideration (though they will receive attention) as bodily life and the desires and fantasies that attend it. In other words, teleological narratives that harmonize everything under the watchful eyes of canon and civil law and the diffuse ideals of behavior proper to men or *andres* are not what the reader will find in this book. Rather there will be reparative narratives of individual contexts that are askew to broader prospects and which even run athwart them. But this is not a bad thing, as it is clear from the source material that Byzantium was a place of multiple discourses.[17]

Discussions to come are predicated on four assumptions about the evidence. The first and second assumptions are that the men spoken of in this book possessed high degrees of education or *paideia* and that intertextuality in the written records to be discussed is therefore interpretable. In terms of *paideia*, these were men who knew the New Testament and the Septuagint[18] well. They also knew the Greek classics, frequently better than scholars do now and bodies of work from late antiquity by writers such as Gregory Nazianzenus or Gregory of Nyssa.[19] The assumption about *paideia* naturally supports the assumption about intertextuality. Intertextual analysis assumes that quotation or reference to an earlier text, Christian or pagan, was recognizable *and* interpretable. This meant that when these men were communicating with one another via a text that alluded to an earlier text or texts, there is reason to believe that the reader would have awareness of what was said in the earlier text and how it compared to the situation in the later text. Intertextuality is a common feature of Byzantine texts,[20] and is discernable in many of the texts appearing in this book. The comparison between these texts in the reader's mind provides semantic depth and an additional way to make meaning then *and now*. While it is speculative to a degree, and calls to mind things not visible, i.e., actions "off-stage" and desires/thoughts/fantasies, interpretation of intertextuality is both a resource to the scholar now and is true to the mode of communication of the men of this educated milieu. Analysis of intertextuality mirrors what happened in the tenth and early eleventh centuries.[21]

The third assumption is that texts don't just reflect reality, they also help make it. Letters and histories that have same-sex desire and intimations of same-sex relations in them, don't just tell what was being thought of, they would have provoked such things. The textual and occasional material evidence[22] in this book are viewed from the angle that they both reflected *and* created the realities in which they played a part.[23]

The fourth assumption is that same-sex desire and same-sex sexual behavior have no necessary character, i.e., are indeterminate, or, alternatively, possess indeterminacy. This means that they have discernable existence prior to any judgment of their significance or morality; they exist and acquire meaning only in context. This assumption is difficult to hold on to, as it demands analytical distance on things (desire, sexual behavior) that often attract judgment in the sources. But measured appraisal of the Byzantine evidence shows that same-sex desire and intimations of sexual behavior are to be seen in the sources with happy affect associated with them, even as civil law and church canon forbid the behavior. This divergence of views on desire and sexual behavior points to their nature as prior to judgment and to their indeterminacy, for they are associated not only with sin and illegality, but also with pleasure, friendship, brotherhood, and religion. An important corollary to this non-necessary, indeterminate character is that reparative narratives free of the need to genuflect to teleologies of civil law or ecclesiastical stricture can be written. While prohibition and censure are certainly to be found in the sources, not all narratives need to end in the semantic closure of prohibition.[24]

A Christian Empire

This book *at times* sets aside church teachings on same-sex desire and sexual behavior because differing valuations of sex present in the sources show

6 *Introduction*

that it was indeterminate, i.e., sex and desire were perceptibly prior to moral judgment and possessed no necessary meaning or significance. However, because Byzantium was an assertively Christian state, it will not do to move blithely from this phenomenological fact to reparative narration of this counter-discourse that views matters of desire and sex differently. There is need to pause and work through how these two discourses, one offering a negative valuation and the other a positive one, coexisted in devout Byzantium. Respect for what was true of many Byzantine persons' lives and for decades of scholarship that mostly has centered prohibition demands this.[25] In the end, the position of this book is that while there was a dominant negative discourse with civil and ecclesiastical power behind it, it shared the stage with another perspective. Indeed, as will be seen in the third chapter, an elaborate prayer for brotherhood is arguably intertextual with the language of same-sex desire seen in epistolography and historiography from court circles. And in the fourth chapter, a reparative presentation of contemporary thoughts about the bachelorhood of Emperor Basil II showcases the surprising role that same-sex desire plays in the formation of properly religious masculinity in Symeon the New Theologian's directions to his monks.[26] But at this moment, it is time for another letter of Nikephoros Ouranos. This letter shows the coexistence of devotion to the church with both practices of desire and intimations of physical activities at odds with this devotion.

Letter 26 of **Nikephoros Ouranos**

Nikephoros wrote *Letter 26*, like *Letter 44*, probably in the first decade 1000s.[27] The addressee is Nicholas, Metropolitan of Neokaisareia in Pontus, who was likely somewhat younger than Nikephoros[28]:

> To Nicholas, Metropolitan of Neokaisareia:
>   As much as I am frozen, my dear soul, by this bitterness of winter as I go about my daily business, to that extent do I every time bloom/sprout/bud (*thallomen*/θάλλομεν) with the hopes that the sweet spring of friendship, which straight up is time spent with you, already smiles upon me. Bloom/sprout/bud (*thalle*/θάλλε), therefore, for me, for the visit of your friend abandoning each sorrowful thing (if there are any), and anything autumnal or wintry. Let us, each other, together spend a spring prior to the season with our unifying God.
>   (Nikephoros Ouranos, *Letter 26*)[29]

In this warm letter written in a cold time, Nikephoros cheers himself with hopes of being with his friend Nicholas again. The calendar's progress promises eventual change to this situation, and Nikephoros, a flower in bud, has sprouted in anticipation. Portraying their friendship as Spring itself no matter the season, Nikephoros and Nicholas, encouraged by Nikephoros, are happy flowers that unfurl from bud into bloom or shoots that grow in their happy relation, which God blesses.

This letter, which attests to warm, man-to-man homosociality between these men of exalted rank, invites analysis. As these men are men of *paideia*, what understandings could they, educated and subtle readers, generate from this text? What kind of intertextualities might be present?

To start with, there are sexual double-entendres. At the surface level, the notion of blooming/budding/sprouting connects to male tumescence with ease. Viewing the already blooming Nikephoros asking Nicholas to bloom for him in a desiring and sexual register perhaps seems audacious, but audacity gains credibility when we consider the fact that these men are steeped in scripture and pagan literature. A survey of *thallo*/θάλλω and compounded and cognate forms in both scripture and the pagan literature shows why. "Time spent with" along with "straight-up" is indicative also.

In scripture, *thallo*/θάλλω and related forms more than once designate the growth of plant life.[30] Fire can, as it were, bloom.[31] It appears in relation to the human body that has been restored with the help of God:

> The Lord is my helper and my shieldsman. My heart hopes with his help. I have been aided and my flesh sprouted forth (*anethalen*/ἀνέθαλεν). From my will I shall sing forth grateful praises to him.
>
> (Ps 27/28:7)[32]

At Phil 4:10, *anathallo* has a figurative meaning: "You made your concern for me sprout/bud/blossom forth."[33] And at Pr 15:13, *thallo* designates an interconnected relationship between feelings and physicality: "when the heart is rejoicing, the countenance blooms."[34]

And so, scripture shows the stirring of plant life and human body. There is also a connection between this physical stirring and emotional engagement. Phenomenologically, scripture suggests the possibility of male tumescence, and especially if emotions and feelings are erotic. But Nikephoros and Nicholas were not only knowledgeable about scripture, they were educated in pagan literature. Two epigrams in the *Greek Anthology* may have inflected Nicholas' understanding and inspired Nikephoros' writing of *Letter 26*.

The *Greek Anthology*, compiled by Constantine Kephalas around 900,[35] was present in educated circles throughout the tenth century.[36] This collection of epigrams, many of which are sexual in nature (especially the fifth and twelfth books), provides evidence of how the language of sprouting forth/ blooming and Spring was adjacent to same-sex desire and, by implication, to male tumescence. Here are two epigrams from the anthology that feature desirable boys as flowers that sprout and bloom in Spring:

> The Zephyr-loving meadows don't thrive with such flowers, the glories of spring present everywhere, as the well-born boys you will see, Dionysius, things made by the hand of the Cyprus-Born and Graces. But

perhaps, outstanding among them, Milesios blooms (*thallei*/θάλλει), as a rose shining among the fragrant leaves. He perhaps does not know, like the fair flower in the heat, that his season hangs on by a hair.

(Strato, *Greek Anthology* 12.195)[37]

Having gathered with his hand the flower of boys, Eros arranged for you, Aphrodite, a garland to deceive a soul. For he twined Diodorus, the pleasing lily, and Asclepiades, the sweet white-violet. Yes indeed he plaited Herakleitos, as from thorn to rose, while a certain Dion, translucent on the vine, was blooming/budding (*ethalle*/ἔθαλλε). He joined together Theron, saffron-gold flowered in his foliage, and he pitched in Ouliades, a sprig of thyme. He plucked off luxuriously-leafed Myïskos, the always-blooming/sprouting (*aeithales*/ἀειθαλές) shoot of olive, and the sprays of Aretos that inspire desire. Happiest of islands, holy Tyre, which holds Kypris' myrrh-suffused flower-bearing grove of boys.

(Meleager, *Greek Anthology* 12.256)[38]

Strato (second century CE), whose male-directed epigrams predominate in the twelfth book of the anthology (which is devoted to the love of boys), and Meleager (first century BCE), whose interests range to women in addition, trope their desirable boys as flowers. In the case of Strato, he concludes his poem with the remark, via the metaphor of a Spring flower burned by Summer heat, that Milesios' beard will arrive and his desirability will at the same moment depart. Meleager presents the fanciful idea of a garland of eight boys that Eros has plaited for his mother Aphrodite. In both of these poems, there is desire for young men or boys as flowers or sprouting plant life. It is also the case that being a flower in bloom is to be the object of desire. Given that sprouting and blooming can be associated with male tumescence, it also suggests the desirability of an erect penis. Lastly, the second poem packs an erotic punch with the presence of both Eros and his mother Aphrodite.

There is another intertextuality in *Letter 26*, this time with Homer, in the phrases, "the sweet spring of friendship, which straight up is time spent with you."[39] This moment is significant because it reads as a double-entendre for sexual intercourse. "Time spent with you" (*he se suntuchia*/ἡ σὴ συντυχία) is sexualized by the word for "straight-up," *antikrus*/ἄντικρυς, if one remembers the *Iliad*. *Antikrus*/ἄντικρυς is a later variant of a word, *antikru*/ἄντικρύ, which occurs over 25 times in Homer. This word is memorable, as it is there when warriors die, designating the thrust of the warrior's weapon that delivers a piercing to finish an opponent off. Here to illustrate is an instance, chosen to drive home the present point especially. It is the slaughter of Phereklos by Meriones: "When indeed Meriones caught him [Phereklos] as he pursued, he struck him through the right buttock; the point went straight up through the bladder to the bone."[40] *Antikru*/ἄντικρύ is always describing something pointy going into flesh. It's a memorable adverb and in the context of Nikephoros' letter, this adverb imports penetrative gestural energy into the letter, giving point to *suntuchia*/συντυχία and sexualizing it.

Some summary observations now about this analysis of *Letter 26*. In the first place, it centers same-sex desire, regarding it as something to discover and measure, since it was a notable feature of this elite masculine culture. Second, knowledge from scripture and *paideia* enabled Nikephoros and Nicholas to craft, share, and/or receive understandings of their world. Third, the analysis is reparative. It starts from traces, in this case both talk of blooming/budding amid warm affect and the plausible presence of intertextualities, to imagine a relation that extended to carnal expression. It is of interest that these men write *in this way* in the letters (and there will be more about epistolography at the beginning of Chapter 1). And this leads to a fourth and final point: as texts both reflect and create reality, this letter, and indeed other texts produced by these men and men like them, both indicated the presence of same-sex desire in Byzantine masculine homosociality and helped produce it as a possibility to be pursued. The language did not merely record desire's presence, it provoked it.

While the enlacement of homoerotic discourse in *Letter 26* is considerable, there is the matter the letter's end. The togetherness to come of Nicholas and Nikephoros happens under the sign of divine approval: "let us, each other, together spend a spring prior to the season with our unifying God."[41] This ending imparts a religious aura to the letter at its end. Is it a possible reference to ritual or spiritual brotherhood (*adelphopoiesis*),[42] given that Nikephoros refers to a unifying God? A possible way to read this letter is to allow this last moment, through its mention of God, to drive interpretation of the entire letter and render the language of sex and desire as decarnalized. On this basis, it is all spiritual and there is nothing else to see here. A much better way to proceed is to keep both body/desire and God in view, as they are present together in this letter: let juxtaposition abide.

A Comparison

Althaus-Reid's book, *Indecent Theology*, offers a useful and clarifying comparison. She considers queer culture in Argentina of the later decades of the twentieth century and her ultimate goal is the elaboration of a changed and more humane theology that welcomes the broadest range possible of human sexual practices. She foregrounds sexuality and intimacy in the search to understand the sacred. Starting from the body to address theological questions is, in her varying formulations, sexual or indecent theology.[43] There are commonalities between with what she does and the reparative mode of reading being practiced in this book about Byzantine men. And while there are real differences, to put it mildly, between medieval Byzantium and modern Argentina, the comparison helps with perceiving the presence of something that is not supposed to be there, as it were. In the story of Father Mario, sexuality that is not approved of by a strong church achieves a degree of approval.[44] His story exemplifies how "indecent" theological thinking can be at work in people's notions of sexuality and, apropos to the strongly religious Byzantine Empire, how societies with powerful ecclesiastical hierarchies can nonetheless have dissent and zones where the usual rules don't apply.

In 1996, Father Mario, a young priest who served the poor in Buenos Aires, was murdered. His funeral was an elaborate occasion. Both persons high in the church hierarchy and his poor parishioners attended. In the weeks that followed, it emerged that he had been killed by a male prostitute in a dispute. There was also discovery of gay pornography in his residence. As this information came out, the church hierarchy distanced itself from Father Mario. It was different in the case of his poor flock, however. Television crews interviewed parishioners who refused to reject Father Mario, and there was even talk of building a chapel to bear his name. It also turned out that his sexual orientation was known and regarded as not worthy of concern, given all the good he had done. One of the parishioners expressed a wish that he could have spoken to them about his loneliness, so that he would not have put himself in danger and stayed among the people who loved him:

> For them, Father Mario was not gay, if by gay you mean that his life was defined only by the fact that he sometimes would sleep with men. He was gay, if by gay we mean a priest who fought for peace and social justice in his Christian Base Community and who was so full of love for his people that he also longed for abundant love in his own life, and for the love and company of another man. That is indecent theological thinking.
>
> (Althaus-Reid 2000, 138)

One could raise the objection that (some of) the parishioners would have wanted him to stay in the area where his ministry was, so that all the more easily he could have been kept in the closet. This is certainly possible, but Althaus-Reid argues for the presence of human understanding and recognition of desire. Many of his parishioners regretted his loneliness, and his sexual orientation was a secondary matter. And talk of a hoped-for chapel and wishes that he had stayed closer to his loving community are expressed after his erotic orientation to men had been made public. Rather than regard Mario's acceptance by his community as something inexplicable, Althaus-Reid explains that ideas of who could be a cherished member of community had been changing by 1996 among conservative poor parishioners in this very Catholic nation.[45] A capacious sense of justice nuanced and led to disregard of principles handed down by an ecclesiastical hierarchy that would cite, as authoritative, the sedimented and centuries-old understandings of sexual matters. In other words, a community may be given universalizing principles by their leadership, but contingent situations and sense of what is fair and just lead to a situation where these principles may be rejected:

> The community does not necessarily use universalizing principles, not even sexual ones, with ease all the time…communities decode the hidden values which are present and discern justice in the relationships already there.
> (Althaus-Reid 2000, 138–139)

What is supposed to be rejected, according to arid and anti-humanist strictures, flourishes because the people perceive a higher moral principle at work that commanded accepting love for Father Mario. The people wished that justice had been done where his desires for intimacy were concerned. "Sexual desire mobilizes people's concept of citizenship, and of justice."[46]

Althaus-Reid's narrative of acceptance and perception of higher justice in contravention of higher authorities is an inspiration. And while there is no need for a liberatory discourse to release Byzantine masculine homoeroticism from oppression (it, verbalized so lavishly by important personages, is hardly beleaguered), it is salutary to start from the facts of desire and imagine a scene in which there are divergent viewpoints on such desire and behavior.[47]

Above, via the letters of Nikephoros Ouranos, this book thus far has spoken of the positive side of the ledger, as it were, and there is much more about the positive presence of same-sex desire and behavior to come. But what of the opposing side that wished for restriction? What was the situation in law and according the church, for it is important to understand both sides of this question?

Civil Law

In these centuries, there were regulations in contemporary civil law codes, mandating execution for anal sex between males (although allowances were made for young offenders), but they appear to have been unused.[48] It has been suggested that the laws were just copied from code to code over the course of the centuries.[49] Here, from the year 741, is the first law:

> Let the *aselgeis*, both the one doing and the one submitting, be punished by the sword. But if the one submitting should be discovered to be less than twelve years old, let him be forgiven, since his age shows that he did not understand that to which he had submitted.
> (*Ekloge* 17.38)[50]

12 *Introduction*

Meant to guide a judge in his actions, this law addresses sexual activity directly. Anal penetration is at issue, and both the one penetrating and the one being penetrated are at fault. The two males are called *aselgeis*, or "shameless ones," and their penalty is execution ("punished by the sword"), though if it is a boy under 12 who is being penetrated, he will not be punished, as the writers of the law feel that he would not have understood the importance of what was happening.

As noted above, this law is the first in a sequence of laws that stretches into the tenth century. *Eklogadion* 17.6 (early ninth century),[51] *Epanagoge* 40.66 (886),[52] and *Prokheiros Nomos* 39.73 (907)[53] are all as terse as *Ekloge* 17.38, and they repeat it with but small variations.[54] The lack of enterprise in the writing of these laws, their apparent lack of use, and no recorded same-sex sex scandals in Byzantium's middle centuries supports what Angeliki Laiou had to say nearly 30 years ago:

> It is possible, despite all the normative zeal to prohibit homosexual acts, that Byzantine society in fact tolerated such acts if they did not cause a scandal.
>
> (1992, 78)[55]

This revolutionary statement, while not unheralded and occasionally followed up,[56] has not affected the study of Byzantine sexuality as much as it should have.

Canon Law/Penitentials

In contrast to inflexible, but brief and unused, enactments in civil law, regulations of a more liberal kind developed around same-sex behavior in canon law. These developments happen in spite the various condemnations of same-sex eroticism in the Septuagint[57] and the New Testament,[58] or even in Plato's *Laws*.[59] Comparison between this developing situation and that in late antiquity places this liberalization in relief.

The fourth century had seen rigorous disapproval of same-sex sexual relations in the penitentials. Basil of Caesarea's Canon 62[60] recommended 15 years of excommunication, and Gregory of Nyssa's Canon 4[61] 18 for same-sex relations between men, referred to as "shamefulness in males" (Basil: ἀσχημοσύνη ἐν τοῖς ἄρρεσιν) and "madness against the male" (Gregory: ἡ κατὰ τοῦ ἄρρενος λύσσα). Later in medieval times, the rigor of the Cappadocian Fathers was left behind. Theodoros the Studite (eighth to ninth century) recommended in his Canon 20 only two years' excommunication,[62] if it was clear that the man would no longer be engaging in "shamefulness in men."[63] Men who paid no mind to this canon were to serve the entire 15 years Basil recommended, however.[64] In the ninth or tenth century, in a collection that had been (incorrectly, as is generally accepted now) attributed to John the Faster (aka patriarch John IV,

582–595),[65] shorter penances also appeared.[66] Canon 18 specified three years instead of Nyssa's 18 or Basil's 15 for "madness for the male" (*arrenomania*/ἀρρενομανία), and, as in the case of Theodoros the Studite's recommendations, the unrepentant could serve Basil's 15 years.[67] In another canon, sex against nature between men (and the reference is to anal penetration: *eis andra pesontes*/εἰς ἄνδρα πεσόντες) drew two years of penance for those who did it only "once, twice or three times" (3: *hapax e dis e tris*/ ἅπαξ ἢ δὶς ἢ τρίς) and who were under 30 years of age or illiterate, or not in possession of a wife.[68] Still another canon specified three years for those who were older and who were guilty of "doing this only once, twice or three times."[69] A careful reading of the canons also yields the conclusion that anal sex with another man was less serious than anal sex with one's own wife: the mildest penance for anal sex with a wife was five years and could go as high as ten.[70]

The level of detail in these penitentials is also notable. Mutual masturbation between men is mentioned in one,[71] and another features a discussion of anal sex (*arsenokoitia*/ἀρσενοκοιτία) that considers the respective statuses of those who receive, those who give, and those who like both:

> Concerning *arsenokoitia*. *Arsenokoitia* has three different kinds. One is to suffer it from another. This is less serious, whether on account of being under age, or poverty, or rape, or other various reasons. Another is doing it, and this is more serious than suffering it. Then there is suffering it from someone else and doing it to another. This will not be pardoned.[72]

There are details and mitigating factors, and even what we call versatility among gay men today is a recognized possibility. A take-away, then, is the evident ease about discussing same-sex sexual relations that one will not find, say, in early modern western Europe, or earlier among the Cappadocian Fathers. This is not a situation where desire cannot speak its name: routes to carnal satisfaction are known and discussed. Same-sex sexual acts between men are temptations of the flesh and, as such, are to be avoided, but commission of mutual masturbation or *arsenokoitia* is not an unspeakable failing, as there is, well, speech.

Men in the *Life of Mary the Younger*

A look at another text, also from the ambit of the church, further supports the idea that the Byzantine Empire at this time had a degree of relaxation and frankness around same-sex relations between men. In an anonymous work of hagiography, the *Life of Mary the Younger*, from either the tenth or eleventh century,[73] the narrative turns to one of the sons of Mary: Baanes.[74] Though married, the soldier Baanes, beloved by the other soldiers,[75] was particularly close to Theodoros. He was "yoked" to this man,

14 *Introduction*

and description of their life together features metaphorical language that is curiously graphic and even coarse:

> [Baanes] had a certain Theodoros as fellow ascetic and helper in all his excellent exploits...a man brave and strong in military matters but braver still in conducting his life for God. Yoked to him, like a bull of good lineage and strong, they were ploughing in/within one another (*erotrion en heautois*/ἠροτρίων ἐν ἑαυτοῖς) as though into rich farmland, and they were sowing the seeds of excellences, as though the best of farmers. At the right moment, they harvested with rejoicing. They laid up for themselves fruits beautiful to God in divine vats and got for themselves joy forever.
>
> (*Life of Mary the Younger* 30/704)[76]

The word, "yoked" (*suzeuchtheis*/συζευχθείς), is often used to refer to married couples, and it is difficult to suppress thoughts of anal sex as they plough in or within one another. And the writer does not make it easy for thoughts of anal sex to be left behind. At the beginning of the next section, less than 100 words away, Baanes' final illness was a diseased bowel.[77] Furthermore, this relationship between Baanes and Theodoros was not *sui generis*. Their closeness is prefigured by the relationship that Mary's husband Nikephoros had with a certain Bardas Bratzes.

Bardas was married to Mary's sister and he suggested to his dear friend Nikephoros that he marry Mary. A marriage connection would bring them closer together:

> "Since," he says, "O dearest of men to me, we have become deeply involved with each other and are bound by our intimate relationship (*sunetheias*/συνηθείας). I think it right to make this, our bond of love, stronger and more perfect and to apply the ties of kinship to it, so that we may be joined in two ways, forging a family connection along with our intimate relationship (*sunetheias*/συνηθείας)."
>
> (*Life of Mary the Younger* 2/692)[78]

Nikephoros ultimately followed this advice,[79] and the word Bardas employs to describe the men's intimate relationship, *sunetheia*/συνηθεία, is capable of designating both close friendship and sexual relations.[80] And of course, it is a bond of love too (*desmon...tes agapes*/δεσμὸν...τῆς ἀγάπης).

Accordingly, then, two generations of men in this saint's life have strong relationships with other men, and the depiction of these connections have in the case of Nikephoros and Bardas hints of corporeal closeness and, in the case of Theodoros and Baanes, boldly sexualizing imagery.[81] The conclusion to draw is that intimations of sexual behavior, and even strong images of carnality, can be unremarkable in ecclesiastical contexts. And such a collocation is visible in *Letter 26* of Nikephoros Ouranos, and will be seen later in Symeon the New Theologian's writings. Furthermore, there is the liberalizing of the penitentials and desuetude of civil law. All these things imply a variety of viewpoints on desire and sexual behavior between Byzantine men.

Prospect

The chapters to follow center desire, connection, and happy affect in a reparative approach to the evidence. Relying on the assumption that desire and sexual behavior are indeterminate, and part of the time were viewed in positive terms, the reparative narratives to come draw pictures of wholes from fragments. The subject is how the elite men in this book, who were not strangers to same-sex desire and who were a group of men of differing bodily morphologies, both eunuchs and intact, related to one another and built connection in a scene that had contradictions: things somatic were both valued and disdained; same-sex desire and same-sex sexual behavior were valued and capable of being invoked with scant euphemism, while at the same time subject to ecclesiastical and legal sanction. Contemporary readers and writers possessed education in things secular (e.g., the masterpieces of Greek literature) and sacred (e.g., scripture, the writings of the church fathers), and this fact licenses searching intertextual readings of texts that surface subtexts and imagine contemporary Byzantine understandings of things sexual and bodily.

Chapter 1 looks back 50 or so years before Nikephoros Ouranos to the court of Constantine VII Porphyrogennetos. A network of letter writers, involving court figures and including the emperor himself, is considered with the aim of documenting relations that are marked by the kinds of desirous language already seen in the letters discussed in this introduction. These men's carnally provocative letters tell a tale about the nature of these men's relations. And while this tale is valuable in and of itself, it serves a purpose in addition: this network contains men who were also historiographers, including Symeon the Logothete and, quite likely, Theodoros Daphnopates, and Emperor Constantine VII Porphyrogennetos, who commissioned the histories and rewarded the historiographers.

Composing historiographies was one of the ways a man acquired position and achieved promotion in these elite homosocial environs. This matters because the earliest surviving accounts of the rise of Emperor Basil I, who is known, among other things, for his ritual brotherhoods and the sexy contours of his coming to the notice of figures in Michael III's court in the ninth century, are the product of this warmly homosocial group of letter writers/historiographers. Their letters illuminate their history writing, i.e., they conceived of events in the previous century in terms they found plausible: as a homoerotic court milieu obtains in and around the epistolographers/historiographers, so they imagine one extant in the previous century.

The second chapter passes from the networks of letter writers to consider six historiographies written in court circles in the mid-tenth century. These accounts contain narratives of Basil making his way to the throne. The chapter pays attention to moments in these historiographies that feature same-sex desire, masculine beauty, and intimations of carnality. Basil's sexiness and beauty were both an asset and a liability, the former because his good looks and athletic prowess brought him to the attention of powerful men and enabled his rise, and the latter because he resembled a bit too much members of Emperor Michael III's debauched court. The positive and negative valences discernible in the presentation of Basil recall the conflict in Byzantine society around same-sex desire and the body; valuing coexisted with disdain and even legal or ecclesiastical sanction.

Chapter 3 concerns itself with ritual brotherhood or *adelphopoiesis*. It starts with Basil I's brotherhoods in the historiographies, teasing out subtexts in the narrations and speculating about how Byzantine audiences would have understood them. These readings of the historiographers are then contextualized by visualization of the *adelphopoiesis* rite and close reading of an elaborate brotherhood prayer, a prayer that shares vocabulary and depictions of warm man-to-man relations with epistolography and historiography. Ultimately, it must be concluded that brothers are what brothers do. And it appears that carnality was something eminently possible, as both historiography and ritual speak not only of spiritual union but also of bodily closeness in various ways. In the tenth century, the ritual was not a license to have sex, but functioned to bring men together in a scene that frequently, though with ambivalence, called same-sex desire to mind in homosocial settings.

Chapter 4 offers a case study of the bachelorhood of Emperor Basil II (976–1025). This study builds on previous chapters' depiction of Byzantine elite homosociality and the place of same-sex desire in it. On the throne for almost 50 years, the energetic and militarily inclined Basil II notoriously never wed. The chapter first discusses how his demurral to take a wife has been explained in unsatisfactory ways in the scholarly literature. It is better to place Basil's refusal to wed in the context of Byzantine masculine homosociality that at times prizes same-sex relations. Discussion of Symeon the New Theologian's notorious parable of an emperor who, instead of chastising a rebel, takes him to bed for a night of love, shows a way in to placing Basil's bachelorhood in this context. Symeon wrote the parable around 30 years into Basil II's reign, so his readers had a natural referent in Basil. Viewed from within the context of the picture presented in this book of male homosocial relations in the upper reaches of Byzantine society, this parable is not odd. It uses an unremarkable scene in men's lives as a metaphor for God's solicitous concern for humanity and, at most, delivers mild castigation of the emperor for being too devoted to things of the body (with plausible deniability built in, as it is but a parable meant to serve another goal altogether: that of speaking of God's grace). In addition, the parable is evidence of a reading generally abroad in Byzantine society of Basil's decision not to wed. The homoeroticism in the parable involving an emperor should also be seen as being of a piece with, and as uncontroversial as the homoerotic sensuality to be seen in the epistolography and historiography of the time.

The conclusion returns to Nikephoros Ouranos and a reading of one more of his letters. *Letter 29* is another warmly homosocial letter and one that concerns itself with brotherhood. A hitherto overlooked source on *adelphopoiesis*, *Letter 29* offers evidence of multiple connections in this powerful eunuch man's life and of multiple ritual brotherhoods in an extended homosocial group. The letter also attests to how a eunuch man would connect himself to other men and how closely this ritual was embraided with the full range of masculine homosociality that is the object of reparative inquiry in this book.

Notes

1 A corpus of 50 letters, a military *taktika*, hagiography, and poetry survive from his pen.
2 For summary of Nikephoros' life, see Dain (1937, 134–136); Darrouzès (1960, 45–48); Guilland (1967, 1.448); McGeer (1991, 129–131); Masterson (2019a, 405–408). Also, see the entry for Nikephoros on the site, *Prosopographie der mittelbyzantinischen Zeit online* (https://www.degruyter.com/view/PMBZ/PMBZ27771). Darrouzès and McGeer also give details on his various writings.
3 ὁ κρατῶν τῆς Ἀνατολῆς.
4 Skylitzes, *Sunopsis historion: Basil and Constantine* 29/345. Cheynet (2003, 88); Darrouzès (1960, 46); Guilland (1967, 1.220, 448, 2.192); Holmes (2005, 349–352, 383–389, 477); Laurent (1962, 235–236); McGeer (1991, 131, 139). Here is the text of the lead seal that shows him with the title "Master of the East": Θ(εοτό)κε β[οήθει] τῷ [σῷ δούλῳ Νικηφ]όρ(ῳ) μαγίσ[τ]ρ(ῳ) τῷ κρα[τοῦ]ντι τῆς [Ἀν]ατολῆς [τῷ] Οὐ(ρα)νῷ (Nesbitt and Oikonomidès 1996, 177/#91.11).
5 In an important monograph on Emperor Basil II, Catherine Holmes (2005, 523–524) remarks of Nikephoros: "If there was an alter ego whom Basil trusted to rule in regions where he could not be present himself for much of his reign it was Nikephoros." Cf. Amedroz and Margoulith (1921, 25, 30, 31, 33, 34); Cheynet (2003, 89).
6 See Masterson (2019a, 408–411) for arguing that supports the point here that he was a eunuch.
7 Nikephoros Ouranos wrote *Letters 29, 30, 33, 35*, and *44* to Paulos *Krites*.
8 A theme is a military-administrative district of the empire. A synonym would be province.
9 Lit. "first of the sword-bearers," but as with many of the court titles, the language is more evocative than literal at this time in the history of the empire.
10 Paulos is to be found on the "Prosopography of the Byzantine World" site under the entry "Paulos 20106" (http://pbw2016.kdl.kcl.ac.uk/person/Paulos/20106/) and there is a lead seal that has survived from later in his career, dating to second quarter of the eleventh century (http://pbw2016.kdl.kcl.ac.uk/boulloterion/1238/). Here is a reconstruction of the inscription on the back of the seal: "Lord aid Paulos protospatharios kourator / krites of the hippodrome and of the Armenika themata" (Κύριε βοήθει Παύλῳ πρωτοσπαθαρίῳ κουράτωρι / κριτῇ ἐπὶ τοῦ ἱπποδρόμου καὶ τῶν Ἀρμενικῶν θεμάτων), cf. McGeer et al. (2001, 56.10). For further information on Paulos, see Weller (2014, 211–212) (and add *Letter 44* from Nikephoros to her list). (I did not find Paulos in the *Prosopographie der mittelbyzantinischen Zeit online*.)

11 Παύλῳ κριτῇ·

> Εἰ μὲν οὖν ἐμὲ παιδεύων ἢ δοκιμάζων τὴν μέχρι τοῦ νῦν ἀσκεῖς σιωπήν, ἅλις σοι καὶ τῆς παιδείας καὶ τῆς δοκιμασίας, εἴτε πολλῶν σοι καὶ μεγάλων σφαλμάτων δίκας ὀφείλομεν, εἴτε καὶ μηδείς σε περὶ ἡμῶν πρὸ τούτου χρόνος ἐπληροφόρησεν. Ἰδοὺ γὰρ καὶ παιδευόμενοι ἀνεχόμεθα, καὶ μηδὲ προσρήσεως ἀξιούμενοι παρὰ σοῦ, καὶ τῶν σῶν ἐρωτᾶν καὶ πολυπραγμονεῖν ἢ παυόμεθα καὶ πρῶτοι τολμᾶν γράφειν παραβαλλόμεθα, ἵν' ἀμφότερον οἱ μεμφθέντες διὰ τὴν τόλμαν, ἢ καὶ ἀποδεχθέντες διὰ τὸ φίλτρον, γραφῆς μὲν οὖν τύχωμεν ἢ φωνῆς, εἴτε τῆς ποθεινῆς ἡμῖν καὶ ἐπεράστου, εἴτε καὶ τῆς ἀπειλητικῆς καὶ ἐλεγκτικῆς. Ποθεινὴ γὰρ ἡμῖν καὶ αὕτη, καθάπερ καὶ τοῖς ἐρῶσι παρὰ τῶν ἐρωμένων ὕβρις τε καὶ πληγή, ἢ καὶ τοῖς διψῶσι ποταμοῦ πηγή, ἡ φοβερὰ μὲν καὶ πολλὴ καὶ ἀπειλοῦσα παρασῦραι τὸν προσιόντα, διαφανὴς δὲ ὅμως καὶ ψυχρὰ καὶ ἡδίστη· ὡς οὖν οὕτως καὶ ἡμῖν εἴτ' ἐπαινοίης, εἴτε κατηγοροίης καὶ διασύρειν ἐπιχειροίης, ἀρεστὰ ποιῶν καὶ ἀρκετὰ πρὸς παραμυθίαν, γράφοις μόνον καὶ ἐμφοροῖο παιδιᾶς ἢ παιδείας.

12 This element of the letter, that is, the complaint about epistolary silence, has been identified as one of many *topoi*, or commonplaces, to be found in Byzantine epistolography. Chapter 1 has discussion of epistolography as a genre and the challenges and opportunities it offers this study. The position of this book is that *topoi* retain interpretable semantic content.

13 I speak more below of intertextuality, which is an important aspect of analyses throughout this book.

14 καὶ βλέπων πρὸς πολὺ ἤδη τὸ καλὸν μηκέτι τὸ παρ' ἑνί, ὥσπερ οἰκέτης, ἀγαπῶν παιδαρίου κάλλος ἢ ἀνθρώπου τινὸς ἢ ἐπιτηδεύματος ἑνός, δουλεύων φαῦλος ᾖ καὶ σμικρολόγος, ἀλλ' ἐπὶ τὸ πολὺ πέλαγος τετραμμένος τοῦ καλοῦ καὶ θεωρῶν πολλοὺς καὶ καλοὺς λόγους καὶ μεγαλοπρεπεῖς τίκτῃ καὶ διανοήματα ἐν φιλοσοφίᾳ ἀφθόνῳ, ἕως ἂν ἐνταῦθα ῥωσθεὶς καὶ αὐξηθεὶς κατίδῃ τινὰ ἐπιστήμην μίαν....

15 κἄν τε ἔμπορός τις ἔλθω, ποιμαίνειν μοι δοκεῖς καὶ καθῆσθαι πείθων τοὺς λίθους, κἄν τε ἐπὶ θάλατταν ἔλθω, ἀνάγει σε ἡ θάλαττα ὥσπερ τὴν Ἀφροδίτην ὁ βυθός, ἄν τε ἐπὶ λειμῶνα, αὐτῶν τῶν ἀνθῶν ἐξέχεις· καίτοι οὐδὲν τοιοῦτον ἐκεῖ φύεται· καὶ γὰρ εἰ καλὰ καὶ χαρίεντα ἄλλως, ἀλλὰ μιᾶς ἡμέρας. καὶ μὴν καὶ ποταμοῦ πλησίον γενόμενος τὸν μὲν οὐκ οἶδα ὅπως ἠφάνισται, σὲ δὲ ῥεῖν ἀντ' ἐκείνου νομίζω καλὸν καὶ μέγα καὶ πολὺ μεῖζον τῆς θαλάττης.

16 I could discuss a third intertext. An epigram by Paulos Silentiarios (sixth century CE) also plays with notions of fixation on the beloved and with water, sea and river both, and indeed liquids in general:

> They say a man stricken with a dog's raging venom sees the beast's image in water. Perhaps enmaddening Love drove his bitter tooth into me and seized my heart for madness, for the sea makes your image appear to me, as do the eddies of the river and the goblet that brings me my wine.
> (*Greek Anthology* 5.266)

> (Ἀνέρα λυσσητῆρι κυνὸς βεβολημένον ἰῷ
> ὕδασι θηρείην εἰκόνα φασὶ βλέπειν.
> λυσσώων τάχα πικρὸν Ἔρως ἐνέπηξεν ὀδόντα
> εἰς ἐμὲ καὶ μανίαις θυμὸν ἐλῄσατο.
> σὴν γὰρ ἐμοὶ καὶ πόντος ἐπήρατον εἰκόνα φαίνει
> καὶ ποταμῶν δῖναι καὶ δέπας οἰνοχόον.)

17 The impulse in scholarship to offer reparative narratives has been around for a while now. See the following: Dinshaw (1999); Fradenburg (1997); Freccero (2007); Rohy (2006), Sedgwick (2003). I found Doan (2013) particularly helpful for illuminating the reparative impulse and the issues for surrounding it when a scholar is constructing narratives about desire and sexual behavior in history.

Introduction 19

One also can find the essence of reparativeness under a number of names. Besides reparative (e.g., Sedgwick 2003), I have seen "affective connections...across time" (Dinshaw 1999, 12), an ambition "to affirm the pleasures of mortal creatures" (Fradenburg and Freccero 1996, xxi), "erotohistoriography" (Freeman 2005), and even "free-associative detranslation" (Stockton 2011, xii).

18 The Septuagint is the Greek version of the Old Testament used by the Byzantines.
19 It has been a mainstay of Byzantine scholarship for many decades now that knowledge of scripture and pagan *paideia* was to be found in the upper reaches of Byzantine society. Readers can start with the following: Cavallo (2006); Hunger (1969–1970, 1978, 1981, 1989); Jeffreys (2008); Lemerle (1986); Markopoulos (2008); Papaioannou (2021); Ševčenko and Mango (1975); Shawcross and Toth (2018; in this volume, Duffy on Theodoros Daphnopates is particularly helpful); Steckel *et al.* (2014). In analyses to come, I focus most of all on scripture and pagan *paideia*. There are further narratives to be written that focus on the fathers of late antiquity.
20 As a cursory glance at any of the critical editions will reveal and which Messis and Papaioannou (2021, 144) state outright.
21 For more on intertextuality, see the following: Conte (1986); Edmunds (2001); Fowler (2000); Hinds (1998); Kaldellis (2021); Masterson (2014); Messis and Papaioannou (2021).
22 In addition to texts, an illustrated manuscript (the *Madrid Skylitzes*) and two ivory caskets will provide evidence for arguments to come.
23 On just this topic, Gabrielle Spiegel calls texts, such as the ones analyzed in this book, "situated uses of language" (1990, 77, cf. Zeikowitz 2003, 9) that both reflect realities and, at the same time, generate these same realities, cf. Messis (2008, 33), for a similar point.
24 For the indeterminate nature of sex and desire, that it is prior to moral evaluation and has no necessary character, see the following: Bech (1997); Dinshaw (1999); Doan (2013); Masterson (2014); Scott (2007). Also, Ermarth (2007) is clarifying on how opposing discourses can share the same space and time.
25 The study of desire between men in Byzantium has roots in scholarship (in a number of modern languages) going back over 60 years. The important work of collecting evidence from civil law, canon law, scripture, hagiography, other ecclesiastical writings, historiography, and, somewhat less often, epistolography, has been conducted by a number of practitioners throughout this time, including Koukoules (1955), Messis (2006), Pitsakis (1993, 2008), and Troianos (1980, 1989, 1993, 1997). The work of these scholars has identified many sources of interest and outlined the expectations of civil and ecclesiastical authorities towards sexual behavior between men. However, it has mostly focused on the fact that these acts were forbidden and faced disapproval. Furthermore, this secondary literature has not always properly distinguished the love of boys (*paiderastia*), which is more a feature of late antiquity and earlier, from discussions of sex and desire between/for men. Essential as it is, this work has been mostly content to report the facts of illegality and disapproval and leave it at that.

Still, given the historical fact that some Byzantine men desired one another, and that sexual acts certainly occurred between them, some scholars have endeavored to find evidence of same-sex desire beyond the lists of prohibitions and expressions of disapproval. Beck (1984) believes that the norms governing behavior are not the whole story (e.g., 99), while Laiou states her belief that same-sex intimacies were of little concern in the medieval empire, only attracting attention if there were a scandal (1992, 78). Smythe (1999) is interested in identifying possibilities, as is Tougher (1999, 2010a). In an audacious *tour de force*, Odorico (1995) identifies mutual masturbation as a salient subject in Theodoros Daphnopates' 17th letter (a letter to be discussed in Chapter 1). Levin (1996) believes

20 *Introduction*

that cosmopolitan Byzantine circles disregarded norms around sex and desire at times. Another scholar, Demosthenous (2004, 175), while being opposed to seeing same-sex desire in the context of Byzantine men's friendships, wonders whether desire of at least a kind is present in the letters that passed between Emperor Constantine VII Porphyrogennetos and Theodoros of Kyzikos, and cf. Angelidi (2002, 228n.28) who is rather more certain that it is present. (I also discuss Constantine and Theodoros' correspondence in Chapter 1.) Focusing on the single-sex milieu of the monks, Krueger (2006, 2011) reveals the presence of same-sex desire in monastic settings, both as a reality and as an object of contemplation among the monks.

But there has also been opposition to seeing same-sex desire present in the sources beyond evidence derived from prohibition and disapproval. This opposition frequently sees current narratives that move beyond narration of prohibition and similar things as compromised by wishful thinking that reads too much into the medieval evidence (e.g., Messis 2006, 2008, 2014b; Rapp 2016, 45–47). Obviously, I disagree and believe that careful reparative narratives can be written.

26 As will be seen, I add to the important work of Derek Krueger (2006) on Symeon the New Theologian in this regard.
27 Darrouzès (1960, 45).
28 Vinson (1985, 111); Weller (2014, 211); "Nikolaos." *Prosopographie der mittelbyzantinischen Zeit Online*. Berlin, Boston: De Gruyter, 2013. https://www.degruyter.com/document/database/PMBZ/entry/PMBZ28194/html. Accessed 2021-06-22. In addition to *Letter 26*, Nikephoros' *Letters 15* and *21* (Darrouzès 1960, 224 and 227 respectively) are also addressed to Nicholas.
29 Νικολάῳ μητροπολίτῃ Νεοκαισαρείας·

> Ὅσῳ ταῖς τοῦ χειμῶνος ταύταις δριμύτησιν, ὦ φίλη ψυχή, πηγνύμεθα, πορείᾳ καθημερινῇ χρώμενοι, τοσούτῳ ταῖς ἐλπίσιν ἑκάστοτε θάλλομεν, ὅτι τὸ γλυκὺ τῆς φιλίας ἔαρ ἡμῖν ἤδη προσμειδιᾷ, ὅπερ ἄντικρύς ἐστιν ἡ σὴ συντυχία. Θάλλε μοι καὶ σὺ τοιγαροῦν, πρὸς τὴν ἐπιδημίαν τοῦ φίλου πᾶν εἴ τι κατηφὲς ἀποβαλών, εἴ τι μετοπωρινὸν ἢ χειμέριον, καὶ κοινῇ πρὸ τῆς ὥρας ἑκάτεροι τῷ ἑνοποιῷ Θεῷ καὶ ἀλλήλους ἐνεαρίσωμεν.

30 E.g., Gen 40:10 (the dream of the chief cup-bearer [ἀρχιοινοχόος]: the blossoming/budding/sprouting [θάλλουσα] vine), Job 8:11 ("the papyrus does not sprout without water" [μὴ θάλλει πάπυρος ἄνευ ὕδατος]), Sir 14:18 (a leaf sprouting on a leafy tree [φύλλον θάλλον ἐπὶ δένδρου δασέος]), Dan 4:21 (the leaves sprouting well [τὰ φύλλα...εὐθαλῇ]); 2 Mac 14:4 ("of blooms/sprouting things thought essential" [τῶν νομιζομένων θαλλῶν] for performance of a rite).
31 Pr 26:20: "fire blooms amid much wood" (ἐν πολλοῖς ξύλοις θάλλει πῦρ).
32 κύριος βοηθός μου καὶ ὑπερασπιστής μου· ἐπ᾽ αὐτῷ ἤλπισεν ἡ καρδία μου, καὶ ἐβοηθήθην, καὶ ἀνέθαλεν ἡ σάρξ μου· καὶ ἐκ θελήματός μου ἐξομολογήσομαι αὐτῷ. Somewhat similar is Nabuchodonosor "flourishing" (εὐθαλῶν) (Dan 4:4), cf. Hos 8:9: "Ephraim flourished against himself" (ἀνέθαλεν καθ᾽ ἑαυτὸν Εφραιμ).
33 ἀνεθάλετε τὸ ὑπὲρ ἐμοῦ φρονεῖν.
34 καρδίας εὐφραινομένης πρόσωπον θάλλει.
35 Lemerle (1986, 310); Cameron (1993, 292).
36 A cursory search of the *Suda*, the tenth-century encyclopedia which figures in arguments throughout this book, reveals a great number of references to the *Greek Anthology*. I speak more of the *Suda* when the emperor who superintended its writing, Constantine VII Porphyrogennetos, enters the narrative in Chapter 1.
37

> Ἄνθεσιν οὐ τόσσοισι φιλοζέφυροι χλοάουσι
> λειμῶνες, πυκιναῖς εἴαρος ἀγλαΐαις,

ὅσσους εὐγενέτας, Διονύσιε, παῖδας ἀθρήσεις,
χειρῶν Κυπρογενεῦς πλάσματα καὶ Χαρίτων.
ἔξοχα δ' ἐν τούτοις Μιλήσιος ἠνίδε θάλλει
ὡς ῥόδον εὐόδμοις λαμπόμενον πετάλοις.
ἀλλ' οὐκ οἶδεν ἴσως, ἐκ καύματος ὡς καλὸν ἄνθος,
οὕτω τὴν ὥρην ἐκ τριχὸς ὀλλυμένην.

38

Πάγκαρπόν σοι, Κύπρι, καθήρμοσε χειρὶ τρυγήσας
παίδων ἄνθος Ἔρως ψυχαπάτην στέφανον.
ἐν μὲν γὰρ κρίνον ἡδὺ κατέπλεξεν Διόδωρον,
ἐν δ' Ἀσκληπιάδην, τὸ γλυκὺ λευκόιον.
ναὶ μὴν Ἡράκλειτον ἐπέπλεκεν, ὡς ἀπ' ἀκάνθης
<εἰς> ῥόδον, οἰνάνθη δ' ὥς τις ἔθαλλε Δίων·
χρυσανθῆ δὲ κόμαισι κρόκον, Θήρωνα, συνῆψεν,
ἐν δ' ἔβαλ' ἑρπύλλου κλωνίον Οὐλιάδην·
ἁβροκόμην δὲ Μυΐσκον, ἀειθαλὲς ἔρνος ἐλαίης,
ἱμερτοὺς Ἀρέτου κλῶνας ἀπεδρέπετο.
ὀλβίστη νήσων ἱερὰ Τύρος, ἢ τὸ μυρόπνουν
ἄλσος ἔχει παίδων Κύπριδος ἀνθοφόρον.

39 τὸ γλυκὺ τῆς φιλίας ἔαρ...ὅπερ ἄντικρύς ἐστιν ἡ σὴ συντυχία.
40 *Iliad* 5.65-67: τὸν μὲν Μηριόνης ὅτε δὴ κατέμαρπτε διώκων / βεβλήκει γλουτὸν κατὰ δεξιόν· ἡ δὲ διαπρὸ / ἀντικρὺ κατὰ κύστιν ὑπ' ὀστέον ἦλυθ' ἀκωκή.
41 κοινῇ πρὸ τῆς ὥρας ἑκάτεροι τῷ ἑνοποιῷ Θεῷ καὶ ἀλλήλους ἐνεαρίσωμεν.
42 Ritual brotherhood (*adelphopoiesis*) is the focus of Chapter 3. It is interesting to compare this moment in *Letter 26* to the end of Prayer A in the Appendix of Prayers: "Because you, Christ our Lord, are *the oneness*, safety, and the binding of peace, we send up to you glory and thanks" (Ὅτι σὺ εἶ *ἡ ἕνωσις* καὶ ἀσφάλεια καὶ δεσμὸς τῆς εἰρήνης, Χριστὲ ὁ θεὸς ἡμῶν, καὶ σοὶ τὴν δόξαν καὶ εὐχαριστείαν ἀναπέμπομεν).
43 Althaus-Reid (2000, 146) (emphases added):

> Sexual theologies are the opposite of idealistic processes. They are materialist theologies, which *have their starting points in people's actions, or sexual acts* without polarizing the social from the [heterosexual-centric] symbolic. *It is from human sexuality that theology starts* to search [for] and understand the sacred, and not vice versa. Indecent theologies are sexual theologies without pages cut from the books of our sexual experiences.

44 Althaus-Reid (2000, 137–139).
45 Althaus-Reid (2000, 138).
46 Althaus-Reid (2000, 139).
47 Cf. Althaus-Reid (2000, 146). Fradenburg makes a similar point about writing history that will be sensitive to sexuality: "the passional register, the locus of passions, is a position from which to know [about the past]" (1997, 216). Similarly, Mills proposes that a history that does well by desire and sexuality will be one that tells "stories that take as their point of departure *sexual intensities, tastes and roles*, gender dissonances, dispositions and styles, queer feelings, *emotions and desires*" (2006, 262, emphases added).
48 Laiou (1992, 68); Messis (2006, 779n170); Pitsakis (2008, 8). I am not discussing Emperor Justinian's *Novellae* 77 and 141 (sixth century) and *Codex Theodosianus* 9.7.3 and 9.7.6 (fourth century), as they have for the most part been eclipsed by laws dating to the eighth century and later.
49 Messis (2006, 781).

50 Οἱ ἀσελγεῖς, ὅ τε ποιῶν καὶ ὁ ὑπομένων, ξίφει τιμωρείσθωσαν· εἰ δὲ ὁ ὑπομένων ἥττων τῶν δώδεκα ἐτῶν εὑρεθῇ, συγχωρείσθω, ὡς τῆς ἡλικίας δηλούσης μὴ εἰδέναι αὐτόν, τί ὑπέμεινεν (text=Burgmann 1983, 238).

51 Ὁ ἀσελγῆς ὅ τε ποιῶν καὶ ὁ ὑπομένων ξίφει τιμωρείσθω· ὁ δὲ ἥττων τῶν δεκαπέντε ἐτῶν τυπτέσθω καὶ μοναστηρίῳ εἰσαγέσθω, ὡς τῆς ἡλικίας δηλούσης τοῦτο ἀκουσίως πεπονθέναι αὐτόν (text=Simon and Troianos 1977, 71).

52 Οἱ ἀσελγεῖς, ὅ τε ποιῶν καὶ ὁ πάσχων, ξίφει τιμωρείσθωσαν· εἰ μὴ ἄρα ὁ πεπονθὼς ἔλαττον ᾖ τῶν ιβ΄ χρόνων. τότε γὰρ τὸ ἐνδεὲς τῆς ἡλικίας αὐτοῦ τῆς τοιαύτης αὐτὸν ἐξαρπάζει ποινῆς (text=Zepos and Zepos 1931, 365).

53 Οἱ ἀσελγεῖς, ὅ τε ποιῶν καὶ ὁ πάσχων, ξίφει τιμωρείσθωσαν, εἰ μὴ ἄρα ὁ πεπονθὼς ἔλαττον εἴη τῶν ιβ΄ χρόνων. τότε γὰρ τὸ ἐνδεὲς τῆς ἡλικίας αὐτοῦ τῆς τοιαύτης αὐτὸν ἀπαλλάττει ποινῆς (text=Zepos and Zepos 1931, 225–226).

54 *Eklogadion* 17.6 exhibits the greatest distance from the other three: the one submitting can avoid punishment if he is less than 15 years old (in the others, he has to be less than 12 years old). Furthermore, the boy is to be beaten and sent to a monastery, where, presumably, he will become a monk. For further discussion of these laws, see Troianos (1989, 35–37); Messis (2006, 776–778, 781).

55 "Il est possible que, en dépit de tout son zèle normatif pour prohiber les actes homosexuels, la société byzantine les ait en fait tolérés tant qu'ils ne faisaient pas scandale."

56 Prefiguring this comment, Mullett (1988, 11n41), notes that possible sexual expression between men was not as weighty an issue as we now might imagine it was. Pitsakis (2008, 9), underscores the nonchalance in the sources about sex between men, while being uncertain whether this means that same-sex desire was thought unimportant or if there was wide-ranging tolerance that we, dealing with the weight of our history, can hardly understand now. Smythe (1999, 144), followed up on Laiou's analysis, but then speaks of Byzantium as the "first closet society," citing Sedgwick (1990). As the closet in Sedgwick's formulation is a structure of paranoid concealment with the possibility of catastrophic revelation, it does not suit this Byzantine evidence. Tougher (1999, 158), speaks of "detect[ing] ripples of homosexuality sounding Basil [I]" in a number of histories of his rise to power.

57 Gen 9:20–27, 19:1–11; Lev 18:22, 20:13.

58 1 Cor 6:9–10; 1 Tim 1:10; Rom 1:26–27.

59 1.636C; 8.841D.

60 See Joannou (1963, 147), and Rhalle and Potle (1854, 220), for Canon 62, and Joannou (1963, 103–104), and Rhalle and Potle (1854, 110), for Canon 7, which gives the length of the penalty. Cf. Troianos (1989, 41); Messis (2006, 781–782).

61 Joannou (1963, 212–216); Rhalle and Potle (1854, 308–311). Cf. Troianos (1989, 42–43); Messis (2006, 782).

62 *PG* 99: 1728: ἡμεῖς δὲ [*sc.* ὡρίσαμεν] ἐάν ἀποστῇ τοῦ κακοῦ μετὰ πληροφορίας, διετῆ χρόνον ἀκοινώνητον ("But I order that, if he should stay clear of the sin with assurance given, that he be excommunicated for a two year period"). Cf. Troianos (1989, 43); Messis (2006, 783).

63 *PG* 99: 1728: τὴν ἀσχημοσύνην ἐν τοῖς ἄρρεσιν.

64 *PG* 99: 1728: εἰ δὲ ἀμελῇ, τὰ δεκαπέντε ἔτη ἐκτελείτω τὸ ἐπιτίμιον.

65 Arranz (1993, 20–22), who assembled an edition that contains two of the three canons to be discussed presently, attributes the collection to John the Monk and suggests that it could be as late as the eleventh century but prefers the ninth or early tenth, cf. Troianos (1989, 43), who does not believe the sixth-century patriarch wrote these canons either. I also consulted Paverd (2006) when making translations.

66 Troianos (1989, 43).

67 Rhalle and Potle (1854, 441–442): Περὶ ἀρρενομανίας· Ὁ τὴν ἀσχημοσύνην ἐν ἄρρεσι διαπραξάμενος, τῷ μὲν γ΄. τοῦ Νύσσης Κανόνι ἔτη ιη΄. τῆς κοινωνίας ἐκβάλλεται· τῷ δε ξβ΄. του μεγαλου Βασιλειου ιε΄. Ἡμῖν δὲ τρία ἔτη τῆς κοινωνίας εἴργεσθαι τὸν τοιοῦτον ἔδοξε, κλαίοντα καὶ νηστεύοντα, καὶ πρὸς ἑσεπέραν ξηροφαγοῦντα, καὶ μετανοίας διακοσίας ποιοῦντα. Περὶ πλείονος δὲ τὴν ῥᾳστώνην ποιούμενος, τὰ ιε΄ ἔτη πληρούτω.
68 Arranz (1993, 72.2–8).
69 9: ταῦτα ἅπαξ ... ποιήσαντες, ἢ δὶς ἢ τρίς (Arranz 1993, 72.9–12). Elsewhere in these canons, and with possible inconsistency, sex against nature with a man (Arranz 1993, 68.10 and 14–15) nets simply a three-year penance with no qualification.
70 Messis (2006, 786); Arranz (1993, 70.8, 70.21–72.1).
71 Arranz (1993, 50.26–32).
72 Arranz (1993, 54.10–17): Περὶ ἀρσενοκοιτίας. Ἡ δὲ ἀρσενοκοιτία τρεῖς ἔχει τὰς διαφοράς. Ἄλλο γὰρ τὸ παθεῖν παρ' ἑτέρου· τόδε κουφότερον· ἢ διὰ τὴν ἀνηλικιότητα. ἢ διὰ πτωχείαν, ἢ διὰ βίαν, ἢ πολλὰς τὰς διαφοράς. Ἕτερον δὲ τὸ ποιῆσαι· ὃ καὶ βαρύτερον τοῦ παθεῖν. Τὸ δὲ παρ' ἄλλου παθεῖν καὶ ποιῆσαι εἰς ἕτερον· πάσης ἂν εἴη ἀπολογίας ἀλλότριον.
73 For the dating of the life, see Talbot (1996, 242–245).
74 See Rapp (2016, 220–222), for discussion of this life. I also thank her for drawing my attention to this work.
75 *Life of Mary the Younger* 30/704: προσφιλὴς ... αὐτοῖς.
76 Ἔσχε καὶ συνασκητὴν καὶ συνεργὸν ἁπάντων τῶν καλλίστων κατορθωμάτων Θεόδωρόν τινα...ἄνδρα γενναῖον τὰ στρατιωτικὰ καὶ ῥωμαλέον, γενναιότερον δὲ τοῖς κατὰ Θεὸν πολιτεύμασιν· ᾧ δὴ συζευχθείς, οἷα μόσχος εὐγενής τε καὶ ἰσχυρός, ὡς εἰς πίονα γῆν ἠροτρίων ἐν ἑαυτοῖς καὶ τῶν ἀρετῶν τὰ σπέρματα ὡς ἄριστοι γεωργοὶ κατεβάλλοντο, οἳ κατὰ καιρὸν εὐφροσύνως ἐθέρισαν, καρποὺς ὡρίμους Θεῷ καὶ τοῖς θείοις ληνοῖς ἐναπέθεντο καὶ ἀγαλλίασιν αἰώνιον ἐκομίσαντο.
77 *Life of Mary the Younger* 31/704: κοιλιακῷ νοσήματι περιπίπτει.
78 "'Ἐπειδή,'' φησιν, ''φίλτατέ μοι ἀνδρῶν, οὕτως ἐκ συνηθείας ἀλλήλοις συνεκράθημέν τε καὶ συνεδέθημεν, δίκαιον ἥγημαι τὸν δεσμὸν τοῦτον τῆς ἀγάπης βιαιότερον θεῖναι καὶ τελεώτερον καὶ τὰ τῆς ἀγχιστείας τούτῳ προσθεῖναι ἅμματα, ἵνα διπλῇ συνδεσμώμεθα, μετὰ τῆς συνηθείας προσλαβόντες καὶ τὴν συγγένειαν."
79 For the record, it was not good for Mary to have this man for a husband. Violent, Nikephoros beat Mary so badly (9/696) that she died from her injuries (10/696).
80 Talbot (1996, 256 n.52); also, and of critical interest: *LSJ* offer up the following in its entry for συνηθεία: "sexual intercourse...; ἔχειν μετὰ γυναικός Plu.2.310e; πρὸς γυναῖκα Vett. Val.288.23."
81 The *Life of Mary the Younger* may need to take its place as a central text on modes of interpersonal connection in Byzantium. Men and women become connected in marriage and men become connected through marriage, even as their relations, one on one, feature emotional and corporeal intensity. The regrettable violence of Nikephoros is worth some thought too: is there something to be said about his possible primary connection to Bardas and a marriage that was an afterthought? There is also the martyrdom of Mary to violence coming at her, in a way, from a tightly connected and sexualized world of masculine homosociality.

1 Eroticism and Desire in Epistolography

Byzantine epistolography is a valuable resource for understanding relations between Byzantine elite men in the tenth century. A notable aspect of their letters is the frequent appearance of language of affection, desire, and sexual activity. This chapter features reparative readings of seven letters, readings that surface wishes for connection and happy affect. These letters attest to the unremarkableness of the language of same-sex desire and intimations of sexual behavior among these men, especially since Byzantine letters are not private like personal letters are in modern times. These letters were part of the public face of these men. Lastly, the letters are by men of education who quote and allude to both scripture and pagan literature to create intertextuality that is interpretable.[1]

The seven letters are by four men from the imperial court of the mid-tenth century: Theodoros Daphnopates, Emperor Constantine VII Porphyrogennetos, Theodoros of Kyzikos, and Symeon the Logothete. And while the expressions of love and desire are the substantial and important focus of this chapter, who these men were and their other writings matter also. Three of the selected epistolographers either wrote or were involved in the earliest surviving historiographies that tell of the rise of Emperor Basil I, which is the focus of Chapters 2 and 3. See Figure 1.1 for this network of letter writers, some of whom, Theodoros Daphnopates and Symeon the Logothete, also composed historiographies. Furthermore, Nikephoros Ouranos was connected to this group at two points. Theodoros Daphnopates wrote three letters, *Letters 17, 18,* and *31,*—discussion of which leads off this chapter— to and for a man who plausibly was one of Nikephoros' forebears, Basil Ouranos. Theodoros Daphnopates was also, most likely, the author of two of the historiographies to be considered in the two chapters that follow this one: the *Life of Basil* and *Theophanes Continuatus*. Emperor Constantine VII Porphyrogennetos, who oversaw and commissioned the writing of the historiographies to be analyzed in the two chapters that follow this one, was also a participant in this letter-writing scene. Two warmly homosocial and erotic letters, one he wrote to Theodoros of Kyzikos and a letter he received from him in return, are next.[2] Nikephoros Ouranos was also friends with the last letter writer: Symeon the Logothete.[3] Symeon wrote a historiography,

DOI: 10.4324/9781351135238-2

Connections between Epistolographers and Historiographers

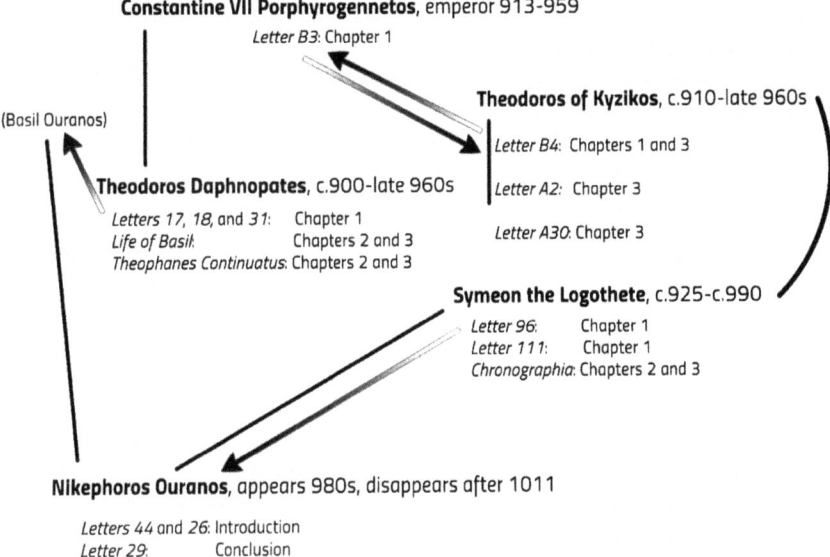

Figure 1.1

his *Chronographia*, which also appears in Chapters 2 and 3. Symeon the Logothete's *Letter 111* possesses remarkable warmth and intertextual intensity that fits with the other letters under consideration in this chapter, and shares significant vocabulary with his description in his historiography of Emperor Basil I's ritual brotherhood. A connection not discussed in detail in this chapter, which is already long enough, is one between Theodoros of Kyzikos and Symeon the Logothete. *Letter 109* in the collection of Symeon's letters is one to Symeon from Theodoros,[4] and *Letter 110* is Symeon's answer.[5]

How to Read Byzantine Epistolography

Epistolography was an important genre of Byzantine writing.[6] There has been considerable admiration of its high level of polish and learned accomplishment.[7] The attractive suggestion has been made that epistolography occupies a place in Byzantine literary productions that lyric poetry occupied in the earlier classical cultures.[8] In addition, the androcentric focus of the genre,[9] that is, the overwhelming majority of writers and recipients are men, suggests that this genre will be useful to investigations of relations between Byzantine men. Still, its value to narratives about Byzantine society and, in particular, relations between men, has been a point of contention. There has been a persisting position in the scholarship that regards the language in the letters as too rhetoricized and formalized to canvass for meaningful information about Byzantine society,[10] and the presence of same-sex desire, while often noticed and occasionally taken seriously, has more often evoked strong reactions against seeing anything "real" about it.[11]

Attention to the milieu of receiving a letter which featured the bearer, or *komistes*, who would have a message he delivered orally,[12] has also allowed additional scope for some scholars to imagine that the contents of a letter do not matter much. The *komistes* delivered the "real" message and the letter can safely be disregarded as only an *objet d'art*, as the story goes. But a doctrinaire insistence that there is nothing to see here should be resisted. It does not pay due attention to the dynamics of reception, that is, what a reader/listener understands from a text is up to them. Furthermore, seeing a letter as a gesture so formalized and instrumentalized that there is practically no meaning to be acquired from the text itself ignores the refrain in what little Byzantine theorizing of epistolography we have[13] that a letter, an "icon of the soul,"[14] is meant to convey something personal, that there is in fact content.[15] It is therefore an attractive position that holds that a letter bears an impress of the personality of the writer and that there is something personal, even "real," present, even if its presence is subtle.[16] It therefore also is attractive to take the risk both to think about how the recipient might have understood a letter and to offer informed speculation about the general social situation of which a letter was a part.[17] In that spirit, here are reparative readings of seven letters from a group of men meant to convey a picture of how they wanted their connections to one another to be seen by each other and others.

Letters of Theodoros Daphnopates

Like Nikephoros Ouranos, Theodoros Daphnopates had a glorious career. He was born about 900 and held various high offices over a long period, commencing in 925, when he held the ranks of *patrikios* (a high ranking dignity) and *protoasekretis* ("head of the college of imperial scribes").[18] He likely composed two historiographies: the *Life of Basil* and *Theophanes Continuatus*.[19] In 959, he was promoted to military logothete[20] and in 961 he became Eparch[21] of Constantinople.[22] There are 40 letters surviving from his pen, which appear in an authoritative edition.[23] The three letters to be discussed presently, the 17th, 18th, and 31st, are concerned with the *protospatharios* (a dignity in the imperial hierarchy) and *asekretis* ("imperial scribe"), Basil Ouranos.[24] Given that he is an Ouranos, it is quite possible he is a relative of Nikephoros Ouranos. *Letter 31* is addressed to Basil, while *Letter 17*, certainly, and *18*, probably, were written by Theodoros for Basil to send out under his own name.[25] And as there is reference to the fact that Theodoros is eparch, these three letters probably date to the early 960s.

First up is the brief *Letter 31*. Theodoros thanks Basil for gifts and a beautiful feast at the time of the winter-solstice festival, the *Brumalia*:

> To Basil Ouranos, *protospatharios* and *asekretis*:
> It was allowed to the men of ancient times and especially in the times of Kronos to enjoy any food they might desire. But you have done so much through the sweetness and worthy-of-wonderment-ness of your most beautiful gifts, and, as far as this Winter solstice table is concerned, you charmed me, so it would lack little but that it would turn me to the nonsense of the pagans. But be well and may it be that you do well for a long time, strengthening through more lavish gifts my/our...[26] of which I am exorbitantly proud and my love which is very hot (*to tes agapes diapuron*/τὸ τῆς ἀγάπης διάπυρον).
>
> (Theodoros Daphnopates, *Letter 31*)[27]

This is no *Letter 26* from Nikephoros Ouranos. It does not speak of friendship blessed by God. Instead, there is a nod to the pagan Golden Age of which Hesiod speaks memorably: parties and the earth giving freely of its bounty[28] in a universe ruled by Kronos.[29] The presence of Kronos is redoubled by reference to the winter festival, *Brumalia*, that also goes by the name of *Kronia*. There are gifts and a festal board that Daphnopates says are liable to turn him, charmed, away from God to paganism. This letter of thanks concludes with wishes for Basil's health and then for more gifts that will strengthen both something of his or theirs which is a source of pride (this moment is obscure: a problem with the text) and, and this is clearer, the undoubted warmth of love. This letter is about sensual delights, gifts, and love that increases, all of which are *not* the province of God. What the church might wish to say about their love is, pointedly, far away, and Theodoros is content to at least pretend to be led away from God.

With this sensual letter left behind, it is time for *Letters 17* and *18*. Both of these letters, but especially *Letter 17*, deserve to be much better known for the light they shine on Byzantine homosociality and a relation it has to same-sex desire. *Letter 18* is first, as one better appreciates the extravagance of *Letter 17*, if one first experiences what appears to be a scaled-back version of it.

Letter 18

It is probable that Theodoros wrote *Letter 18* for Basil Ouranos to send to a friend who had gotten married, which is what is specified for *Letter 17*. The editors of the 1978 collection of the letters proposed that *Letter 18* replaced *Letter 17*, because the latter may have been judged as excessive by Basil.[30] This congenial judgment[31] allows a reader now to assume that this letter comes across as a more buttoned-up version of

28 *Eroticism and Desire in Epistolography*

Letter 17 and that *Letter 17* should not be seen as a sexy and inexplicable outlier, but instead on a continuum with *Letter 18*. This duplicates an effect the letters would have had in their manuscript[32] in any case. Here is *Letter 18*:

> [A letter] of the same one [i.e., of Basil Ouranos but written by Theodoros (?)]:
>
> An announcement has been heard by me about you, o my most excellent and most educated friend, how you yourself are wholly married, having plaited the flowered bridal bedroom and artistically arranged the silver-ceilinged wedding chamber, and, along with these things, having put at the ready the musical instruments because they are friendly to the deed, through all of which kindled desire will fulfill the mystery of the marriage festival. But Kypris did not withdraw far from the things being perfected. We believe that she herself danced all around, smiled, was guiding the bride by the right hand, and was leading her into the innermost parts of the wedding chamber. [We also believe] Erotes and Graces were dancing around, and that the Graces were crowning the bride's head, and that Erotes were flying overhead to sprinkle her with blooms and roses. And if any other thing has customarily accompanied the marriage festival, it did not stand aside from the realization of and companionship with things similar to it.[33] And if you have boldly completed your Herculean Labor, how noble a one you are, one without rival, and one not taking second place to the marvels of Herakles.
>
> While being ill and as your friend I have written these things to you, on the one hand fulfilling the debt owed to the intimacies of our love/friendship (*t[a sune]the tes philias*/τ[ὰ συνή]θη τῆς φιλίας), and, on the other hand, honoring one who has acted temperately. May you remain within the established terms of our love, and may you continue to be supported by them, and may you stretch yourself to the increase of it [i.e., our love].
>
> (Theodoros Daphnopates, *Letter 18*)[34]

Writing for Basil, Theodoros imagines the groom on his wedding night, describing the wedding chamber and decorously referring to entities appropriate to the moment: Aphrodite, Erotes, and the Graces. And the groom, a Herakles, has completed his labor. In the second paragraph, and in contrast to the triumphant athleticism of the groom, the letter writer feels weak and ill. And this is followed by mention of their friendship in terms that emphasize the closeness of writer and groom: "fulfilling the debt owed to the intimacies of our love/friendship." The mention of "intimacies" (*ta sunethe*/τ[ὰ συνή]θη), which granted is conjecture on the part of the editors, so what is said at this moment must be taken as a suggestion, recalls the intimate relationship (*sunetheia*/συνηθεία) of Bardas Bratzes and Nikephoros from the *Life of Mary the Younger*[35]:

> "Since," [Bardas Bratzes] says [to Nikephoros], "O dearest of men to me, we have become deeply involved with each other and are bound by our *intimate relationship* (*sunetheias*/συνηθείας). I think it right to make this, our bond of love, stronger and more perfect and to apply the ties of kinship to it, so that we may be joined in two ways, forging a family connection along with our *intimate relationship* (*sunetheias*/συνηθείας)."
> (*Life of Mary the Younger* 2/692)[36]

The writer also honors the groom, who, he says, has acted temperately. The marriage therefore is a moment of temperance and wise behavior. This observation of Theodoros opens up the question as to intemperance in the past, in the present, or in the future. Is there a broader terrain here? The final sentence returns to the love (*tes agapes*/τῆς ἀγάπης) they share and the hope that it will continue. The focus of the letter has shifted from the wedding to the letter writer and his relationship with the groom. By letter's end the bodies of groom and writer have both been staged and there seems precariousness in the friendship of the two men, as the writer, evidencing some insecurity, wants the groom to remain mindful of their relationship and to nurture it.

Remarks of Menander Rhetor (third century CE), from one of his treatises on epideictic oratory, provide intertexts to measure the semantics of this letter further. Menander and his two treatises or handbooks on how to make speeches of praise were well known in Byzantium at all periods.[37] It is eye-opening to compare *Letter 18* to what Menander says about what a rhetor should do if he would provide remarks (*logoi*) prior to a wedding, i.e., the Wedding Speech (*ho epithalamios logos*/ὁ ἐπιθαλάμιος λόγος or *gamelios logos*/γαμήλιος λόγος),[38] or just prior to the newlyweds sharing their bed for the first time, i.e., the Bedding Speech (*ho kateunastikos logos*/ὁ κατευναστικὸς λόγος).[39] In the Bedding Speech, Menander makes a comment that Theodoros plausibly took to heart in constructing his letter:

> May you exhort him [i.e., the young man about to take his new wife to bed] via the beauty of the wedding chamber, which the Graces adorn, and via the ripe beauty of the maiden, and [observing] what marriage deities there are all around her.
> (Menander Rhetor 2.6.7/407 [Loeb 244])[40]

But both speeches have references to things that will be familiar to a reader of *Letter 18*: the bridal bedroom (*pastas*/παστάς[41]) and the wedding chamber (*thalamos*/θάλαμος[42]), Aphrodite,[43] Erotes,[44] and Graces.[45] A place where the resemblance ends, though, is where the emphasis changes from

30   *Eroticism and Desire in Epistolography*

celebrating the newlyweds to speaking of the relation between letter writer and groom. As Menander's prescriptions do not include foregrounding the speaker, the change in focus highlights the personal bond. As a model is ostentatiously no longer being followed, the letter arguably performs genuineness and sincerity here.

And it is at this moment that focus moves from *Letter 18* to *Letter 17*. The centering of the relation between writer and recipient seen at the end of *Letter 18* pervades *Letter 17*. Indeed, *Letter 17* makes the wedding an occasion for much talk about the connection between letter writer and groom, and the groom's new marriage is all but forgotten. What is a final thought in *Letter 18* blooms into a corporeal and emotional extravaganza in *Letter 17*.

Letter 17

Letter 17 comes with a title that says he wrote this letter for Basil to send to one of his friends on the occasion of the friend's "wedding festival." The letter depicts the exertions of the groom on his first night in the marital bed, and, in tandem with these exertions, the sexy bodily disturbances the letter writer was feeling at the same time:

> A letter of Theodoros Daphnopates, *patrikios* and *eparchos*, so as [to be] from the person of Basil the *protospatharios* to one of his friends who was having his wedding festival:
> Oh you of my friends the one most to be marvelled at (and I will add, in the present moment also, the one most initiated), something happened to me which I would have to reveal in the case of someone else, but really in your case. Around the time of dawn's rays, a slumber sweeter than usual was coming upon me and it was, as it seems, a most un-mendacious prophet of things about to happen. For certain itchings, exertions of hands, the excitement of innards entire, and desire placed by nature in the liver were throwing [my] whole [body], roused awake, into confusion and causing a pitching, as though they were tossing a raft in the waves in a storm and crushing it to pieces. But such things, as I am able to surmise, were most un-mendacious tokens of the things that happened to you. For *when* you were already leaving off from your erotic exercise, *when* the Erotes, bidding farewell, were departing, *when* Aphrodite with coaxing words was granting you victory in that moment, *when* the laborer of the night, a Hermes, was going down/settling, having disposed of all the things of his assistance well, *when* the things of your hopes were at last safe and beyond question, with you having manfully set yourself to those Herculean battles, having sufficiently satisfied your desire, and having been warmed sufficiently by the breezes of erotic desire—*at that moment* swarms from bows of erotic desire, being loosed invisibly, were wounding poor me in my liver, they were striking against my heart, they were being launched against my mind. And when you

yourself were having a share of the things of completion, I was being aroused by them to the beginning of sweet pain. When coming into my sight, you announced your feat and I marvelled at the similar power of *pathos* and the companionability and sociability of the marvelous Erotes extending through all men.

But you, dear and honorable soul, and whoever, like you, is mastered by such a praise-worthy and blessed *pathos*, may you be for me lucky amid such endeavours, secretly and according to proper ritual bringing to completion the concealed and not-to-be spoken mysteries of the goddess (*sc*. Aphrodite). Let there be in your heart consideration for me and fellow-feeling, because I am being deprived of the things I desire and I am enduring being far away and bereft of them. Guard the things of our friendship and be a good manager of them. May statues and bronze *stelai* utter words before any of these sorts of things between us be made known.

(Theodoros Daphnopates, *Letter 17*)[46]

These two men, according to this letter, felt sexual excitement magically at the same time. The (purported) letter writer's thoughts and feelings feature much carnality: hands exerting themselves suggesting masturbation, and innards' turmoil pointing to strong desire and even to memories of penetrations, as he was like a raft mastered by forces greater than he. There is extensive visualization of the climax and postlude of the groom's successful completion of his "erotic exercise" (*erotikou gumnasiou*/ἐρωτικοῦ γυμνασίου) and "Herculean battles" (*Herakleotikou[s]...agonas*/Ἡρακλεωτικοῦ[ς]... ἀγῶνας). Aphrodite and Erotes are on hand, logically enough in this scene, and, specifically for the period of detumescence, there is the appearance of Hermes, as "laborer of the night." Laborer of the night seems a logical phrase to designate the groom's genitalia which are going down. There is more to say about Hermes, including why the translation says "a Hermes," but that is for later in the general interpretive commentary on the letter.

The letter continues with the almost but not quite parallel sexual excitements of letter writer and groom. The letter writer apparently only progresses some way down the road toward an orgasm,[47] while the groom completes his journey (and "Hermes," successful, sags). All of this, according to the conceit of the letter, came out later when writer and groom met, perhaps later that morning, and compared notes, as it were.[48] It is surely, the letter continues, a testament to the companionable and sociable[49] power of Erotes who make their way through all peoples to cause sexual feeling, *pathos*/πάθος, which is experienced similarly in disparate places.

In the second paragraph of the letter, there is more talk of *pathos*, which is worth holding in esteem, even as it also needs to be hidden and perhaps has something pagan about it (which calls to mind *Letter 31*). Indeed, that *pathos* had something sexual about it was well known from antiquity going forward.[50] It could indicate literally the feeling of desire and even the sensation of being penetrated (through its relation to the verb *pascho*/πάσχω ["to endure"]),[51] or speak to the mental unmooring that occurs on account of feelings of desire and infatuation. Then, the letter writer hopes that there will be a thought for him in his friend's heart, as he, having to do without at a distance, does not have what he desires. The letter concludes with a wish that the writer's friend keep secret from others what they have together. Let statues and steles speak before the details of their relationship might be known. This wish for discretion is ironic, as it already involves three men and is in a letter, which, of course, is not actually private.

Unlike a number of the letters under discussion in this book, *Letter 17* has received some scholarly attention. It has been found to be too fantastical *and*, at the same time, exemplary of a prevalent fault of fabulation in Byzantine epistolography against which critics need to guard themselves.[52] It has also been suggested that Basil is a eunuch[53] because he does not orgasm[54] and speaks of how he is far away from the (desirable) sexual arena in which his friend is excelling.[55] Other approaches, more congenial, have focused on the connection between letter writer and the recipient.[56]

Privileging homosociality is preferable because the wedding and conjugal sex become an occasion for placing bodies and relations between men front and center: at the end of *Letter 18* and throughout *Letter 17*. And appearing in *Letter 17* are body parts, bodily sensations, a primary relation between at least two men (and maybe more, if Theodoros is included), certainly one successful ejaculation, a perhaps unsuccessful attempt at another, a man to man meeting to speak of sexual matters, and one man narrating the affairs of two other men, giving the words to one of them to send to the other. The sum total of these things hints at other instances of similar activities that would be against civil law and ecclesiastical canon, and indeed to attitudes opposed to carnality elsewhere. But worries over exciting the concerns of authorities or community opinions is but unconvincingly signaled at the end of the letter, when mention is made of *stelai* and statue. Odorico says that the letter offers a view into an individual response to strictures and indeed into ways that a Byzantine man could think about forbidden practices:

> It [*sc.* the letter] allows us to note the distance the individual has from the values that society officially supports, not only in individual practice, but in the way of conceiving of these practices.
> (Odorico 1995, 311)[57]

And it ultimately amounts to more than an individual response. These letters are public documents that partake of a general set of expectations about the performance of relations for current and indeed future audiences. For this reason, then, these two letters are not idiosyncratic but representative. Indeed, Odorico sees *Letter 17* as indicative of a "diffuse mentality" (*mentalité diffuse*) about these man-to-man matters:

> Because the letters of Byzantine men of letters (*rhetors*) are not only personal documents but are also (and principally) literary works with

exemplary value both in terms of stylistic excellence and in terms of reflecting shared attitudes in a homogeneous environment, the testimony of Daphnopates turns out to be highly representative of a diffuse mentality.
(Odorico 1995, 312)[58]

And this "diffuse mentality" is as follows: the culture of homosociality of these Byzantine men features occasional unblushing talk of carnal matters. This is visible in other letters in various ways and emerges in the historiographies too. At the overt end of a continuum, these instances of frank representation are to be seen as instances of greater directness that illuminate subtexts in more oblique depictions elsewhere of same-sex desire and same-sex sexual behavior.

Discussion of *Letter 18* mentioned that interpretation of intertextuality with Menander Rhetor's prescriptions for the wedding and bedding *logoi* reveals depths in that letter. Interpretation of intertextuality with Menander Rhetor also highlights the audacity and extravagance of *Letter 17*, which, in turn, attests to this "diffuse mentality" that is contestatory of moralizing strictures around carnal matters.

The reader of *Letter 17* will see much that recalls what Menander says. For example, as letter writer and groom meet at some point after his first night with his bride, so a similar debriefing is envisaged toward the beginning of the remarks for the bedding *logos*:

> We offer praise... of the bravery and strength of the young man, exhorting him not to shame them when there will be so many witnesses present on the morning after his initiation.
> (Menander Rhetor 2.6.2/405–406 [Loeb 240])[59]

Present too in *Letter 17* are deities of love and Herakles, which were noted as commonalities between Menander and *Letter 18*. Indeed, there is a moment in the recommendations for the Wedding Speech that has Erotes with arrows notched and ready, which recalls the arrows that assail the letter writer in *Letter 17*:

> The fourth topic[60] is speaking of items concerned with the wedding chamber and bridal bedrooms and wedding deities; and like so, when we would speak: "Therefore the city has come together. All of it is celebrating the festival, while the bridal bedrooms, of a kind as never before for another, stand ready, and the wedding chamber has been adorned with flowers and paintings of all kinds and it holds a surfeit of Aphrodite [in it]. I am convinced that Erotes are present stretching taut[61] their bows, notching their arrows, having annointed the tips with drugs of desire through which they make souls breathe as one. Hymenaios will light the lamps and torches with marriage fire for us." You should also mention the Graces and Aphrodite...
> (Menander Rhetor 2.5.21–22/404 [Loeb 236–238])[62]

With this talk of arrows, a way *Letter 17* departs from the recommendations of Menander Rhetor becomes visible. The letter writer, and not the bride or groom, is the most evident recipient of the arrows of love in the letter. It is not usual for an interested bystander at a wedding to become infactuated, as this is not their day. And this departure from Menander's remarks puts a spotlight on the letter writer and his feelings for the groom through a now refused imitation of the rhetorical occasion.

But this is not the only departure that would be perceptible to an educated audience. Menander recommends that the bedding *logos* have an easy paratactic flow[63]:

> For the speech must be unadorned and for the most part be unconnected, not in clauses and periods, but proceeding more according to prose (i.e., not with an excess of poetical conceits), as in the genre of the chat.
>
> (Menander Rhetor 2.6.26/411 [Loeb 256])[64]

Letter 17 does not follow this directive. In particular, a sentence of over 80 words in the middle of the letter begins with a "when" (ὅτε) that waits for its "then" (τότε [translated as "at that moment"]) for over 60 words and across 5 subordinate clauses.[65]

But there is yet one more departure that is probably the most important: the prevalence of indiscretion in the letter, a thing against which Menander cautions. The bedding *logos*, herald and prelude to a night of sex, must not cross a line and become too carnal: "Care must be taken in this [*logos*], lest we seem say anything base, cheap, or bad, dropping to base and paltry things" (2.6.3/406 [Loeb 242]).[66] It is clear that *Letter 17* crosses the line here, what with talk of pathos and body parts. If we have this rhetorical occasion in mind, this is surely not what Menander intended for *this* rhetorical occasion.[67] To further illustrate this carnal excess and finish discussion of *Letter 17*, a return to Hermes, "the laborer of the night."

Just after mention of Erotes and Aphrodite in *Letter 17*, Hermes appears: "the laborer of the night, a Hermes, was going down/settling, having disposed of all the things of his assistance well."[68] As was remarked above, it is clear enough that the laborer of the night can refer to the groom's genitalia, the reference to detumescence is evident: duty done, he settles. Still, the presence of Hermes, especially with the unparalleled epithet "the laborer of the night," is somewhat puzzling, a situation noted by editors of the scholarly edition.[69] They suggest a passage from Plutarch's *Coniugalia Praecepta* as a way to make sense of the grouping of Hermes with deities of love and desire: "men of old put Hermes in place next to Aphrodite, as the pleasure of the marriage was especially in need of *logos*/reason" (*Coniugalia Praecepta* 138C-D).[70] Plutarch does provide an explanation for the collocation with Aphrodite and the Erotes—Hermes, the interpreter/translator god, will, say, put erotic pleasure in language that can be understood, will make this

Eroticism and Desire in Epistolography 35

pleasure explicable—but this moment from the *Coniugalia Praecepta* does not explain the epithete, "laborer of the night." Thought about the laborer of the night and the graphic nature what accompanies his appearance—he "was going down/settling"—leads to revelation of another explanation. Is this a reference to a herm, which were in the built environment of Classical Greece and were, in any case, known from literature?

A herm was a bust of a mature bearded man mounted on top of an almost featureless rectangular pediment that was taller than it was wide (see Figure 1.2). The one feature that the pediment possessed was an erect penis about where it would be, if it were on a man's naked body sculpted in full. That one of these stone herms, which were used as property markers in

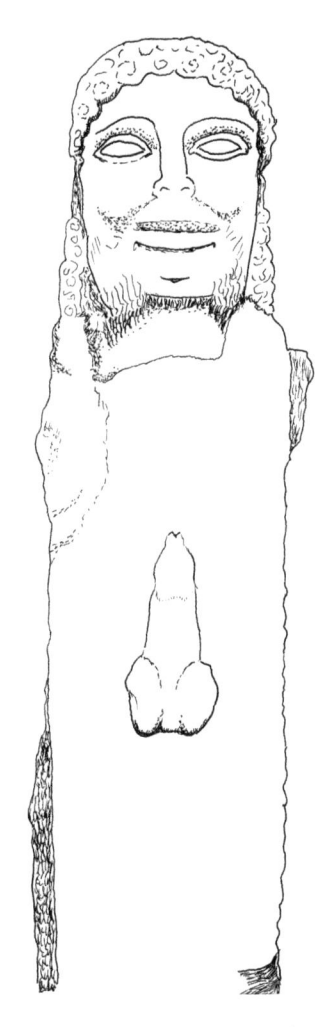

Figure 1.2 Drawing of a sixth-century BCE herm from Siphnos (original in the National Archaeological Museum of Athens). Artist: Jonathan Else.

classical times, could be called to mind for a reader of *Letter 17* is backed up by the fact of the word for the god Hermes and a herm being the same in Classical and Byzantine Greek sources. English has two words, one for the god and the other for the sculpted boundary marker, while Greek has the one, hence the translation of the word as "a Hermes," which reproduces the ambiguity of the Greek. Furthermore, there are discussions of herms in the literature being preserved and collected by the Byzantines at this period. There was awareness of these statues in the texts, if there were not many to be seen anymore in the built environment.

For example, the *Suda*,[71] the encyclopedia compiled within Daphnopates' milieu about 20 years prior to *Letter 17*, has occasion to mention herm/Hermes a number of times. For example, herms (for which, read "Hermes") were in the past to be seen all around Athens:

> Of Herms: Herms, of stone, were in the city of Athens in the doorways and shrines. They say that since Hermes is the guardian of speech and truth, for this reason they made the images rectangular and cubic, conveying via a riddling medium with respect to this sort of shape, on whichever side it should fall, that it on all sides is stable and upright. Thus too speech and truth are on all sides similar to themselves, while falsehood is diffuse, riven, and most of all discordant with itself.
>
> (*Suda*, Epsilon 3051)[72]

Missing in this allegorical reading is the phallus, but there is much evidence of it elsewhere. For example, the first-century Lucaeus Annaeus Cornutus speaks of the custom of the older Greeks to make these representations:

> The ancients used to make older and bearded [representations of] Hermes that had erect penises[73]...
>
> (*Theologiae Graecae Compendium* 23)[74]

Diogenes Laertius speaks of the philosopher Demetrius (late fourth century to early third century BCE) who compared a dissolute young man to a herm:

> At one point, having caught sight of a dissolute young man, he said, "behold a rectangular Hermes! He has robe, ass, cock, and beard!"
>
> (*Lives of the Eminent Philosophers* 5.82)[75]

Aristophanes' *Lysistrata* has two relevant lines, addressed by the chorus leader to a Spartan and Athenian, who are both sporting prominent erections:

> ...if you are wise, you will put on cloaks, so that none of the "herm-choppers" will catch sight of you. (1093–1094)[76]

Eroticism and Desire in Epistolography 37

And there was, of course, the famous mutilation of the herms in 415 BCE in Athens prior to Sicilian Expedition, to which Aristophanes is clearly referring and which is famous from Thucydides.[77]

Lastly a return to the *Suda* for one more entry to close out discussion of herm/Hermes in *Letter 17*. The entry Psi 99[78] offers an interesting definition for "whispering Hermes, Eros and Aphrodite." The collocation of Hermes, Eros, and Aphrodite in a roughly contemporaneous text naturally attracts the attention of a reader of *Letter 17*:

> Of whispering Hermes, Eros, and Aphrodite: what Theseus did first, as Zopyros says, since Phaedra, as the story goes, whispered to Theseus against Hippolytus, slandering him. But they say [i.e., *communis opinio* is] something more human (*anthropinoteron*/ἀνθρωπινώτερον) in the matter of Hermes the Whisperer, as to how people coming together there [probably in front of Hermes/a herm] propose not-to-be-spoken things (*ta aporreta*/τὰ ἀπόρρητα) and whisper to each other, all about what they wish [to do]. Also: whispering is the slandering of those being present according to the Apostle.[79]
>
> (*Suda*, Psi 99)[80]

There are two emphases in Psi 99. One is the whispering that happens among groups of people that presages communal disorder, an aspect the conclusion from Paul ("the Apostle") brings home, when he says he fears dissension among the Corinthians, of which "whisperings" will be a part.[81] The other emphasis is on the things related to sexual desire, which is already suggested by the presence of Eros and Aphrodite. The reference to the sad house of Theseus, brought to grief by desire and Aphrodite, also underscrores this. In the middle of the entry, there is moral complexity in evidence, however, with a tone perceptedly at odds with the beginning with Theseus and the end with Paul. It speaks of something that is "more human." At this point, the entry highlights Hermes the Whisperer. People come together at a temple for Hermes, or, more probably, in front of a herm, and propose "not-to-be spoken things" and whisper to each other about what they desire. It is worth noting that things not-to-be spoken are often sexual secrets, and further that this term, *ta aporreta*/τὰ ἀπόρρητα, is a euphemisn for the genitals, *ta aidoia*/τὰ αἰδοῖα in earlier literature.[82] And the reader of *Letter 17* will remember the "not-to-be spoken mysteries of the goddess (*sc*. Aphrodite)," also using the word *aporreta*/ἀπόρρητα.[83]

And so this entry from the *Suda*, which speaks of Hermes, deities of love, desire, and secrecy, has much in common with the letter. Is the letter writer in essence whispering to the groom about what he wants to do? Does the reader scan the letter but cannot make out precisely what is being said, although they don't have nothing either? The reader "sees" them talking but not all is clear about what the ostensible writer "wishes [to do]," as he speaks of the Erotes, Aphrodite, and Hermes, all three of which are explicitly associated with desire in the letter. Indeed, the final words of the letter, "may statues and bronze *stelai* utter words before any of these sorts of things between us will be made known,"[84] make the reader think of the built environment, and they might begin to wonder if the only solution is to find a Hermes to interpret these communications that have some obscurities, or a herm to spit them out.

Desire's Dreams and Visions in Letters of an Emperor and His Friend

In his *Letter 17*, Theodoros Daphnopates set the scene for the narration of parallel sexual scenarios with reference to "slumber":

> Around the time of dawn's rays, a slumber sweeter than usual was coming upon me and it was, as it seems, a most un-mendacious prophet of things about to happen.[85]

This pleasurable and premonitory sleep dissipated and led to "certain itchings" and "exertions of hands."[86] This slumber, a *hupnos* (ὕπνος), was the obscure but pleasant impetus to physical and wide-awake descriptions. Two letters to be analyzed presently, one by Emperor Constantine VII Porphyrogennetos and the other by Theodoros of Kyzikos, explore this zone of sleep, probing and explaining it, and, like Daphnopates' letter, the reveries that follow when one is awake. The two letters chosen not only speak of dreams and waking visions, they also place desire front and center, manipulating its phenomenology. Indeed, in one of them, a metaphor of rose and thorn appears whose bodily correlate is anal eroticism.[87]

A sequence of 18 letters that passed between Emperor Constantine VII Porphyrogennetos and Theodoros of Kyzikos has survived.[88] These letters answer one another and it is precious and rare to have a conversation documented like this. Relying on evidence internal to the letters (mention of a Russian incursion[89] and general anxiety around rulership, which suggests that Emperor Romanos I Lekapenos, who was the overshadowing emperor through much of Constantine's youth, was still around or Constantine was but freshly in charge[90]), scholars have thought the letters date from the 940s.[91]

Proclaimed emperor while still a boy in 913, Constantine VII Porphyrogennetos was emperor until his death in 959. That said, Emperor Romanos I Lekapenos consigned Constantine to the sidelines in 920, taking over as lead emperor until 944. This meant that Constantine, denied political power, had leisure to develop his intellectual interests. Once he was sole emperor and probably before that, he superintended important intellectual projects. He guided the writing of the immense encyclopedia, the *Suda*, which has already been cited in this book. This work of over 600,000 words pulls together much information that goes back as far as early Greece in the

BCE centuries. It gives an indication of the level of *paideia* in Constantine's court. He also commissioned histories,[92] the *De Ceremoniis* (the invaluable guide to imperial ceremonial), the *Excerpta de Sententiis* (a massive project of excerpting earlier literature), and much else besides.[93] Constantine was a leading figure in an intensely intellectual milieu that lasted for decades.

Not as much is known about Theodoros of Kyzikos. He was a churchman whose star shone bright for as long as Constantine was emperor. Later, he seems to have run afoul of the new regime that came to power after the death of Constantine's son, Emperor Romanos II, in 963. He was exiled that year, and we hear nothing more of him after 965.[94] As is the case with Constantine, he clearly had attained a high degree of education.

Dreams and Visions in the Suda

Dreams and waking visions enliven the two letters to be discussed below. They provide phenomenologically varied ways for Constantine and Theodoros to present desire for one another. It is relevant that Constantine's own encyclopedia, the *Suda*, provides definitions for both dreams and waking visions. A look at the *Suda*'s entries on the "dream" (*Oneiron*/Ὄνειρον) and "waking vision" (*Hupar*/Ὕπαρ) underscores the significance of their appearances in the letters. According to the *Suda*, the distinction between visions to keep in mind is whether one is asleep and dreaming, or one is awake and experiencing a waking vision.

The *Suda* defines the "dream" (*oneiron*/ὄνειρον) in relation to the "vision-in-sleep" (*enupnion*/ἐνύπνιον).[95] The entry itself is confused, that is, a quotation from Homer at the end contradicts the definition being developed. Nevertheless, it is safe to say that the difference between dreams and visions-in-sleep is that dreams have a pronounced connection to reality and predict what will be:

> A dream differs from a vision-in-sleep. It is something else and not the same. But someone can say not objectionably that a dream is a vision-in-sleep. But whenever someone speaks with skillful precision, it is necessary to use each word in its proper sense, and the one meaningless and not foretelling anything, having its power during sleep alone, and coming into being because of an irrational desire or an overarching fear or satiety or poverty: this one it is necessary to call a vision-in-sleep. With respect to a good or bad dream there is effectivity in reality or soon to eventuate. Often [*sc.* both of the] nouns must be used, just as Homer [says]: "a divine dream came to me as a vision-in-sleep."
> (*Suda*, Omicron 345)[96]

The dream (*oneiron*/ὄνειρον) addresses reality and has predicative power ("effectivity in reality or soon to eventuate"), whereas the vision-in-sleep (*enupnion*/ἐνύπνιον) comes from something irrational in the mind or from

40 *Eroticism and Desire in Epistolography*

the way the body is feeling, and therefore has, according to the *Suda*, no address to reality. It is debatable, of course, whether a dream driven by, say, the reality of one's own indigestion is not somehow connected to reality. But rather than question too exactingly, it is best to accept the distinction and allow mental or somatic solipsism define the vision-in-sleep. The quotation from Homer confuses things. As the vision-in-sleep (ἐνύπνιον) plays in the mind while one is asleep, a divine dream (*theios...oneiros*/θεῖος ...ὄνειρος) can appear within this envelope, as it were. This has to be understood as a mistake of the *Suda*.

The other type of vision is one that appears to someone who is not asleep: the "waking vision" (*hupar*/ὕπαρ):

> A waking vision is truth and not [a vision] in a dream; a dream during the day. [A waking vision] is existent obviously and truly. "You tell me my dream and I seem to relate [to you] your waking vision" [writes Emperor Julian in a letter].[97] A waking vision designates a dream during the day as evidently existent, a true thing; [also] according to the removal of the final syllable, the *chon*/χον; [to whit, *huparchon*/ὑπάρχον ("thing existing") has become *hupar*/ὕπαρ].
>
> (*Suda*, Upsilon 155)[98]

The waking vision (*hupar*/ὕπαρ) is distinct from the dream (ὄνειρον), and especially from the vision-in-sleep (*enupnion*/ἐνύπνιον). It has a closer relationship to reality, as it is truth (*aletheia*/ἀλήθεια). The *Suda* entry strengthens the point about truth through asserting that the word for waking vision, *hupar*/ὕπαρ, is an abbreviation of *huparchon*/ὑπάρχον, which means "thing existing." The waking vision also happens during the day while one is awake. As a daytime envisioning, it has, on this basis, an attachment to things that are real: consciousness establishes credibility. Still though, a tension is present in this word, and, as above with the dream, it is best not to try to resolve it. It is a tension between, on the one hand, the reality of envisioning things while awake, that is, the fact of consciousness, and, on the other hand, an oblique connection the waking vision has to things that are real, which is occult and even supernatural. Quoted in the *Suda*, Emperor Julian highlights this tension: magically, and from a distance, he tells Ecdicius, the recipient of his *Letter 108*, what the truth is:

> Emperor Julian to the Ecdicius, the Prefect of Egypt:
> The proverb says: "You tell me my dream (*onar*/ὄναρ)," and I seem to relate to you your waking vision (*hupar*/ὕπαρ). The Nile, they say, great raised aloft by cubits has filled up all of Egypt. If you desire to hear an accounting, it is fifteen [cubits] on the twentieth of September. Theophilus, the *stratopedarch*, discloses this. If, accordingly, you did not know this, hearing it from me, rejoice!
>
> (Emperor Julian, *Letter 108* [362 CE])[99]

It is not known what Ecdicius wrote before, perhaps a request of some kind. In any case, Julian relates facts that have come to him in a dream, and he miraculously tells what was before Ecdicius' eyes, that is, the Nile in flood. This letter and the *Suda* entry on *hupar*, therefore, underscore the close relation that the dream and waking vision have to reality.

A Letter from Constantine

Constantine voices desire for Theodoros often in *Letter B3*. He approaches his desire via dream and waking vision:

> These things of mine are not a letter, by your virtue, but something small has done service, characteristic of a little priest and cheap, in answer to the sort of letter [you have written]! The idea [that this is so], even if I will deny it, is surely clear to those who know what I'm like. Indeed, the shoddy state of my mind and the barbarity and incorrect usage of my muse-less state are not unknown to many and it's not hidden from them either. It is clear and evident, even if I should venture to deny it.
>
> Having received the summer fruit, truly sweet and dripping with honey, and the wine scented with flowers, which was called in very ancient times nectar, I have tasted it as though having received some small kiss from your sweet lips. But, while filled up by this all the more and as though, according to what has been written, made to rejoice (*euphranthentes*/εὐφρανθέντες), I found constriction and distress in my heart arising in the company of my wine glass, just as, I suppose, the thorn thrives, somehow, near the rose. This is the law of *eros* and of *philia* that's unbastardized, true, sweet, and lovable/erotic. What is more wounding than thorns, or a two-edged sword, unless it be the loss of one's *eromenos*, the absence and being away of a friend, and of such a one so trustworthy, wisdom-loving, and holding the first place surely in all things? For I am, as it turns out, an *erastes* maddened as regards those who have *philia* for me, for I am mad but [I am mad] temperately, for *philia* [as far as I am concerned] knows how to innovate (*kainotomein*/καινοτομεῖν) in all things. But I allow more to you, as I know that you are well-disposed to me and will remain so.
>
> Many times and in many ways, dreams shake me up and make me rejoice (*euphrainousi*/εὐφραίνουσι). And just as if they put my dearest one in my hands, they counterfeit conversation/intercourse and deceive me about kissing. But then I curse many times the waking vision (*hupar*/ὕπαρ) and believe it a bringer of loss, for what I enjoy in dreams and however much of desire I am filled with, I, awakened, discover myself bereft of such pleasure and I pray to my Lord God to give me the moment to kiss my dear friend and the moment to desire my desired one and to bite him not in a hostile way but in a friendly way, for those who

feel *philia* bite not so much so that they may harm but so that they may desire all the more. Pray therefore for the moment to come so that we may satisfy our desire.

(Constantine VII Porphyrogennetos, *Letter B3*)[100]

There is much to say about this letter. First, Constantine affects rusticity with the evident aim of lowering Theodoros' expectations. The letter then gains homoerotic warmth as it proceeds. He speaks of Theodoros' gift of summer fruit and wine, likening them to a kiss from his lips. He expands on the emotion, feeling filled up and rejoicing: "and as though, according to what has been written, 'made to rejoice.'"[101] "Made to rejoice" is meant to be read intertextually, as Constantine signals by saying "according to what has been written." As Tziatzi-Papagianni suggests,[102] a probable intertext is a portion of Ps 103/104, a psalm which enumerates benefits that God brings to the world:

...raising up grass for the cattle and the shoots for the slavery of men to bring forth bread from the earth. Wine makes the heart of a man rejoice (*euphrainei*/εὐφραίνει) to make the face shine with oil, and bread makes the heart of man strong. The trees of the plain will be made to grow lushly, the cedars of Lebanon which he planted.

(Ps 103/104:14–16)[103]

Recollection of this psalm leads to further reflections, for there are additional commonalities between these two texts. They have pleasant elements in common and there are accompanying items that qualify pleasure: things in the psalm and the letter come with a catch.

Heart and wine are present in both the psalm[104] and the letter.[105] There also are good things to eat: summer fruit in the letter and sustaining bread in the psalm. Good things do not come free, however. In the psalm, the slavery of men[106] accompanies the things to be enjoyed. In the letter, wine and summer fruit are accompanied by "constriction and distress."[107] The acknowledgment of a downside then leads Constantine to reflect further on other instances in which the good is accompanied by the unwanted. Constantine provides an explanatory metaphor: that of the rose and thorn.

Constantine's mention of the rose and thorn intensifies the erotic content of his letter, placed as it is between the thought of Theodoros' kiss and musings on *eros* and *philia* and the introduction of the terms *eromenos* (ἐρώμενος, "beloved boy" [lit.: "beloved male"]) and *erastes* (ἐραστής, "lover"). In the *Greek Anthology*, the anus of the boy was the rosebud and the thorn was the hair on the backside that would arrive to mark the supposed end of a boy's desirability. For example, in the anonymous fortieth epigram from Book 12, a young man past the age of boyish desirability wishes to be worshipped as a statue might be. But he wants to be a particular kind a statue: one whose extremities are made of marble, but the rest, made of wood (probably) and covered with a cloak, is not:

> "Don't take off my little cloak, man, but look at me as if I were a god's statue with marble extremities." Seeking the naked grace of Antiphilos, you will discover his blooming rosebud, as it were, amid thorns!
> (*Greek Anthology* 12.40)[108]

Antiphilos, whose words in quotation commence the epigram, does not want his cloak removed, for it will reveal that he has sprouted hairs on his rear.[109] A work like this epigram would occur to an educated Byzantine reader, and Theodoros was certainly one of those, not only because of the compilation and circulation of pederastic poetry in the *Greek Anthology* at this time but also because of the mention of beloved boy and lover, who appear soon in the letter.

Next, Constantine writes of "the law of *eros* and of *philia* that's unbastardized, true, sweet, and lovable/erotic."[110] One could be forgiven for imagining that Constantine was going to expand on the "law" of maturity bringing an end to desirability, given what he was just writing about. But it turns out that the primary aspect of this law about which he wishes to speak is the pain of being apart, for this is what causes "constriction and distress in [his] heart."[111] In any case, he no sooner mentions the law than the thorns reappear, but they are not as wounding as absence. And as the thorns cannot compete with absence, neither can a new metaphor, that of the two-edged sword (*rhomphaia distomos*/ρομφαία δίστομος): "What is more wounding than thorns, or a two-edged sword, unless it be the loss of one's *eromenos*…?"[112] The two-edged sword appears in both the Septuagint[113] and in the New Testament[114] and moves the letter into intertextuality with scripture and away from pederastic literature. What is the valence of this image? Thorns and roses speak of pederasty in a certain way, a way which is interrupted in the letter. What does the two-edged sword say?

In the Septuagint, the two-edged sword appears in the Psalms and Sirach. In the bloodthirsty Ps 149, the two-edged sword is a weapon of righteous aggression that holy men wield after they have praised God and taken carnal enjoyment in their bedchambers:

> …the holy men will speak loud in glory and they will enjoy themselves exceedingly in their bedchambers. The exaltations of God will be in their throats and the two-edged swords will be in their hands to bring vengeance to the nations, to refute the peoples, to bind their kings in fetters and their nobles in iron chains, to bring to them the judgement that has been written. This glory will be for all His holy men.
> (Ps 149:5–9)[115]

44   *Eroticism and Desire in Epistolography*

This weapon of the righteous men appears with nearly opposite valence in Sirach. Here, the two-edged sword is not a weapon wielded by the holy ones, it is, instead, among the metaphors for soul-destroying sin:

> Have you sinned child? Do so no longer and ask for pardon for your previous [sins]. As from the face of a serpent, flee from sin. For if you will approach, it will bite you: its teeth are those of a lion carrying off souls of people, just as the two-edged sword is all lawlessness, there is no cure for its blow.
>
> (Sir 21:1–3)[116]

These two occurrences from the Septuagint show that the two-edged sword has a double valence. On the one hand, it is a weapon of the carnal fathers who fight with divine sanction, and, on the other, it is "all lawlessness" (*pasa anomia*/πᾶσα ἀνομία) that will destroy a soul, similar to a savage beast that bites or a malady for which there is no remedy. Interestingly, sin will "bite." Constantine says later in the letter he hopes to bite Theodoros, and Theodoros, in his letter, will hope to return the favor.

The two-edged also occurs in the Apocalypse of John 1 and 2. As is well known, this section of the New Testament claims to be a quotation of a letter that John has written to the seven churches in Asia.[117] In this letter, he relates what an angel sent by Christ told him about last things. Hearing a voice telling him to write,[118] John turns around to see the source of that voice:

> I turned to look to the voice which was speaking with me. Having turned I saw seven gold candle-stands and, in the midst of the candle-stands, one like the son of man, clothed to his feet and wearing a gold sash across his breast. His head and hair are white as wool is white, as snow is white, and his eyes are as the fire's flame. His feet are like brass, as though in the furnace of the glowing [flame], and his voice is like the voice of many waters. He is holding in his right hand seven stars, and from his mouth a sharp two-edged sword is jutting out. The appearance of him shines as the sun does in its power.
>
> (Apoc 1:12–16)[119]

Here, the two-edged sword juts out from the mouth. It is a difficult image, but surely gestures in the direction of language that is aggressive. The words out of the mouth of the "one like the son of man" will be violent and punishing. The partly metaphorical nature of the sword discernible in Sirach ("all lawlessness") has been realized here, as the sword is as metaphorical as can be at this point in the text.

In the next section of the Apocalypse, the two-edged sword appears again. There are further directions for John:

> And to the angel of the church in Pergamum [John, I want you to] write the following: "The one holding the sharp two-edged sword says the

following: 'I know where you live, where the throne of Satan is, and you honor my name. You did not deny faith in me during the days faithful Antipas was a martyr, who was killed among you, in the place where Satan lives. But I do have some things against you. You have those who honor the teachings of Balaam, who taught Balak to pitch a snare in the face of the sons of Israel, to eat the sacrifices to the idols, and to fornicate. In the same moment you also have those honoring the teaching of the Nicolaitians. Repent therefore. If you don't, I will come for you swiftly, and I will make war against them with the sword of my mouth."

(Apoc 2:12–16)[120]

Here, the two-edged sword appears first as an actual weapon in the hand but at the end of the passage it is issuing from his mouth again.[121] There is movement toward physicality and then back toward the metaphor that characterized the two-edged sword in the first section of the Apocalypse. The two-edged sword, an instrument of physical and verbal chastisement, means to sharpen the resolve to repent of consuming sacrificial meats and fornicating (*phagein eidolothuta kai porneusai*/φαγεῖν εἰδωλόθυτα καὶ πορνεῦσαι), the latter of which is relevant in comparison with the desire-filled context of Constantine's letter.

When Constantine mentions the two-edged sword, he wields an image that, when in the Septuagint, is both an actual weapon of the carnal fathers and a metaphor for the damage that sin can do to the soul. In the New Testament, the two-edged sword is not only a physical weapon but also a metaphor for the punishing word of Christ that condemns fornication. This image from authoritative scripture brings moral and phenomenological complexity to this scene of desire in a medieval letter: carnality, chastisement of fornication, and lawlessness on one hand, and, on the other, a dichotomy between physicality and metaphoricity.

Comparison of the two-edged sword to the thorn (*akantha*/ἄκανθα) is revealing and appropriate, for Constantine presents them both as less vexatious than being apart from Theodoros is. The thorn encapsulates a limitation on desire according to the general protocols around pederasty: a hairy man is not to be desired. The threat posed by the two-edged sword to desire is more nebulous. It is certainly reasonable to imagine that the two-edged sword embodies strictures against carnal expression of desire, though it is not a simple image, on account of the references to carnality, lawlessness, *and* upholding God's law. But Constantine worries less about desire improper (thorn) or illicit (sword) than he does about being apart. He does not worry about prohibition, whether it is based on age—for hair on his beloved (*eromenos*) will not bother him—or on religion. Rather, absence is the worst thing. Indeed, he expands on this rule-breaking position when he says the following: "I am mad but [I am mad] temperately, for *philia* [as far as I am concerned] knows how to innovate in all things."[122] In their relations with one other another, paradoxes abound. Madness is temperate. There is a law of *eros* and *philia*, according to which rulebooks are thrown out amid innovation and renegotiation. Established law is innovation and the rule is that there is no rule.

Now having broken free of constraints, Constantine becomes direct and speaks of his desire as perceptible in dreams and in a waking vision, both of which of course, as noted above in the discussion of their respective entries in the *Suda*, had a particular address to reality and truth. In the letter, he remarks that dreams (*oneiroi*/ὄνειροι) often disturb his sleep. They make him rejoice, however, when he thinks his "dearest one" has been put in his hands, for then there is an opportunity for intercourse/conversation—a double-entendre: *prosomilein*/προσομιλεῖν—and kissing. Then he wakes and the visions he had while asleep yield to the kind one has while awake. The illusion of presence that unconsciousness made available is no longer present for him. And, he expresses dissatisfaction with being in the domain of the waking vision (*hupar*/ὕπαρ), as he is no longer enjoying the pleasure (*hedone*/ἡδονή) that the dreams were offering him, and which were bodily. A reader might expect that things will be more chaste going forward. This expectation is not met when the same things are written into the register of the waking vision; all these feelings turn out to be truth (*aletheia*/ἀλήθεια), even a thing existing (ὑπάρχον), as it were.[123] The waking vision, initially the chilly waters of reality, becomes an increasingly warm bath as kissing, friendly biting (*dakein...philikos*/δακεῖν...φιλικῶς), and the satisfaction of desire become "truth and not [a vision] in a dream," as the *Suda* would put it.[124]

In sum, Constantine outlines a place for his desire for Theodoros outside of strictures recoverable from both earlier Greek literature and scripture. The letter concludes with a phenomenologically varied depiction of this desire, which appears both in dream and waking vision. While a modern reader of this letter might be tempted to think Constantine's talk of dreams and visions is illusory, the *Suda* discourages such a view. Dreams and waking visions have a connection to truth and there is the fact that Constantine has spent much time considering his desire from a number of angles.

A Letter from Theodoros

Theodoros' answer to Constantine's letter is responsive and also interested in desire:

> Your letter, which honors me and is all knowing and quite smart, arrived today [and] has dispelled yesterday's gloom over being apart from you. It has changed [the gloom] to cheerfulness and sets alight and causes the flame in my heart to burn, [as well as the flame] of desire for the crowned and divine head of our imperial one. Already my soul is on fire, as it desires and seeks hoped for things. The sources of the sweet-mouthed and honey-dripping spring of you, of your wise and all-golden mouth, [the sources] lavish for me not only quench the flame, they enkindle it.

Hence then, during the day I envision for myself my desired one, gold gleaming for me and beyond light-filled, and during the night you, a dream (*oneiros*/ὄνειρος), stood at my right, and I see you in your nobility and in the beloved marvelousness of your always valiant and imperial smile. And at the moment I urged you to run faster in my dreams so that no one would beat you and close the palace to you, and I took zealous part so as not to be left behind. All things were second to "the snorting" of your "horse."[125]

But these things fall short of true rejoicing, for however much one seems to rejoice in a vision, to that extent one rages against the truth. May it happen that I be filled with your true intercourse and conversation, O God and Lord who converts everything to a better state.

I have received recompense many times over for yesterday's fruits, these fruits that have nothing brilliant about them other than the fact that they were chosen [for you by me], [recompense that is these] ripe and sweet words of yours, words that, through desirous/erotic biting and turning over my soul have a sweet scent, more than how the praised scent of flowers knows how to make the hearts of men rejoice or even nectar itself, on which the blessed ones used to get drunk.

(Theodoros of Kyzikos, *Letter B4*)[126]

In his answer, Theodoros prefers the flames of desire and, more egalitarian, he does not talk of lovers and beloved boys, thereby avoiding the asymmetries of pederasty which were a prominent theme in Constantine's letter. Nor does he speak of thorns and roses. Theodoros focuses instead on Constantine's sweet mouth and depicts the emperor as a spring, honeyed and golden, that does not quench a fire but makes it flame higher and hotter. Also depicting his thoughts about the emperor as happening both in an unconscious dream and in conscious visions, Theodoros articulates his desire via the dream/waking vision dichotomy in a manner similar to Constantine's. He thinks of Constantine during the day. Constantine also appears to Theodoros in a dream in which a running or horse-back riding Constantine is pursued. His dream is not as erotic as Constantine's. The running, perhaps a race, with overtones of political allegory, does not seem sexy. But the admiring lead-in, which features Theodoros' delight in Constantine's smile, perhaps is. There also might be a double-entendre with "stood" when he says, "during the night you, a dream, stood at my right."[127]

The verb in question *parestekas*/παρέστηκας is intransitive in this form and can refer to an erection, as resort to the *Greek Anthology* shows. In an epigram attributed to Skythinos (fifth or fourth century BCE), an impatient narrator addresses his erect penis:

Now you have stood (*hestekas*/ἔστηκας) straight up, nameless one, nor do you fail: you strain as though you would never cease. But when Nemesenos stretched out his entire self next to me on the bed, offering

48 *Eroticism and Desire in Epistolography*

everything I might have wanted, a dead thing you hung there. Strain, burst, and cry! It's all in vain. You will not receive mercy from my hand.
(*Greek Anthology* 12.232)[128]

The narrator berates his member for being hard now ("now you have stood straight up"[129]) when it only had erectile dysfunction to offer a willing boy at a previous moment. He will now let his penis suffer in an unrelieved erect state by refusing it masturbation.

Still, Theodoros' letter dismisses much of the content of the dream, as it merely contains things that appear "in a vision" and not the truth.[130] Although he rejoices in the dream, it is ultimately unfulfilling.[131] He prefers to picture his desired one during the day, in what could be termed a waking vision, though he does not call it a *hupar*. He wishes for "true intercourse and conversation," both of which are double-entendres.[132] He is also grateful for the words in Constantine's letters, calling them "ripe" (*horaious*/ὡραίους), a word often associated with sexually desirable persons.[133] And these words come on like an insistent lover. In speaking of how these words affect him, Theodoros corrects Constantine's friendly biting (*dakein...philikos*/δακεῖν... φιλικῶς) to say, instead, that they bite him in a desirous or erotic way (*daknein erotikos*/δάκνειν ἐρωτικῶς), and also that they are "turning over his soul." And this turning over is also worth attention. In this increasingly erotic milieu, that is, biting has just been made desirous/erotic, "turning over" (*strephein*/στρέφειν) turns out to have a relevant sexual life.

It will be useful to reprint the final words of the letter here:

I have received recompense many times over for yesterday's fruits, these fruits that have nothing brilliant about them other than the fact that they were chosen [for you by me], [recompense that is these] ripe and sweet words of yours, words that, through desirous/erotic biting and turning over my soul have a sweet scent, more than how the praised scent of flowers knows how to make the hearts of men rejoice or even nectar itself, on which the blessed ones used to get drunk.
(Theodoros of Kyzikos, *Letter B4*)[134]

A carnal vision is called up here: the emperor biting Theodoros on, what?, the neck and then turning him over to...oh wait, it's the soul (*psyche*/ψυχή). The arrival of the soul is deflating and decorporealizing, but it does not evacuate the immediately preceding words of semantic content. The reader has been on a journey that the late appearance of the soul cannot erase. Indeed, turning to "turning over" in the *Greek Anthology* reveals that this verb refers to anal penetration on four occasions.

Four epigrams, two from Book 5 and two from Book 12, show that this verb can be construed as designating a man turning someone, male or female, over or around in order to penetrate them anally. At 5.54.5–6, Dioscorides (originally third century BCE) suggests that if one's wife (or concubine) is pregnant, anal sex provides a good substitute enjoyment: "[H]aving turned your bed-partner over (*strepsas/στρέψας*), enjoy her buttocks that are like the rose, practicing boyish Kypris"[135] (note too the presence of the rose). In another poem, also from Book 5, Markos Argentarios (originally first century CE [?]) addressing devotees of male love, assures them that if they don't have a boy to hand and only a girl or a woman, anal intercourse is a remedy: "... having turned over Menophila of the beautiful hips, suppose in your mind that you possess male Menophilos himself in his recesses."[136] There is an epigram by Kallimakhos (originally third century BCE) in Book 12, which is one of the few poems in this book of the anthology not concerned with the love of younger men or boys. After telling some young men that they should not spend time with a female runaway slave,[137] Kallimakhos concludes the poem by implying that she is (probably) being anally penetrated: "For I know that she, worthy to be stoned, is in some kind of way being turned over around here and badly loved."[138] In another poem from Book 12, Rhianos (originally third century BCE) makes a list of dazzling boys who can command a man's attention. Theodoros or Philokles are truly beautiful to gaze upon.[139] The next boy mentioned, Leptines, is the point of interest. His gorgeous body is the object of a compound verb built on *strephein, epistrephein*. This verb refers both to turning things over (it is close in meaning to the uncompounded verb, στρέφειν) and to perception:

> If you turn over/gaze upon (*epi...strepseis/ἐπὶ...στρέψῃς*) the body of Leptines, no longer will you move your limbs, but you stay on account of adamant that cannot be dissolved, stopped in your steps...
> (*Greek Anthology* 12.93.7–9)[140]

Epistrephein is polysemous here, able to be understood either as the handling of the boy's body or as the perception of it. These lines speak of the narrator walking no further, but the language teases and suspicion that an erection has arisen also hovers at the margins of a reader's perception: perhaps the glans does not flop at this point and has an impressive hardness? Accordingly, when Theodoros speaks of erotic biting from his emperor and then to a turning over, the reader perceives via a vision, even a waking vision, a coincidence of the physical (body) and the dematerialized (soul), which is only the latest instance of such a thing, for, to take another example, fruits and words are made equivalent too. In these letters, then, Constantine and Theodoros play a teasing and corporealizing game that turns on perception and desire which they evoke only to thwart it, and then, redoubling it, they evoke it again.

Two Letters of Symeon the Logothete

Letters by Symeon the Logothete, who also is known as Symeon Metaphrastes, conclude this survey of masculine epistolographic culture in the tenth century.[141] Symeon the Logothete was born about 925. He was *asekretis* in 945 and *protoasekretis* in 952. He completed the two editions of his *Chronographia*, the historiography to be considered in the next two chapters, in rapid succession in 968 (first edition) and 969 (second edition).[142] He was also *magistros* ("a high ranking Dignity"[143]) prior to 969 and was *logothete* around 976. At some point after 976, as directed by Emperor Basil II, he supervised the rewriting in many volumes of saints' lives in more sophisticated Greek for a *menologion* or "a collection of *vitae* of saints arranged according to the date of each saint's celebration."[144] This work late in life is why he is also known as Symeon Metaphrastes, i.e., "Symeon the Rephraser" or "Paraphraser."[145] Toward the end of the century, his passing was commemorated in a dirge by Nikephoros Ouranos.[146] Symeon's *Letter 96* may be a letter to Nikephoros Ouranos, written to him when he held of the office of *magistros*[147]:

> To the *magistros*:
> I introduce this man to you, you who are a hunter of handsome and good men, and I don't know if up to now he has been outside your nets, or whether already seized on account of being known to you. One of the "huntables," a man gentle and humane, he might have escaped either the notice of men good at hunting or your solicitude in such matters.
>
> (Symeon the Logothete, *Letter 96*)[148]

There is homosocial warmth here. The man being recommended by Symeon is one to attract the attention of Nikephoros, who has a keen interest in men of good character and good looks. Indeed he no sooner becomes aware of such a man than he is seized. This letter gives a view of a situation similar to the one that will enable the rise of Basil I. A young man whose personal and physical qualities are attractive is one to be hunted and netted. He will be brought into association with more powerful men to become part of the powerful man's entourage.

Many letters survive from Symeon's pen,[149] and a good number of them contain warm language.[150] *Letter 111* has interpretable and relevant intertextuality with Plato and, like other evidence already seen in this chapter, speaks in terms of dreaming and waking visions and envisions communions with the addressee that are spiritual *and* carnal:

> Foolish in reality and filled with silliness is he who does not choose this thing before the others and makes much of it, [namely] being with (*suneinai*/συνεῖναι) you all the time. And, like the mythological creatures who had two heads grown together/united (*sumpephukenai*/συμπεφυκέναι) on one body, wouldn't this also be the case with us, if it were possible somehow to be constructed to fit (*sc.* with each other), and that the inventive constructor of supernatural marvels could be seen?

On account of our love, solid and understood in the same way to the greatest degree, I think even the imperial halls to be sweet because of you, not before having such an opinion about them, and I say that every thing, whatever it may be, that carries you to me is good and most beneficial. But, when we have been deprived of this [sc. closeness of physical association] through reversals of affairs, we will not fall far from the concord of our souls.

For souls, inasmuch as they are bodiless and are not enslaved to bodily necessities, and indeed not hindered by any physical impediment, mingling (*epimignumenai*/ἐπιμιγνύμεναι) with each another, they grow, on the one hand, as they will and are joined to each other at the root, and, on the other hand, they, dripping the sweetness of love in our hearts, rekindle, enflame, entirely arouse them [sc. our hearts] to bodily affection. Thus I am with (*suneimi*/σύνειμι) you for all time, and I will be with (*sunesomai*/συνέσομαι) you, having set up you, all of you, in my mind, and rejoicing thoroughly (*kateuphrainomenos*/κατευφραινόμενος) in the Graces emanating off of you. And may you be undivided from me for all time, being envisioned in my mind, visualized in a dream, seen in a waking vision, being together (*sungenomenoi*/συγγενόμενοι) always in the other's totality—intelligible as to the unifying (mental) part, and sensible as to the part that sees [each of us] at one and the same time—so that I will be able to take pleasure in you that is pleasure via both (ways [i.e., in my mind and through your physical presence]), if I may but find a remedy of consolation in my other.

(Symeon the Logothete, *Letter 111*)[151]

Letter 111 starts with a picture of a thoughtless man who does not prioritize being always and enthusiastically with the addressee, whose name is not given in the manuscript. This picture gives way to imagining closeness in a way influenced by *paideia*. Symeon makes reference to Plato's *Symposium*, specifically the speech of Aristophanes. His narration of primeval beings composed of two male or two female halves, or of one male and one female half is offered as mythical explanation for the desire that men can have for one another, or women for women, or women and men for each other.[152] In possession of two heads, two pairs of genitals, four arms, four legs, *and* aggressive temperaments, they were ordered split into two by Zeus because they were too dangerous. This led to a poignant situation:

And so, when their nature had been cut in two, each, desiring its half, would come together, and throwing their hands around (each other) and being locked together with one another, desiring to grow together/be united (*sumphunai*/συμφῦναι), they were perishing from hunger and lack of activity on account of their unwillingness to do anything separate from one another.

(Plato, *Symposium* 191A-B)[153]

This traumatic separation is the origin of human sexual desire and defines desire as a search for lost wholeness[154] and a desiring to grow together, which is what is said in *Letter 111* too. And the remedy of sexual intercourse was given to the bereft beings so they could have some taste of their primeval togetherness.[155] The reader of Plato remembers that Aristophanes envisions the god Hephaistos appearing to two male lovers and asking them whether they would like to be welded together.[156] This moment, which is sexual and memorable, also appears in the letter: "wouldn't this also be the case with us, if it were possible somehow to be constructed to fit (*sc.* with each other) and that the inventive constructor of supernatural marvels could be seen?"[157] The opening of *Letter 111*, indubitably intertextual with Plato, has sex on its mind.

As the letter continues, Symeon observes that this other man and their love and concord made the tiresome corridors of power a place of good associations for him. But they have been separated physically. All is not lost, though. They have their mental connection via the harmonious agreement of their souls. They blend and grow together (lightly touching on the *Symposium* again[158]) even if they cannot touch each other's body, and Symeon's language is bodily. Their souls are joined at the root; they drip; they are on fire. And the connection to thoughts of bodily expression of such feelings is expressly owned when Symeon writes that "souls... dripping the sweetness of love in our hearts...arouse them [*sc.* our hearts] to bodily affection."[159] The verb *erethizo*/ἐρεθίζω ("I arouse"), also appeared in *Letter 17* of Theodoros Daphnopates at moment also connected to eroticism: "*I was being aroused* by them to the beginning of sweet pain."[160] Lastly, there are a number of words that are double-entendres for sexual union: *epimignumi*/ἐπιμίγνυμι/"I mingle with, have (sexual) intercourse with" (as *epimignumenai*/ἐπιμιγνύμεναι)[161] *Suneimi*/σύνειμι ("I am with, have (sexual) intercourse with") (as *suneinai*/συνεῖναι in the first paragraph and *suneimi*/σύνειμι and *sunesomai*/συνέσομαι in the second)[162] and *sungignomai*/συγγίγνομαι "I keep company with, am together with, have (sexual) intercourse with" (as *sungenomenoi*/συγγενόμενοι).[163] Lastly, when Symeon says that he is "rejoicing thoroughly in the Graces emanating off of" the recipient of the letter, "rejoicing thoroughly" (*kateuphrainomenos*/κατευφραινόμενος) is a form of the verb *kateuphraino*/κατευφραίνω, which is related to another verb, *suneuphraino*/συνευφραίνω ("rejoice together with"). "Rejoice together with" describes a sexual dimension to Basil I's ritual brotherhood in Symeon's *Chronographia* and also appears in Proverbs 5, where a young man is counseled to rejoice together with the wife of his youth, all of which points to a broader discursive situation that connects "rejoice thoroughly" to the carnality elsewhere in *Letter 111*.

After this physicalization of their mental communion ("joined...at the root," "dripping," "bodily affection," "being-with," "rejoicing"), the letter concludes with emphasizing that not only does Symeon desire mental communion, he wishes for bodily contact too. Symeon wishes to see his friend

Eroticism and Desire in Epistolography 53

not only in dreams and waking visions (which recalls letters of Constantine and Theodoros above) but also in person: he will be a man to think of but also a man to be with physically ("being together always in the other's totality—intelligible as to the unifying [mental] part, and sensible as to the part that sees [each of us] at one and the same time"[164]). If a friend can provide consolation in this life, Symeon wants the pleasure of his friend's presence in his mind and in his physical space: "so that I will be able to take pleasure in you that is pleasure via both (ways [i.e., in my mind and through your physical presence]), if I may but find a remedy of consolation in my other."[165]

Conclusion

It has been said in reference to the letters that passed between Constantine and Theodoros, *Letter 17* of Daphnopates, and of letters of the tenth century in general, that these men of empire were interested in mapping the contours of erotic desire for each other and were pushing at the boundary between licit and forbidden through their lively untrammeled narratives in the first person.[166] The evidence of these letters, when engaged, shows this to be so, and furthermore, it is best to regard the letters appearing in this chapter not as outliers but as examples of greater explicitness that surface subtexts in other letters. One might say that Hermes' whispers vary in audibility, and that historians listening now with reparative attention can use them as indicative evidence.

Accepting the evidence of these letters and coming to an understanding of relations between these men on these bases enable a better understanding of the frankly carnal historiography these men were happy to write and regard as definitive. They reimagined the ninth century in terms they were familiar with and depictions of masculine environments that had same-sex desire and behavior in them were credible.

Notes

1 Material from this chapter has appeared in earlier publications: see Masterson (2018 and 2019a).
2 Emperor Constantine and Theodoros wrote, respectively, *Letters B3* and *B4*.
3 Logothete (*logothetes*/λογοθέτης) is a generic term for a high official in the ninth and tenth centuries.
4 Tziatzi-Papagianni (2012, 121–123); Darrouzès (1960, 160–161).
5 Tziatzi-Papagianni (2012, 123–124); Darrouzès (1960, 161–162).
6 This fact is generally acknowledged and the many letters we still have are a fraction of the ones that were written. In developing my understanding of Byzantine epistolography, I have found the following discussions (among others) helpful: Papaioannou (2010b); Mullett (2008); Mullett (1997, 1–43); Hatlie (1996); Littlewood (1976). For general background and scholarship from earlier in the twentieth century, see Hunger (1978, 1.199–239). Most helpful in explicating the situation in the manuscripts of the letter collections and individual letters is Papaioannou (2012).

54 *Eroticism and Desire in Epistolography*

7 Polish, see, e.g., Hatlie (1996, 227); Littlewood (1976, 201). Learned accomplishment: Littlewood's analysis of a number of major letter collections suggested to him both that the letter writers in general were seeking out-of-the-way quotations to use in their letters and that they were not relying on handbooks:

> [visible is a] desire on the part of many writers to seek out unusual quotations, especially in non-biblical literature [on account of] the range of sources used....The many still extant manuscripts of complete theological and secular Byzantine works, including a considerable number that preserve collections of letters chosen from a variety of writers, suggest that both epistolographers and other authors obtained the majority of their quotations from perusal of complete texts rather than of *florilegia*.
>
> (1988, 151, 153)

8 Mullett (1981, 82), cf. Mullett (1995, 48).
9 As emphasized by Papaioannou (2010b, 190).
10 E.g., Jenkins (1963, 45): "a Byzantine letter is an impersonal rhetorical flourish, which either contains no message at all, or, if it does, the message is couched in so obscure and allusive a fashion as to be nearly unintelligible," or Karlsson (1962, 14):

> Dans toutes ces correspondances auxquelles les Byzantins ont attaché une valeur littéraire, qui ont été recueillies et éditées par leurs auteurs ou par leurs contemporains, on s'attend à trouver –comme on la trouve par exemple dans Cicéron ou dans les épistoliers plus récents –une abondante documentation autobiographique ou historique. Avant d'en déceler quelque trace dans les épîtres byzantines, il faut cependant chercher très longtemps parmi les clichés et les formules générales.

Also, see similar remarks reported in the following: Mullett (1997, 23–25); Mullett (1981, 81); Littlewood (1988, 137); Weller (2014, 2): "The Byzantine letter has often been considered too recursive, elusive, and self-referential to shed much light on Byzantine social and political 'realities.'"

11 Over the years, the erotic/friendly language in Byzantine epistolography has been noted (e.g., Karlsson 1962, 21–23, 58–78; Patlagean 1985, 603–605; Tomadakis 1993, 116–118; Mullett 1999; Grünbart 2005, 113–122; Schneider 2008). The general trend has been to interpret the language of same-sex desire as a performative and semantically inert convention of the genre being performed in a Christian context which does not allow such carnality, e.g., Messis (2006, 823; 2008, 33–34) and Demosthenous (2004, 173–175). That said, there has been some tentative resistance to this position on the erotic language in the letters. Mullett (1999, 20–21), e.g., believes it is worth thinking carefully in terms of referentiality to actual desire (cf. Schneider 2008, 95). Odorico (1995) also offers a challenge to this general approach to same-sex desire in Byzantine epistolography.

12 For the scene of receiving a letter, see the following: Littlewood (1976, 219); Mullett (1981, 81, 84; 1997, 31–39; 2008, 882).

13 There is hardly any theorizing by the Byzantines of what a letter is supposed to be. Theorizations from late antiquity and before seem to have been the most important ones, at least until much later in the empire. For more, see Mullett (2008, 883, 885); Papaioannou (2010b, 194; 2012, 298). Malherbe (1988) assembles the evidence from late antiquity and before.

14 Karlsson (1962, 94–99), speaks of "le portrait de l'âme" but regards it as a *topos* with little content that expresses anything about the writer. In recent decades, following the lead of Littlewood (1976, 197–226), there has been an inclination to regard this and similar formulations as having at least some meaning and personal qualities, e.g., Mullett (2008, 885); Mullett (1981, 80, 89); Papaioannou

Eroticism and Desire in Epistolography 55

(2010b, 192); Weller (2014, 52, 132). The phrase, "ikon of the soul," is from Demetrios of Phaleron, *On Style* (Περὶ ἑρμηνείας) 227: "each writes a letter to be an ikon of his own soul" (εἰκόνα ἕκαστος τῆς ἑαυτοῦ ψυχῆς γράφει τὴν ἐπιστολήν).

15 For Littlewood (1976, 217), something is there: "Our conceits, fostered by both rhetorical theory and the Eastern Church's conviction of the distinctiveness of the individual, accord ill with the prevailing modern criticism of Byzantine letters as impersonal documents." Mullett (1981, 89), suggests we see in the letters "the expression of the corporate mentality of the elite which was composed of all who were rhetorically educated at any one time...[r]eading their letters is the best way to observe the interactions of the members of this elite," cf. Mullett (2003, 66); Odorico (1995, 312). Papaioannou (2012, 296), speaks of the "inescapable embeddedness of Byzantine letters in the socio-political moment of their creation." Papaioannou (2010b, 195), also notes the ways in which letters could engage with real issues: "letter-writing [for the Byzantines] is not merely a discursive site where social norms, expectations and hierarchies are confirmed and perpetually replicated; rather, this is a discursive world where such norms can also be negotiated, and often transgressed."

16 Littlewood (1988, 154), suggests that the canny variation of quotations observable in the letter writers shows an "artistry with which they sedulously placed their barely perceptible personal impress upon quotations both commonplace and recondite," cf. Littlewood (1976, 201): "...all letters, except sometimes those of officialdom, were believed to bear the impress of their authors' personalities."

17 Mullett had the following to say in 1997:

> Every letter must be interpreted in terms of what is known of the recipient as well as the writer... If we read letters carefully we may learn a great deal about the shared aspirations and values of an enclosed group...
>
> (18, 30)

18 Treadgold (2013, 178); also see Darrouzès and Westerink (1978, 1–4) for further biographical details on Theodoros Daphnopates.
19 Evidence points to Theodoros Daphnopates being the author of both the *Life of Basil* and *Theophanes Continuatus* (Treadgold 2013, 178). There is some debate; see Treadgold for its contours.
20 A military logothete was a high official in the military (the term is generic).
21 He was "governor/prefect of the city" (*eparchos tes poleos*/ἔπαρχος τῆς πόλεως), and by "the city" is meant, of course, Constantinople.
22 Treadgold (2013, 179).
23 Darrouzès and Westerink (1978).
24 For Basil Ouranos in general, see Cheynet (2003, 89); Darrouzès and Westerink (1978, 21, 23); Messis (2006, 824–826; 2014a, 235–237); Odorico (1995).
25 Masterson (2019a, 407) incorrectly states that Basil is the addressee of all three of these letters. Basil is the addressee only in the case of *Letter 31*.
26 Darrouzès and Westerink (1978, 193) added φιλίας to the text, as will be seen in the entire Greek text printed below. Something is needed grammatically but I don't feel comfortable accepting this as a basis from which to argue. The last words of the letter with their addition read as follows: ...δεξιώσεσι δαψιλεστέραις τ[ὸ] τῆς ἡμετέρας <φιλίας> [φιλ]ότιμον καὶ τὸ τῆς ἀγάπης διάπυρον [ἐ]πικρ[ατύν]ων, "...strengthening through more lavish gifts my/our friendship of which I am exorbitantly proud and my love which is very hot."
27 Βασιλείῳ πρωτοσπαθαρίῳ καὶ ἀσηκρῆτις τῷ Οὐρανῷ·

> [Ἐφ]εῖτο τοῖς πάλαι τῶν ἀνθρώπων ἔν γε ταῖς Κρονίαις μόναις ἡμέραις πᾶν ὅτι καὶ θέλοιεν τῶν βρωμάτων ἐπαπολαύειν. Σὺ δὲ τῶν καλλίστων δώρων τῷ ἡδεῖ καὶ ἀξιοθαυμάστ[ῳ τ]οσοῦτον ὑπηγάγου καὶ πρὸς τὴν βρουμάλιον τράπεζαν

ἡμᾶς ἔθελξας, ὡς μικροῦ ἂν ἐδέησε πρὸς τὴν Ἑλληνικὴν ἡμᾶς εἰκαιομυθίαν ἐκτραπῆναι. Ἀλλ' ἔρρωσο καὶ γένοιτό σοι χαίρειν ἐπὶ μακρόν, δεξιώσεσι δαψιλεστέραις τ[ὸ] τῆς ἡμετέρας... [φιλ]ότιμον καὶ τὸ τῆς ἀγάπης διάπυρον [ἐ] πικρ[ατύν]ων (Text=Darrouzès and Westerink 1978, 193, altered slightly).

Also see remarks and French translation (and text) in Darrouzès and Westerink (1978, 23, 192–193).

28 Hesiod, *Works and Days*, 115–118: "They used to delight in festivities... and all good things were theirs. The grain-giving field of its own accord was giving produce, much of it and unlimited" (τέρποντ' ἐν θαλίῃσι.../...ἐσθλὰ δὲ πάντα / τοῖσιν ἔην· καρπὸν δ' ἔφερε ζείδωρος ἄρουρα / αὐτομάτη πολλόν τε καὶ ἄφθονον).

29 Hesiod, *Works and Days*, 109–126.

30 Darrouzès and Westerink (1978, 21). See Odorico (1995, 308), for further suggestions on the title of *Letter 17* and its relation to both *Letters 17* and *18*.

31 The reason for the confusion lies in the title, Τοῦ αὐτοῦ (lit. "of the same one") that is placed at the head of *Letter 18*. It is a question not able to be answered whether this letter was also a letter that Basil Ouranos could send under his own name, as "of the same one" could mean that, but not necessarily. Here for reference is the title of *Letter 17*:

> A letter of Theodoros Daphnopates, *patrikios* and *eparchos*, so as [to be] from the person of Basil the *protospatharios* to one of his friends who was having his wedding festival:
> (Ἐπιστολὴ τοῦ πατρικίου Θεοδώρου καὶ ἐπάρχου τοῦ Δαφνοπάτου ὡς ἐκ προσώπου Βασιλείου πρωτοσπαθαρίου πρός τινα τῶν φίλων αὐτοῦ γαμήλιον ἑορτὴν ἔχοντα·)

And here is the title of *Letter 18* (to which much must added):

> [A letter] of the same one [i.e., of Basil Ouranos but written by Theodoros (?)]:
> (Τοῦ αὐτοῦ·)

Besides the titles, though, marriage is front and center in *Letter 18*, which makes the idea of it being another letter to congratulate the groom plausible. *Letter 18* is also concerned with the relation between letter writer and groom, which strengthens the narrative that it is a "buttoning-up" redo of the previous letter.

32 Patmos 706 (Darrouzès and Westerink 1978, 11).

33 Cf. *Letter 17* (discussed below): "I marvelled at the similar power of *pathos* and the companionability and sociability of the marvelous Erotes extending through all men" (ἐθαύμασα τοῦ πάθους τὸ ἰσοδύναμον καὶ τῶν θαυμαστῶν Ἐρώτων τὸ περὶ πάντας κοινωνικὸν καὶ εὐόμιλον).

34 Τοῦ αὐτοῦ·

> Ἀγγελία τις ἤκουσταί μοι περὶ σοῦ, ὦ φίλων ἄριστε καὶ φιλολογώτατε, ὡς αὐτὸς ὅλος εἴης γεγαμηκώς, ἀνθοφόρον παστάδα ὑποπλεξάμενος καὶ ἀργυροστεγώδη θάλαμον φιλοτεχνησάμενος, μεθ' ὧν καὶ τὰ μουσικῆς ὄργανα ὡς φίλα τῷ πράγματι παραστησάμενος, ὑφ' ὧν τὸ ἐπιθυμητικὸν ἀναπτόμενον τῆς γαμηλίου ἑορτῆς ἀποπληροῖ τὸ μυστήριον. Ἀλλ' οὐδὲ Κύπρις μακρὰν τῶν τελουμένων ἀφειστήκει· καὐτὴν γὰρ ἐκείνην περιχορεύειν καὶ γεγηθέναι καὶ κατὰ δεξιὰν φέρειν τὴν νυμφευθεῖσαν καὶ πρὸς τὰ τοῦ θαλάμου εἰσάγειν ἐνδότατα πεπιστεύκαμεν, Ἐρωτάς τε καὶ Χάριτας περιχορεύειν, καὶ τὰς μὲν στεφανοῦν τὴν νυμφικὴν κορυφήν, τοὺς δ' ἄνωθεν περιΐπταμένους ἄνθεσι καὶ ῥόδοις αὐτὴν ἐπιπάττειν· καὶ εἴ τι ἄλλο τῇ γαμηλίῳ ἑορτῇ καθέστηκε παρεπόμενον, οὐδ' αὐτὸ τῆς τῶν ὁμοίων ἀφέστηκεν ἐνεργείας καὶ κοινωνίας. Εἰ δὲ καὶ τὸν Ἡράκλειον ἆθλον θαρσαλέως διήνυσας, ὡς γενναῖός τις εἶ καὶ ἀγανταγώνιστος καὶ τῶν ἐκείνου θαυμάτων μ]ὴ φέρων τὰ δεύτερα.

Ταῦτά ϛοι καὶ νοσῶν καὶ φιλῶν ἔγραψα, ὁμοῦ μὲν τ[ὰ συνή]θη τῆς φιλίας ἀπ[ο]πληρῶν, ὁμ[οῦ] δὲ ϰαὶ σωφρόνως πεποιηκότι τιμῶν· καὶ εἴη [ϛ] ἡμῖν τοῖς τῆς ἀγάπης ἐμμένων θεσμοῖς καὶ τούτοις ἐπιστηριζόμενος καὶ πρὸς ἐπίδοσιν ταύτης ἐπεκτεινόμενος.

35 *Ta sunethe*/τὰ συνήθη is a substantive use of the adjective *sunethes*/συνήθης which is the adjective form of the noun, *sunetheia*/συνηθεία, employed in the *Life of Mary the Younger*.
36 "Ἐπειδή," φησιν, "φίλτατέ μοι ἀνδρῶν, οὕτως ἐκ συνηθείας ἀλλήλοις συνεκράθημέν τε καὶ συνεδέθημεν, δίκαιον ἥγημαι τὸν δεσμὸν τοῦτον τῆς ἀγάπης βιαιότερον θεῖναι καὶ τελεώτερον καὶ τὰ τῆς ἀγχιστείας τούτῳ προσθεῖναι ἄμματα, ἵνα διπλῆ συνδεσμώμεθα, μετὰ τῆς συνηθείας προσλαβόντες καὶ τὴν συγγένειαν."
37 It is possible that the two treatises on epideictic oratory that come down under Menander Rhetor's name are not even by him, but the authorship question is not important in the present instance. What is important is that these treatises were clearly important in Byzantine educated circle at every period (*ODB*, "Menander Rhetor"), and so constitute a reservoir of expectations against which epistolography may be measured when there are close thematic similarities, as there are here. The *Suda* is aware of him, having a brief entry on him (Mu 590). In short, the two sections from the second treatise to be discussed shortly, directions for the Wedding Speech and for the Bedding Speech, are chattily arranged sets of recommendations, cautions, and examples meant to be of use to a *rhetor* or speaker who wishes to make a speech at a wedding or in the (unexpected to modern sensibilities context of the) bridal chamber just prior to bride and groom consummating their union.
38 Menander Rhetor 2.5/399–405 [Loeb 224–239].
39 Menander Rhetor 2.6/405–412 [Loeb 240–257].
40 Προτρέψῃ δ' αὐτὸν καὶ ἀπὸ τοῦ κάλλους τοῦ θαλάμου, ὃν αἱ Χάριτες κατεποίκιλαν, καὶ ἀπὸ τῆς ὥρας τῆς κόρης καὶ ὁποῖοι περὶ ἐκείνην θεοὶ γαμήλιοι.
41 E.g., at 2.5.15/403 [Loeb 234]; 2.5.21/404 [Loeb 236]; 2.6.1/405 [Loeb 240]; 2.6.24/411 [Loeb 254].
42 E.g., at 2.5.21/404 [Loeb 236]; 2.6.1/405 [Loeb 240]; 2.6.7/407 [Loeb 244]; 2.6.22/410 [Loeb 252]; 2.6.24/411 [Loeb 254].
43 E.g., at 2.5.3/400 [Loeb 226]; 2.5.21–22/404 [Loeb 236]; 2.6.7/407 [Loeb 244].
44 E.g., 2.5.3/400 [Loeb 226]; 2.5.22/404 [Loeb 236]; 2.6.1/405 [Loeb 240].
45 E.g., 2.5.18/403 [Loeb 236]; 2.5.22/404 [Loeb 238]; 2.6.7/407 [Loeb 244].
46 Ἐπιστολὴ τοῦ πατρικίου Θεοδώρου καὶ ἐπάρχου τοῦ Δαφνυπάτου ὡς ἐκ προσώπου Βασιλείου πρωτοσπαθαρίου πρός τινα τῶν φίλων αὐτοῦ γαμήλιον ἑορτὴν ἔχοντα·

> Ἐγένετό τι περὶ ἡμᾶς, ὦ φίλων θαυμασιώτατε (προσθήσω δὲ τῷ καιρῷ καὶ μυστικώτατε), ὅπερ εἰ καί τινι ἄλλῳ, σοὶ μᾶλλον ἀνακαλύπτειν χρεών. Περὶ τὰς ἑωθινὰς αὐγὰς ὕπνος μέ τις ὑπεισήει τοῦ συνήθο[υ]ς ἡδύτερος καὶ τῶν μελλόντων ὡς ἔοικε πρόμαντις ἀψευδέστατος. Γαργαλισμοὶ γάρ τινες καὶ διατάσεις χειρῶν ἐγκάτων τε ὅλων συστροφὴ καὶ ἡ φυσικῶς ἐγκειμένη τῷ ἥπατι ἔφεσις διαναστάντα ὅλον ἐκλόνουν καὶ διεσάλευον καὶ ὡς ὑπὸ κυμάτων σκάφος ἐχείμαζον καὶ συνέθρ[αυ]ον. Τὰ δὲ ἦν, ὡς εἰκάζειν ἔχω, τῶν ἐπὶ σοὶ συμβεβηκότων ἀψευδέστατα σύμβολα· ὅτε γὰρ αὐτὸς ἤδη τοῦ ἐρωτικοῦ γυμνασίου ἔληγες, καὶ χαίροντες μὲν ἀπῄεσαν Ἔρωτες, Ἀφροδίτη δ' ὑποκοριζ[ο]μένη [τὴν ν]ίκην τέως σοι παρετίθετο, [ὁ] δὲ νυκτὸς ἐργάτης Ἑρμῆς ὑπεν[ό]στει [τὰ] τῆς χ[ει]ραγωγίας εὖ διαθέμενος, καὶ ἦν τὸ λ[ο]ιπ[ὸν] ἐγ τῷ ἀσφαλεῖ καὶ ἀκινδύνῳ τὰ τῶν ἐλπίδων, ἀνδρικῶς πρὸς τοὺς Ἡρακλεωτικοὺ[ς] ἐκείνους ἀγῶνας ἐπαπoδυσαμένῳ καὶ ἱκανῶς τῆς ἐφέσεως ἐμπλησθέντι καὶ ταῖς ἐρωτικαῖς αὔραις ἀρκούντως ἐπιθαλφθέντι, τότε μοι τῷ δυστυχεῖ ἀκροβολισμοί τινες τῶν ἐρωτικῶν τοξευμάτων ἀφανῶς ἐπιπεμπόμενοι ἐτίτρωσκον καθ' ἧπαρ, ἔβαλλον κατὰ καρδίαν, ἐτόξευον κατὰ νοῦν· καὶ ὧν αὐτὸς μετεῖχες τῆς τελειώσεως, τούτοις ἐγὼ πρὸς ἀπαρχὴν γλυκείας ὀδύνης

ἠρεθιζόμην. Ὡς δὲ καὶ εἰς ὄψιν ἐλθὼν διήγγειλας τὸ ἀγώνισμα, ἐθαύμασα τοῦ πάθους τὸ ἰσοδύναμον καὶ τῶν θαυμαστῶν Ἐρώτων τὸ περὶ πάντας κοινωνικὸν καὶ εὐόμιλον.

Ἀλλὰ σὺ μέν, φίλη ἐμοὶ καὶ τιμία ψυχή, καὶ ὃς κατὰ σὲ τῷ τοιούτῳ ἐπαινετῷ καὶ μακαρίῳ πάθει κεκράτηται, εἴης μοι εὐτυχῶν ἐπὶ τοιούτοις, κρυφίως καὶ μυστικῶς τὰ κρυπτὰ καὶ ἀπόρρητα τῆς θεοῦ μυστήρια τελεσιουργούμενος. Περὶ δὲ ἡμῶν ἔστω σοὶ μὲν φροντὶς καὶ συμπάθεια, ὡς ἀποστερουμ[έ]νων μὲν ὧν ποθοῦμεν, καρτερούντων δὲ καὶ ὧν ἀπῳκίσμεθα καὶ στερούμεθα· φυλάξαι δὲ τὰ φιλικὰ καὶ παρ' ἑαυτοῖς ταμιεύσασθαι. [Ἀν]δριάντες ἂν πρότερον καὶ στῆλαι χαλκαῖ φωνὴν ἀπορρήξωσιν ἤ τι τῶν τοιούτων παρ' ἡμῶν ἔκφορον ἔσται.

(I found the translations into French by Darrouzès and Westerink [1978, 168–170], and by Odorico [1995, 304], helpful in preparing my own.).

47 "I was being aroused by them ['bows of erotic desire, being loosed invisibly' etc.] to the beginning of sweet pain" (τούτοις ἐγὼ πρὸς ἀπαρχὴν γλυκείας ὀδύνης ἠρεθιζόμην).

48 "When coming into my sight, you announced your feat..." (Ὡς δὲ καὶ εἰς ὄψιν ἐλθὼν διήγγειλας τὸ ἀγώνισμα...).

49 κοινωνικὸν καὶ εὐόμιλον.

50 For πάθος referring to sexual feeling, see, e.g., *LSJ* πάθος 2.II.

51 Examples that show that *pathos*/πάθος referring to penetration are easy to find. There is this letter of course. But there are also two germane examples, employing the verb *pascho*/πάσχω, from civil law, which were discussed in the introduction to this book: *Epanagoge* 40.66 and *Prokheiros* 39.73 both begin with the following: "The *aselgeis*, both the one doing and *the one receiving/enduring...*" (Οἱ ἀσελγεῖς, ὅ τε ποιῶν καὶ ὁ *πάσχων*...).

52 Provoked by *Letter 17*'s exuberance, Darrouzès and Westerink have the following to say: "La rencontre que Basile aurait eue avec son correspondant dès le matin...a l'air d'être une fiction littéraire...dans toute les épistolographie byzantine, il faut tenir compte des libertés que les auteurs se permettent avec la réalité" (1978, 21 ["The meeting that Basil would have had with his correspondent in the morning...has the air of being a literary fiction...throughout all Byzantine epistolography, it is necessary to take into account the freedoms that the authors allow themselves with reality."]).

53 Messis (2014, 235–237); cf. Messis (2006, 824–826), which is an earlier version of this later argument.

54 "I was being aroused by them [i.e., the things attending the groom's climax] to the beginning of sweet pain" (τούτοις ἐγὼ πρὸς ἀπαρχὴν γλυκείας ὀδύνης ἠρεθιζόμην).

55 "Let there be in your heart consideration for me and fellow-feeling, because I am being deprived of the things I desire and I am enduring being far away and bereft of them" (Περὶ δὲ ἡμῶν ἔστω σοὶ μὲν φροντὶς καὶ συμπάθεια, ὡς ἀποστερουμ[έ]νων μὲν ὧν ποθοῦμεν, καρτερούντων δὲ καὶ ὧν ἀπῳκίσμεθα καὶ στερούμεθα).

56 Angelidi (2002, 228); Laiou (1992, 84n76); Odorico (1995).

57 "...elle [sc. la lettre] permet constater l'éloignement de l'individu face aux valeurs que la société officiellement soutient pas seulement dans la pratique individuelle, mais auusi dans la façon de concervoir ces pratiques."

58 "Puisque les lettres des rhéteurs byzantins ne sont pas seulement des documents personnels, mais aussi et principalement des ouvrages littéraires avec une valeur d'exemple au niveau de l'expression et de reflet d'attitudes partagées dans un milieu homogène, le témoignage de Daphnopatès résulte hautement représentatif d'une mentalité diffuse."

59 ἐροῦμεν δὲ ἐγκώμιον...τοῦ δὲ νεανίσκου τὴν ἀλκὴν καὶ τὴν ῥώμην, παραινοῦντες μὴ καταισχῦναι ταῦτα τοσούτων μαρτύρων γενησομένων τῇ ὑστεραίᾳ τῆς τελετῆς.
60 The first topic in the Wedding Speech (2.5.6 ff.) is concerned with the creation of marriage and its prevalence among gods and humans. The second topic is praise of the families hosting the wedding (2.5.13 ff.) and third is a suite of recommendations for how to praise the bride and groom (2.5.18 ff.).
61 This stretching taut (ἐντειναμένους) recalls the end of *Letter 18* also: "may you remain within the established terms of our love, and may you continue to to be supported by them, and may you *stretch yourself* (ἐπεκτεινόμενος) to the increase of it [i.e., our love]" (καὶ εἴη [ς] ἡμῖν τοῖς τῆς ἀγάπης ἐμμένων θεσμοῖς καὶ τούτοις ἐπιστηριζόμενος καὶ πρὸς ἐπίδοσιν ταύτης *ἐπεκτεινόμενος*).
62 Τέταρτος τόπος ἐστὶν ἀπὸ τοῦ <τὰ> περὶ τὸν θάλαμον καὶ παστάδας καὶ θεοὺς γαμηλίους ἐρεῖν, ὡς ὅταν λέγωμεν, συνελήλυθε μὲν οὖν ἡ πόλις, συνεορτάζει δὲ ἅπασα, πεπήγασι δὲ παστάδες οἷαι οὐχ ἑτέρῳ ποτέ, θάλαμος δὲ πεποίκιλται ἄνθεσι καὶ γραφαῖς παντοίαις, πολλὴν δὲ τὴν Ἀφροδίτην ἔχει· πείθομαι δὲ καὶ Ἔρωτας παρεῖναι τόξα μὲν ἐντειναμένους, βέλη δὲ ἐφαρμόττοντας, φαρμάκοις πόθων τὰς ἀκίδας χρίσαντας, δι' ὧν τὰς ψυχὰς συγκυρώσουσιν ἀναπνεῖν ἀλλήλαις, Ὑμέναιος δὲ ἀνάψει λαμπάδας ἡμῖν καὶ δᾷδας γαμηλίῳ πυρί· χαρίτων τε μνημονεύσεις καὶ Ἀφροδίτης... (I found the translation in the Loeb by William Race helpful in composing my own.)
63 I.e., a series of short sentences that are easy to understand, one by one.
64 ἀκατάσκευον γὰρ τὸν λόγον εἶναι δεῖ καὶ τὰ πολλὰ ἀσύνδετον, οὐ κώλοις οὐδὲ περιόδοις συγκείμενον, ἀλλὰ συγγραφικώτερον, οἷόν ἐστι καὶ τὸ τῆς λαλιᾶς εἶδος.
65 One can see this in the translation by tracking the italicized "when's" and the "at that moment."
66 Φυλακτέον δ' ἐν τούτῳ, μή τι τῶν αἰσχρῶν μηδὲ τῶν εὐτελῶν ἢ φαύλων λέγειν δόξωμεν, καθιέντες εἰς τὰ αἰσχρὰ καὶ μικρά....
67 The letter writer rubs salt in the wound, as it were, with all the talk of discretion, *stelai,* and statues at the end of the letter. He wishes that revelation of inappropriate things will never happen, *right after* being decidedly unreserved.
68 [ὁ] δὲ νυκτὸς ἐργάτης Ἑρμῆς ὑπεν[ό]στει [τὰ] τῆς χ[ει]ραγωγίας εὖ διαθέμενος.
69 Darrouzès and Westerink (1978, 168–169).
70 οἱ παλαιοὶ τῇ Ἀφροδίτῃ τὸν Ἑρμῆν συγκαθίδρυσαν, ὡς τῆς περὶ τὸν γάμον ἡδονῆς μάλιστα λόγου δεομένης.
71 There will be more on the *Suda* when Emperor Constantine VII Porphyrogennetos, the emperor who oversaw its compilation, arrives below.
72 Ἑρμῶν. Ἑρμοῖ ἦσαν ἐν τῇ Ἀθηναίων πόλει λίθινοι ἐν προθύροις καὶ ἱεροῖς· ἐπειδὴ φασι τὸν Ἑρμῆν λόγου καὶ ἀληθείας. ἔφορον εἶναι, διὰ τοῦτο καὶ τὰς εἰκόνας αὐτοῦ τετραγώνους καὶ κυβοειδεῖς κατεσκεύαζον, αἰνιττόμενοι τὸ τοιοῦτον σχῆμα, ἐφ' ἃ μέρη πέσῃ, πανταχόθεν βάσιμον καὶ ὄρθιον εἶναι. οὕτω καὶ ὁ λόγος καὶ ἡ ἀλήθεια ὁμοία ἐστὶ πανταχόθεν αὐτὴ ἑαυτῇ, τὸ δὲ ψεῦδος πολύχουν καὶ πολυσχιδὲς καὶ ἑαυτῷ μάλιστα ἀσύμφωνον.
73 It is necessary to address the choice to translate the euphemism, τὰ αἰδοῖα (lit. "shameful bits") graphically. I opt to name, here and elsewhere, the organ according to the context, as this particular euphemism in Greek from ancient times is but the scantiest of coverings. Accordingly, "erect penises" captures better the mental image being called to mind than trying to say "erect shameful bits," though I also recognize that opinions on this could vary.
74 οἱ δ' ἀρχαῖοι τοὺς μὲν πρεσβυτέρους καὶ γενειῶντας Ἑρμᾶς ὀρθὰ ἐποίουν τὰ αἰδοῖα ἔχοντας...
75 ἰδών ποτε νεανίσκον ἄσωτον, "ἰδού," ἔφη, "τετράγωνος Ἑρμῆς ἔχων σύρμα, κοιλίαν, αἰδοῖον, πώγωνα."
76 ...εἰ σωφρονεῖτε, θαἰμάτια λήψεσθ', ὅπως / τῶν Ἑρμοκοπιδῶν μή τις ὑμᾶς ὄψεται.

60 Eroticism and Desire in Epistolography

77 For the mutlilation of the herms during the Peloponnesian War, Thucydides 6.27 is the place to start. For secondary literature on this affair, and other places in Classical Greek sources, see Furley (1996) or Hamel (2012). This affair appears a number of times in the *Suda* (Alpha 1280, Epsilon 3047, Pi 2006). One thing to note is that Thucydides says that the heads of the herms were damaged. Hamel and other ancient sources feel it was the head *and* the notable phalloi. Aristophanes' *Lysistrata* (see above in text) indicates that phalloi were at issue. In his *Compilation of Attic Names* (Ἀττικῶν ὀνομάτων συναγωγή), Pausanias also believes this incident involved the genitals of the herms: "Hermchoppers: the ones who cut away the throats and genitals of the herms" (Epsilon 72: Ἑρμοκοπίδαι· οἱ τῶν Ἑρμῶν τοὺς τραχήλους καὶ τὰ αἰδοῖα ἀποκόψαντες).

78 And cf. *Suda*, chi 100 for a briefer mention of the same topic, i.e., Hermes the Whisperer is honored with cult, as is Aphrodite the Whisperer and, almost certainly, Eros the Whisperer too.

79 2 Cor 12:20.

80 Ψιθυριστοῦ Ἑρμοῦ καὶ Ἔρωτος καὶ Ἀφροδίτης: ἅπερ πρῶτος ἐποίησεν, ὥς φησι Ζώπυρος, Θησεύς, ἐπεὶ Φαῖδρα, ὥς φασιν, ἐψιθύριζε Θησεῖ κατὰ Ἱππολύτου, διαβάλλουσα αὐτόν. οἱ δὲ ἀνθρωπινώτερόν φασιν Ἑρμῆν Ψιθυριστήν, παρὰ τὸ ἀνθρώπους ἐκεῖ συνερχομένους τὰ ἀπόρρητα συντίθεσθαι καὶ ψιθυρίζειν ἀλλήλοις, περὶ ὧν βούλονται. Ψιθυρισμὸς δὲ ἡ τῶν παρόντων κακολογία παρὰ τῷ Ἀποστόλῳ.

81 These are what Paul fears to find among the Corinthians: "strife, jealousy, angers, quarrels, slanders, *whisperings*, instances of pride, instances of anarchy" (2 Cor 12:20: ἔρις, ζῆλος, θυμοί, ἐριθεῖαι, καταλαλιαί, *ψιθυρισμοί*, φυσιώσεις, ἀκαταστασίαι).

82 τὰ ἀπόρρητα, = τὰ αἰδοῖα, Plu.2.284a, cf. Ar.Ec.12, Longin. 43.5.

83 ἀπόρρητα τῆς θεοῦ μυστήρια.

84 [Ἀν]δριάντες ἂν πρότερον καὶ στῆλαι χαλκαῖ φωνὴν ἀπορρήξωσιν ἤ τι τῶν τοιούτων παρ' ἡμῶν ἔκφορον ἔσται.

85 Περὶ τὰς ἑωθινὰς αὐγὰς ὕπνος μέ τις ὑπεισήει τοῦ συνήθο[υ]ς ἡδύτερος καὶ τῶν μελλόντων ὡς ἔοικε πρόμαντις ἀψευδέστατος.

86 γαργαλισμοί...τινες; διατάσεις χειρῶν.

87 *Letter B3* (Tziatzi-Papagianni 2012, 87).

88 Tziatzi-Papagianni (2012 (B1–18), 83–108); Darrouzès (1960, 317–332). A note about the letters that are associated with these two men will be welcome, especially as there are so many. (Indeed, I feel there is much more to be said about them in an absolute sense, given all the text we have.) The letters that feature dialogue between Constantine and Theodoros come from Codex Athous Laura Ω 126. Constantine writes letters B1, B3, B5, B7, B10, B12, B15, and B18, while Theodoros writes B2, B4, B6, B8, B9, B11, B13, B14, B16, and B17. Tziatzi-Papagianni discusses Codex Athous Laura Ω 126 (and two other codices that contain the letters) on pp. *20–*29. The letters from Codex Athous Laura Ω 126, their numbers preceded by the letter B, appear on pp. 83–120 of Tziatzi-Papagianni's edition, as noted above. Darrouzès edition (1960) has been superseded by this collection.

Another collection of letters, found in Codex Vindobonensis phil. Graecus 342 (V), contains a number of letters that Theodoros wrote to Constantine: nos. A1-6, A17, A47, A51, and A52. There are, alas, no answers from Constantine in this collection. Tziatzi-Papagianni discusses Codex Vindobonensis phil. Graecus 342 (V) on pp. *30–*36. The letters from this codex, their numbers preceded by the letter A, appear on pp. 5–82 of Tziatzi-Papagianni's edition. I discuss a few letters from the ones in Codex Vindobonensis phil. Graecus 342 (V) in Chapter 3.

89 Emperor Constantine, *Letter B5* (Tziatzi-Papagianni 2012, 90–91).

Eroticism and Desire in Epistolography 61

90 In *Letter B4*, Theodoros has a dream, discussed below, that may allegorize anxiety about palace politics (Tziatzi-Papagianni 2012, 89).
91 Tziatzi-Papagianni (2012, *4).
92 There were *On Imperial Reigns*, written by Ioseph Genesios, and the anonymous *Life of Basil* and *Theophanes Continuatus*, both likely written by Theodoros Daphnopates (Treadgold 2013, 178). These works are central to Chapters 2 and 3.
93 See Treadgold's discussion (2013, 156–167) of the hub of intellectual activity that was Constantine's court. See also Lemerle (1986, 309–353).
94 See Tziatzi-Papagianni (2012, *3–*16), for a sketch of Theodoros' life.
95 Greek has three nouns that mean "dream," *onar*/ὄναρ, *oneiron*/ὄνειρον, and *oneiros*/ὄνειρος, with no appreciable difference in meaning between them.
96 Ὄνειρον ἐνυπνίου διαφέρει· ἕτερον γάρ ἐστι καὶ οὐ ταὐτό. ἀλλὰ καὶ τὸ ὄνειρον καὶ ἐνύπνιον καλῶς εἴποι τις ἄν· ὅταν δὲ τεχνικῶς λέγῃ τις, κυρίως ἕκαστον χρὴ καλεῖν, καὶ τὸ μὲν ἀσήμαντον καὶ οὐδενὸς προαγορευτικόν, ἀλλ᾽ ἐν μόνῳ τῷ ὕπνῳ τὴν δύναμιν ἔχον, γινόμενον δὲ ἐξ ἐπιθυμίας ἀλόγου ἢ ὑπερβάλλοντος φόβου ἢ πλησμονῆς ἢ ἐνδείας, ἐνύπνιον χρὴ καλεῖν, τὸ δὲ μετὰ τὸν ὕπνον ἐνέργεια ὂν καὶ ἀποβησόμενόν ἐστιν ἀγαθὸν ἢ κακὸν ὄνειρον. πολλάκις δὲ καταχρηστέον τοῖς ὀνόμασιν, ὡς καὶ Ὅμηρος· "θεῖός μοι ἐνύπνιον ἦλθεν ὄνειρος" (Homer, *Iliad* 2.56; *Odyssey* 14.495).
97 Emperor Julian, *Letter 108* (*TLG*).
98 Ὕπαρ· ἀλήθεια, οὐκ ἐν ὀνείρῳ. τὸ μεθ᾽ ἡμέραν ὄναρ. οἷον φανερῶς, ἀληθῶς ὑπάρχον. "ἐμοὶ διηγοῦ σὺ τοὐμὸν ὄναρ· ἐγὼ δ᾽ ἔοικα [σοὶ] τὸ σὸν ὕπαρ ἀφηγεῖσθαι." Ὕπαρ λέγει τὸ μεθ᾽ ἡμέραν ὄναρ· ὡς ἐναργῶς ὑπάρχον, ἀληθές. κατὰ ἀποκοπὴν τῆς τελευταίας συλλαβῆς τῆς χον.
99 Ἰουλιανὸς Ἐκδικίῳ ἐπάρχῳ Αἰγύπτου·

Ἡμὲν παροιμία φησίν· "ἐμοὶ σὺ διηγεῖ τοὐμὸν ὄναρ," ἐγὼ δὲ ἔοικα σοὶ τὸ σὸν ὕπαρ ἀφηγεῖσθαι. Πολύς, φασίν, ὁ Νεῖλος ἀρθεὶς μετέωρος τοῖς πήχεσιν ἐπλήρωσε πᾶσαν τὴν Αἴγυπτον· εἰ δὲ καὶ τὸν ἀριθμὸν ἀκοῦσαι ποθεῖς, εἰς τὴν εἰκάδα τοῦ Σεπτεμβρίου τρὶς πέντε. Μηνύει δὲ ταῦτα Θεόφιλος ὁ στρατοπεδάρχης· εἰ τοίνυν ἠγνόησας αὐτό, παρ᾽ ἡμῶν ἀκούων εὐφραίνου.

100 Οὐκ εἰσὶν ἐμὰ τὰ γράμματα, μὰ τὴν σὴν ἀρετήν, ἀλλά τι σμικρὸν παπαδύλλιον καὶ εὐτελὲς πρὸς τὴν τοιαύτην γραφὴν διηκόνησεν· ἡ δὲ ὑπαγόρευσις, εἰ καὶ ἡμεῖς ἀρνησόμεθα, ἀλλὰ δήλη τυγχάνει τοῖς τὸν ἡμέτερον ἤδη χαρακτῆρα γινώσκουσι· καὶ γὰρ τὸ σαθρὸν τοῦ ἡμετέρου νοὸς καὶ τὸ βάρβαρον καὶ σόλοικον τῆς ἡμετέρας ἀμουσίας οὐ τοῖς πολλοῖς ἄγνωστον καὶ κεκρυμμένον ἐστί, ἀλλὰ δῆλον καὶ προφανές, κἂν ἡμεῖς ἀπαρνώμεθα.

Τὰς δὲ γλυκείας ὄντως καὶ μελιρρύτους ὀπώρας δεξάμενοι καὶ τὸν ἀνθοσμίαν οἶνον, τὸ<ν> ὑπὲρ τὸ πάλαι λαλούμενον νέκταρ, ἀπεγευσάμεθα μὲν οἱονεὶ τῶν σῶν γλυκερῶν χειλέων σμικρόν τινα ἀσπασμὸν εἰσδεξάμενοι, ἐπὶ πλέον δὲ τούτου ἐμφορηθέντες καὶ οἱονεὶ κατὰ τὸ γεγραμμένον εὐφρανθέντες, τὸ θλῖβον καὶ τρύχον τὴν ἡμετέραν καρδίαν ἐγγὺς τῆς κύλικος ἐπιφυόμενον εὕρομεν, ὥσπερ, ὡς οἶμαι, τῷ ῥόδῳ πως ἀναφύεται καὶ ἡ ἄκανθα. Νόμος γὰρ οὗτος ἔρωτος καὶ φιλίας ἀνοθεύτου καὶ ἀληθοῦς καὶ γλυκείας καὶ ἐρασμίας. Τί γὰρ ἀκάνθης ἢ ῥομφαίας διστόμου πληκτικώτερον, εἰ μὴ στέρησις ἐρωμένου καὶ φίλου ἀποικία καὶ ἀπουσία, καὶ τοιούτου οὕτω πιστοῦ καὶ φιλοσόφου καὶ κατὰ πάντα ἤδη τὸ πρωτεῖον ἔχοντος; Μανικὸς γὰρ ὄντως ἐραστής τυγχάνω πρὸς τοὺς ἐμὲ οὕτω φιλοῦντας—μαίνομαι γάρ, ἀλλὰ σωφρόνως· οἶδε γὰρ φιλία πάντα καινοτομεῖν. Σοὶ δὲ τὰ πλείονα παραχωροῦμεν ὡς εἰδότες οὕτω πρὸς ἡμᾶς καὶ διακείμενον καὶ διακεισόμενον.

Ἐμὲ δὲ καὶ πολλὰ καὶ πολλάκις οἱ ὄνειροι καὶ ταράσσουσι καὶ εὐφραίνουσι, καὶ ὡσπερεὶ τὸν φίλτατον ἐν χερσὶ διδόασι καὶ προσομιλεῖν πλανῶσι καὶ καταφιλεῖν ἀπατῶσι. Τὸ δὲ ὕπαρ πολλὰ καταρῶμαι καὶ ζημίας πρόξενον ἡγοῦμαι· οὐ γὰρ καθ᾽

ὕπνους ἀπολαύω καὶ ποσῶς τῆς ἐφέσεως ἐμφοροῦμαι {καὶ} ἀφυπνισθεὶς μάταιος τῆς τοιαύτης ἡδονῆς εὑρίσκομαι, καὶ εὔχομαι Κυρίῳ τῷ Θεῷ μου δοῦναι καιρὸν φιλῆσαι τὸν φιλούμενον καὶ ποθῆσαι τὸν ποθούμενον καὶ δακεῖν οὐχὶ πληκτικῶς ἀλλὰ φιλικῶς· δάκνουσι γὰρ καὶ οἱ φιλοῦντες, οὐχ ἵνα πλήξωσιν, ἀλλ᾽ ἵνα πλέον ποθήσωσιν. Εὔχου τοίνυν τὸν καιρὸν ἐλθεῖν ἵνα τῆς ἐφέσεως ἀπολαύσωμεν (Text=Tziatzi-Papagianni 2012, 87–88).

101 Tziatzi-Papagianni (2012, 87): καὶ οἱονεί κατὰ τὸ γεγραμμένον εὐφρανθέντες.
102 Tziatzi-Papagianni 2012, 87.
103 …ἐξανατέλλων χόρτον τοῖς κτήνεσιν καὶ χλόην τῇ δουλείᾳ τῶν ἀνθρώπων τοῦ ἐξαγαγεῖν ἄρτον ἐκ τῆς γῆς· καὶ οἶνος εὐφραίνει καρδίαν ἀνθρώπου τοῦ ἱλαρῦναι πρόσωπον ἐν ἐλαίῳ, καὶ ἄρτος καρδίαν ἀνθρώπου στηρίζει. Χορτασθήσεται τὰ ξύλα τοῦ πεδίου, αἱ κέδροι τοῦ Λιβάνου, ἃς ἐφύτευσεν….
104 οἶνος εὐφραίνει καρδίαν.
105 καρδίαν; οἶνον, ἐγγὺς τῆς κύλικος.
106 τῇ δουλείᾳ τῶν ἀνθρώπων.
107 θλίβον καὶ τρύχον.
108 "Μὴ 'κδύσῃς, ἄνθρωπε, τὸ χλαινίον, ἀλλὰ θεώρει
οὕτως ἀκρολίθου κἀμὲ τρόπον ξοάνου."
Γυμνὴν Ἀντιφίλου ζητῶν χάριν, ὡς ἐπ᾽ ἀκάνθαις
εὑρήσεις ῥοδέαν φυσμένην κάλυκα.
109 See Richlin (1992, 35–36). The reader will also remember one of Strato's epigrams (Greek Anthology 12.195), discussed in the introduction as an intertext to Nikephoros Ouranos' Letter 26, that also speaks of the damaging arrival of hair.
110 νόμος…ἔρωτος καὶ φιλίας ἀνοθεύτου καὶ ἀληθοῦς καὶ γλυκείας καὶ ἐρασμίας.
111 τὸ θλίβον καὶ τρύχον τήν…καρδίαν.
112 Τί γὰρ ἀκάνθης ἢ ῥομφαίας διστόμου πληκτικώτερον, εἰ μὴ στέρησις ἐρωμένου….
113 Ῥομφαία δίστομος appears at Ps 149:6 (plural there) and Sir 21:3.
114 Ῥομφαία δίστομος appears in Apoc 1:16 and 2:12.
115 …καυχήσονται ὅσιοι ἐν δόξῃ καὶ ἀγαλλιάσονται ἐπὶ τῶν κοιτῶν αὐτῶν· αἱ ὑψώσεις τοῦ θεοῦ ἐν τῷ λάρυγγι αὐτῶν, καὶ ῥομφαῖαι δίστομοι ἐν ταῖς χερσὶν αὐτῶν τοῦ ποιῆσαι ἐκδίκησιν ἐν τοῖς ἔθνεσιν, ἐλεγμοὺς ἐν τοῖς λαοῖς, τοῦ δῆσαι τοὺς βασιλεῖς αὐτῶν ἐν πέδαις καὶ τοὺς ἐνδόξους αὐτῶν ἐν χειροπέδαις σιδηραῖς, τοῦ ποιῆσαι ἐν αὐτοῖς κρίμα ἔγγραπτον· δόξα αὕτη ἐστὶν πᾶσι τοῖς ὁσίοις αὐτοῦ.
116 Τέκνον, ἥμαρτες; μὴ προσθῇς μηκέτι καὶ περὶ τῶν προτέρων σου δεήθητι. ὡς ἀπὸ προσώπου ὄφεως φεῦγε ἀπὸ ἁμαρτίας· ἐὰν γὰρ προσέλθῃς, δήξεταί σε· ὀδόντες λέοντος οἱ ὀδόντες αὐτῆς ἀναιροῦντες ψυχὰς ἀνθρώπων. ὡς ῥομφαία δίστομος πᾶσα ἀνομία, τῇ πληγῇ αὐτῆς οὐκ ἔστιν ἴασις.
117 Apoc 1:4.
118 Apoc 1:10–11.
119 Καὶ ἐπέστρεψα βλέπειν τὴν φωνὴν ἥτις ἐλάλει μετ᾽ ἐμοῦ· καὶ ἐπιστρέψας εἶδον ἑπτὰ λυχνίας χρυσᾶς, καὶ ἐν μέσῳ τῶν λυχνιῶν ὅμοιον υἱὸν ἀνθρώπου, ἐνδεδυμένον ποδήρη καὶ περιεζωσμένον πρὸς τοῖς μαστοῖς ζώνην χρυσᾶν· ἡ δὲ κεφαλὴ αὐτοῦ καὶ αἱ τρίχες λευκαὶ ὡς ἔριον λευκόν, ὡς χιών, καὶ οἱ ὀφθαλμοὶ αὐτοῦ ὡς φλὸξ πυρός, καὶ οἱ πόδες αὐτοῦ ὅμοιοι χαλκολιβάνῳ ὡς ἐν καμίνῳ πεπυρωμένης, καὶ ἡ φωνὴ αὐτοῦ ὡς φωνὴ ὑδάτων πολλῶν, καὶ ἔχων ἐν τῇ δεξιᾷ χειρὶ αὐτοῦ ἀστέρας ἑπτά, καὶ ἐκ τοῦ στόματος αὐτοῦ ῥομφαία δίστομος ὀξεῖα ἐκπορευομένη, καὶ ἡ ὄψις αὐτοῦ ὡς ὁ ἥλιος φαίνει ἐν τῇ δυνάμει αὐτοῦ.
120 Καὶ τῷ ἀγγέλῳ τῆς ἐν Περγάμῳ ἐκκλησίας γράψον· Τάδε λέγει ὁ ἔχων τὴν ῥομφαίαν τὴν δίστομον τὴν ὀξεῖαν· Οἶδα ποῦ κατοικεῖς, ὅπου ὁ θρόνος τοῦ Σατανᾶ, καὶ κρατεῖς τὸ ὄνομά μου, καὶ οὐκ ἠρνήσω τὴν πίστιν μου καὶ ἐν ταῖς ἡμέραις Ἀντιπᾶς ὁ μάρτυς μου ὁ πιστός μου, ὃς ἀπεκτάνθη παρ᾽ ὑμῖν, ὅπου ὁ Σατανᾶς κατοικεῖ. ἀλλ᾽ ἔχω κατὰ σοῦ ὀλίγα, ὅτι ἔχεις ἐκεῖ κρατοῦντας τὴν διδαχὴν Βαλαάμ, ὃς ἐδίδασκεν τῷ Βαλὰκ

βαλεῖν σκάνδαλον ἐνώπιον τῶν υἱῶν Ἰσραήλ, φαγεῖν εἰδωλόθυτα καὶ πορνεῦσαι· οὕτως ἔχεις καὶ σὺ κρατοῦντας τὴν διδαχὴν Νικολαϊτῶν ὁμοίως. μετανόησον οὖν· εἰ δὲ μή, ἔρχομαί σοι ταχύ, καὶ πολεμήσω μετ' αὐτῶν ἐν τῇ ῥομφαίᾳ τοῦ στόματός μου.
121 The adjective 'two-edged' is missing in the later verse but may be presumed.
122 μαίνομαι γάρ, ἀλλὰ σωφρόνως οἶδε γὰρ φιλία πάντα καινοτομεῖν.
123 *Suda*, Upsilon 155 (Ὕπαρ).
124 *Suda*, Upsilon 155 (Ὕπαρ).
125 cf. Jer 8:16.
126 Τὴν ἐκ τῆς ἀπουσίας ὑμῶν χθεσινὴν κατήφειαν ἡ σήμερον ἐλθοῦσά μοι τιμία καὶ πάνσοφος καὶ φρονιμωτάτη γραφὴ διεσκέδασε καὶ πρὸς εὐθυμίαν μετήμειψε, καὶ τὴν ἐν τῇ καρδίᾳ μου φλόγα τοῦ πόθου τῆς βασιλείου ὑμῶν στεφηφόρου καὶ θείας κεφαλῆς ἐπὶ πλεῖον ἀνῆψέ τε καὶ ἐξέκαυσε, καὶ ἤδη μου φλέγεται ἡ ψυχὴ ἐπιθυμοῦσα καὶ ζητοῦσα τὰ ἐλπιζόμενα· οἱ δὲ ἐκ τῆς γλυκοστόμου καὶ μελιρρύτου σου πηγῆς, τοῦ σωφρονοῦντος καὶ παγχρύσου σου στόματος, ἐπιδαψιλευόμενοί μοι κρουνοὶ οὐ μόνον <οὐ> σβεννύουσι τὴν φλόγα, ἀλλὰ καὶ προσανάπτουσιν. Ὅθεν καὶ μεθ' ἡμέραν φαντάζομαι τὸν ποθούμενον, τὸν χρυσαυγῆ μοι καὶ ὑπέρλαμπρον, καὶ νύκτωρ δεξιός μοι παρέστηκας ὄνειρος, καὶ σὲ βλέπω μετὰ τοῦ γενναίου καὶ μετὰ θαύματος ἀγαπωμένου ἀεὶ βλοσυροῦ καὶ βασιλικοῦ μειδιάματος· καί ποτέ σε κατὰ τοὺς ὕπνους προετρεψάμην ταχύτερον θεῖν, ἵνα μή τις προφθάσῃ σε καὶ ἀποκλείσῃ σοι τὰ βασίλεια, καὶ αὐτὸς συμπροεθυμούμην μὴ ἀπολείπεσθαι, ἀλλὰ τῆς ὀξύτητος τοῦ ὑμετέρου ἵππου παντ' ἐγίνετο δεύτερα.
Ἀλλὰ ταῦτα μὲν τῆς ἀληθινῆς εὐφροσύνης ἀπολειπόμενα, ὅσον εὐφραίνειν κατὰ τὴν φαντασίαν δοκεῖ, τοσοῦτον ἀνιᾷ κατὰ τὴν ἀλήθειαν. Ἡμᾶς δὲ εἴη τῆς ἀληθοῦς ἐμφορηθῆναι συνουσίας καὶ ὁμιλίας σου, ὦ Θεὲ καὶ Κύριε, ὁ πάντα μετασκευάζων ἐπὶ τὸ βέλτιον.
Τῶν δὲ χθίζων ὀπωρῶν, οὐδὲν ἐχουσῶν λαμπρὸν ἢ μόνην τὴν προαίρεσιν, πολλαπλασίαν ἐδεξάμην τὴν ἀμοιβήν, τοὺς ὡραίους σου λόγους καὶ γλυκερούς, οἵπερ ἐν τῷ δάκνειν ἐρωτικῶς καὶ στρέφειν μου τὴν ψυχὴν πλέον εὐωδιάζουσιν ἤπερ ὁ ἐπαινεθεὶς ἀνθοσμίας οἶδεν εὐφραίνειν καρδίαν ἀνθρώπων ἢ καὶ τὸ νέκταρ αὐτό, ᾧπερ οἱ μάκαρες ἐμεθύσκοντο (Text=Tziatzi-Papagianni 2012, 88–90).
127 καὶ νύκτωρ δεξιός μοι παρέστηκας ὄνειρος.
128 Ὀρθὸν νῦν ἔστηκας, ἀνώνυμον, οὐδὲ μαραίνῃ,
  ἐντέτασαι δ' ὡς ἂν μήποτε παυσόμενον·
ἀλλ' ὅτε μοι Νεμεσηνὸς ὅλον παρέκλινεν ἑαυτὸν
  πάντα διδούς, ἃ θέλω, νεκρὸν ἀπεκρέμασο.
τείνεο καὶ ῥήσσου καὶ δάκρυε· πάντα ματαίως
  οὐχ ἕξεις ἔλεον χειρὸς ἀφ' ἡμετέρης.
129 ὀρθὸν νῦν ἔστηκας.
130 κατὰ τὴν φαντασίαν.
131 Be it noted, too, that εὐφροσύνης/*euphrosunes* and εὐφραίνειν/*euphrainein* ("rejoicing" and "to rejoice," the latter appearing twice) are echoes of εὐφρανθέντες/ *euphranthentes* ("made to rejoice") and εὐφραίνουσι/*euphrainousi* (make...rejoice) in Constantine's letter.
132 ἀληθοῦς... συνουσίας καὶ ὁμιλίας. Συνουσία (*sunousia*) can mean sexual intercourse from early Classical times (*LSJ* I.4) and this continues into late antiquity, so there are many *loci* available to educated Byzantine men: e.g., *Lampe* 2; John Chrysostom *Oppugn*. 1.3 (*PG* 47 323), 2.3 (*PG* 47 335), 2.10 (*PG* 47 346); Athanasius, *Inc.* 8.23 (Thomson 1971, 152); Porphyry, *Antr.* 16. It is the same with ὁμιλία (*homilia*): e.g., *LSJ* I.2; *Lampe* A2a; John Chrysostom, *Oppugn*. 3.15 (*PG* 47 375).
133 *LSJ* III; *Lampe* 2.
134 ...πολλαπλασίαν ἐδεξάμην τὴν ἀμοιβήν, τοὺς ὡραίους σου λόγους καὶ γλυκερούς, οἵπερ ἐν τῷ δάκνειν ἐρωτικῶς καὶ στρέφειν μου τὴν ψυχὴν πλέον εὐωδιάζουσιν

ἥπερ ὁ ἐπαινεθεὶς ἀνθοσμίας οἶδεν εὐφραίνειν καρδίαν ἀνθρώπων ἢ καὶ τὸ νέκταρ αὐτό, ᾧπερ οἱ μάκαρες ἐμεθύσκοντο.
135 ...στρέψας ῥοδοειδέι τέρπεο πυγῇ / τὴν ἄλοχον, νομίσας ἀρσενόπαιδα Κύπριν.
136 *Greek Anthology* 5.116.5–6....στρέψας Μηνοφίλαν εὐίσχιον ἐν φρεσὶν ἕλπου / αὐτὸν ἔχειν κόλποις ἄρσενα Μηνόφιλον.
137 *Greek Anthology* 12.73.4: τὴν δρῆστιν μὴ ὑποδέχεσθε, νέοι.
138 *Greek Anthology* 12.73.5–6: ...ἐκεῖσε γὰρ ἡ λιθόλευστος / κείνη καὶ δύσερως οἶδ' ὅτι που στρέφεται. NOTE: It is possible that it is not anal penetration simply; it could be rape, if δύσερως ("badly loved") can be seen to drive interpretation past the "unproductive" pleasures of anal sex into unspecific sexual coercion.
139 *Greek Anthology* 12.93.3–6.
140 ἢν δ' ἐπὶ Λεπτίνεω στρέψῃς δέμας, οὐκέτι γυῖα / κινήσεις, ἀλύτῳ δ' ὡς ἀδάμαντι μένεις / ἴχνια κολληθείς...
141 I follow Treadgold's narrative of his life (2013, 203–210, especially 208–209). For differing views, including the position that Symeon the Metaphrast *may* be different from Symeon the Logothete, start with Høgel (2002) and also consult references in Treadgold. This is a contentious area, but I note that *Letter 111* (discussed below) is identified as being by the Symeon who is both Symeon the Logothete and Symeon Metaphrastes. The attribution in the manuscript which contains *Letter 111*, Codex Baroccianus 131 (f. 178), reads "of the logothete, lord Symeon Metaphrastes" (τοῦ λογοθέτου κῦρ Συμεὼν τοῦ Μεταφραστοῦ) (Darrouzès 1960, 34).
142 Treadgold (2013, 211).
143 *ODB, ad loc.*
144 "Menologion" in *ODB*.
145 See Høgel (2002) and Papaioannou (2021, 502–511), for much more on Symeon the Metaphrast.
146 See Mercati (1950) for text and commentary. Also, see Papaioannou (2021) for remarks on this dirge (502–504) and translation (513–514). This dirge is another moment, to go with the attribution in the Codex Baroccianus 131, when Symeon is both *logothete* and Metaphrast: it's title reads thus: "Verses of Ouranos for Symeon the Metaphrast and *Logothete of the Drome*" (Στίχοι τοῦ Οὐρανοῦ πρὸς τὸν Συμεῶνα τὸν Μεταφραστὴν καὶ λογοθέτην τοῦ δρόμου).
147 As per suggestion of Darrouzès (1960, 156).
148 Εἰς τὸν μάγιστρον·

> Τουτονί σοι προσάγω τὸν ἄνδρα, τῷ τῶν καλῶν τε καὶ ἀγαθῶν θηρευτῇ, οὐκ οἶδα εἰ μέχρι τοῦ νῦν ἔξω τῶν σῶν δικτύων ὑπάρχοντα, εἴτ' οὖν τῆς περὶ τοῦ γνώριμον εἶναί σοι καταλήψεως· λάθοι δ' ἂν πρότερον τοὺς περὶ τὴν κυνηγίαν δεινούς τι τῶν θηρευομένων, ἢ τὸ σὸν περὶ ταῦτα ἐπιμελὲς ἄνθρωπος ἐπιεικὴς καὶ φιλάνθρωπος. (Text= Darrouzès 1960, 156; Note: I altered the text: I have γνώριμον for γνώριμος).

149 The letters of Symeon the Logothete are to be found in Darrouzès (1960, 99–163) (with some letters of Nicholas Mystikos, patriarch from 901 to 907 and again 912 to 925, mixed in).
150 *Letters 1, 2, 18, 51, 54, 71, 78, 84, 85, 89, 97, 104* (in addition to *111*, which is discussed below) all contain warm language. There is much work possible on this corpus.
151 Ἠλίθιος τῷ ὄντι καὶ εὐηθείας ἀνάμεστος ὃς οὐ τοῦτο πρὸ τῶν ἄλλων αἱρεῖται καὶ περὶ πολλοῦ τίθεται, συνεῖναί σοι διὰ παντὸς καί, κατὰ τὰ μυθευόμενα τέρατα ἐν ἑνὶ σώματι δύο συμπεφυκέναι τὰς κεφαλάς, τοῦτο καὶ ἐφ' ἡμῖν, εἴ πως ἐνῆν ἀντιδημιουργηθῆναι καὶ καινουργὸν ὀφθῆναι μὲν τὸν πλάστην θαυμάτων ὑπερφυῶν; Διὰ τὸ τῆς ἀγάπης ἀρραγὲς καὶ ὁμοφραδέστατον, ἐγὼ καὶ τὰς βασιλείους αὐλὰς διὰ σὲ γλυκείας ἡγοῦμαι, μὴ πρότερον οὕτως ἔχων περὶ αὐτῶν, καὶ πᾶν ὅ τι σε

τῶν πρὸς ἡμᾶς διαβιβαζόντων ἀγαθόν τέ φημι καὶ εὐεργετικώτατον· ἀλλ', ἐπεὶ καὶ τοῦτο διά τινας πραγμάτων περιπετείας ἀποστερούμεθα, οὐκ ἂν καὶ τῆς κατὰ ψυχὴν συναινέσεως πόρρω πεσούμεθα.

Αἱ γὰρ ψυχαί, ἅτε δὴ ἀσώματοι οὖσαι καὶ μὴ σωματικαῖς ἀνάγκαις δουλεύουσαι, μὴ δήπου τινὸς ὑλικοῦ κωλύματος παρεμποδιζόμεναι, ἀλλήλοις ἐπιμιγνύμεναι, φύονται μὲν καθ' ἑαυτὰς καὶ συρριζοῦνται, τὸ δὲ τῆς ἀγάπης ἡδὺ ταῖς καρδίαις ἐναποστάζουσαι ἀναζωπυροῦσιν αὐτὰς καὶ ἀναφλέγουσιν καὶ παντοίως πρὸς φίλτρον σωματικὸν ἐρεθίζουσιν. Οὕτως ἐγὼ σύνειμι διὰ παντὸς καὶ συνέσομαι ὅλον σε κατὰ τὸν ἐμαυτοῦ νοῦν ἀναστηλώσας καὶ ταῖς παρὰ σοῦ πεμπομέναις κατευφραινόμενος χάρισι· καὶ εἴης διὰ παντὸς ἀφ' ἡμῶν ἀδιαίρετος κατὰ νοῦν φανταζόμενος, κατ' ὄναρ ὀπταζόμενος, καθ' ὕπαρ βλεπόμενος, κατὰ πᾶν ἕτερόν τι νοητόν τε καὶ αἰσθητὸν ἐνωτικοῦ τε καὶ συνοπτικοῦ μέρους ἀεὶ συγγενόμενοι, ἵνα ἔχωμεν ἐπὶ σοὶ χαίρειν ἐπ' ἄμφω, εἰ γοῦν ἀλλὰ τῷ ἑτέρῳ παραμυθίας ἐφευρίσκοιμεν φάρμακον. (Note: I found Karlsson's 1962, 68, translation into French, which has a text that differs at times, helpful for my translation of this letter.)

152 Pederasty, age discrepant and asymmetrical, is not in evidence at this moment in this mythical story, which assumes the equality of the halves in two out of the three beings, though pederasty is added incongruously at 192B.

153 ἐπειδὴ οὖν ἡ φύσις δίχα ἐτμήθη, ποθοῦν ἕκαστον τὸ ἥμισυ τὸ αὑτοῦ συνῄει, καὶ περιβάλλοντες τὰς χεῖρας καὶ συμπλεκόμενοι ἀλλήλοις, ἐπιθυμοῦντες συμφῦναι, ἀπέθνησκον ὑπὸ λιμοῦ καὶ τῆς ἄλλης ἀργίας διὰ τὸ μηδὲν ἐθέλειν χωρὶς ἀλλήλων ποιεῖν.

154 Plato, *Symposium* 192E: "This is the reason—that our primeval nature was this and we were whole. Therefore the name for this desire and pursuit of the whole is Eros" (τοῦτο γάρ ἐστι τὸ αἴτιον, ὅτι ἡ ἀρχαία φύσις ἡμῶν ἦν αὕτη καὶ ἦμεν ὅλοι· τοῦ ὅλου οὖν τῇ ἐπιθυμίᾳ καὶ διώξει ἔρως ὄνομα).

155 Plato, *Symposium* 191C-D: "...if male [should happen] upon male, there would be the full satisfaction of intercourse...it indeed is from so great an event [i.e., the primeval cutting in two] that desire for each other is innate in humans, and (desire) is the reuniter of ancient nature and tries to make one out of two and to heal human nature. Therefore each of us is a token (fitting with another token) of a person... indeed each always is seeking its own token (with which it will fit)" (εἰ καὶ ἄρρην ἄρρενι, πλησμονὴ γοῦν γίγνοιτο τῆς συνουσίας...ἔστι δὴ οὖν ἐκ τόσου ὁ ἔρως ἔμφυτος ἀλλήλων τοῖς ἀνθρώποις καὶ τῆς ἀρχαίας φύσεως συναγωγεὺς καὶ ἐπιχειρῶν ποιῆσαι ἓν ἐκ δυοῖν καὶ ἰάσασθαι τὴν φύσιν τὴν ἀνθρωπίνην. ἕκαστος οὖν ἡμῶν ἐστιν ἀνθρώπου σύμβολον...ζητεῖ δὴ ἀεὶ τὸ αὑτοῦ ἕκαστος σύμβολον.).

156 Plato, *Symposium* 192D-E: [Hephaistos speaks] do you desire this, to be with one another as much as possible, so that night and day you are not apart from one another? If you desire this, I am willing to fuse and weld you into the same being, with the result that you, being two, become one, and as long as you live, you, each other, will live in common, being one.... (Ἆρά γε τοῦδε ἐπιθυμεῖτε, ἐν τῷ αὐτῷ γενέσθαι ὅτι μάλιστα ἀλλήλοις, ὥστε καὶ νύκτα καὶ ἡμέραν μὴ ἀπολείπεσθαι ἀλλήλων; εἰ γὰρ τούτου ἐπιθυμεῖτε, θέλω ὑμᾶς συντῆξαι καὶ συμφυσῆσαι εἰς τὸ αὐτό, ὥστε δύ' ὄντας ἕνα γεγονέναι καὶ ἕως τ' ἂν ζῆτε, ὡς ἕνα ὄντα, κοινῇ ἀμφοτέρους ζῆν....).

157 τοῦτο καὶ ἐφ' ἡμῖν, εἴ πως ἐνῇ ἀντιδημιουργηθῆναι καὶ καινουργὸν ὀφθῆναι μὲν τὸν πλάστην θαυμάτων ὑπερφυῶν; In relation to this reference to Plato's Hephaistos and indeed to Symeon's entire nod to the *Symposium*, Karlsson (1962, 62–78), discusses the prevalence of Plato's fused primeval beings across Byzantine epistolography (and provides a French translation of this very letter on page 68). In a substantial note (74–76) about this Greek, he also provides a discussion that avoids engagement with the presence of desire in the text and opts to understand the letter primarily in terms of the sublimations of Neoplatonism,

which has the effect of suppressing the *Symposium* as intertext to an appreciable extent. While the discussion is interesting, and thoughts of Neoplatonism certainly might have occurred to readers of this letter, I think readers were going to be thinking of the *Symposium* first and primarily because of the language of desire in the letter: language *and* content are directly applicable.

158 Cf. *Symposium* 191A, sumphunai/συμφῦναι and, from *Letter 111* (second paragraph), *phuantai*/φύονται.
159 Ψυχαί...τὸ δὲ τῆς ἀγάπης ἡδὺ ταῖς καρδίαις ἐναποστάζουσαι...παντοίως πρὸς φίλτρον σωματικὸν ἐρεθίζουσιν.
160 τούτοις ἐγὼ πρὸς ἀπαρχὴν γλυκείας ὀδύνης *ἠρεθιζόμην*.
161 See *LSJ* ἐπιμείγνυμι II. (NOTE: ἐπιμίγνυμι is the later Greek version of this word.).
162 See *LSJ* σύνειμι II.1 and .2.
163 See *LSJ* συγγίγνομαι II.3. There is also Gen 19:5 (Sodom and Gomorrah): "so that we may 'be with' them" (ἵνα *συγγενώμεθα* αὐτοῖς) is what the men of the town are asking Lot for. In response, he offers them his daughters instead.
164 κατὰ πᾶν ἕτερόν τι νοητόν τε καὶ αἰσθητὸν ἑνωτικοῦ τε καὶ συνοπτικοῦ μέρους ἀεὶ συγγενόμενοι.
165 ...ἵνα ἔχωμεν ἐπὶ σοὶ χαίρειν ἐπ' ἄμφω, εἰ γοῦν ἀλλὰ τῷ ἑτέρῳ παραμυθίας ἐφευρίσκοιμεν φάρμακον.
166 Angelidi (2002, 228–229):

> The learned men and highest officials go further in their mappings of erotic desire. Indeed a series of letters written in the first person with verbal freedom and active descriptions indicate that new boundaries were being drawn between the permissible and forbidden. A systematic analysis of our texts would point, I think, to interesting discoveries related to the understanding and experience of the physiology of the body and the senses; it would document a transformed treatment of sexual experience...

> (Οι λόγιοι λαϊκοί και ανώτατοι αξιωματούχοι προχωρούν περισσότερο στη χαρτογράφηση του ερωτικού πόθου. Πράγματι, σειρά επιστολών που συντάσσονται σε πρώτο πρόσωπο με λεκτική ελευθερία και εναργείς περιγραφές υποδεικνύει ότι χαράσσονται νέα όρια ανάμεσα στο επιτρεπτό και το απαγορευμένο. Μια συστηματική ανάλυση των κειμένων μας θα οδηγούσε, νομίζω, σε ενδιαφέρουσες διαπιστώσεις σχετικά με την πρόσληψη και τη βίωση της φυσιολογίας του σώματος και των αισθήσεων, θα κατέγραψε τη μετασχηματισμένη αντιμετώπιση της σεξουαλικής εμπειρίας...)

2 Histories of Masculine Beauty and Desire

The Case of Emperor Basil I

Three of the letter writers from the previous chapter, Symeon the Logothete, Theodoros Daphnopates, and Emperor Constantine VII Porphyrogennetos, either produced or commissioned historiographies. They are part of a broader group that includes one more named historiographer, Ioseph Genesios, and another who lacks a name but is known as Pseudo-Symeon. Surviving from this group of four writers and one commissioning emperor are a total of six historiographies written in the middle of the tenth century that portray the rise to the throne of Emperor Basil I, the founder of the glorious Macedonian dynasty. These texts all feature warm homosociality and same-sex desire in the life of this poor, ambitious, and attractive young man who made his way to the throne. And as is always the case with historiography, these accounts tell not only a story about the past, they also reflect the present of their writing.[1] These men, for whom historiographical writing was vital career-building activity, craft their narratives in terms plausible to them and depict a warm homosocial culture that is of a piece with their letters. Indeed these works are interested in making an impression on readers: readers are not to acquire so much "an understanding of the past" as they are to receive "a direct sensation of it."[2] These texts want to depict not only events but also the impression the events made, i.e., they cultivate vividness (*enargeia*).[3] The focus on the follies of Michael III's court, which are discussed in some detail toward the end of this chapter and which can seem lacking in propriety, has a warrant here.

Considering these depictions in detail is worthwhile because Basil I is the most famous participant in the rite of ritual brotherhood, *adelphopoiesis*, in history, which will be the focus of the chapter following this one. These historiographies show the kind of man who could be ritual brother and the kind of context in which he could be found. And as always: "texts both mirror *and* generate social realities, are constituted by *and* constitute the social and discursive formations which they may sustain, resist, contest, or seek to transform."[4] These texts not only look to the past, they also mold the present and look to the future, and read reparatively, tell about social expectations and the differing valuations that can adhere to intimate relations between men.

DOI: 10.4324/9781351135238-3

Historiographies from the Mid-Tenth Century

This first of these historiographies is the *Life of Basil*, likely by Theodoros Daphnopates. It is a panegyrical biography of Basil I and has been dated to 950.[5] The second is *On Imperial Reigns* by Ioseph Genesios. It is in four books and tells of the reigns of Emperors Leo V (813–820), Michael II (820–829), Theophilos (829–842), and Michael III (842–867), each in one book. The fourth book on Michael III contains the material on the rise of Basil. Born about 910, Genesios was connected to the educated and cultivated milieu of the imperial court. He was *patrikios* and keeper of the imperial inkstand[6] in 969.[7] Constantine likely commissioned him to write *On Imperial Reigns* around 954.[8]

Theodoros Daphnopates has been said to be the author of the third historiography, *Theophanes Continuatus*.[9] As its title suggests, it is a continuation of Theophanes the Confessor's *Chronographia*, and the first four books of it, like Genesios' historiography, cover, respectively, the reigns of Leo V, Michael II, Theophilos, and Michael III. And again like Genesios', it is the fourth book that contains information on the rise of Basil. *Theophanes Continuatus* has been dated to the year 958.[10]

Two editions of Symeon the Logothete's *Chronographia* are the fourth and fifth historiographies.[11] The *Chronographia* commences with the creation of the world and is arranged, as the title would indicate, chronologically. The material on Basil appears when the narrative comes to the ninth century. It has been suggested, based on internal evidence and the vagaries of imperial politics, that the two editions date respectively to the years 968 and 969.[12]

The sixth and final historiography is a *Chronographia* that used to be attributed to Symeon the Logothete but is now believed to be by another man altogether. There is no name for this person, whose current and perhaps forever name is Pseudo-Symeon. This work, most of which remains in manuscript, is in need of a critical edition, though sections that include the rise of Basil were brought out in 1838.[13] The *Chronographia* of Pseudo-Symeon starts with Adam and continues to the time of purple-born power, as it proclaims in an opening frontispiece couplet.[14] This historiography seems to have been completed in 978 or 979.[15] We know nothing about Pseudo-Symeon beyond the probable time of the writing of the *Chronographia* and his likely social position, given the fact that he could write this work at all. The author clearly was educated, though he also was very much a copier.[16] The reason to bother with this work at all is that Pseudo-Symeon's readings are occasionally different, and also because his version is the sixth presentation in less than 30 years of sexy material about Basil I. Pseudo-Symeon, whoever he was, was most likely younger than Genesios, Daphnopates, and Symeon the Logothete but he probably knew all of them, as did all of them know each other. His is another voice from this extended group that attests to a sustained interest in Basil I.

Lastly, these sources vary somewhat in their attitude toward Basil. The *Life of Basil*, *Theophanes Continuatus*, and Genesios are pro-Basil (and the Macedonian dynasty). At moments that are mostly not a concern here, e.g., the assassination of Michael, there are efforts to minimize his involvement. In contrast, Symeon the Logothete's two editions depend on source material originally written during the minority of Constantine VII Porphyrogennetos,[17] when he had to share the throne with Romanos I Lekapenos, who was overshadowing him. This source material, lost now, evidently did not have a pro-Macedonian brief. On top of this, the two editions of Symeon the Logothete's *Chronographia* came out during the reigns of Nikephoros II Phokas and John I Tzimiskes and while Basil II was a minor, so there were uncertainties again about the dynasty. In any case, Symeon does not minimize Basil's key role in the assassination of Michael, and emphasizes brutality there and elsewhere.[18] He also reports that Eudokia Ingerina was pregnant with Leo VI by Michael when she married Basil, which makes the Macedonian dynasty a mirage and but a continuation of the Amorian.[19] Relying on Symeon the Logothete and *Life of Basil*, and on still other sources which are lost, Pseudo-Symeon displays, not surprisingly, an inconsistent attitude toward Basil in his *Chronographia* when it is compared to the five works which preceded it. But these differences turn out not to matter that much when attention is on Basil the young man making his way to power amid the warm homo-sociality in and adjacent to Michael III's court. Across all the historiographies, male same-sex desire and the beauty of Basil play important roles in tenth-century understandings of the establishment of the dynasty in the ninth century. Before the focus on the things of desire and sex in these accounts, which fragments them, as it were, under a microscope, an account of Basil's rise distilled from the six historiographies will anchor discussions to come: discussions of amorous language, an important man who appreciated masculine beauty, the taming of a horse, a wrestling match, a scourging, competition from another "pretty boy," an eagle that recalls Zeus, and some flatulence.

Narrative of the Rise of Basil I

Basil enters history when he is but a child at an unspecified year in the early decades of the ninth century.[20] His humble Armenian family had been recently moved to the west or northwest of Constantinople, and they were in territory controlled by Bulgarians. These early years have fantastical details that build the legend of the founder of the Macedonian dynasty. For example, a young Basil charms the Bulgarian Tsar, who even puts him on his lap (see Figure 2.1). Of particular interest is an eagle coming to Basil when he is quite young and shading him while his parents work the fields. Basil's mother found this eagle alarming and chased it away. It nonetheless returned to him repeatedly as he matured.

70 *Histories of Masculine Beauty and Desire*

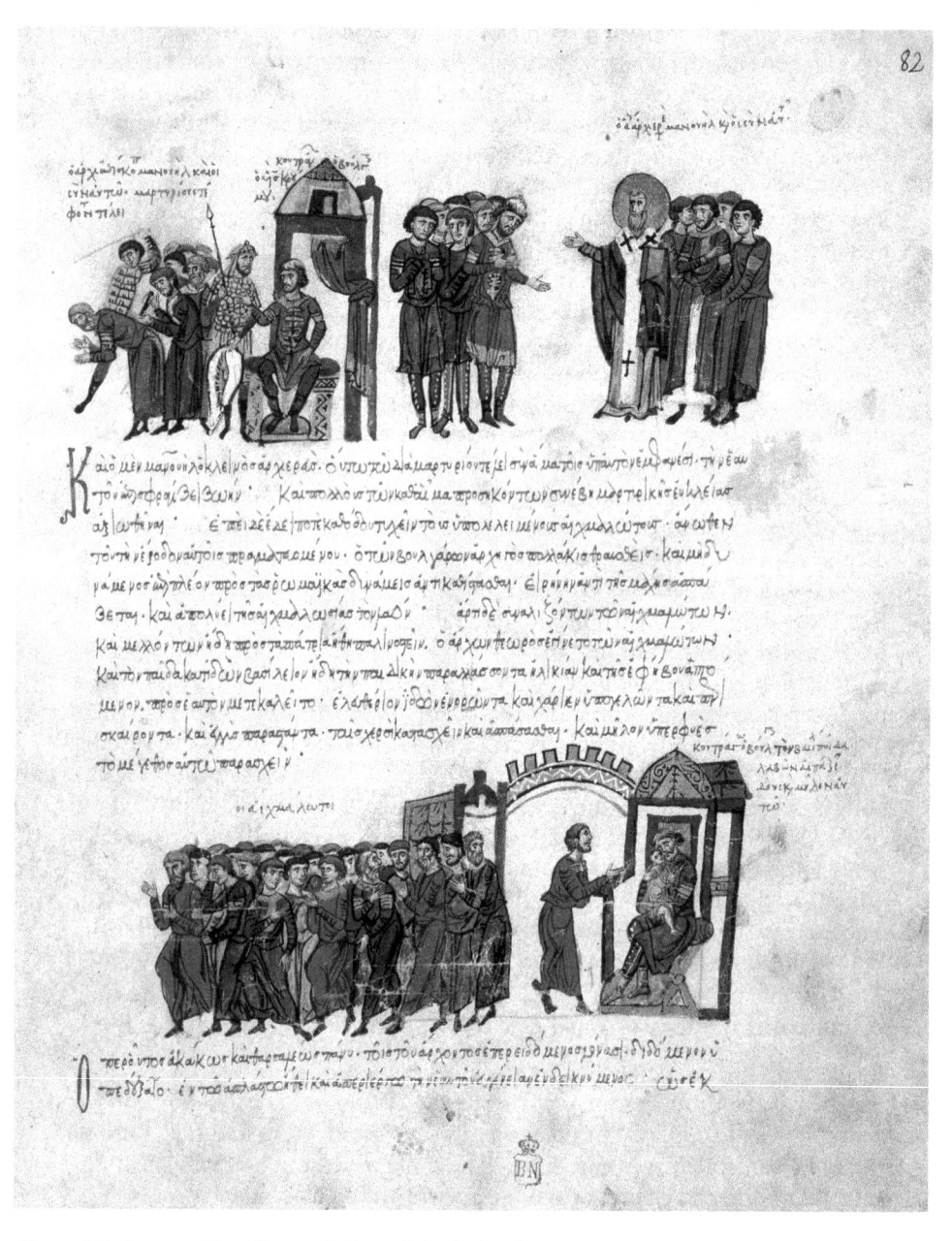

Figure 2.1 A young Basil is on the lap of the Bulgarian Tsar at bottom right (Skylitzes Manuscript fo. 82r. Biblioteca Nacional, Madrid).

When he had grown up, Basil made his way to Constantinople in the hopes of making something of himself. Upon arrival, he paused to rest and fell asleep in the forecourt or threshold of the monastery of St. Diomedes. Nicholas, the sacristan or overseer of the monastery, had a dream in which a heavenly voice told him to go outside and find someone named Basil who would be important, even an emperor. At first Nicholas didn't believe the exhausted and grubby young man could the person destined by the dream or voice for greatness. But the divine signs insisted, and Nikolaus, convinced, took Basil under his wing. Some of the accounts say Basil and Nicholas became ritual brothers.[21] Now, in any case, joined up with Nicholas, Basil came to the attention of Nicholas' brother who was a doctor who served Theophilitzes,[22] a relative of the currently reigning Emperor Michael III. As a strong and athletic young man, Basil naturally became a member of a *hetaireia* or group of young men that Theophilitzes had about himself. While in Theophilitzes' *hetaireia*, and looking good in the silks Theophilitzes provided to all his men, Basil tamed a high-spirited horse of Emperor Michael III, thereby coming to imperial notice. Basil also had a heralded success wrestling a Bulgarian.

Also during his time in Theophilitzes' entourage, the *Life of Basil* tells how Basil journeyed to the Peloponnese in southern Greece, and met Danelis, a rich widow who was politically powerful there. She had heard that he was destined for greatness from a priest. She gave Basil gifts and had him become ritual brothers with her son, John. Danelis and her son were later honored by Basil when he was emperor. She received great marks of respect when she later visited Basil, now emperor, in Constantinople, and was even called "Mother of the Emperor."[23] John was made *protospatharios* by his ritual brother Basil. And Nicholas, Basil's other ritual brother, later became *oikonomos* and *sunkellos*.[24]

But returning to the story, this handsome and powerful man, building connections in various ways, then went from Theophilitzes' employ and became part of the imperial court—a court that gets some heavy weather in the sources for being debauched, a characterization that cannot fail to implicate Basil, who had become an insider. He was made *parakoimomenos*, "the one who sleeps beside (the emperor)" (a great honor), was adopted by Emperor Michael III, was given a wife (the emperor's ex-mistress, Eudokia Ingerina), and eventually (after a private ritual whipping while naked, according to Genesios) became co-emperor. In time, however, things began to sour between Co-Emperors Michael and Basil. Michael went so far as to attempt to crown another co-emperor, a man named Basilikinos.[25] Michael did not get a chance follow through on his intention, however. Shortly afterwards, Michael was assassinated by Basil and Basil's own *hetaireia*, as most of the accounts say. Handsome Basil became sole emperor and founder of the Macedonian dynasty in 867.

Summary of Things to Come

Although with some departures from one another, the six historiographies have many things in common, for which see Figure 2.2. Most salient are the

Notable Persons and Things in the Historiographies

Work, Author, Date, as per Treadgold 2013, in parentheses	Amorous Language	Theophilitzes, Theophiliskos, Theophilidion, or Theophilos	Horse Taming	Wrestling Match	Naked Scourging	Basilikinos, Basiliskianos	Eagle	Male Backsides and Flatulence	Brotherhoods (to be discussed in Chapter 3)
Life of Basil, Theodoros Daphnopates (950)	X	X	X	X		X	X	X	John (τὸ ποιήσασθαι πνευματικῆς ἀδελφότητος σύνδεσμον πρὸς Ἰωάννην)
On Imperial Reigns, Ioseph Genesios (954)	X	X	X	X	X				
Theophanes Continuatus, Theodoros Daphnopates (958)						X		X	
Chronographia, Symeon the Logothete (first edition) (968)	X	X	X			X			Nicholas (ἐλθὼν ἐν τῇ ἐκκλησίᾳ ἐποίησεν ἀδελφοποίησιν) **Other brothers**
Chronographia, Symeon the Logothete (second edition, Bekkerus) (969)	X	X	X			X			Nicholas (ἐλθὼν ἐν τῇ ἐκκλησίᾳ ἐποίησεν ἀδελφοποίησιν) **Other brothers**
Chronographia, Symeon the Logothete (second edition, Istrin) (969)	X	X	X			X			Nicholas (πνευματικὸν ἀδελφὸν ἐποιήσατο) **Other brothers**
Chronographia, Symeon the Logothete (second edition, Featherstone) (969)	X	X	X			X			Nicholas (πνευματικὸν ἀδελφὸν ἐποιήσατο) No other brothers (abbreviated edited text)
Chronographia, Pseudo-Symeon (978/979)	X	X	X			X		X	Nicholas (ἀδελφοποιητὸν ποιήσας) **Other brothers**

Figure 2.2

depictions of men bonding at the highest levels of Byzantine society and the beauty and physique of Basil. All the historiographers give instances of amorous language that Basil inspires. Object of desire and love, Basil makes connections and advances, becoming a member of in-groups (in Greek *hetaireiai* or *phatriai*), Theophilitzes' first and then Michael III's. The historiographers variously share spectacularizations of Basil's body in the scenes of his taming the emperor's horse, a wrestling match, and a ritual naked scourging. A number of them also narrate Michael's attempt to replace Basil with the handsome Basilikinos, who appears to have leveraged his looks, so fetching to men's eyes, for advancement like Basil did.

But these things imagined about the nature of the reactions Basil caused and the relations he developed are not the only places where same-sex desire becomes evident to a reader of these accounts. At the point of reception of the historiographies, knowledge of pagan mythology brings Zeus and Ganymede to mind for readers of the narration of the eagle that takes an interest in Basil as a very young child, but then returns throughout his life. The scatological investments on display in the hi-jinks of Michael's debauched court indicate same-sex sexual interest in anal matters all on their own. The *Life of Basil* intensifies this when it includes intertextuality with Paul's Letter to the Romans.

Amorous Language

Five of the six historiographies emphasize how handsome and charismatic Basil is.[26] He causes wonder, fosters affection, and inspires desire and love in other men. To begin with, there is marveling or wonderment. *Thaumazo* (θαυμάζω)[27] and *thambeo* (θαμβέω),[28] both of which mean "to (stare in) wonder at," often show the reaction his size and masculinity evoke. His appearance can cause an even stronger reaction, as is shown by the occasional use of *ekplesso* (ἐκπλήσσω), with means "to be deeply astonished (at)," and even "struck with desire."[29]

Marvel and astonishment lead in these accounts to fond emotional reactions. "Loving goodwill" (*philostorgos protheseos*/φιλοστόργου προθέσεως)[30] and "affection" (*philtron*/φίλτρον) appear in Genesios.[31] Also in Genesios, Basil acquires considerable power "on account of the marked tender loving (*philostorgeo*/φιλοστοργέω) of the emperor."[32] The verb *epipotheo* (ἐπιποθέω, "to desire") and the related noun *pothos* (πόθος, "desire") also describe the feelings that Basil inspires and occasionally returns. Theophilitzes is told of the accomplished Basil, "that he is of the sort you desire and seek."[33] Basil is also "the sort your [*sc.* Michael III's] rule desires."[34] Basil becomes Michael's *parakoimomenos*, "the one who sleeps beside," because, among other reasons, Basil has shown desire for Michael: "I wish Basil to be *parakoimomenos* because he has great desire for me," Michael said.[35]

Agapao (ἀγαπάω, "to love") and the related noun, *agape* (ἀγάπη, "love") also describe the feelings that Basil evokes. In the *Life of Basil*, "Theophilos made [Basil] his *protostrator*[36] and was loved by him more and more each day."[37] It was similar with Emperor Michael. "The love the emperor

[Michael] had for Basil overflowed" in Symeon the Logothete's *Chronographia*.[38] After Basil tames a wayward horse belonging the emperor, Michael loved him.[39] And later, after Basil marries Eudokia Ingerina, *Kaisar*[40] Bardas perceives that Michael's love for Basil was increasing:

> When this had happened (*sc.* the marriage) and the love (*agape*/ἀγάπη) of the emperor for Basil was growing each day, the *Kaisar* [Bardas] seeing, being both bitten with jealousy and fearing what was to come...
> (*Life of Basil* 16/235)[41]

In Genesios, Emperor Michael "loved the sight"[42] of Basil and two other young men (and Basil especially of course[43]), and after he tames the emperor's horse, the evidence of the emperor's love for him increases.[44] Pseudo-Symeon reports that Michael is told that Basil is the sort of man his rule loves.[45]

Lastly, and perhaps most significantly, the verb *agapao*/ἀγαπάω also designates an undoubted sexual relationship between Michael III and Eudokia Ingerina. All versions of Symeon's *Chronographia* and Pseudo-Symeon's make this clear, for in all of them *agapao* is the word to designate the feelings Michael had for Eudokia Ingerina: "She was the mistress of the emperor and he loved her thoroughly, as she was beautiful."[46] Pseudo-Symeon elsewhere has an occasional preference for the verb *eramai*/ἔραμαι which means "to love" with an emphasis on the sexual aspect. For example, in Pseudo-Symeon, Theophilitzes saw Basil and "loved" (*erasthe*/ἠράσθη) him, which is tantamount to "felt strong physical desire" for him,[47] and this is a moment where the other authors are using *agapao*. The point of this observation is that it is crucial to note that the hoary dichotomy between carnal love/desire as *eros* and non-carnal love/desire as *agape* is irrelevant in these historiographies (and in epistolography). The historiographers are happy to use *agapao* and *agape* in places where other authors, especially earlier ones prefer *eramai* and *eros*.

Theophilitzes and *Hetaireiai*

In five of the six historiographies, a notable moment in Basil's career progression was becoming a member of a *hetaireia*, or group of young men, that Theophilitzes led. Basil's membership in this *hetaireia* led by a relative of Emperor Michael III was brought about by love inspired by his physique and abilities. There is some variation in the historiographers as to how he came to be in the group.

In Symeon the Logothete and Pseudo-Symeon, Basil came to Constantinople because his association with Tzantzes, a general (*strategos*), had not helped him.[48] And so after arriving at the monastery and having met and becoming intimate with its overseer or sacristan, Nicholas, Basil then came to the attention of Nicholas' brother, a doctor in the service of Theophilitzes.[49] Nicholas' brother then sent him on to Theophilitzes, who had a group of young men whom he led. At this point in Symeon and Pseudo-Symeon, Basil was swiftly taken into the emperor's *hetaireia*.

In the *Life of Basil*, young Basil came to Constantinople to make a connection with a powerful man, "to mingle" (*prosmixai*/προσμῖξαι[50]), which is a double-entendre, in the hopes of getting ahead:

> Having set out from Macedonia in Thrace, he made his way to this city that rules all the cities, wishing to mingle with some one of the powerful and illustrious men and enlist and establish himself in that man's entourage and service.
>
> (*Life of Basil* 9/223)[51]

Indeed, after meeting the abbot of the monastery of St. Diomedes,[52] who told him about how he had dreamed that Basil was destined for greatness, Basil took no notice of that and asked instead that the abbot help him so that he might "be handed over into the service of one of the more illustrious men,"[53] a task to which the abbot happily set himself.[54] No brother is mentioned here and it is, rather, the abbot himself who introduced Basil to Theophilitzes.[55] In Genesios, the overseer of the monks recommended Basil to Theophiliskos.[56] So what is the nature of this homosocial group and how does a poor young man from the provinces become a member?

A group of young men that a powerful elite man could have around himself was called a *hetaireia*/ἑταιρεία, which translates as "gathering of comrades."[57] These gatherings of comrades, whose loyalties were to the leader/sponsor who chose the young men for the group, sat for the most part to the side of the official governing structures, though there was a place for them in imperial ceremonial.[58] And as they were mostly extralegal, these associations did on occasion wind up introducing political instability, as was the case with the group around Bardanes Tourkos in the early ninth century,[59] or indeed with the one that Basil acquired, which helped him assassinate Michael III.[60] Indeed, when historiographers wish to underline the sinister role these groups could play, they often use the term *phatria*/φατρία.[61] Even more intense opprobrium of a group emerges in relation to Michael III's own group, from which he drew Basil's proposed replacement, Basilikinos, when it is called an "abominable association."[62] But a *hetaireia* was not just an armed gang. The remit of *hetaireiai* was broader and included social activities.[63] Young men were chosen by the leader on the basis of both shared interests in, e.g., hunting or horsemanship, and manliness.[64] And there is a possible role for same-sex desire as a factor leading to successful entry into a *hetaireia*, as looks did appear to be a consideration.[65]

In the *Life of Basil*, Theophilitzes "had a strong interest to keep about him excellent men, who were handsome and of good stature and who were notable for bravery and strength of body."[66] He also wanted the crew of men in his *hetaireia*[67] looking good in silks:

> ...and it was possible, to take an example, to see these [men of his] made handsome in their silk clothes and standing out with the rest of their ensembles.
>
> (*Life of Basil* 9/225)[68]

These men, chosen for manliness and using their bodies for various tasks and feats, are also costumed to be a pleasing spectacle engineered by one man for other men. Fitting right in and becoming the star of the show, Basil was notable "for his bodily strength and soulful manliness" and "he turned out to be excellent with his hands, intelligent in his soul, and keen and handy for everything that might be requested [of him]."[69] Theophilitzes made Basil chief groom for his horses (*protostrator*), while, as previously noted, his love for Basil increased daily and he felt a sense of wonder at Basil's excellence.[70]

A final thing to note about the portrayal of Theophilitzes in the *Life of Basil* is his nickname, "the educated" (*paideuomenon*).[71] This moniker attributes to him excellence in literature, oratory and learning in general. This means that the man who heads this *hetaireia*, with its masculine homosociality and fetching displays of the male form, will know of earlier literature, including earlier Greek productions that feature same-sex desire. Theophilitzes will also resemble the epistolographers of the first chapter, including Theodoros Daphnopates.

There are similar gatherings of comrades in the other historiographies. In Genesios, the leader of the monks attached Basil to a band led by Theophiliskos (*sc.* Theophilitzes), who, again, is related to the imperial family,[72] and Theophiliskos' band (*sulloge*/συλλογή)[73] was manly and youthful.[74] In the various versions of Symeon the Logothete and Pseudo-Symeon, Nicholas' brother, the doctor tells Theophilitzes, his master, about Basil's desirable and useful masculinity:

> The doctor spoke to his master about the manliness of Basil and [said], "he is the sort you desire and seek..."
> (Symeon the Logothete, *Chronographia* [first edition] 131.15)[75]

Pseudo-Symeon's version is also worth quotation for the increase in the warmth of the language:

> ...when Theophilitzes was asking about a manly man for his horses, the doctor was present and told [him] all about Basil. And so Basil was led there forthwith, and having gazed upon him, Theophilitzes loved (*erasthe*/ἠράσθη). And since he had curly hair and a big head, he called him "The Head" and detailed him to take care of his horses.
> (Pseudo-Symeon, *Chronographia* 656/11)[76]

A clever man who also looked good and, once seen, inspired love—and it is *eramai*, the more erotic verb, being used. Singled out for particular mention is his hair and big head. These were clearly attractive features, and he is also known as "The Head" across the versions of Symeon the Logothete's *Chronographia*.[77]

Basil's membership in Theophilitzes' *hetaireia* eventually brought him to the attention of the emperor. Key parts of his coming to imperial notice were his public displays of excellence in horse-taming and wrestling.

The Emperor's Horse

When Basil is taken into Theophilitzes *hetaireia*, he is to take care of the horses. There is a related development that appears in five of the six accounts. Basil tames an unruly horse of Emperor Michael. In Genesios, it provides confirmation to Michael of Basil's excellence, as in *On Imperial Reigns* Basil has already come to notice of the emperor.[78] In the accounts of Symeon the Logothete, Pseudo-Symeon, and the *Life of Basil*, his success in this task brings him into the emperor's close orbit once and for all. In all the accounts, Basil's mounting of the emperor's horse that causes the emperor to love him is therefore a carnal metaphor, and the version in the *Life of Basil* intensifies this via intertextuality with the Septuagint.

In Genesios, Basil is compared to Alexander the Great and Bellerophon and his feat of taming this wild (but evidently lovable) horse is the cause of great wonder (and note the presence of wonder):

> And so Michael made Basil the *protostates* of his grooms and gave him a wild horse, which he loved a great deal, to mount. He, leaping upon it, like another Alexander onto Boukephalos, as Bellerophon on Pegasus, rides excellently, leaving (in his wake) thunderstruck wonder in the glances of all. After that benefactions for him from the emperor's love increased even more...
>
> (Genesios, *On Imperial Reigns* 4.26)[79]

The hero Basil, object of wonder, receives offices and honors that attest to Michael's love for him: he is made *patrikios*, receives Eudokia Ingerina as wife, is adopted by Michael, becomes *magistros* and *parakoimomenos*, and, finally, after a ritual whipping (about which: more below) is crowned co-emperor with Michael.

In the accounts of Symeon the Logothete and Pseudo-Symeon, the taming of a fine horse also appears.[80] The five versions follow the same basic outline. Emperor Michael has a horse, sent to him by a *strategos*, that is so high-spirited that it will not even allow its teeth to be inspected. Michael is irritated by this. Theophilitzes is present and says that he has a young man who is manly and most skilled as regards horses. Theophilitzes uses the language of desire in two of the renditions of Symeon the Logothete's *Chronographia*,[81] and the language of love in Pseudo-Symeon's.[82] Basil gentles the horse, making it tamer than a sheep, for an admiring audience, among whom is the emperor. And then in all the versions of Symeon and in Pseudo-Symeon, the emperor issues the directions to his *hetaireiarch*[83] Andrew that Basil is to become a member of his *hetaireia*.[84]

In the *Life of Basil*, the horse is danger of being destroyed, as it has been misbehaving: when Michael dismounted, it ran off. Michael commands that its hind legs be hamstrung. *Kaisar* Bardas pleads with the emperor not to maim the horse, which is a fine animal.[85] Basil at this point offers to help, but worries, speaking to Theophilitzes, that Michael may take it badly if he mounts the horse while it bears the imperial insignia. Assured that Michael allows it, Basil mounts the horse and, taming it, is loved:

> And so, Basil, present with his master (Theophilitzes), speaks to him, "if I should ride along side the emperor's horse and, launched from my horse, should come to be mounted upon his, will there not come to be irritation from the emperor against me because it (*sc.* the emperor's horse) is adorned with imperial insignia?" When the emperor had been apprised of (Basil's offer) and ordered that it be done, Basil did it readily and with natural ability. When the emperor had seen (the feat) and conceived a love for Basil's handsome body/excellent disposition endowed with manliness and his intelligence, he immediately took him away from Theophilitzes and enrolled him among the imperial *stratores* [grooms]. He was obsessed with and loved him, seeing his quality of surpassing by much all the other men in every way. Accordingly he (Michael) made him (Basil), who had many times displayed himself in his presence, mount to the dignity of *protostrator*.
> (*Life of Basil* 13/231)[86]

The *Life of Basil* makes for interesting reading here, as it stages in addition to the obvious status transgression, sexual transgression in two ways.

The sight of Basil mounting the imperial horse plays with the impropriety of the lower-status man going where he should not, and it is Basil himself who worries about this. Also to the extent that the horse is a proxy for the emperor, then this brings to mind anal sex between men, as Basil with ease is able to master the emperor['s horse], and the emperor loves it and, indeed, him (which fits with insinuations about Michael's court to be discussed below). But this line of thinking is supported by more than a bald metaphorics of mounting and resultant emotions. There is intertextuality with the Septuagint at the end of the passage.

The passage from *Life of Basil* concludes with the following sentence: "Accordingly he (Michael) made him (Basil), who had many times displayed himself in his presence, mount to the dignity of *protostrator*." The Greek for "mount to the dignity": *eis ten axian anebibasen*/εἰς τὴν ἀξίαν ἀνεβίβασεν uses the verb *anabibazo*/ἀναβιβάζω which recalls a famous moment from Leviticus via its resemblance to the verb *bibazo*/βιβάζω ("to mount") that appears there. *Bibazo* speaks of forbidden relations between animals and people in Leviticus and, significantly, just after one of the anathematizations of relations between males:

> Do not have intercourse with the male as with a women. It is an abomination. And as regards every four-footed creature, you will not have

intercourse to make your seed filthy in it. And woman will not position herself up against a four-footed creature to be mounted (*bibasthenai/* βιβασθῆναι), for that is disgusting.

(Lev 18:22–23)[87]

This scene with the horse is an environment already strong in metaphor, as mounting the emperor's horse is about status and a sexual charge is present. The conclusion of the passage intensifies this, when the literal mounting is made metaphoric again, as Basil "mounts" to the dignity of *protostrator*. And feeling the power of Leviticus is the most natural thing in the world. There is concern about a possible transgressive mounting of an animal and that brings to mind other possible transgressive mountings, like that of a woman by an animal or that between two men in anal sex.

Grappling and a Naked Scourging

The historiographies contain two other moments of physical visibility of young and able Basil: the depiction of him as a wrestling champ, in both the *Life of Basil* and in Genesios, and his ritual scourging prior to being made co-emperor, which appears only in Genesios. Both of these episodes attest yet again to the presence of masculine same-sex desire in Basil's rise to the throne. Furthermore, Basil the wrestler excites the interest of not only the audience internal to the account and readers and authors in the tenth century, but also in a later, but not much later, Byzantine reception: an illustration in the *Madrid Skylitzes*, a manuscript from probably the 1100s (discussed below).

The Bulgarians are in Constantinople after Basil has been added to Theophilitzes' entourage and they are being insufferable, praising their wrestling champion to the skies. In the *Life of Basil*, Theophilitzes offers Basil to *Kaisar* Bardas as the man to put the Bulgarians in their place:

> Since the Bulgarians, always being fairly overly confident and braggarts, happened to have with them at that time a Bulgarian puffing himself up on account of the manliness of his body and being the best at wrestling, and one whom no one of those who had wrestled him had defeated, I think, until that time, they seemed to bet on him to an unbearable extent and were carrying on beyond all measure. While the drinking was proceeding and the good cheer was dancing across the tables, that little Theophilos [*sc.* Theophilitzes] says to the *Kaisar* (Bardas), "I have, master, a man who, if you should command it, will wrestle with this Bulgarian who is heralded all around. For this will be a great reproach to the Romans and no one will be able to bear their bragging, if this one, unconquerable, should return to Bulgaria.
>
> (*Life of Basil* 12/229)[88]

80 *Histories of Masculine Beauty and Desire*

Bardas agrees and an area in the feasting hall is prepared for the match. The young men, Basil and the Bulgarian, then have their match, which Basil wins handily:

> And when this had happened (i.e., the wrestling space had been prepared), Basil, locked together with the Bulgarian (*sumplakeis toi Boulagaroi*/συμπλακεὶς τῷ Βουλγάρῳ) and having swiftly squeezed and bound him up, as though a bundle of hay, insubstantial and lifeless, or a tuft of wool, dry and light, and thus having easily lifted him aloft over the table, he slammed him down (*sc.* on the table). When this had happened, there was no one of those at hand who did not speak all about Basil and stare in wonderment at him. And the Bulgarians, astounded at the abundance of his skill and ability—some of them stayed [in Constantinople]. From that day, the fame of Basil began more and more to spread about the City, all of it, and he was on the lips of all, already firmly admired.
> (*Life of Basil* 12/230)[89]

Two men grappling is a spectacle this audience wants. The Bulgarians carry on so they can have it. Furthermore, the language employed is suggestive, as wrestling language always is. After the wrestlers have first closed in on one another, and Basil is "locked together with the Bulgarian" (*sumplakeis toi Boulagaroi*/συμπλακεὶς τῷ Βουλγάρῳ), the word *sumplakeis* (συμπλακείς) is a form of the verb *sumpleko* (συμπλέκω). This verb, in addition to its use in narrations of wrestling, is redolent of sexual coupling,[90] and indeed shows up with just such a meaning in Plato's *Symposium*.

Already discussed in relation to *Letter 111* of Symeon the Logothete in Chapter 1, Aristophanes' famous speech speaks of primal beings—beings made of two males, two females, and of one male and one female—that had been cut in half on the orders of Zeus. These beings, traumatized by this, are bereft and also looking for their other half:

> And so, when their nature had been cut in two, each, desiring its half, would come together, and throwing their hands around (each other) and being locked together with one another (*sumplekomenoi allelois*/συμπλεκόμενοι ἀλλήλοις), desiring to grow together/be united...
> (Plato, *Symposium* 191A)[91]

Driven by desire, the beings when they find their half, embrace tightly to replicate their lost unity. But they do nothing but embrace until one of them dies. Then the survivor, no doubt weakened, looks for another half that matches the half they have lost:

> The one left behind (after the other half has died) was seeking another and was locking itself together (*sunepleketo*/συνεπλέκετο) (with them), whether it would get with the half of the woman whole, which we now

most assuredly call a woman, or whether it would get with the part of the man whole, thus they were perishing.

(Plato, *Symposium* 191B)[92]

Zeus pitied them and moved humans' genitals to the front of the body, which would allow them to have sex, for both reasons of continuing the race and for general satisfaction and pleasure that make work easier:

And so, he (Zeus) changed their (genitals [191B: *ta aidoia*/τὰ αἰδοῖα]) in this way to the front and through these things he made it so that they would beget in one another, by means of the male in the female, with the following in mind: partly so that if a man should get with a woman in an embrace [lit. a lock together (*en tei sumplokei*/ἐν τῇ συμπλοκῇ)], they may make a child and the race comes into being, and partly so that if a male (should get with) a male (in an embrace), at least then there will be the satisfaction of intercourse, and they may rest themselves and they may turn to labors and pay attention to the rest of life.

(Plato, *Symposium* 191C)[93]

And so, educated readers of the *Life of Basil*, when reading of the grappling Bulgarian and Basil locked together, quite likely remembered the possibility of intercourse granted to the refigured primal beings and which was a scene of satisfying and relaxing reunification for the separated male/male being. There is also evidence that the closeness of wrestling and sex in this match was known in a reception not long after the writing of this text.

One of the illustrations from the *Madrid Skylitzes* manuscript shows this wrestling scene. This manuscript dates probably from the twelfth century and is an edition of Skylitzes' *Sunopsis Historion*. John Skylitzes, an eleventh-century historiography, copied the text of the *Life of Basil* and other texts with small changes and put them into his narrative of the years 811–1057.[94] In any case, the artist in the manuscript depicted the Bulgarian on his back on the table and Basil's crotch right up against his buttocks, when it came time to illustrate "having easily lifted him aloft over the table, he slammed him down (*sc.* on the table)," and that is the language that appears just above the illustration in the last partial line of text.[95] This significant reception of the text of the *Life of Basil* comes as close to showing an actual anal penetration as decorum will allow (see Figure 2.3). The manuscript illustrates a coincidence of man-on-man wrestling with man-on-man copulation prompted by (1) the general sexualizing context on display in the *Life of Basil*, (2) the Greek language, through *sumpleko*/συμπλέκω (which is also copied by Skylitzes), and (3) perception of intertextuality with the *Symposium* enabled by this verb.

Basil also appears as a wrestler in Genesios' *On Imperial Reigns*.[96] Similar to the *Life of Basil*, it is a raucous agonistic context, but instead of Bulgarians against Romans, it is a contest of wrestling champions sponsored by the

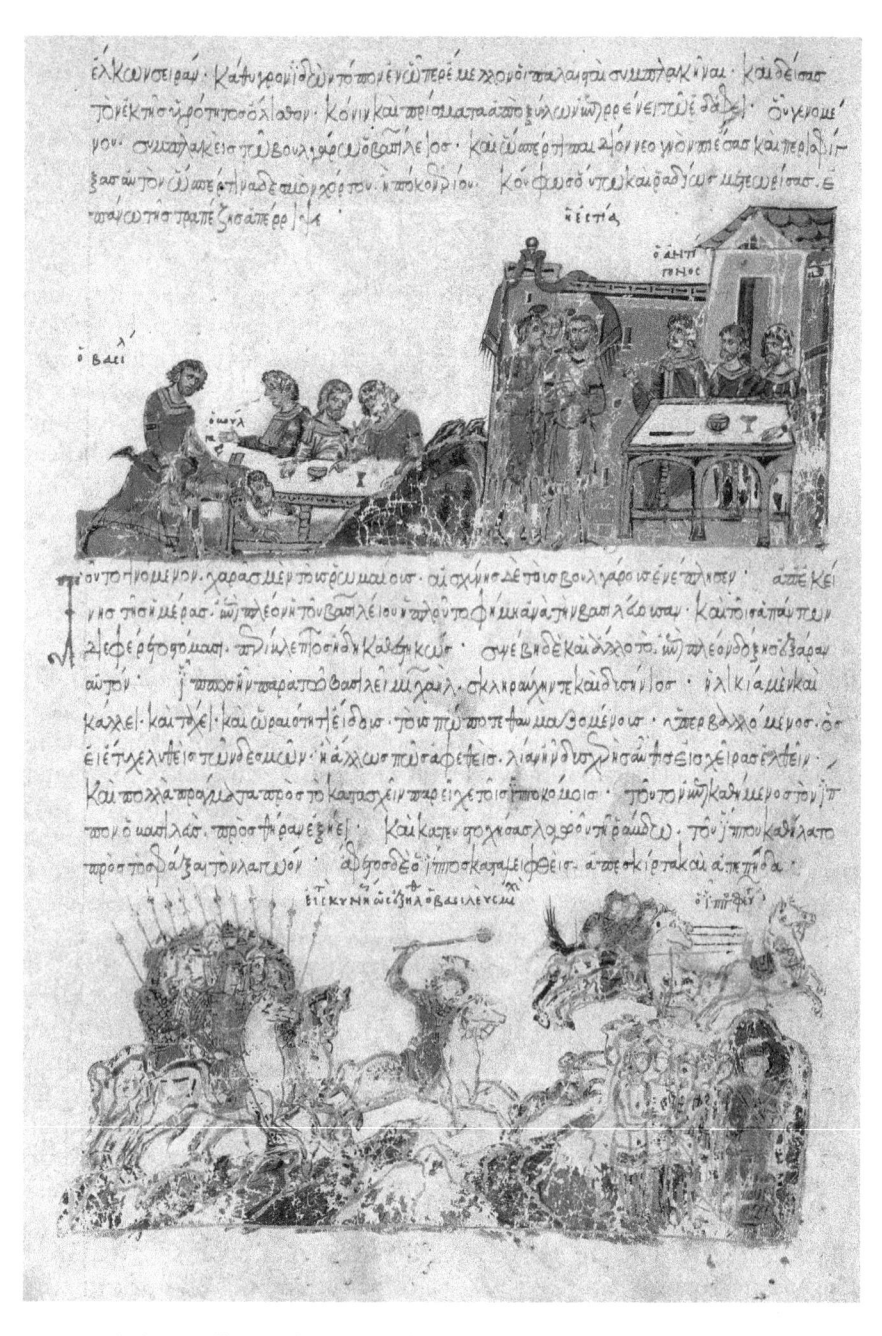

Figure 2.3 A wrestling Basil slams defeated Bulgarian down on the table. See top, far left (Skylitzes Manuscript fo. 85v. Biblioteca Nacional, Madrid).

emperor and *Kaisar* Bardas against those of Theophiliskos. Theophiliskos' men are getting the worst of it until Basil is called up. Basil makes short work of the competition:

> ...the two of them (Basil and his opponent) came together on the wrestling floor. The other tried to lift Basil aloft, but he, not able to endure the resistance of Basil, is most masterfully lifted aloft immediately and is turned around with the swiftest of motions. By means of a locking hold (*prospolkei*/προσπλοκῇ), called the *podreza*, as the local terminology has it, he is plunged to the ground, having experienced an obvious fall, such as was said to be to the satisfaction of all, even if he revived only with difficulty after a good long while, sprinkled with much water.
> (Genesios, *On Imperial Reigns* 4.26)[97]

As noted above, this match is somewhat different from the one in the *Life of Basil*. Not only is it an intra-Roman affair, there is no table on which Basil throws his opponent, and he also uses a special move, a locking hold called the *podreza*. This term is obscure, probably from some proto-Slavic dialect.[98] But the exact meaning of *podreza* does not matter much, as Genesios offers a synonym: "locking hold." A locking hold is a *prosploke*/προσπλοκή, which is from the family of words based on *pleko*/πλέκω, to which *sumpleko*/συμπλέκω, seen in the *Life of Basil* and the *Symposium*, also belongs. It therefore also calls to mind sexual contact. In any case, wrestling success leads to Emperor Michael taking an interest in Basil:

> In time Emperor Michael became apprised of these things and he summons him (Basil) with two (other wrestlers) of the same age. And when he had gazed upon them, he loved the sight. He praised this company of young men all the same age, but he had admired Basil much more than the other two. He achieves greater ranks and he is honored with greater favors.
> (Genesios, *On Imperial Reigns* 4.26)[99]

As so often, Basil's physique attracts attention and, furthermore, the sight of his youthful manliness causes love in the emperor. This love born of sight then translates into advantages, which are the various offices he holds on his way up the ladder to being made co-emperor. And as Genesios immediately remarks, the body powerfully employed in man-to-man combat is symbolic and even an allegory of the glorious imperial future:

> Those whom God has perceived to be future emperors, he has predestined them, and in all ways he arranges for symbols of this fact (to appear) beforehand.
> (Genesios, *On Imperial Reigns* 4.26)[100]

But Genesios presents more than premonition of imperial office.[101] His account, like those of the other historiographers, embodies a male gaze that finds in Basil a favored object. The reader admires Basil's superior physique, like the people did as they watched Basil wrestling, or Michael did, when he summoned Basil with two of his age-mates.

And there is another display in Genesios of Basil's body for the delectation of men's eyes. *On Imperial Reigns* contains an episode that appears in none of the other historiographers. Just prior to crowning Basil co-emperor with him, and right after the wrestling match and subsequent inspection in which Basil outshines the two other youths, Michael has Basil stripped, whips him, and this is his way of showing affection:

> Having locked Basil in one of the imperial sleeping chambers, he [Michael] with a nod orders those with him to strip him naked and to stretch out both his hands. When this had happened in accordance with the order, Basil is shocked, but all the same, being vigorously youthful, he recovers from shock. He is positioned by the emperor himself and is whipped by him with a double whip thirty times, to provide him with an engraved memory of loving goodwill toward him. And then having gone to the greatest church, [i.e., Hagia Sophia,] that very early morning, he presents a crowned leader to the people on the 26th of May in the fourteenth indiction. He gives to him all the things appropriate to the second in rank in the imperial office. And giving to him in addition much affection, he also bestows (upon Basil) equal prerogatives, and even things in excess.
> (Genesios, *On Imperial Reigns* 4.27)[102]

This curious scene of Basil's naked and scourged body says a number of things at once. The outstretched arms and scourging bring Christ to mind. A Byzantine reader might also think of martyrologies, which feature literal and yet symbolic torture. Martyrs suffer persecution that is not only destruction of their physical bodies; it is also the means to sanctity as one of God's elect. Here Basil suffers torture and it is leading him to splendor as co-emperor.

But Michael says he engages in this physical abuse to demonstrate affection and love. This whipping of the young and vigorous Basil's naked body is not torture; it gives Basil "an engraved memory of loving goodwill toward him."[103] From this angle, an understanding in homoerotic terms is possible. Basil's clothes are removed, his arms held out and his body positioned by the emperor and then a whipping follows. These actions resemble a gay sadomasochistic scene now. While speaking of sadomasochism in Byzantium is anachronism perhaps to beat them all, it is clarifying: the resignification of the infliction of pain as a showing of affection and love is an underlying mechanism in sadomasochistic scenarios, and suggests homoeroticism in this extravagant scene prior to a coronation. At the end of this passage, the scene of Basil's being crowned and receiving "much affection" makes this resignifying point again[104]: there are many ways to show affection and love and preferment and violation are among them.

Basilikinos/Basiliskianos: Handsome Competition

So far, this chapter has been surveying things that connect Basil and his milieu to same-sex desire: language that shows the regard and interest that Basil inspires; his membership in Theophilitzes' *hetaireia*; subtexts that attend the depiction of Basil as a horse-tamer and wrestler; and, finally, as a participant in polysemous scene that includes a blending of ritualized violence with affection. In various ways, all the narratives so far surveyed have been interested in displaying Basil's body for the readership. It is worthwhile to keep all these things in mind when coming to an episode that appears in seven out the eight accounts (Genesios is the one that omits it): Michael's attempt to make another man, Basilikinos or Basiliskianos, co-emperor. This man is a threat to Basil. In all the accounts Michael's attempt leads in short order to the assassination of Michael and the beginning of the Macedonian dynasty with Basil I as sole emperor. The rationale for Basilikinos being made emperor and the descriptions of him lay bare Basil's ambitions and reinscribe homoerotic subtexts already discernable in the rise of Basil himself.[105]

Basil had been co-emperor for some time when Michael decided to make another man emperor in addition. His name is Basilikinos in *Life of Basil* and *Theophanes Continuatus*, and Basiliskianos in both editions of Symeon the Logothete's *Chronographia* and in Pseudo-Symeon's. The way the historiographers handle this man, proposed for the throne and competition for Basil, puts into even sharper relief the power of male beauty and the circulation of same-sex desire in court circles. A stand-in for Basil, Basilikinos has the qualities Basil does and his life circumstances are similar to those of Basil. In the first place, the *Life of Basil* and *Theophanes Continuatus* reveal that Basilikinos' background is modest and, like Basil, he has come up in the world: he had been an oarsman of the imperial trireme or *dromon*.[106] The spin here is that the low status of Basilikinos makes him undeserving to replace Basil, who is destined for greatness. In the various versions of Symeon the Logothete and in Pseudo-Symeon, Basiliskianos is, in contrast, a *patrikios* who praises the emperor for a horse race well done.[107] Symeon the Logothete and Pseudo-Symeon attribute higher status to Basiliskianos and thus make him more deserving of honor; still on a(n ill-fated) journey to eminence, he does not have far to go and may be more deserving than Basil. Lastly, their names are similar: Basileios (in Greek) as opposed to Basilikinos/Basiliskianos, with Basilikinos and Basiliskianos coming across as parodic. Still, though, while all present a Basilikinos that differs occasionally in the details, all offer up a figure in him who has beauty and provokes same-sex desire, and uses both of them to advance to higher position and, therefore, has similarity to Basil on these bases. See Figure 2.4 for an image from the *Madrid Skylitzes* that shows Basilikinos and Basil looking similar.

Both editions of Symeon the Logothete tell of a well-attended banquet given after Michael has successfully raced his horses.[108] Basil, as Michael's

86 *Histories of Masculine Beauty and Desire*

Figure 2.4 Basilikinos (left) and Basil (right) in the top bank of figures don't look that different (Skylitzes Manuscript fo. 80v. Biblioteca Nacional, Madrid).

Histories of Masculine Beauty and Desire 87

co-emperor, is there, along with wife Eudokia Ingerina. Basiliskianos praises Michael's excellence in the races. This leads Michael to order Basiliskianos to take the imperial red shoes, the *tzangia*, off him and put them on himself.[109] This is a serious political suggestion. There is a tense moment when Basiliskianos isn't sure whether he should obey this order to wear the red imperial shoes, because Basil is right there watching. Michael angrily reiterates his order. Basil assents with a nod, and when the shoes are on Basiliskianos, Michael announces his plans. Here is this moment from the first edition of Symeon the Logothete *Chronographia* (which appears with trivial differences in the second edition[110]):

> Having ordered him (Basiliskianos) to rise, the emperor told him to pull off his *tzangia* and to put them on. While he was refusing and looking away over at Basil, in anger the emperor told him to do it. After Basil gave him the approving nod, he put the *tzangia* on himself. And the emperor with an oath said to Basil, "how they suit him more beautifully than you! And do I not have the power, as I have made you emperor to make another also?" And he was furious, being angry with Basil. While crying, Eudokia [Ingerina] said to the emperor, "the worthiness of your rule, my master, is great, even we have been honored beyond our worth. But it is not right that it be despised." [In answer,] the emperor said, "don't be vexed [*sc.* to no purpose] over this; I intend to make Basiliskianos emperor." Basil was plunged into anger and great pain.
>
> (131.46–47)[111]

This donning of imperial shoes creates, Michael says, a sight more beautiful than anything Basil could offer. This beauty will translate forthwith into imperial majesty if Michael gets his way. Basil and Eudokia Ingerina are distressed by this, and the murder of Michael comes soon.

In the *Life of Basil* and *Theophanes Continuatus*, Michael puts Basilikinos in imperial raiment, but it isn't to confront Basil and Eudokia Ingerina at a banquet, he instead presents Basilikinos to the senate:

> And so he (Michael) clothes this Basilikinos of the bad name in the once much-famed-in-poetry imperial purple, the visually arresting and enviable crown, the completely golden *paludamentum*, the shoes red and stoned, and all the other emblems of rule. He leads him out to the senate, grasping him by the hand and fawning on him, like that Nero long ago did with the much-talked-about Eros and he speaks [thus] word for word:
>
> "All of you, see and stare in wonderment (*thaumasate*/θαυμάσατε)!
>
> Does it not suit him to be emperor?
>
> First his beauty is worthy of the rule.

88 *Histories of Masculine Beauty and Desire*

>   Second the crown is naturally his
>
>   and all things fit (him) to the office."

And [he also says,] "how much more beautiful a thing it is that I make him emperor rather than Basil!" All those about the palace, seeing and hearing of these things, remained close-lipped, astounded at the illogical stupidity and delirium of the emperor that was a result of his folly. He was thus a man, on account of his excessive drunkenness and unlawful and *aselges* deeds, situated entirely outside of where he should be, insane, and carried away.

(Life of Basil 25/250–251)[112]

As in Symeon's versions, Basilikinos wears the red shoes, and an addition is all the other finery that make Basilikinos look every inch a co-emperor. Then with attentive physicality (holding his hand, the fawning) that argues for intimacy between them, he presents Basilikinos to the senate. Reference to an otherwise unknown story of Nero and Eros emphasizes that this intimacy is erotic.[113] While the lack of evidence elsewhere of Nero and Eros makes it a challenge to evaluate, some conclusions can be drawn. It is clear enough that this comparison signals both Michael III's debauchery (Michael *is* Nero) and the sexual nature of the connection between Michael and Basilikinos (Basilikinos *is* Eros, i.e., "sexual desire"). There then follows Michael's pronouncement, in verse, that demands first that the senators stare in wonderment (*thaumasate*/θαυμάσατε), which is a reaction Basil is said to elicit over and over again both in *Life of Basil* and in other sources.[114] As Michael continues, the beauty of Basilikinos accredits him for the role, as does the fact he is wearing imperial finery. The references to beauty continue after the poem is complete with the words "how much more beautiful a thing is it that I make him emperor..."), which recalls Symeon the Logothete's Michael saying to Basil that the *tzangia* suit Basiliskianos more beautifully. The final thing to note is the mention of the *aselges* deeds Michael has been engaging in. *Aselges* recurs in descriptions of men in Michael's circle (discussed below) and also, highly salient in the present instance, calls to mind regulations against anal sex between males in civil law.[115]

This episode with its poetry from the emperor appears also in *Theophanes Continuatus* in substantially the same format as the *Life of Basil*. It does not contain the reference to Nero and Eros though.[116] The verse pronouncement also appears in Pseudo-Symeon's version. He clearly synthesized the *Life of Basil*/*Theophanes Continuatus* with the various versions of Symeon the Logothete:

> [Just after Basiliskianos finished praising Michael for excellent racing], the emperor straightaway ordered him [Basiliskianos] to rise, to pull off his *tzangia* and put them on himself. But as he was refusing, while looking at Basil, at that moment the emperor with anger ordered, and Basil gave the approving nod. He put them on. The emperor says with an oath

to Basil, "they suit him more beautifully. And do I not have the power? As I made you emperor, [I have the power] to make another!" And he was furious, being angry with Basil. While crying, Eudokia [Ingerina] said to the emperor, the worthiness of your rule, my master is great, even we have been honored beyond our worth. But it is not right that it be despised." And to Basil he said, "don't be vexed [*sc.* to no purpose] over this; I intend to make Basiliskianos emperor." And to those present he said,

"Does it not suit him to be emperor?

First his beauty is worthy of the rule.

Second the crown is naturally his

and all things fit [him] to the office."

And [he said further]: "how much more beautiful a thing it is, therefore, that I make him emperor." Basil was plunged into anger and great pain.
(Pseudo-Symeon, *Chronographia* 682–683/47)[117]

The post-horseracing banquet that figured in Symeon the Logothete's versions of this story is back. As in those accounts, the main audience for Basiliskianos' elevation is Basil and Eudokia. But the poem that figures in *Life of Basil* and *Theophanes Continuatus* appears and this tells a reader that Pseudo-Symeon had access to at least one of these works and/or even to their sources. It is clear that these earlier sources were available and, further, that thoughts about the rise of Basil I in the mid-tenth century embraced all of them, as the synthesis of Pseudo-Symeon shows.

In summation, Basiliskianos provides a template by which to judge Basil. In all the accounts, Michael believes that Basiliskianos is a credible replacement for Basil. He is beautiful. And Basil, while a member of the *hetaireia* of Theophilitzes, is handsome in his silk clothing. The *Life of Basil* criticizes Basilikinos as generally worthless, not manly enough, and vain about his head of hair: "worthless, accursed, effeminate and enamored of his locks."[118] The mention of hair recalls the nice curly hair that Basil has and the moniker, "head," given to him by Theophilitzes on account of his locks.[119] Young men such as Basiliskianos (or Basil) who make their way up the ladder in Byzantium can credibly be charged with having used their looks to advance their careers. There also is the language of desire discussed above that identifies of Basil as the object of same-sex desire and this can be put alongside the conclusion of the passage from the *Life of Basil* that mentions *"aselges* deeds" that Michael engaged in.[120] Basilikinos/Basiliskianos adds to the portrait of Basil.

These historiographical texts, showing masculine beauty and desirability leading to associations that benefitted Basil on his way to the throne, reveal more when intertextual dynamics are analyzed. An eagle appearing in the *Life of Basil* and Genesios recalls Zeus and Ganymede, especially given the way the narratives subsequently stage same-sex desire. Ganymede would have come to mind, given his presence both in other texts and in the environment around the writers. The scatological antics of Michael's "abominable association,"[121] which is associated in the *Life of Basil*, *Theophanes Continuatus*, and Pseudo-Symeon with sexual desire, receives a denunciation from Empress Theodora which is intertextual with Paul's Letter to the Romans.

Eagle and Ganymede

In the *Life of Basil*, the remarks about what happened with young Basil and an eagle start with these words:

> There happened to him at a young age something which caused wonder (*thaumasion*/θαυμάσιον), a thing revealing his fate to come, a thing which I think it would not be right to pass over in silence.
>
> (*Life of Basil* 5/218)[122]

The one who would cause wonder often when older, started early. As the story continues, the time was the middle of summer and the harsh rays of the sun were pouring down. Basil's parents were supervising the threshers at their work in the fields. Basil a very young child, a *paidion*/παιδίον, needed to be shielded from the sun. A shelter made from the sheaves was constructed and Basil was in it (see Figure 2.5).

While his parents were away with the reapers, an eagle flew down and "shaded the child with its spead-out wings."[123] Basil's mother, alerted by the shouts of those who saw the eagle "making shade all about the child with its wings,"[124] chased the eagle away three times. She could not bring herself to trust it. While the eagle could be chased off, it nonetheless was not particularly frightened of Basil's mother, even as she was preparing to throw a rock at it: "it was looking at her intently and yet in a favoring way."[125] These encounters with the eagle were signs of things to come,[126] and significantly, the eagle would return again and again to Basil as matured:

> This thing [the eagle shielding him] happened to him not a few times as he matured, and many times he was discovered being shaded in his sleep by the eagle.
>
> (*Life of Basil* 5/219)[127]

The eagle also makes a brief appearance in Genesios' *On Imperial Reigns*. Basil's mother was told that an eagle had alighted on young Basil's head and covered it with his wings:

> And in addition to these things, a good word was given to her from someone that an eagle had flown down upon her boy's head while he was at play with agemates at the water's edge, and clapping its wings, it was covering his head.
>
> (Genesios, *On Imperial Reigns* 4.24)[128]

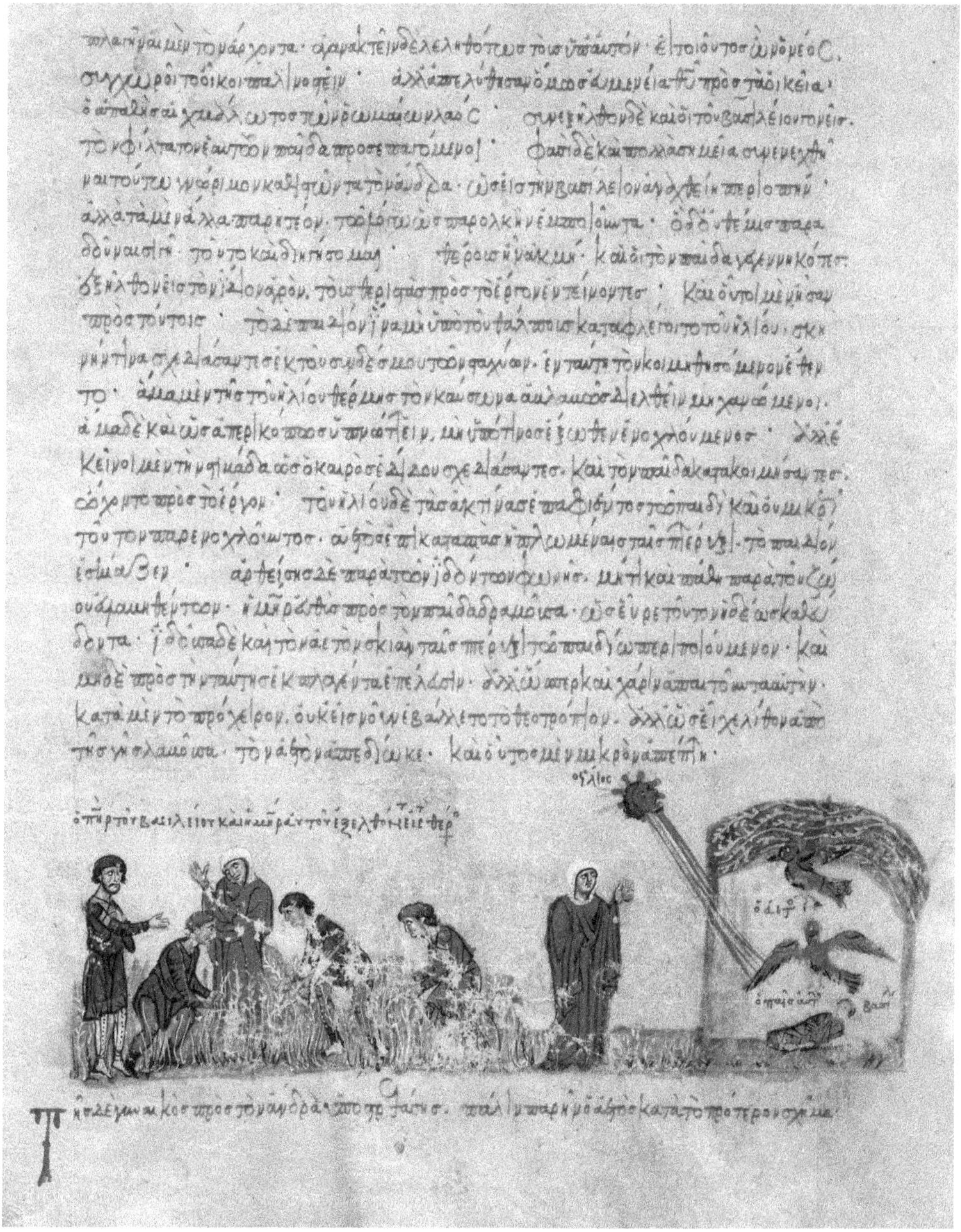

Figure 2.5 The eagle shields baby Basil from the sun in his shelter. Basil's mother looks on. See bottom, far right (Skylitzes Manuscript fo. 82v. Biblioteca Nacional, Madrid).

As the eagle promises greatness in the *Life of Basil*, it does in *On Imperial Reigns*. Indeed, in the "good word" she received was just not report of this appearance of an eagle; the Greek, *rhesin euangelon*/ῥῆσιν εὐάγγελον is redolent of scripture. Genesios places this story about the eagle between a premonitary dream Basil's mother had and a prophecy from an old man that Basil would be emperor. Genesios outlines the stakes of the dream Basil's mother had:

> And subsequently (the dream) was interpreted under oath to her that for her child there would be a marching forward into possession of the rule, into a greatness of it, and into a span stretched into length with offspring and descendants and that, through him, sufficent wealth would spring up upon the land from which he had been born.
>
> (Genesios, *On Imperial Reigns* 4.24)[129]

This glorious future mediates interpretation of this vignette with eagle and boy; a great rule is coming and that makes the moment with an eagle significant. Much meaning crowds around this eagle.

In the first place, this story of an eagle shielding a future ruler from the hot sun had been reported in historiography before.[130] Prokopios (sixth century) reports that when Marcian (emperor 450–457) was on campaign in North Africa against the Vandal kingdom, the Roman troops, who had been captured, were made to gather under guard in a courtyard at midday in the full sun and an eagle shaded Marcian as slept,[131] and this portended that he would be emperor.[132] The *Chronographia* of Theophanes the Confessor (eighth to ninth century) has Marcian shaded by his eagle twice. The first time Tatianos, later city prefect of Constantinople in 450–452, and his brother Julius note the solicitous eagle while they are on campaign in the east with Marcian.[133] Then, Theophanes repeats the story in Prokopios of the eagle shading Marcian with his wings in North Africa.[134]

The *Suda* mentions a story "from the Macedonians" in which an eagle blocks the clear light of the sun:

> Pure: clear, unmixed. A story flows down from the Macdonians, which says that an eagle, hanging about, stretching out out its wings, keeps both the pure ray from him, while holding itself aloft, and, when it might rain, the copious rain.
>
> (*Suda*, Alpha 963)[135]

This plausibly is an abbreviated story of the eagle sheltering Basil, as mention of the Macedonians is made.[136]

These three references to Prokopios, Theophanes the Confessor, and the *Suda* hardly exhaust the political resonances which were possible to feel when reading this story about Basil.[137] But it is significant that in these earlier historiographies, it is a man who has the eagle interested in him, while in the *Life of Basil* and *On Imperial Reigns*, it is a boy.[138] Thoughts naturally turn to the famous mythical story of Zeus as an eagle and Ganymede.

The Trojan prince Ganymede, who, as a young boy, was seized by Zeus, made wine-pourer of the gods, took his place in Zeus' bed, and became a founding figure for pederasty in mythological imagination,[139] has not been associated with young Basil in discussion of these historiographies. But he should be, as neither author is shy about speaking about mythological figures in relation to Basil. Genesios mentions Chiron's education of Achilles as similar to the upbringing Basil's parents gave him in the lead-in to his remarks on the eagle.[140] In the *Life of Basil*, just after the story of the eagle, Basil's education by his father is said to be superior to the instruction Achilles received from Chiron and to whatever he hypothetically might have learned from Lycurgus or Solon, had they instructed him.[141] Furthermore, visited in the *Life of Basil* at various times later in his life by the eagle,[142] Basil would have been the proper Ganymede age at some point and a reader's thoughts would turn in the direction of pederasty, especially as Basil's beauty was undeniable later. Lastly, famous Ganymede was a presence in tenth-century Byzantium, able to be found in representations of various kinds, including ivory caskets and written productions that were available to writers and readers of these historiographies.

Two famous ivory caskets, one, the "Veroli Casket" (see Figure 2.6), located at the Victoria and Albert Museum,[143] and the other, at the Museée de Cluny,[144] have relevant programs of images. And these programs both include a depiction of a boy or youth, ages are hard to judge, riding an eagle. These representations call Ganymede and Zeus to mind.[145] Both caskets are from the tenth or the very early eleventh century,[146] and therefore are roughly contemporaneous with composition of the historiographies.

Before discussion of the probable depictions of Zeus and Ganymede on these caskets, it is necessary to speak briefly about Byzantine ivory caskets in general. The construction of these caskets was two-step process. First was the construction of a box out of wood and then the selection and application of both ivory borders (the Veroli has flowers, while the Cluny has faces in profile alternating with flowers) and ivory plaquettes of various sizes that had figures on them.[147] The image of boy/youth on the eagle was likely popular, or, at any rate one that was seen often.[148]

The boy and eagle appear on one of the long sides of the Veroli casket (see Figure 2.7). They are at the top right of the left plaquette that contains a total of ten different figures. This panel has two Erotes/Cupids,[149] four boys/youths, a female panther or lioness, a greyhound, a deer, and the eagle. The two Erotes to the right of the panel are attempting to bridle the deer. The boy on his eagle is just above them (see Figure 2.7.1). To the left is a youth grasping the dog, and then, continuing to the left, the panther with one boy underneath her suckling on one her teats, and another boy kissing her, while evidently attempting to bridle her. In summation, this panel contains divine beings, mortals, and assorted animals—and the identification of Zeus and Ganymede in boy and eagle grows stronger when more of the casket is considered.

94 *Histories of Masculine Beauty and Desire*

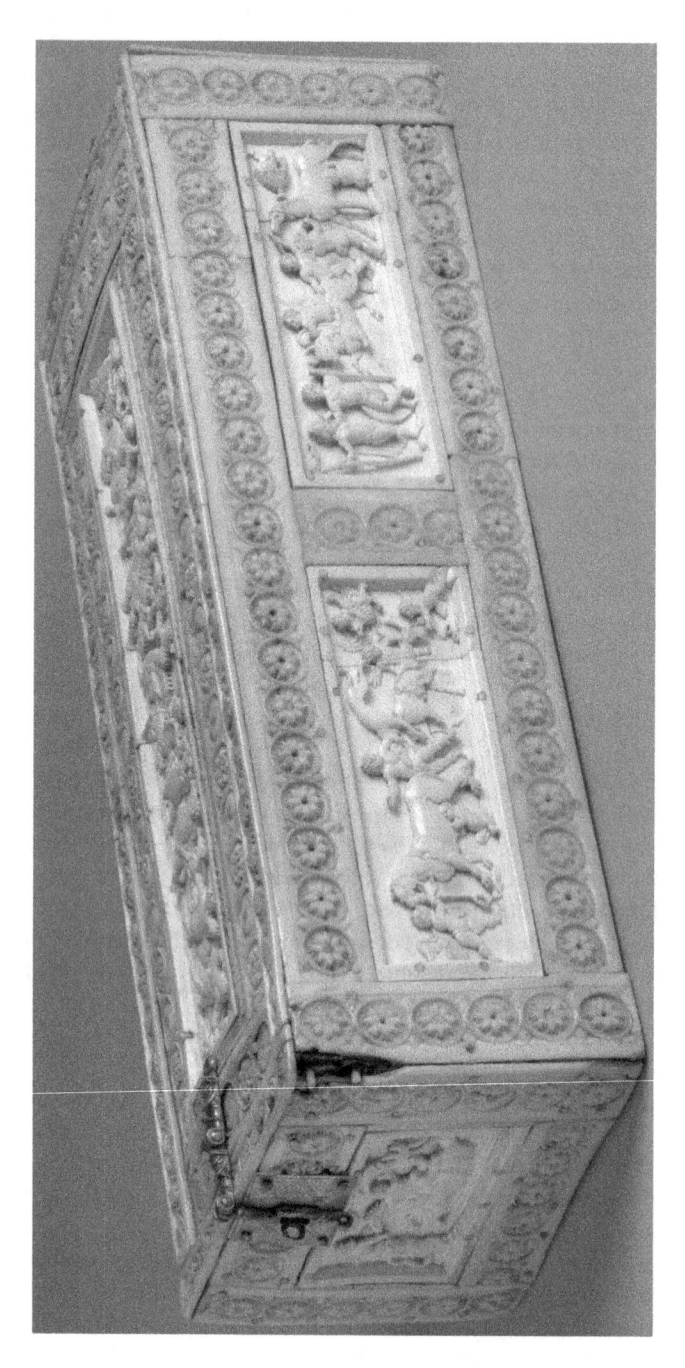

Figure 2.6 Side angle of the Veroli Casket (Victoria and Albert Museum, London).

Histories of Masculine Beauty and Desire   95

Figure 2.7 Side of the Veroli Casket, straight on (Victoria and Albert Museum, London).

96 *Histories of Masculine Beauty and Desire*

Figure 2.7.1 Detail of a side of the Veroli Casket, straight on: boy/Ganymede on his eagle (Victoria and Albert Museum, London).

Figure 2.7.2 Detail of a side of the Veroli Casket, straight on: figures in the right two thirds of the right panel/plaquette (Victoria and Albert Museum, London).

On the right plaquette, a nearly naked woman and a man[150] clothed in martial garb appear. These figures have been identified as Aphrodite and Ares.[151] Given the eroticism, explicit and hinted at, shortly to be seen both to right of this couple and on the top of the casket, identification of the nude female figure as Aphrodite is justified, an identification which then supports seeing the other figure as Ares.

To the right of the couple, are a number of boys/youths and animals (see Figure 2.7.2). There is a boy on a bull with his back to the viewer, and this echoes the probable appearance of Europa on a bull on the top of the casket (discussed below). To the right, a youth goads the bull on which the boy is riding. Next to him, another youth is restraining a horse that is, and this is a challenging image, being fellated by still another boy. The last figure on this panel, and in the same position as the boy on the eagle in the panel to the left, is a boy, though possibly an Eros, who has fallen head-first into a basket. The basket might even be flying through the air and his naked backside is the feature that captures the eye. Indeed, there is a total of four bared male backsides on this plaquette.

Consideration of the top completes this survey of the Veroli casket (see Figure 2.8). On the far left are two women rushing to help (?) a woman on a bull that is being charged menacingly by a group of men. This woman on the bull is surely Europa. To the right of the hostile men, are three Erotes,

Figure 2.8 Top of the Veroli Casket (Victoria and Albert Museum, London).

98 *Histories of Masculine Beauty and Desire*

two of which appear to be flying, and underneath one of the flying Erotes is old man playing what looks to be a lyre and who has been identified as a "Herakles type."[152] To the right of the man playing the lyre, two centaurs caper, while playing an aulos (the one on the left) and the pan-pipes (the one on the right). The centaur on the left possibly has wings, while the one on the right has a boy on his shoulder. The panel concludes at the far right with three maenads.[153]

The boy on his eagle is likely to recall Ganymede with Zeus for a number of reasons. In the first place, a viewer is primed to read Ganymede into the depiction of the boy on eagle because they are already seeing myths and mythical creatures elsewhere on the casket.[154] Second, Zeus arguably appears twice, once as the bull and then again as the eagle. Furthermore, Zeus' appearance as a bull enables a viewer to be thinking of a Zeus who is on the prowl, and so the sexualized reading of the eagle gains strength on this basis. There are also instances of bestiality on the box, implied, i.e., the story of Europa and the bull, and explicit, i.e., the boy fellating the horse, which likewise make a reading of Ganymede and Zeus/eagle likely.

The Musée Cluny casket, dating from around the same time as the Veroli casket,[155] has marked similarities with it in terms of the modeling of the characters.[156] Similar also is the occurrence of stories and figures from myth. There is likely a siege of Troy on the top.[157] Herakles also appears twice, once as young man wrestling the Nemean Lion on one of the short sides of the casket, and on the long side opposite[158] the side to be discussed presently, he appears, mature, carrying his club, on which is attached the hide of the Nemean lion.

On the opposite long side of this casket is the boy on the eagle, which is familiar from the Veroli.[159] This side of the casket has a row of five square plaquettes, which are separated and framed by borders of faces in profile alternating with flowers (see Figure 2.9). The boy on his eagle is the central one. On the far left is a soldier rushing forward and apparently getting ready to bring his sword down. To the right of him, the next plaquette probably features the centaur Nessus' attempt to rape Dejanira,[160] though it has also been suggested that it is Achilles on the back of Chiron.[161] Just on the other side of boy and eagle, a winged Eros rides a sea horse and then, to the right in the last plaquette, what looks to be a rape scene. The woman on this plaquette holds two torches, and therefore reads as a maenad.

When this side of the casket and indeed the whole casket is considered, the boy and eagle recall Ganymede and Zeus for a number of reason. In the first place, the frequent presence of mythical figures and stories on the box as a whole primes a viewer to think in terms of myth. Next, desire in the form of an Eros on his sea horse, is present. And desire with compulsion is certainly also present, appearing on the last plaquette to the right with the rape of the probable maenad, and on the second plaquette from the left, which likely shows Nessus and Dejanira.[162] Myth, desire, and sexual compulsion make the reading of the boy on eagle as Ganymede on Zeus nearly inescapable.

Figure 2.9 Side of the casket from the Musée de Cluny (photo © RMN-Grand Palais (musée de Cluny - musée national du Moyen Âge) / Thierry Ollivier).

There is more evidence of Ganymede in the environment around the historiographers and their readers. As noted earlier, the *Greek Anthology* reached its milestone compilation around the year 900 and was known in educated circles supported by Emperor Constantine VII. The anthology contains 12 epigrams that mention Ganymede and Zeus. Most of them state or strongly imply that Zeus is an eagle,[163] while in two epigrams, the eagle is viewed as separate entity from Zeus.[164] There are four epigrams in which the fact of the connection post-rape between Ganymede and Zeus is mentioned.[165] Ganymede's attractive backside, which evidently is being surpassed by a young man that the epigrammatist has seen[166]—which recalls the backsides on the Veroli casket. In still another one, Hera remarks that it was Troy, through Ganymede, that introduced Zeus to "masculine fire."[167] And lastly, the most famous of the pederastic epigrammaticists, Strato, depicts a scene where the narrator of the poem encounters a group of handsome lads, whom he calls Erotes and whose master he judges is greater than Zeus because he has so many young men, while Zeus only had Ganymede:

> Out of what sort of temple, from where this troop of Erotes, all dazzling? Men, I see poorly! Who of these is a slave? Who is free? I cannot say. The guy who is master of these? I cannot [say]. But if there is [a master of all these handsome lads], he greater than Zeus by a lot, he who had Ganymede alone, although he was a god so great. And this one [has] so many!
>
> (Strato, *Greek Anthology* 12.254)[168]

Theophilitzes and his men handsome in silk come to mind.

The presence of Ganymede can also be found in texts written in the ninth and tenth centuries. He appears in Photios' *Bibliotheca* from the mid-800s. In his epitome of Conon's (lost) *Narrationes/Diegeseis* from the time of Augustus, Photios notes that Ganymede was seized by Zeus.[169] Writing around the year 900, Emperor Leo VI (Basil I's son and Constantine VII's father) seems to have the Veroli casket in front of him, as he finds fault with stories from myth:

> As they say, is there any shame or any excess of insanity that the supreme one of the gods has less of, who becoming a bull and carrying his beloved on his back and, a bull god, cleaving the watery way and enticing the maiden with gentle lowing and persuading her to climb on as though onto a wagon. Or the evilly-desiring desire for a lad directing the bird so that, thus seized aloft, Ganymede might pour out nectar for him?
>
> (Leo VI, *Homilia* 4.51–57)[170]

Lastly, and contemporary with the writing of the histories, are various entries in the *Suda*. Ganymede features in four of them. At the end of the entry for Ilion/Ἴλιον, there is the following remark: "the poets wrote that

Ganymede was seized by Zeus, mythologizing the bitter thing of his death," which was caused by a misunderstanding with Tantalos (*Suda*, Iota 320).[171] In the entry for Minos/Μίνως, Ganymede inspires desire in the Cretan king instead of Zeus. Having seized Ganymede, Minos is frustrated in his erotic hopes when Ganymede kills himself. Minos buried Ganymede on sacred ground and hence, according to this entry, came his traditional association with Zeus:

> Minos interred him in a temple and, on account of this event, it is said that Ganymede lives with Zeus.
> (*Suda*, Mu 1092)[172]

The entry on the poet and mythical forebear to Homer, Thamuris/Thamuras (Θάμυρις ἢ Θαμύρας) speaks of his reputation for starting the practice of pederasty: "he was the first man make love to a boy, Hymenaios by name, the son of Kalliope and Magnes" (*Suda*, Theta 41).[173] But, as the entry continues, the Cretans don't see him as the first lover of a boy. They speak of Talon, who made love to Rhadamanthys, and of Laios, who made love to Chrysippos, the son of Pelops (*Suda*, Theta 41).[174] Another possibility is offered and then there is a final judgment:

> But others says that it was the Italiotes who first invented this [practice of loving boys] on account of military exigency. But according to truth, Zeus, himself the first, made love to Ganymede.
> (*Suda*, Theta 41)[175]

Ganymede appears for a fourth time in the entry for the word, *eupeteia/* εὐπέτεια. One of the illustrations of how to use this word, which means "ease," speaks of the suicide of Ganymede: "Ganymede with ease did himself in with a sword" (*Suda*, Epsilon 3646).[176]

The reader of the *Life of Basil* and of *On Imperial Reigns* was therefore going to be thinking of the eagle's power to designate a man for future imperial greatness and also, because of the age of Basil when the story starts, of the rape of Ganymede. A mother's anxiety, the presence of other mythologizing elements in the historiographies, and the penumbra of sexual attractiveness that Basil would have made this moment in both histioriographies recall the mythological Ganymede.

Male Backsides and Romans

The love and desire Basil inspires, his feats of physicality, his beauty variously on display, a doppelgänger in the attractive and upwardly mobile Basilikinos, and a Ganymedean backstory are not the only things that attest to the presence of same-sex desire in the biography of Basil. Michael III's court is characterized as a place where *aselges* men may be found and there is male bonding over shared interests in male backsides and flatulence. Already characterizing Michael's court as place where *aselgeia* is practiced, the *Life of Basil* surfaces the sexual subtext of these bonding hi-jinks when it depicts Empress Theodora quoting Paul's Letter to the Romans in reaction to an insult, a choice of text that lays bear the sexual stakes in this homosocial play. And lastly, it is key that Basil was a consummate insider of this mileu.

The court of Michael III liked its amusements.[177] The *Life of Basil*, *Theophanes Continuatus*, and Pseudo-Symeon speak of these activities in judgmental and no doubt exaggerated fashion, emphasizing debauchery, desire, and scatological aspects of the rowdiness.[178] The *Life of Basil* provides a most critical portratryal of Michael's *hetaireia*, using the term *phatria*, and terms even more critical,[179] to underscore its suspect nature:

> Oh, to what extent did he [Michael III] allow himself to stray from fitting things, and to such an extent did he rage with Bacchic frenzy for every illegal deed! And in this way he disgraced religious things and committed offenses against the laws of the state and of nature together. Having put about himself an impious band of *aselgeis*, defiled, and all-around criminal men, and having disrespected the dignity of imperial greatness, the wretched man was spending his days amid parties, drinking, *aselges* desires (*erotas aselgeis*/ἔρωτας ἀσελγεῖς), and disgusting chatter, and, further, around charioteers, horses, and chariots, and, from that point, madness and frenzy devoid of good sense. And for these sorts of men he unstintingly empties the public treasury.
>
> (*Life of Basil* 20/242–243)[180]

Michael strenuously chases after diversion, leaving behind "fitting things," which is a preview of Rom 1:28 which Theodora will have occasion to quote. Law, religious scruples, and nature cannot restrain him. His *phatria*, an "impious band," is criminal and some or all of them are *aselgeis*, whom civil law designates as engaging in anal intercourse. Days are spent in activities that are not befitting of imperial dignity: drinking, partying, *aselges* sex, and things that empty the treasury, like horse racing.

Continuing, the *Life of Basil* tells of "theatrical danced pantomimes" Michael and his group, including one man named "Grullos,"[181] enjoyed putting on. These mimes were impious:

> ...and Roman wealth was poured out away from military units and into theatrical danced pantomimes that were the talk of the town. And the imperial treasures were wantonly and profligately turned over to *aselges* and illegal Bacchic revels and desires (*aselgeis kai paranomous bakkheias kai erotas*/ἀσελγεῖς καὶ παρανόμους βακχείας καὶ ἔρωτας). As all this is well known and obvious to all, I will pass it by. That he (sc. Michael) mocked sacred things, and from defiled and *aselges* effeminates,

Histories of Masculine Beauty and Desire 103

intimates (*synonton*/συνόντων) of his, he named one of them patriarch and eleven metropolitans, while he himself was filling out the count to twelve: this I will relate! For having given that polluted and most defiled Grullos the title of patriarch, having adorned him with gold-embroidered and brilliant episcopal raiment, and having placed the pallium around his shoulders; and having dressed up eleven others (from the same association of those like-minded to him) [to be] in the rank of metropolitans, as was said; and having named himself the twelfth Archbishop of Asstown (*lit.* Koloneia)...

(*Life of Basil* 21/243–244)[182]

Again a prominent feature of the *phatria*'s behavior is an interest in same-sex sexual matters. "*Aselges* and illegal Bacchic revels and desires (*erotas*/ ἔρωτας)" call to mind drunken anal sex between men. This point is underlined again when mention is made of effeminates who are *aselges* a few words later. Furthermore, Grullos and the others are the emperor's "intimates": *sunonton*/συνόντων. *Synonton* is a participial form of the verb *suneimi*/σύνειμι, which can refer to sexual intercourse,[183] and it arguably does so here, given that it follows mention of *aselgeis* men and *eros*. Lastly, the role that Michael takes in this miming board of bishops also strengthens visibility of sexual matters. When he calls himself Archbishop of Asstown (*lit.* Koloneia), the translation foregrounds anality present in the Greek. The town name *Koloneia*/Κολωνεία is a double-entendre that works through perception of the noun *kolon*/κόλον which means colon in the name of this town.[184] Asstown retroactively intensifies the sexual energy coursing through the passage.

As the *Life of Basil* continues, this mime troupe takes their show on the road. Dressed up in mock ecclesiastical garb with lutes under their robes, they give mock holy services and commununion of mustard and vinegar from actual sacred vessels "accompanied with much jollity, base words, and ill-omened and disgusting gestures."[185] This *phatria*, for Grullos is "the emperor's *phatriarch*,"[186] even harass the actual patriarch, Ignatios, as he is leading a procession,[187] behaving like satyrs and letting loose with "whoreish words and songs."[188] And these songs, suitable to prostitutes ("whoreish," *pornika*/πορνικά), i.e., meant to stimulate and keep an erection hard, of course reinscribe sexual energy yet again.[189]

The narrative of this carnivaleque *phatria*, already smelly from the emphases on anality, becomes even smellier. Himerios' great fart blows out a substantial candle at a banquet:

And then [Michael gave money] to the *patrikios* Himerios, whom the emperor called "hog" on account of the feral ferocity of his face, but he was worthy of this designation on account of the swinish nature of his life or rather the filth of it. And so to this one speaking basely in his presence, retailing the nonsense things from the stage, and out of an entirely shameless disposition, and not shrinking from reproaches at all, and having let loose with an incontinent sound from his cursed belly, a thing so massive and rushing out so forcefully like a storm, that a shining great candle was blown out...this one he honored with a gift of fifty pounds, as though to one accomplishing a Herculean labor by doing this sort of thing.

(*Life of Basil* 27/253–254)[190]

This story also appears with trivial variations in *Theophanes Continuatus* and Pseudo-Symeon. One difference is that at the end of each of these other accounts, instead of a reference to Herakles, it is an incredible wonder, a *thauma*:

...on account of the incredible nature of this wonder (*thaumatos*/θαύματος), he gave 100 pounds of gold.

(*Theophanes Continuatus* 4.21/172)[191]

...on account of the incredible wonder (*thaumati*/θαύματι), he gave 100 nomismata of gold.

(Pseudo-Symeon, *Chronographia* 659/14)[192]

A reader of these accounts will remember that young Basil caused wonder too.

This laddish (and lucrative!) horseplay benefits from contextualization. The *Life of Basil* reports—and this is similar to what was said prior to the assembling of the board of fake metropolitans—that Michael's priority was lavishing resources on "men who were *aselges*" (in addition to charioteers and prostitutes)[193] and further that money "was being spent in an *aselges* fashion and wantonly."[194] Again, there is a connection to *aselgeia* and the *aselgeis*, which calls to mind sexual behavior and desire forbidden by civil law.

The tenth-century authors found it plausible that men in *hetaireiai*/*phatriai* were going to find male backsides and flatulence interesting and the author of the *Life of Basil* implicitly and explicitly connected this interest to actual illegal sexual behavior through his frequent use of the word *aselges*/ἀσελγής and reference to "desires" that were "*aselges* and illegal."[195] But it was not merely civil law that stitches this anal horseplay, via *aselges* and *eros*, to actual sexual interest. There is an additional anal moment that connects these activities of Michael's *phatria* to sexual interests, and it is via intertextuality with Paul's Letter to the Romans and its denunciation of same-sex sexual behavior.

In *Theophanes Continuatus*,[196] Pseudo-Symeon,[197] and the *Life of Basil*[198] is a story that strains credulity as a historical document. But it invites contemplation because of what it says about the masculine homosociality around Michael and the historiographers' understandings of the nature of the anal horseplay that is a prominent feature in this milieu.

Michael and his *phatria* came up with another entertainment for themselves. The plan was to have Grullos disguise himself as the Patriarch Ignatios, who was a eunuch, which meant Grullos hid his beard. Empress Theodora, Michael's mother, was told that she could come and receive a blessing from "Ignatios." As she knelt to receive a blessing, Grullos turned his backside to her and broke wind in her face:

> ...having lept up and let loose with a sudden sound full of stench and some improper words, he called down curses from her and from ones more pious against themselves [*sc.* Grullos and Michael].
> (*Theophanes Continuatus* 4.39/202)[199]

Pseudo-Symeon adds what the unseemly words of Grullos were:

> Readily—having jumped up—and letting loose with a sound and also having offered improper words, [he said,] "what I've got, mistress, I provide it to you!" He filled everything up with stench.
> (Pseudo-Symeon, *Chronographia* 663–664/20)[200]

The *Life of Basil* has the longest telling of this story of insult to Theodora. The preparations of Michael and Grullos to deceive Theodora are narrated at some length.[201] And then there is the repellent flatulence:

> That entirely defiled one, having risen a little from the episcopal throne, having turned opposite her, and having let loose with the sound of a donkey from his foul entrails, said to her, "so that you won't say, mistress, that we did not deem you worthy of even this!"
> (*Life of Basil* 23/247)[202]

At this moment there is general merriment at Theodora's expense, and the *Life of Basil* renders judgment too:

> At that moment the emperor broke out in laughter and that utterly impure one burst out with a great laugh, and they were joking a whole bunch or, rather, in the disorder of their minds they were maddened illogically to the utmost...
> (*Life of Basil* 23/247)[203]

The *Life of Basil* presents this behavior as deranged and worthy of censure. Resonances in the phrase, "in the disorder of their minds they were maddened illogically to the utmost,"[204] are worth teasing out.

"Illogically to the utmost" is a translation of the superlative form, i.e., *alogotata*/ἀλογώτατα, of the adjective, *alogos*/ἄλογος. *Alogos* has a base meaning of "without reason, illogical." Looked at from this angle, *alogotata* shows the historiographer throwing up his hands and designating this activity meaningless and pointless, except for, one may suppose, the fostering of masculine homosociality. But as Christ is The Logos, *alogotata* is therefore able to be translated thus: "being without The Logos/Christ, to the utmost degree." This translation indicates something more serious than masculine horseplay that fosters camaraderie.

Seeing a reference to The Logos/Christ in *alogotata*/ἀλογώτατα is made more likely by what Empress Theodora says in reaction to Grullos' flatulence and the merriment at her expense:

> ...when the empress had recognized (*epignousa*/ἐπιγνοῦσα) the plot and deception and groaning deeply over the current circumstances, and having lobbed the greatest of curses at her son, she at last said this to him, "see here, my evil son! God has taken his hand from you and 'a worthless mind, [one such as] to do unfitting things' has been given to you."
>
> (*Life of Basil* 23/247)[205]

This passage is intertextual with Paul's Letter to the Romans at 1:28:

> And just as they did not think it worthwhile to keep God in their thoughts (*epignosei*/ἐπιγνώσει), so God gave them to a worthless mind, [one such as] to do unfitting things.[206]

There are a number of similarities between these passages from historiography and scripture. In the first place, the word translated as "thoughts" in Paul, *epignosei*/ἐπιγνώσει, is echoed by "having recognized" in the life, *epignousa*/ἐπιγνοῦσα: the noun *epignosis*/ἐπίγνωσις is merely a nominalization of the verb *epigignosko*/ἐπιγιγνώσκω. God, ὁ θεός, appears in both passages also. The last six words of both passages, however, leave no doubt about intertexutality with Romans; they are identical except for a trivial change of case, Nominative instead of Accusative, for the first two words:

Life of Basil 23/247: ἀδόκιμος νοῦς ποιεῖν τὰ μὴ καθήκοντα
Rom 1:28: ἀδόκιμον νοῦν ποιεῖν τὰ μὴ καθήκοντα

A Byzantine person who read or heard this passage therefore would remember the context from which these words came[207]: they come directly after the famous denunciation of same-sex sexual behavior between women and then men at Rom 1:26–27:

> On account of this God gave them over to passions of dishonor. For their women changed the natural use of the female to one that was against nature. Likewise did the men, leaving behind the natural use of women, burn in their desire for each other, men practicing shamelessness in men

and receiving in themselves the recompense which was necessary for their error.

(Rom 1:26–27)[208]

In providing this undeniable intertextuality with Romans, the *Life of Basil* makes the stakes of these insulting and juvenile anal hi-jinks higher and also connects them once and for all to same-sex sexual behavior.[209] Indeed this intertextuality is previewed at 20/242 with the words, "oh, to what extent did he [Michael III] allow himself to stray from fitting things (*ton kathekonton*/τῶν καθηκόντων)" (discussed above).

This narrative of scatological behavior that connects it to men's desire for other men shows how, in tenth-century understandings, a *hetaireia* or *phatria* can tarry with "unfitting things." It also implicates the authors, revealing levels of knowledge in Theodoros Daphnopates and authors like him about the messiness of reality. The historiographers understand the ways and means of these men in groups, even out to a rather challenging place for us now, and the *Life of Basil* shows these writers and their milieu in possession of the broad and even staining experience needed to articulate an understanding such as this one. It is also the case that Basil was in with this group, a consummate insider and Michael's co-emperor, at the time of these shenanigans.[210] He is stained also.

Conclusion

The historiographies composed close together in time in the mid-tenth century draw a picture of the power of Basil's beauty and of the presence of same-sex desire around him, a presence that both enabled his rise and was a constitutive part of the *hetaireiai/phatriai* he was involved in. Language of love and desire exists alongside Theophilitzes looking for handsome and manly lads to dress in silks, a horse-taming, a wrestling scene, and a semantically complex scourging that offer Basil's body up to readers. Basil has a scandalous double in Basilikinos. Two of the historiographers make readers think of Ganymede. Basil is a member of a *phatria* whose laddish and debauched homosociality is condemned via Paul's Romans, making evident the sexual stakes in the horseplay.

While some of the historiographers in these sources are interested in praising Basil and so invective, the underside of panegyric, comes Michael's way, they don't save their hero from insinuation, since invective exposes the lie of panegyric's glittering surface. Basil cannot stand outside the context in which he became a consummate insider. The desire to praise will take the writer down one path, and the one of criticism a different one. What both paths have in common, however, is that they tell stories that have perceptible links to what is possible. No story is going to be told that is utterly untethered from an address to what is possible in these *hetaireiai* or *phatriai*. There accordingly is much relevant in these stories for developing an understanding of (1) Byzantine elite male homosociality's enmeshment in same-sex desire itself, (2) the kind of man Basil had to be so that he could get ahead, and (3) what the men themselves were aware of about the homosociality in which they themselves played a part, i.e., the knowing analyses by the writers are anchored in conscious understandings of experiences close to home. It is essential to keep these three points in mind when approaching ritual brotherhood, which is firmly anchored in masculine homosociality and whose poster-boy, for us now, is Basil. The stories told about ritual brothers reflect the experiences of brothers *and* tellers in and outside of church.

Notes

1. Nilsson (2006, 48) (cf. 51 and 56): "[These Byzantine historiographies are] consciously devised compositions that may be read both as sources of historical information and as textual products of their time."
2. Papaioannou (2010a, 10).
3. Webb's discussions of *ekphrasis* offer a way to understand the focuses of these historiographers. With their works being visual extravaganzas, it is useful to think of the historiographers as interested in "mental impressions left by perception" of events, persons, of objects (1999b, 18), and wanting "to convey the effect that the perception of [an] object [or person or event] worked upon the viewer" (1999a, 64).
4. Spiegel (1990, 77).
5. For the date of *Life of Basil*: Treadgold (2013, 165, 179). Details about Theodoros Daphnopates can be found in Chapter 1.
6. *Ho epi tou kanikleiou*/ὁ ἐπὶ τοῦ κανικλείου was a high dignity. The man who held this office was in charge of the ink the emperor would use to sign documents.
7. Treadgold (2013, 184–185). Kaldellis (1998) is essential on Genesios.
8. Treadgold (2013, 184).
9. Treadgold (2013, 176–179, 188–190) argues vigorously for this. That said, there is debate (see Treadgold's discussions) and about the only thing relatively certain is that *Theophanes Continuatus* is mid-tenth century. If we lose Theodoros as the author, we at least have Symeon the Logothete and Constantine, and the context from which these historiographers write is still present. I will note that in the new critical edition, Featherstone and Signes-Codoñer (2015), which is the text I use, it is stated that we don't know who the author is.
10. Treadgold (2013, 165, 179).
11. The first edition narrates down to the year 948, and the second ends with the year 963.
12. Treadgold (2013, 208) for the dates. There has been a modern critical edition by Wahlgren of the first edition, which was formerly attributed to Theodosius Melissenus and Leo Grammaticus. There has not been a critical edition of the second edition, which has, in addition, two divergent redactions: redaction A and redaction B. The sections treating Michael and Basil were passed down in the continuation of the *Chronicon* of George the Monk (*Georgius Monachus Continuatus*), with redaction A appearing in Bekkerus (1838) and redaction B brought out by Istrin in 1920. A manuscript, Vat. gr.163, has a combination of redactions A and B and also attributes the *Chronographia* to Symeon the Logothete. An edition of selections from this manuscript, containing the material on Basil, appeared in 1998 from Featherstone. I have consulted the first edition and all three versions of the second edition of Symeon the Logothete's *Chronographia*.

13 Bekkerus (1838, 603–760), prints this portion of Pseudo-Symeon's *Chronographia* under the incorrect name of Symeon Magister (Treadgold 2013, 498).
14 Here is the couplet which begins the entire history, and this is reported by Markopoulos (Treadgold 2013, 217), as these earlier sections of the manuscript remain to be published: "The book had Adam as its start and as its end pious purple-born power "(Ἀρχὴ[ν] μὲν Ἀδὰμ ἔσχε βίβλος καὶ τέλος / τὸ πορφυρογέννητον εὐσεβὲς κράτος).
15 Treadgold (2013, 222).
16 Treadgold (2013, 218). Much of Pseudo-Symeon is also contained in Kedrenos' *Sunopsis Historion*, an historiography from the eleventh century (Treadgold 2013, 218). I did not consult this later work.
17 Treadgold (2013, 197–203).
18 Symeon the Logothete, *Chronographia* (first edition), 131.51.
19 Symeon the Logothete, *Chronographia* (first edition), 131.45; Symeon the Logothete, *Chronographia* (second edition), Bekkerus 835/33, Istrin 15, Featherstone 431/30.
20 For general background on Basil I's rise to throne, see Adontz (1933); Karlin-Hayter (1991); Moravcsik (1961); Markopoulos (2013); Tobias (1969).
21 We read of Nicholas and Basil becoming ritual brothers in Symeon the Logothete and Pseudo-Symeon.
22 He is called Theophilitzes in the *Life of Basil*, all versions of Symeon the Logothete, and Pseudo-Symeon. He called Theophiliskos by Genesios. In the *Life of Basil* he also is referred to as Theophilidion and Theophilos.
23 *Life of Basil* 75/318: *meter... basileos*/μήτηρ...βασιλέως.
24 An *oikonomos* is a cleric who manages the finances of a religious establishment and a *sunkellos* is a close advisor to the Patriarch of the church.
25 Some of the sources call him Basiliskianos.
26 *Theophanes Continuatus* is the outlier here, as many of the details about Basil are farmed out into the *Life of Basil*, a work with which it appears to be co-ordinated (which is another reason why it probably is the work of Theodoros Daphnopates).
27 *Life of Basil* 9/225: ἠγαπᾶτο παρ' αὐτῷ καὶ ἐπὶ τοῖς οἰκείοις προτερήμασιν ἐθαυμάζετο; *Life of Basil* 12/230: οὐδεὶς τῶν παρόντων ἦν ὃς οὐ περιεῖπεν καὶ ἐθαύμαζεν τὸν Βασίλειον; Symeon the Logothete, *Chronographia* (first edition) 131.15: ἰδὼν τὸν Βασίλειον θαυμάσας τὸ μέγεθος καὶ τὴν ἀνδρείαν αὐτοῦ. Cf. Symeon the Logothete, *Chronographia* (second edition), Bekkerus 820/10: ἰδὼν τὸν Βασίλειον καὶ θαυμάσας τὸ μέγεθος καὶ τὴν ἀνδρίαν αὐτοῦ; Pseudo-Symeon, *Chronographia* 656/11: εἶδε τὸν Βασίλειον, καὶ θαυμάσας τό τε ἀνάστημα τῆς ἡλικίας αὐτοῦ καὶ τὸ εἶδος.
28 Genesios, *On Imperial Reigns* 4.26: ἐτεθαμβήκει Βασίλειον and θάμβος... ἐγκατάπληκτον.
29 Symeon the Logothete, *Chronographia* (second edition), Istrin 6 and Featherstone 424/10: τὸ τοῦ ἀνδρὸς εὐειδὲς ἐκπλαγείς.
30 *On Imperial Reigns* 4.27: Michael III characterizes the 30 lashes he gives the naked Basil as marks of his "loving goodwill."
31 *On Imperial Reigns* 4.27: πολὺ φίλτρον ἐπιδιδούς.
32 Genesios, *On Imperial Reigns* 4.23: διὰ τὸ πεφιλοστοργῆσθαι λίαν παρὰ τοῦ αὐτοκράτορος.
33 Symeon the Logothete, *Chronographia* (first edition), 131.15: ὅτι τοιοῦτός ἐστιν, οἷον ἐπιποθεῖς καὶ ζητεῖς. Cf. Symeon the Logothete, *Chronographia* (second edition), Bekkerus 820/10: ὅτι τοιοῦτός ἐστιν οἷον ἐπιποθεῖς καὶ ζητεῖς; Istrin 6: ὡς εἴη ἀνὴρ περιδέξιος καὶ "οἷον ἐπιποθεῖς"; Featherstone 424/10: ὡς "Εἴη ἀνὴρ περιδέξιος καὶ οἷον ἐπιποθεῖς."

34 Symeon the Logothete, *Chronographia* (first edition), 131.7: ἔχω νεώτερον ἐμπειρότατον καὶ ἀνδρεῖον εἰς τοὺς ἵππους, οἷον *ἐπιποθεῖ* ἡ βασιλεία σου, τοὔνομα Βασίλειον.
35 Symeon the Logothete, *Chronographia* (first edition), 131.40: θέλω δὲ Βασίλειον παρακοιμώμενον, ὡς... *πόθον* πρός με πολὺν ἔχοντα. Cf. Symeon the Logothete, *Chronographia* (second edition), Bekkerus 832/30: *πόθον* πολὺν πρός με ἔχοντα; Pseudo-Symeon, *Chronographia* 679/43: "θέλω δὲ Βασίλειον τὸν παρακοιμώμενον, ὡς...*πόθον* πρός με πολὺν ἔχοντα.
36 A *protostrator* is a man appointed to accompany his master while on horseback and to manage the stables. Elite men, and especially emperors, had *protostratores*. Genesios has *protostates* instead.
37 *Life of Basil* 9/225: πρωτοστράτορα αὐτοῦ πεποίηκεν ὁ Θεόφιλος· καὶ ἡμέραν ἐξ ἡμέρας ἐπὶ πλέον *ἠγαπᾶτο* παρ' αὐτῷ....
38 Symeon the Logothete, *Chronographia* (first edition), 131.26: ἡ δὲ τοῦ βασιλέως *ἀγάπη* πρὸς τὸν Βασίλειον ἐξεκέχυτο. Cf. Symeon the Logothete, *Chronographia* (second edition), Bekkerus 825/18: ἡ δὲ τοῦ βασιλέως *ἀγάπη* πρὸς τὸν Βασίλειον ἐξέχυτο; Pseudo-Symeon, *Chronographia* 666/26: ἡ δὲ τοῦ βασιλέως *ἀγάπη* πρὸς τὸν Βασίλειον ἐξεκέχυτο.
39 *Life of Basil* 13/231:

> When the emperor had seen (the feat) and *conceived a love* for Basil's handsome body/excellent disposition (endowed with manliness) and his intelligence, he immediately took him away from Theophilitzes and enrolled him in the *stratores*. He was obsessed with and loved him...
>
> (ὃ θεασάμενος ὁ βασιλεύς, καὶ *ἀγαπήσας* τὴν μετ' ἀνδρείας εὐφυΐαν αὐτοῦ καὶ σύνεσιν, εὐθέως ἀπὸ τοῦ Θεοφιλίτζι αὐτὸν ἀνέλαβέ τε καὶ εἰς τοὺς βασιλικοὺς κατέταξε στράτωρας. Προσεῖχεν δὲ καὶ *ἠγάπα* αὐτόν....).

40 *Kaisar* was a very lofty court title at this time in the empire.
41 τούτου δὲ γενομένου, καὶ καθ' ἑκάστην ἐπιδιδούσης τῆς τοῦ βασιλέως *ἀγάπης* πρὸς τὸν Βασίλειον, ὁρῶν ὁ Καῖσαρ καὶ τῷ φθόνῳ δακνόμενος καὶ ὑπὲρ τοῦ μέλλοντος ὀρρωδῶν....
42 Genesios, *On Imperial Reigns* 4.26: ἠγάσθη τῆς ὄψεως.
43 Genesios, *On Imperial Reigns* 4.26: "and he stared in wonder at Basil more than the other two by a lot" (καὶ τῶν δύο πολλῷ πλέον ἐτεθαμβήκει Βασίλειον).
44 "After that, benefactions for him from the emperor's *love* increased even more ...[a list of the offices and various honors that came Basil's way from Michael follows]" (*On Imperial Reigns* 4.26: ἐντεῦθεν καὶ κρεῖττον αὐτῷ τῆς δεσποτικῆς *ἀγάπης* τὰ πρακτέα διηύξητο...).
45 Pseudo-Symeon, *Chronographia* 655/10: οἷον *ἀγαπᾷ* ἡ βασιλεία σου.
46 These exact words occur in all versions of Symeon the Logothete and in Pseudo-Symeon: ἦν γὰρ αὐτὴ τοῦ βασιλέως παλλακή, καὶ πάνυ *ἠγάπα* αὐτὴν ὡς εὐπρεπῆ (Symeon the Logothete, *Chronographia* [first edition], 131.32; Symeon the Logothete, *Chronographia* [second edition], Bekkerus 828/23, Istrin 11, Featherstone 427/25; Pseudo-Symeon, *Chronographia* 675/40).
47 Pseudo-Symeon, *Chronographia* 656/11: θεασάμενος αὐτὸν Θεοφιλίτζης *ἠράσθη*.
48 Symeon the Logothete, *Chronographia* (first edition), 131.13; Symeon the Logothete, *Chronographia* (second edition), Bekkerus 819/9, Istrin 5, Featherstone 423/10; Pseudo-Symeon, *Chronographia* 655/11.
49 Symeon the Logothete, *Chronographia* (first edition) 131.15; Symeon the Logothete, *Chronographia* (second edition), Bekkerus 820/10, Istrin 5–6, Featherstone 424/10; Pseudo-Symeon, *Chronographia* 656/11.
50 *LSJ* προσμείγνυμι IIA and *Lampe* μ(ε)ίγνυμι B both make clear the potential of this word to designate carnality.

51 Ἄρας οὖν ἐκ Μακεδονίας τῆς Θράκης πρὸς τὴν ἄρχουσαν ταύτην τῶν πόλεων πασῶν ἐπορεύετο, τῶν δυνατῶν τινὶ καὶ περιφανῶν προσμῖξαι βουλόμενος καὶ εἰς θεραπείαν καὶ δουλείαν αὐτοῦ ἑαυτὸν ἀποτάξαι καὶ καταστῆσαι.
52 The name Nicholas does not appear here.
53 *Life of Basil* 9/224: πρὸς δουλείαν δοθῆναι τῶν ἐμφανεστέρων τινί.
54 *Life of Basil* 9/224: προθύμως ἑαυτὸν εἰς τοῦτο ἐπέδωκεν ὁ ἡγούμενος.
55 *Life of Basil* 9/225.
56 *On Imperial Reigns* 4.26.
57 Beck in his "Byzantinisches Gefolgschaftswesen" (1965) surveyed Byzantine historiography, including the six works in the current argument, and took as his subject the repeated spectacle of elite men having about themselves groups of younger men, who were frequently of lower social status. The story of the rise of Basil I is the centerpiece of his analysis and he presents it as exemplary of broader trends before, during and after the tenth century (1965, 4–18).
58 Oikonomidès (1972, 35, 63).
59 Beck (1965, 18–22).
60 Beck (1965, 17).
61 Beck (1965, 15–16). Note: there can be variations in the terminology and in spelling (though the words remain basically recognizable). In addition to φατρία (*phatria*), the following appear in the sources: φάτρα (*phatra*), φράτρα (*phratra*), and φρατρία (*phratria*). See also Messis (2008, 37) and Rapp (1997, 288–289).
62 *Life of Basil* 25/250: παλαμναίου συνεδρίου.
63 Beck remarks, "der Charakter dieser Hetairien ist nicht durchwegs politisch" (1965, 29).
64 Beck (1965, 10, 12).
65 Beck (1965, 10).
66 *Life of Basil* 9/225: σπουδὴν ἔχων γενναίους ἄνδρας καὶ εὐειδεῖς καὶ εὐήλικας καὶ ἐπ' ἀνδρείᾳ μάλιστα καὶ ῥώμῃ σώματος διαφέροντας κεκτῆσθαι περὶ αὐτόν.
67 The term *hetaireia* does not occur here or elsewhere in the *Life of Basil*, but it occurs when Symeon the Logothete (first edition, 131.7; second edition: Bekkerus 817/7, Istrin 5, Featherstone 422/9) and Pseudo-Symeon (655/10) refer to the group of men around the emperor. Indeed there is no word offered for this group around Theophilitzes in the *Life of Basil*. I therefore use *hetaireia* for ease of discussion, a move with which Beck would agree. However, *phatria*, which Beck points out as having a negative valence, does appear in the *Life of Basil* to designate the band of men around Emperor Michael III (discussed below).
68 οὓς εὐθὺς ἦν ὁρᾶν σηρικαῖς τε κοσμουμένους ἐσθῆσι καὶ τῇ ἄλλῃ καταστολῇ διαπρέποντας.
69 *Life of Basil* 9/225: ...κατά τε σωματικὴν ἀλκὴν καὶ ψυχικὴν ἀνδρείαν...ἐφαίνετο... κατὰ χεῖρα γενναῖος καὶ κατὰ ψυχὴν συνετὸς καὶ πρὸς τὸ κελευόμενον πᾶν ὀξύς τε καὶ ἐπιτήδειος.
70 *Life of Basil* 9/225: "Theophilos (*sc.* Theophilitzes) made [him] his *protostrator*, and he both was loving him more and more day by day and was marveling at his [Basil's] superior qualities" (πρωτοστράτορα αὐτοῦ πεποίηκεν ὁ Θεόφιλος· καὶ ἡμέραν ἐξ ἡμέρας ἐπὶ πλέον ἠγαπᾶτο παρ' αὐτῷ καὶ ἐπὶ τοῖς οἰκείοις προτερήμασιν ἐθαυμάζετο).
71 *Life of Basil* 9/224–225.
72 Genesios, *On Imperial Reigns* 4.26: "He (Basil) was then added, through the efforts of the leader of the monks, to one of the lofty men from the imperial family" (Τότε δέ τινι προσκεκόλληται τῶν πρὸς γένους βασιλικοῦ μεγιστάνων διὰ τοῦ προστατοῦντος τῶν μοναχῶν).
73 *Sulloge*/συλλογή is Genesios' word for *hetaireia*. Genesios frequently has peculiar vocabulary.

74 Genesios, *On Imperial Reigns* 4.26: ἐπάνδρου καὶ νεανικῆς συλλογῆς.
75 ὁ ἰατρὸς εἶπεν τῷ κυρίῳ περὶ τῆς ἀνδρείας τοῦ Βασιλείου, καὶ ὅτι τοιοῦτός ἐστιν, οἷον ἐπιποθεῖς καὶ ζητεῖς... cf., with minor changes in phrasing, the following: Symeon the Logothete, *Chronographia* (second edition), Bekkerus 820/10, Istrin 6, Featherstone 424/10.
76 ...τοῦ Θεοφιλίτζη ζητοῦντος ἄνθρωπον ἀνδρεῖον εἰς τοὺς ἵππους αὐτοῦ, παρῆν ὁ ἰατρὸς καὶ τὰ περὶ τοῦ Βασιλείου διηγήσατο. ἤχθη οὖν ὁ Βασίλειος συντόμως, καὶ θεασάμενος αὐτὸν Θεοφιλίτζης ἠράσθη. ἐπεὶ δὲ ἐπιάγουρος ἦν καὶ μεγαλοκέφαλος, καλεῖ αὐτὸν Κεφαλάν, καὶ δέδωκεν αὐτῷ δουλεύειν τοὺς ἵππους αὐτοῦ.
77 Symeon the Logothete, *Chronographia* (first edition), 131.15; Symeon the Logothete, *Chronographia* (second edition), Bekkerus 820/10, Istrin 6, Featherstone 424/10.
78 The first of two wrestling matches (to be discussed below) that Basil has in *On Imperial Reigns* occurs in 4.26 just before the horse-taming scene. This leads to Basil being summoned by Michael and brought into imperial service.
79 πρωτοστάτην οὖν αὐτοῦ τῶν ἱπποκόμων [sc. ὁ Μιχαὴλ] καθίστησι τὸν Βασίλειον, καὶ ἵππον αὐτῷ δυσήνιον ἐπιδίδωσι διοχήσασθαι, ὃν ἐπεφιλήκει τὰ μάλιστα. οὗτος αὐτοῦ ἐφαλλόμενος, ὡς εἴ τις ἄλλος Βουκεφάλου Ἀλέξανδρος, ὡς Βελλεροφόντης Πηγάσῳ γενναίως ἱππάζεται, θάμβος λιπὼν ἁπάσαις ἐν ὄψεσιν ἐγκατάπληκτον. ἐντεῦθεν καὶ κρεῖττον αὐτῷ τῆς δεσποτικῆς ἀγάπης τὰ πρακτέα διηύξητο...
80 Symeon the Logothete, *Chronographia* (first edition), 131.7; Symeon the Logothete, *Chronographia* (second edition), Bekkerus 816–817/7, Istrin 5, Featherstone 422/9; Pseudo-Symeon, *Chronographia* 655/10.
81 Symeon the Logothete, *Chronographia* (first edition), 131.7: "I have a younger man most skilled and manly as regards the horses, *the sort of man your reign desires*, and his name is Basil" (ἔχω νεώτερον ἐμπειρότατον καὶ ἀνδρεῖον εἰς τοὺς ἵππους, *οἷον ἐπιποθεῖ ἡ βασιλεία σου,* τοὔνομα Βασίλειον); Symeon the Logothete, *Chronographia* (second edition), Bekkerus 817/7: "I have a younger man most skilled and most manly as regards the horses, *the sort of man your reign desires*, and his name is Basil" (ἔχω νεώτερον ἐμπειρότατον καὶ ἀνδρειότατον εἰς τοὺς ἵππους, *οἷον ἐπιποθεῖ ἡ βασιλεία σου,* τοὔνομα Βασίλειον).
82 Pseudo-Symeon, *Chronographia* 655/10: "I have a younger man most skilled and manly as regards the horses, *the sort of man your reign loves*, and his name is Basil" (ἔχω νεώτερον ἐμπειρότατον καὶ ἀνδρεῖον εἰς τοὺς ἵππους, *οἷον ἀγαπᾷ ἡ βασιλεία σου,* τοὔνομα Βασίλειον).
83 A *hetaireiarch* is the leader of a *hetaireia*.
84 Symeon the Logothete, *Chronographia* (first edition), 131.7: "the emperor handed him (Basil) over to Andrew, who was the *hetaireiarch*, to be a member of his *hetaireia*" (ὁ βασιλεὺς παρέδωκεν αὐτὸν Ἀνδρέᾳ ὄντι ἑταιρειάρχῃ τοῦ εἶναι εἰς τὴν ἑταιρείαν); Symeon the Logothete, *Chronographia* (second edition), Bekkerus 817/7: "The emperor handed him (Basil) to the *hetaireiarch* Andrew to be a member of his *hetaireia*" (ὁ βασιλεὺς παραδέδωκεν αὐτὸν τῷ ἑταιρειάρχῃ Ἀνδρέᾳ τοῦ εἰς τὴν ἑταιρείαν εἶναι); Istrin 5 and Featherstone 422/9 (just a minor difference in punctuation and a typographical error in Featherstone [should have Ἀνδρέᾳ for Ἀνδρέα]): "the emperor ordered him (Basil) to be in his *hetaireia*, handing him over to Andrew the *hetaireiarch*" (ὁ βασιλεὺς ἐν τῇ ἑταιρείᾳ αὐτοῦ τοῦτον κατέταξεν, Ἀνδρέᾳ ἑταιρειάρχῃ παραδούς); Pseudo-Symeon, *Chronographia* 655/10: "the emperor handed him (Basil) over to the *hetaireiarch* Andrew to be a member of his *hetaireia*" (ὁ βασιλεὺς παραδέδωκεν αὐτὸν τῷ ἑταιρειάρχῃ Ἀνδρέᾳ τοῦ εἰς τὴν ἑταιρείαν εἶναι).
85 *Life of Basil* 13/231.
86 ὁ οὖν Βασίλειος συμπαρὼν τῷ κυρίῳ αὐτοῦ λέγει πρὸς αὐτόν, ὅτι· "εἰ παραδράμω τὸν βασιλικὸν ἵππον καὶ ἀπὸ τοῦ ἐμοῦ ἵππου ἐκτιναχθεὶς ἔποχος αὐτοῦ γένωμαι, ἆρα μὴ διὰ τὸ βασιλικοῖς φαλάροις κεκοσμῆσθαι αὐτὸν ἀγανάκτησις παρὰ τοῦ βασιλέως γένηται κατ' ἐμοῦ;" τοῦ δὲ βασιλέως ὑπομνησθέντος καὶ κελεύσαντος

τοῦτο γενέσθαι, ἑτοίμως καὶ εὐφυῶς ὁ Βασίλειος τοῦτο πεποίηκεν. ὃ θεασάμενος ὁ βασιλεύς, καὶ ἀγαπήσας τὴν μετ' ἀνδρείας εὐφυΐαν αὐτοῦ καὶ σύνεσιν, εὐθέως ἀπὸ τοῦ Θεοφιλίτζι αὐτὸν ἀνέλαβέ τε καὶ εἰς τοὺς βασιλικοὺς κατέταξε στράτωρας· προσεῖχεν δὲ καὶ ἡγάπα αὐτόν, ὁρῶν αὐτοῦ τὸ πρὸς τοὺς ἄλλους ἐν πᾶσι διαφέρον κατὰ πολύ. διὸ καὶ πολλάκις ἐπιδειξάμενον κατενώπιον αὐτοῦ εἰς τὴν τοῦ πρωτοστράτορος ἀξί<αν> ἀνεβίβασεν.

87 καὶ μετὰ ἄρσενος οὐ κοιμηθήσῃ κοίτην γυναικός· βδέλυγμα γάρ ἐστιν. καὶ πρὸς πᾶν τετράπουν οὐ δώσεις τὴν κοίτην σου εἰς σπερματισμὸν ἐκμιανθῆναι πρὸς αὐτό, καὶ γυνὴ οὐ στήσεται πρὸς πᾶν τετράπουν βιβασθῆναι· μυσερὸν γάρ ἐστιν.

88 οἱ δὲ Βούλγαροι, ἀεί πως οἰηματίαι καὶ καυχηματίαι τυγχάνοντες, ἐπεὶ ἔτυχον τότε μεθ' ἑαυτῶν ἔχοντες Βούλγαρον ἐπ' ἀνδρείᾳ σεμνυνόμενον σώματος καὶ ἄκρον ἐν παλαισμοσύνῃ ὑπάρχοντα, ὃν οὐδεὶς σχεδὸν μέχρι τότε τῶν προσπαλαιόντων κατέβαλεν, οὐκ ἀνεκτὸν ἐδόκουν ἐπ' αὐτῷ φρονεῖν, ἀλλ' ὑπὲρ τὸ μέτρον ἠλαζονεύοντο. τοῦ δὲ πότου προϊόντος καὶ θυμηδίας χορευούσης κατὰ τὴν τράπεζαν, λέγει ὁ μικρὸς ἐκεῖνος Θεόφιλος πρὸς τὸν Καίσαρα ὅτι· "ἔχω, δέσποτα, ἄνθρωπον, ὅς, ἐὰν κελεύῃς, ἵνα παλαίσῃ μετὰ τοῦ περιβοήτου τούτου Βουλγάρου. μέγα γὰρ ὄνειδος τοῦτο Ῥωμαίοις, καὶ οὐδεὶς ὑποίσει τὴν ἀλαζονείαν αὐτῶν, εἰ οὗτος ἀκαταγώνιστος ἐν Βουλγαρίᾳ παραγένηται.

89 οὗ γενομένου συμπλακεὶς τῷ Βουλγάρῳ ὁ Βασίλειος καὶ θᾶττον συμπιέσας καὶ περισφίγξας αὐτόν, ὡσεὶ δεσμόν τινα χόρτου κοῦφον καὶ ἄψυχον ἢ ἐξ ἐρίου πόκον ξηρόν τε καὶ ἐλαφρόν, οὕτω ῥᾳδίως αὐτὸν ἐπάνω τῆς τραπέζης μετεωρίσας ἀπέρριψεν. τού<του> δὲ γεγονότος, οὐδεὶς τῶν παρόντων ἦν ὃς οὐ περιεῖπεν καὶ ἐθαύμαζεν τὸν Βασίλειον. ἐκπλαγέντες δὲ καὶ οἱ Βούλγαροι τὴν περιουσίαν τῆς εὐχερείας τε καὶ δυνάμεως, ἔμειναν ἐνεοί. ἀπ' ἐκείνης δὲ τῆς ἡμέρας ἤρξατο ἐπὶ πλέον ἡ τοῦ Βασιλείου φήμη εἰς πᾶσαν τὴν Πόλιν διαφοιτᾶν, καὶ τοῖς ἁπάντων διεφέρετο στόμασιν, ἀπόβλεπτος ἤδη καθεστηκώς.

90 A point observed by Poliakoff in the context of a broader discussion of of *pleko/* πλέκω and compound forms of the verb and nouns related to it (1981, 73–85; see, e.g., 73, 77).

91 ἐπειδὴ οὖν ἡ φύσις δίχα ἐτμήθη, ποθοῦν ἕκαστον τὸ ἥμισυ τὸ αὐτοῦ συνῄει, καὶ περιβάλλοντες τὰς χεῖρας καὶ συμπλεκόμενοι ἀλλήλοις, ἐπιθυμοῦντες συμφῦναι….

92 τὸ λειφθὲν ἄλλο ἐζήτει καὶ συνεπλέκετο, εἴτε γυναικὸς τῆς ὅλης ἐντύχοι ἡμίσει – ὃ δὴ νῦν γυναῖκα καλοῦμεν – εἴτε ἀνδρός· καὶ οὕτως ἀπώλλυντο….

93 μετέθηκέ τε οὖν οὕτω αὐτῶν εἰς τὸ πρόσθεν καὶ διὰ τούτων τὴν γένεσιν ἐν ἀλλήλοις ἐποίησεν, διὰ τοῦ ἄρρενος ἐν τῷ θήλει, τῶνδε ἕνεκα, ἵνα ἐν τῇ συμπλοκῇ ἅμα μὲν εἰ ἀνὴρ γυναικὶ ἐντύχοι, γεννῷεν καὶ γίγνοιτο τὸ γένος, ἅμα δ' εἰ καὶ ἄρρην ἄρρενι, πλησμονὴ γοῦν γίγνοιτο τῆς συνουσίας καὶ διαπαύοιντο καὶ ἐπὶ τὰ ἔργα τρέποιντο καὶ τοῦ ἄλλου βίου ἐπιμελοῖντο.

94 For more on Skylitzes, a reader may start with Wortley (2010) and Treadgold (2013).

95 Skylitzes, *Sunopsis Historion*, Basil 1 7/124: μετεωρίσας ἐπάνω τῆς τραπέζης ἀπέρριψε, which is, for all practical purposes, identical to the *Life of Basil* 12/230: ἐπάνω τῆς τραπέζης μετεωρίσας ἀπέρριψεν. There are just a semantically inert change of word position and the removal of a *nu* on the final word in the later text.

96 The match to be discussed presently is but the first one in Genesios. Basil wrestles a second time later in his reign at *On Imperial Reigns* 4.40. Kaldellis (1998, 97) suggested that Genesios was confused and made a doublet out of a single occurrence. This seems likely, as Basil stripping to wrestle as a much older man is worth skepticism. This later spectacularization of Basil's grappling body shows again the interest his physique inspires but will not be the subject of further attention, as it does not play a part in young Basil's rise to power.

97 …συνῆλθον κατὰ παλαίστραν ἀμφότεροι· ὧν ὁ μὲν μετεωρίζειν πειρᾶται Βασίλειον, ὁ δὲ μὴ ἐνεγκὼν τὴν Βασιλείου ἀντίβασιν μετεωρίζεται παραυτὰ γενναιότατα καὶ περιστρέφεται ταχίστῳ κινήματι, καὶ τῇ κατὰ πόδρεζαν προσπλοκῇ, ὡς ὁ ἐγχώριος

λόγος, πρὸς γῆν καταφέρεται, ὑποστὰς πτῶσιν ἀλάθητον, ὡς καὶ παραψυχὴν τοῖς πᾶσιν εἶναι λογίζεσθαι, εἰ καὶ μετὰ πολὺν χρόνον ὕδασι πολλοῖς καταρραντισθεὶς μόλις ἀνέσφηλεν.

98 See Kaldellis (1998, 97) for bibliography. Also see Kislinger (1981, 147–149) and Poliakoff (1981, 6, 13, 155).

99 Δι' οὗ καὶ ὁ βασιλεὺς Μιχαὴλ τούτων ἐγεγόνει κατήκοος, καὶ ἀνακαλεῖται τοῦτον σὺν ἑτέροις ἥλιξι δύο. ὡς δὲ τούτους τεθέατο, ἠγάσθη τῆς ὄψεως, ἐπῄνεσε τὴν ἡλικιῶτιν, καὶ τῶν δύο πολλῷ πλέον ἐτεθαμβήκει Βασίλειον, καὶ διαφόροις βαθμοῖς καταλέγει καὶ πρὸς μείζονας εὐποιΐας ἀρραβωνίζεται.

100 Οὕς...ὁ θεὸς εἰς βασιλέας διέγνωκεν, τούτους προώρισεν καὶ τὰ πρὸς αὐτὴν πάντως προδιατίθησι σύμβολα.

101 This grappling in Basil's life recalls a trope occasionally seen in ancient literatures of the future or present king who wrestles. See Poliakoff (1981, 5–6, 13) for discussion of sporting prowess accrediting future leaders, with Jakob (Septuagint), Gilgamesh, and Ptolemy Philadelphos provided as examples.

102 τινὶ κοιτώνων ἐγκλείσας Βασίλειον τοῖς σὺν αὐτῷ προστάττει ἐν νεύματι ἀπογυμνοῦν τοῦτον τὼ χεῖρέ τε διατεῖναι. τούτου δὲ γινομένου κατὰ τὸ προσταχθέν, ὁ Βασίλειος καταπλήττεται, ἀλλ' ὅμως νεανικὸς ὢν τῆς ἐκπλήξεως ἀνακτᾶται, ἑαυτοῦ τε καὶ τοῦ βασιλέως καθίσταται, καὶ μαστίζεται παρ' αὐτοῦ διπλοῖς ἐν φραγελλίοις λ΄, μνήμην ἔχειν τοῦτον ἀνάγραπτον τῆς πρὸς αὐτὸν φιλοστόργου προθέσεως. καὶ τῷ μεγίστῳ ναῷ ἐπελθὼν πρωΐας αὐτῆς στεφηφόρον ἄνακτα λαοῖς ἀναδείκνυσι, μηνὶ Μαΐῳ κς΄, ἰνδικτιῶνος ιδ΄, καὶ τῆς κατὰ δευτερείαν αὐτῷ βασιλείας τὰ πρόσφορα δίδωσιν. ᾧ καὶ πολὺ φίλτρον ἐπιδιδούς, καὶ τὰ ἴσα, πρὸς δὲ καὶ τὰ καθ' ὑπεροχὴν ἐμπαρέχεται.

103 Genesios, *On Imperial Reigns* 4.27: μνήμην...ἀνάγραπτον τῆς πρὸς αὐτὸν φιλοστόργου προθέσεως.

104 Genesios, *On Imperial Reigns* 4.27: πολὺ φίλτρον.

105 For other discussions of Basilikinos/Basiliskianos, see Tougher (1999) and Karlin-Hayter (1991).

106 *Life of Basil* 25/250 (trireme); *Theophanes Continuatus* 4.44/208 (warship/dromon).

107 Symeon the Logothete, *Chronographia* (first edition), 131.46; Symeon the Logothete, *Chronographia* (second edition), Bekkerus 835/33, Istrin 15, Featherstone 431/30; Pseudo-Symeon, *Chronographia* 682/47.

108 Symeon the Logothete, *Chronographia* (first edition), 131.46; Symeon the Logothete, *Chronographia* (second edition), Bekkerus 835–836/33, Istrin 15–16, Featherstone 431/30.

109 Τὰ τζαγγία at Symeon the Logothete, *Chronographia* (first edition), 131.46; Symeon the Logothete, *Chronographia* (second edition), Bekkerus 835/33. Τὰ βασιλικὰ ὑποδήματα and τὰ κοκκοβαφῆ ὑποδήματα at Symeon the Logothete, *Chronographia* (second edition), Istrin 15; Featherstone 431/30.

110 Cf. Symeon the Logothete, *Chronographia* (second edition), Bekkerus 835–836/33, Istrin 15–16, Featherstone 431/30.

111 τοῦτον ἀναστῆναι κελεύσας ὁ βασιλεὺς τὰ τζαγγία αὐτοῦ προσέταξε σῦραι καὶ ὑποδήσασθαι. τοῦ δὲ ἀνανεύοντος καὶ πρὸς Βασίλειον ἀποβλέποντος ἐν θυμῷ προσέταττεν ὁ βασιλεὺς τοῦτο ποιῆσαι. τοῦ δὲ Βασιλείου ἐπινεύσαντος αὐτῷ ὑπεδήσατο τὰ τζαγγία. ἔφη δὲ ὁ βασιλεὺς μεθ' ὅρκου πρὸς Βασίλειον, ὡς ὑπὲρ σὲ κάλλιον αὐτῷ πρέπουσι. μὴ γὰρ οὐκ ἔχω ἐξουσίαν, ὡς σὲ βασιλέα ἐποίησα, καὶ ἄλλον ποιῆσαι; καὶ ὠργίζετο κατὰ τοῦ Βασιλείου θυμούμενος. δακρύουσα δὲ ἡ Εὐδοκία ἔφη τῷ βασιλεῖ· τὸ τῆς βασιλείας ἀξίωμα, δέσποτά μου, μέγα ἐστίν, καὶ ἀναξίως καὶ ἡμεῖς ἐτιμήθημεν, καὶ οὐ δίκαιόν ἐστι καταφρονεῖσθαι αὐτό. ὁ δὲ βασιλεὺς εἶπεν· μὴ λυποῦ ἐπὶ τούτῳ· καὶ γὰρ καὶ τὸν Βασιλισκιανὸν βασιλέα θέλω ποιῆσαι. Βασίλειος δὲ ἐν θυμῷ καὶ λύπῃ μεγάλῃ γέγονεν.

112 τοῦτον οὖν τὸν δυσώνυμον Βασιλικῖνον ἐνδύει ποτὲ τὴν πολυύμνητον βασιλικὴν πορφύραν καὶ τὸν περίοπτον καὶ ἐπίφθονον στέφανον, χλαμύδα τε πάγχρυσον καὶ τὰ κοκκοβαφῆ καὶ διάλιθα πέδιλα καὶ τἆλλα τῆς βασιλείας ἐπίσημα, ἐξάγει τε αὐτὸν πρὸς τὴν σύγκλητον τῆς χειρὸς ἅμα κρατῶν καὶ ὑπουργῶν αὐτῷ, ὡς ὁ Νέρων ἐκεῖνος πάλαι τὸν πολυθρύλητον Ἔρωτα, καί φησιν ἐπὶ λέξεως

"ἴδετε πάντες ὑμεῖς, καὶ θαυμάσατε!
ἆρα οὐ πρέπει αὐτὸν εἶναι βασιλέα;
πρῶτον μὲν εἶδος ἄξιον τυραννίδος,
τὸ δεύτερον δὲ συμφυὲς πέλει στέφος,
ἅπαντα δ' ἁρμόζουσι πρὸς τὴν ἀξίαν."

καὶ ὅτι· "πόσον ἦν κάλλιον τοῦτόν με ποιῆσαι βασιλέα ἢ τὸν Βασίλειον." ταῦτα πάντες οἱ κατὰ τὰ βασίλεια ἰδόντες τε καὶ ἀκούσαντες ἔμειναν ἀχανεῖς, ἐκπληττόμενοι τὴν παράλογον ἐξ ἀφροσύνης τοῦ βασιλέως ἐμβροντησίαν τε καὶ παρακοπήν. οὕτως ἦν ἄνθρωπος ὑπὸ τῆς κατακοροῦς μέθης καὶ τῶν ἀθέσμων καὶ ἀσελγῶν πράξεων ὅλως τῶν δεόντων ἐξεστηκὼς καὶ φρενοπλὴξ καὶ παράφορος.

113 Jenkins (1948) suggests that this story (and the portrait of Michael III in general) is an amalgam of material from Plutarch. Jenkins also audaciously posits that the author of the *Life of Basil* depends on Plutarch's lost biography of Nero. The more familiar same-sex connections of Nero are to Sporus, to whom he played husband, and to Pythagoras/Doryphoros, to whom he played wife.

114 *Life of Basil* 9/225, 12/230; Symeon the Logothete, *Chronographia* (first edition) 131.15, *Chronographia* (second edition), Bekkerus 820/10; Pseudo-Symeon, *Chronographia* 656/11.

115 The regulations in civil law against the *aselgeis* are discussed in the introduction to this book.

116 Here for reference is *Theophanes Continuatus* 4.44/208-209:
And having brought forth another man who was called Basilikinos, he clothes him in purple and he places the diadem on him, and having put on [him] the grandeurs of the shoes, he leads him to the senate, holding him by the hand. And he says to the senators: "It has long since been necessary, men, that I lead this man to this illustrious adornment [of the state], in his case

First his beauty is worthy of the rule,
second the crown is naturally his
and all things fit [him] to the office.

[and all the more] than Basil: as far as he is concerned I have also repented of those things on the strength of which I made him emperor."

(καί τινα ἄλλον... – Βασ<ιλ>ικῖνος οὗτος ἐλέγετο... – ἀγαγών, τὴν πορφύραν τε ἐνδύει καὶ τὸ διάδημα περιτίθησιν, καὶ τὰ παράσημα τῶν ὑποδημάτων περιβαλὼν ἐξάγει πρὸς τὴν σύγκλητον τῆς χειρὸς ἔχων αὐτόν, καὶ πρὸς τὴν γερουσίαν φησὶν ὡς "ἔδει πάλαι με τοῦτον εἰς τουτονὶ τὸν περίβλεπτον κόσμον, ὦ ἄνδρες, ἐπαγαγεῖν, ᾧ

πρῶτον μὲν εἶδος ἄξιον τυραννίδος,
δεύτερον δὲ συμφυὲς πέλει στέφος,
ἅπαντα δ' ἁρμόζουσι πρὸς τὴν ἀξίαν,

ἢ τὸν Βασίλειον, ἐφ' ᾧ καὶ μεταμεμέλημαι ἐφ' οἷς αὐτὸν ἐβασίλευσα.")

117 εὐθὺς οὖν κελεύει τοῦτον ὁ βασιλεὺς ἀναστῆναι, τὰ τζάγγια δὲ αὐτοῦ σῦραι καὶ ἑαυτῷ ὑποδῆσαι. τοῦ δὲ ἀνανεύοντος καὶ πρὸς Βασίλειον βλέποντος, ἐπεὶ ὁ βασιλεὺς μετὰ θυμοῦ προσέταξεν καὶ ὁ Βασίλειος ἐπένευσεν, ὑπέδησεν τὰ αὐτά. καὶ λέγει ὁ βασιλεὺς μεθ' ὅρκου πρὸς Βασίλειον "κάλλιον αὐτῷ πρέπουσιν. καὶ γὰρ οὐκ ἔχω ἐξουσίαν, ὡς σὲ βασιλέα ἐποίησα, καὶ ἄλλον ποιῆσαι." καὶ ὠργίζετο

κατὰ Βασιλείου θυμούμενος. δακρύουσα δὲ ἡ Εὐδοκία ἔφη τῷ βασιλεῖ, "τὸ τῆς βασιλείας σου ἀξίωμα, δέσποτά μου, μέγα ἐστίν, ᾧ ἀναξίως καὶ ἡμεῖς ἐτιμήθημεν· καὶ οὐ δίκαιόν ἐστι καταφρονεῖσθαι αὐτό." καὶ τῷ Βασιλείῳ ἔφη "μὴ λυποῦ ἐπὶ τούτῳ· καὶ τὸν Βασιλισκιανὸν βασιλέα θέλω ποιεῖν." καὶ πρὸς τοὺς παρόντας εἶπεν,

"ἆρα οὐ πρέπει αὐτὸν εἶναι βασιλέα;
πρῶτον μὲν εἶδος ἄξιον τυραννίδος.
τὸ δεύτερον δὲ συμφυὲς πέλει στέφος.
ἅπαντα δ' ἁρμόζουσι πρὸς τὴν ἀξίαν."

καὶ ὅτι "πόσον οὖν κάλλιον τοῦτόν με ποιῆσαι βασιλέα!" Βασίλειος δὲ ἐν θυμῷ καὶ λύπῃ μεγάλῃ γέγονεν.

118 *Life of Basil* 25/250: φαῦλον καὶ μιαρὸν θηλυδρίαν τε καὶ φιλόκωμον.
119 Symeon the Logothete, *Chronographia* (first edition), 131.15: θεασάμενος οὖν αὐτὸν ἐπίσγουρον καὶ μεγάλην κεφαλὴν ἔχοντα ἐπέθηκε Κεφαλᾶν; Symeon the Logothete, *Chronographia* (second edition), Bekkerus 820/10; θεασάμενος οὖν αὐτὸν ἐπιάγουρον καὶ μεγάλην κεφαλὴν ἔχοντα ἐπέθηκεν αὐτὸν Κεφαλάν; Istrin 6: καὶ θεασάμενος αὐτὸν κομῶντα τὴν κεφαλὴν καὶ ἐπίσγουρον, αὐτὴν δὲ τὴν κεφαλὴν μεγάλη ἔχοντα, Κεφαλᾶν ἐπωνόμασε; Featherstone 424/10: θεασάμενος αὐτὸν κομῶντα τὴν κεφαλὴν καὶ ἐπίσγουρον, αὐτήν τε τὴν κεφαλὴν μεγάλην ἔχοντα, Κεφαλᾶν ἐπωνόμασε; Pseudo-Symeon, *Chronographia* 656/11: ἐπεὶ δὲ ἐπιάγουρος ἦν καὶ μεγαλοκέφαλος, καλεῖ αὐτὸν Κεφαλάν.
120 *Life of Basil* 25/251.
121 *Life of Basil* 25/250: παλαμναίου συνεδρίου.
122 ἐγένετο δέ τι περὶ αὐτὸν εὐθὺς κατὰ τὴν πρώτην ἡλικίαν θαυμάσιον, τὴν εἰς ὕστερον τύχην παραδηλοῦν, ὅπερ οὐ θέμις οἶμαι σιγῇ παρελθεῖν.
123 *Life of Basil* 5/218: ἡπλωμέναις ταῖς πτέρυξι τὸ παιδίον ἐσκίαζεν.
124 *Life of Basil* 5/218: σκιὰν ταῖς πτέρυξι τῷ παιδίῳ περιποιούμενον.
125 *Life of Basil* 5/218: ὥσπερ χαριέντως πρὸς αὐτὴν ἀτενίζοντα.
126 *Life of Basil* 5/219: "Thus does God always before great events sow beforehand certain symbols and tokens of the affairs of the future" (οὕτω τῶν μεγάλων πραγμάτων ἀεὶ πόρρωθεν ὁ θεὸς προκαταβάλλεταί τινα σύμβολα καὶ τεκμήρια τῶν εἰς ὕστερον).
127 τοῦτο δὲ καὶ εἰς τὴν ἐχομένην ἡλικίαν οὐκ ὀλιγάκις γέγονεν ἐπ' αὐτῷ, ἀλλὰ πολλάκις εὑρέθη ὑπὸ ἀετοῦ ἐν τῷ ὑπνοῦν σκιαζόμενος.
128 σὺν τούτοις καὶ προεισηγηθῆναι αὐτῇ παρά τινος ῥῆσιν εὐάγγελον, ὡς τοῦ παιδὸς κατὰ παιγνίαν τῶν ὁμηλίκων ἔν τινι λίμνῃ ἀετὸν ἐπιπτῆσαι τῇ κεφαλῇ, σκέπειν τε ταύτην πτερύσσοντα.
129 καὶ ἐντεῦθεν ἀπομεμαντεῦσθαι σὺν ὅρκῳ ταύτῃ τῷ ἐξ αὐτῆς τὴν τῆς βασιλείας ἐπίτευξιν καὶ ταύτης μεγαλειότητα καὶ τὴν ἐπὶ μῆκος διάτασιν συγγόνοις τε καὶ ἀπογόνοις ἐκβήσεσθαι, καὶ αὐτάρκη πλοῦτον τῇ κατ' αὐτὸν χώρᾳ μεθήσειν, ἐξ ἧς ἐγεγέννητο.
130 Moravcsik (1961, 84–88).
131 Prokopios, *Wars* 3.4.4.3–6.1.
132 Prokopios, *Wars* 3.4.8.3–9.1.
133 Theophanes the Confessor, *Chronographia* 104.8–14.
134 Theophanes the Confessor, *Chronographia* 104.24–27.
135 Ἄκρατον: διειδῆ, ἀκραιφνῆ. διαρρεῖ δὲ λόγος ἐκ Μακεδόνων, ὃς λέγει, ἀετὸν ἐπιφοιτῶντα καὶ τὰς πτέρυγας ὑποτείνοντα ἀποστέγειν αὐτοῦ καὶ τὴν ἄκρατον ἀκτῖνα ἑαυτὸν ἀπαιωροῦντα καὶ ὅτε ὕοι, τὸν πολὺν ὑετόν.
136 A reader of this entry in the mid-tenth century will first sense child Basil, but there is a possible presence of Marcian too.
137 See Moravcsik (1961, 83–88) for more stories of an eagle predicting a man's future political power in the Roman state and in neighboring cultures.

138 The *Suda* is not specific about the age of the shielded masculine person.
139 *Suda*, Theta 41 (discussed below).
140 *On Imperial Reigns* 4.24:

> And he was born in the land of the Macedonians to parents not undistinguished in their lineage, and raised vigorously, as if an Achilles by Chiron, he was educated by them in manly thoughts and deeds, and he turned out to be known and dear to all for both of these things.
>
> (ὃς Μακεδόνων τῆς γῆς ἐκφυεὶς γεννητόρων ἦν κατὰ γενεὰν οὐκ ἀσήμων, τραφείς τε νεανικῶς, ὡς εἴ τις Ἀχιλλεὺς Χείρωνι τῷ Κενταύρῳ, παρ' αὐτῶν τοῖς ἀνδρικοῖς ἐγεγύμναστο φρονήμασί τε καὶ πράγμασι, καὶ πᾶσι μὲν κατ' ἄμφω ἐξάκουστος διετέλει καὶ φίλιος).

141 *Life of Basil* 6/220.
142 *Life of Basil* 5/219.
143 This casket is 40.3 (length) × 15.5/16 (breadth) × 11.5 (height) centimeters (Williamson 2010, 77). See Goldschmidt and Weitzmann (1930/1979, I.30–32); II pls. IX–X for images. Here are some additional discussions of the Veroli Casket: Angelova (2019), Chatterjee (2013), Cutler (1997), James (2018), Maguire (1999), Simon (1964).
144 This casket is 41.5 (length) × 17.5 (breadth) × 11.5 (height) centimeters (Caillet 1985, 147). See Goldschmidt and Weitzmann (1930/1979, I.39–40); II pl. XXIII for images. See Caillet (1985) and Maguire (1999) for more discussion.
145 This is a thought that has appeared now and again in the scholarly literature: Caillet (1985, 148 [Cluny]); Williamson (2010, 80 [Veroli]); Maguire (2004, 12 [Cluny]); Hanson (1999, 176).
146 Veroli: Simon (1964, 279); Williamson (2010, 82); Cutler (1997, 230). Cluny: Caillet (1985, 147).
147 For a discussion of the construction of these caskets, see Cutler (1994 and 1984–1985).
148 Cutler (1994 and 1984–1985, 42) (especially) is of the mind that there is degree of inattentiveness to the process. Other scholars (e.g., James 2013 and 2018) see more authorial intention in the selection of plaquettes. But whatever is happening when the boxes are put together, these patterns are popular.
149 Young male figures with wings or who appear to be flying are, naturally, best called Erotes. Otherwise, I call them boys or youths.
150 I call him a man mostly because he is the same size as the undoubted woman. It seems like it might be better to call him a youth were it not for this.
151 E.g., James (2018, 399).
152 Cutler (1997, 230).
153 Cutler (1997, 230); Williamson (2010, 77).
154 Simon (1964) interprets the entire box as being about the *Dionysiaka*, an the epic poem by Nonnos (fifth century CE). While we may not wish to follow her in saying that the box *must* be an expression of this massive epic from late antiquity, Simon's suggestion is nonetheless believable as a possible reception of the casket (for Nonnos' poem was popular among the Byzantines) *and*, even more relevant in the present instance, suggests that we should feel comfortable reading the casket with mythological meanings in mind.
155 Caillet (1985, 147).
156 Caillet (1985, 147).
157 Weitzmann (1951, 168–169).
158 The side on which this Herakles appears is the *Vorderseite* (Goldschmidt and Weitzman 1930, II pl. XXIIIb) or *la paroi longitudinale antérieure* (Caillet 1985, 147).

118   Histories of Masculine Beauty and Desire

159 The side on which the boy on his eagle appears is the *Rückseite* (Goldschmidt and Weitzman 1930, II pl. XXIIIc) or *la paroi longitudinale postérieure* (Caillet 1985, 148).
160 Caillet (1985, 148).
161 Maguire (2004, 12).
162 If one prefers to think of Achilles and Chiron on this plaquette, same-sex desire still comes to mind on account of Achilles' future and famous connection to Patrokles.
163 *Greek Anthology* 5.65, 9.77, 11.330, 11.407, 12.65, 12.69.
164 *Greek Anthology* 12.220, 12.221.
165 *Greek Anthology* 12.37, 12.133, 12.230, 12.254.
166 *Greek Anthology* 12.37.
167 *Greek Anthology* 9.77.3: "male fire"/ ἄρσεν πῦρ.
168 Ἐκ ποίου ναοῦ, πόθεν ὁ στόλος οὗτος Ἐρώτων
πάντα καταστίλβων; ἄνδρες, ἀμαυρὰ βλέπω.
τίς τούτων δοῦλος, τίς ἐλεύθερος, οὐ δύναμ' εἰπεῖν.
ἄνθρωπος τούτων κύριος; οὐ δύναται.
εἰ δ' ἐστίν, μείζων πολλῷ Διός, ὃς Γανυμήδην
ἔσχε μόνως, θεὸς ὢν πηλίκος· ὃς δὲ πόσους.

169 *Bibliotheca* 186/132b.34–35: Γανυμήδην, ὃν ἥρπασε Ζεύς.
170 Τίνος γὰρ αἴσχους ἢ ποίας ἀνοίας ὑπερβολῆς ἔλαττον ἔχει ὁ τῶν θεῶν, ὡς αὐτοί φασιν, ὕπατος, ταῦρος γινόμενος καὶ τὰ παιδικὰ φέρων ἐπὶ νώτου καὶ τέμνων πορείαν ὑγρὰν ὁ θεόταυρος, μυκήματι ἁπαλῷ δελεάζων τὴν κόρην καὶ πείθων ἀναβαίνειν ὡς ἐν ὀχήματι; Ἠ μειρακίου δύσερως ἔρως ὄρνιν δεικνύων, ἵν' οὕτως ἀναληφθεὶς Γανυμήδης τὸ νέκταρ οἰνοχοήσοι αὐτῷ;
171 *Suda*, Iota 320: οἱ δὲ ποιηταὶ ἁρπαγῆναι τὸν Γαννυμήδην ὑπὸ τοῦ Διὸς ἔγραψαν, τὸ ὀξὺ τοῦ θανάτου μυθολογήσαντες.
172 αὐτὸν ὁ Μίνως ἐν τῷ ναῷ ἔθαψεν. ἐξ οὗ δὴ καὶ λέγεται Γανυμήδην μετὰ Διὸς ὑπάρχειν.
173 πρῶτος ἠράσθη παιδὸς Ὑμεναίου τοὔνομα, υἱοῦ Καλλιόπης καὶ Μάγνητος.
174 οἱ δὲ Κρῆτά φασί τινα Τάλωνα Ῥαδαμάνθυος ἐρασθῆναι. οἱ δὲ Λάϊόν φασιν ἐρασθῆναι πρώτου Χρυσίππου.
175 οἱ δὲ Ἰταλιώτας πρώτους κατ' ἀνάγκην στρατείας εὑρέσθαι τοῦτο. κατὰ δὲ ἀλήθειαν αὐτὸς ὁ Ζεὺς πρῶτος ἠράσθη Γανυμήδους.
176 ὁ οὖν Γανυμήδης κατ' εὐπέτειαν ἑαυτὸν ξίφει διειργάσατο.
177 Tougher (2010b, 140–141); James (2013, 110).
178 Genesios also makes oblique reference to such matters at *On Imperial Reigns* 4.19.
179 Elsewhere in the *Life of Basil*, Michael's *phatria* is called an "impious band" (20/243: χορὸν δυσσεβῆ, immediately below) and an "abominable association" (25/250: παλαμναίου συνεδρίου), which intensify the opprobrium.
180 τοσοῦτον ἑαυτὸν τῶν καθηκόντων ἐξεδιήτησεν, καὶ τοσοῦτον πρὸς πᾶσαν παράνομον ἐξεβακχεύθη πρᾶξιν, καὶ οὕτως τά τε θεῖα ἐξωρχήσατο καὶ πρὸς τοὺς τῆς πολιτείας ὁμοῦ καὶ τῆς φύσεως νόμους ἐξύβρισεν. συστησάμενος γὰρ περὶ ἑαυτὸν ἀσελγῶν καὶ μιαρῶν καὶ παμπονήρων ἀνθρώπων χορὸν δυσσεβῆ καὶ τὴν τοῦ βασιλικοῦ μεγέθους ἀτιμάσας σεμνότητα, περὶ κώμους καὶ μέθας καὶ ἔρωτας ἀσελγεῖς καὶ αἰσχρὰ διηγήματα, ἔτι δὲ περὶ ἡνιόχους καὶ ἵππους καὶ ἅρματα καὶ τὴν ἐντεῦθεν μανίαν καὶ παρακοπὴν τῶν φρενῶν ὁ ἄθλιος διημέρευεν, καὶ εἰς τοὺς τοιούτους ἀνθρώπους ἀφειδῶς ἐξεκένου τὰ δημόσια χρήματα.
181 Ševčenko (2011, 82) directs a reader to Niketas Paphlagonos' *Vita Ignatii* (*PG* 105 528B) where one discovers that Grullos' real name was Theophilos and that he was *protospatharios*. Pseudo-Symeon also notes that his real name was Theophilos (*Chronographia* 663/19). Lastly, his name varies between sources, appearing as Grulos and Groullos also. I print Grullos for all occurrences.

182 ...καὶ ἀπὸ τῶν πολεμικῶν τάξεων εἰς τὰς θυμελικὰς ὀρχήσεις καὶ λέσχας ὁ Ῥωμαϊκὸς ἐξεχεῖτο πλοῦτος, καὶ εἰς ἀσελγεῖς καὶ παρανόμους βακχείας καὶ ἔρωτας ἀσώτως καὶ ῥύδην ἐξεφοροῦντο οἱ βασιλικοὶ θησαυροί, ὡς πᾶσι γνώριμον καὶ καταφανὲς καθεστὼς παρήσειν μοι δοκῶ· ὅτι δὲ τὰ θεῖα κατέπαιζεν, καὶ ἀπὸ τῶν συνόντων αὐτῷ μιαρῶν καὶ ἀσελγῶν ἀνδρογύνων καὶ πατριάρχην ἕνα ὠνόμαζε καὶ μητροπολίτας ἐκ τούτων ἀφώρισεν ἕνδεκα ὡς αὐτοῦ συμπληροῦντος τὸν δωδέκατον ἀριθμόν, τοῦτο δὴ διηγήσομαι. τὸν γὰρ ἐναγῆ καὶ μιαρώτατον ἐκεῖνον Γροῦλλον τὸ τοῦ πατριάρχου ἐπιφημίσας ὄνομα, καὶ ἀρχιερατικῇ τοῦτον χρυσοστίκτῳ καὶ ὑπερλάμπρῳ κοσμήσας στολῇ καὶ ὠμοφόριον περιθείς, καὶ ἐν τάξει μητροπολιτῶν ἑτέρους ἕνα πρὸς τοῖς δέκα, ὡς εἴρηται, ἐκ τοῦ αὐτοῦ τῶν ὁμογνωμόνων αὐτῷ συνεδρίου σκευάσας, καὶ δωδέκατον ἑαυτὸν Κολωνείας ὀνομάσας ἀρχιεπίσκοπον...
183 As has been noted earlier in this book, sexual meanings can be surfaced from σύνειμι (*LSJ* [συνεῖναι] II.2) and its related noun, συνουσία (*LSJ* I.4).
184 Ševčenko provides "of the city's colon/gut" in Latin, i.e., *urbis coli*, in the apparatus of his edition of the *Life of Basil* (2011, 84), where the customary language is Latin. His translation of *Koloneia*/Κολωνεία as "Guttown" is attractive (2011, 85). Lastly, omicron (ο) and omega (ω) are homophonic in medieval Greek, so "ass" is audible no matter what.
185 *Life of Basil* 21/245: μετὰ πολλοῦ τοῦ μεταξὺ γέλωτος καὶ ῥημάτων αἰσχρῶν καὶ σχημάτων ἀποτροπαίων καὶ βδελυρῶν.
186 *Life of Basil* 22/245: τοῦ βασιλέως φατριάρχην.
187 *Life of Basil* 22/245–246.
188 *Life of Basil* 22/245: ῥήματα καὶ ᾄσματα πορνικά.
189 These events appear with less detail in *Theophanes Continuatus* (4.38/200–202) and Pseudo-Symeon (*Chronographia* 661–662/18). Notably, both *Theophanes Continuatus* and Pseudo-Symeon speak of "the *phatria* that he [Michael] had about himself" (ἡ τῶν ὢν εἶχε μεθ' ἑαυτοῦ φατρία). Pseudo-Symeon also intensifies the toilet humour by saying at the end that Michael made himself "the occupier of the first throne of Asstown" (πρωτόθρονος ὁ Κολωνείας).
190 ἀλλὰ καὶ τῷ πατρικίῳ Ἰμερίῳ, ὃν Χοῖρον αὐτὸς μὲν ὁ βασιλεὺς διὰ τὴν τῆς ὄψεως ὠνόμαζεν ἀγριότητα, διὰ δὲ τὸ χοιρῶδες τοῦ βίου μᾶλλον καὶ ῥυπαρὸν ἄξιος ἦν τῆς τοιαύτης προσρήσεως – τούτῳ τοίνυν αἰσχρολογοῦντί ποτε κατενώπιον αὐτοῦ καὶ ταῖς ἀπὸ σκηνῆς φλυαρίαις καταχρωμένῳ ἔκ τε τοῦ παντελῶς ἀπερυθριᾶσαι καὶ μηδὲν τῶν ἐπονειδίστων ὀκνῆσαι – καὶ ψόφον ἀκόλαστον ἀπὸ τῆς μιαρᾶς ἀφέντος γαστρός, οὕτως βαρὺν καὶ σφοδρῶς καταιγίζοντα ὥστε καὶ τὸ φαῖνον φατλίον ἀποσβεσθῆναι, πεντήκοντα λιτρῶν ἐπιδόσει ἐτίμησεν ὡς Ἡράκλειόν τινα τοῦτον ἆθλον ἀνύσαντι.
191 τῷ παραδόξῳ τοῦ τοιούτου θαύματος χρυσίου λίτρας δέδωκεν ἑκατόν.
192 τῷ παραδόξῳ θαύματι, χρυσίου νομίσματα δέδωκεν ρʹ.
193 *Life of Basil* 27/253: ἡνιόχοις καὶ πόρναις καὶ ἀσελγέσιν ἀνθρώποις.
194 *Life of Basil* 27/253: ἀσελγῶς καὶ ἀσώτως διασκιδνάμενα.
195 *Life of Basil* 21/243–244: ἀσελγεῖς καὶ παρανόμους...ἔρωτας, cf. 20/243: ἔρωτας ἀσελγεῖς.
196 *Theophanes Continuatus* 4.39/201–202.
197 *Chronographia* 663–664/20.
198 *Life of Basil* 23/246–247.
199 ψόφον ἀναθορὼν ἐπαφεὶς δυσωδίας πλήρη καὶ ῥήματά τινα ἀπρεπῆ τὰς ἐκείνης καὶ τῶν εὐσεβεστέρων εἰς ἑαυτοὺς ἐξεκαλεῖτο ἀράς.
200 καὶ ἐκ προχείρου ψόφον ἀναθορὼν ἐπαφεὶς καὶ λόγους ἀπρεπεῖς προστεθεικὼς καὶ τὸ "ἡμεῖς ὅπερ ἔχομεν, κυρά, παρέχομέν σοι," τὰ πάντα δυσωδίας ἐπλήρου.
201 *Life of Basil* 23/246–247.
202 ὁ δὲ παμμίαρος ἐκεῖνος τῆς καθέδρας ὀλίγον ὑπεγερθεὶς καὶ ἀπ' αὐτῆς τοὐναντίον ἀποστραφείς, ὀνώδη ψόφον ἀπὸ τῶν μυσαρῶν ἐγκάτων ἀφεὶς πρὸς αὐτὴν ἀπεφθέγξατο, ὅτι· "ἵνα μὴ λέγῃς, κυρά, ὡς οὐδὲ κἂν τούτου σε ἠξιώσαμεν."

203 τοῦ δὲ βασιλέως ἀνακαγχάσαντος καὶ αὐτοῦ τοῦ παμβεβήλου παμμέγεθες ἐκγελάσαντος, καὶ πολλὰ καταφλυαρησάντων, ἢ μᾶλλον τῷ παραφόρῳ τῆς γνώμης ἀλογώτατα ἐξοιστρησάντων...
204 τῷ παραφόρῳ τῆς γνώμης ἀλογώτατα ἐξοιστρησάντων.
205 ...ἐπιγνοῦσα τὸ πλάσμα καὶ τὴν ἀπάτην ἡ βασιλὶς καὶ πολλὰ τῶν παρόντων καταστενάξασα καὶ πλείστας ἀρὰς τῷ υἱῷ ἐπιρρίψασα, τέλος ἐξεῖπεν πρὸς αὐτὸν, ὅτι· "ἰδού, κακὸν τέκνον, ὁ θεὸς τὴν χεῖρα αὐτοῦ ἀφείλετο ἀπὸ σοῦ, καὶ ἐδόθη σοι 'ἀδόκιμος νοῦς ποιεῖν τὰ μὴ καθήκοντα.'"
206 καὶ καθὼς οὐκ ἐδοκίμασαν τὸν θεὸν ἔχειν ἐν ἐπιγνώσει, παρέδωκεν αὐτοὺς ὁ θεὸς εἰς ἀδόκιμον νοῦν, ποιεῖν τὰ μὴ καθήκοντα.
207 And Ševčenko writing in the *apparatus criticus* of his edition certainly did: "cf. etiam Rom. 1:27 vicinum ubi Apostolus masculos in masculos turpitudinem operantes valde increpat" (2011, 90). (A translation of this moralizing remark: "cf. also to Rom 1:27, which is nearby, where the Apostle strongly condemns males working disgracefulness into males.")
208 διὰ τοῦτο παρέδωκεν αὐτοὺς ὁ θεὸς εἰς πάθη ἀτιμίας· αἵ τε γὰρ θήλειαι αὐτῶν μετήλλαξαν τὴν φυσικὴν χρῆσιν εἰς τὴν παρὰ φύσιν, ὁμοίως τε καὶ οἱ ἄρσενες ἀφέντες τὴν φυσικὴν χρῆσιν τῆς θηλείας ἐξεκαύθησαν ἐν τῇ ὀρέξει αὐτῶν εἰς ἀλλήλους, ἄρσενες ἐν ἄρσεσιν τὴν ἀσχημοσύνην κατεργαζόμενοι καὶ τὴν ἀντιμισθίαν ἣν ἔδει τῆς πλάνης αὐτῶν ἐν ἑαυτοῖς ἀπολαμβάνοντες.
209 A cross-cultural comparison is intriguing here. In remarks about late medieval England but relevant to this study, Masten says: "sweet smells, evacuation, anality, and desire are often inextricably bound in this culture..." (2016, 75).
210 Basil's proximity to this behavior is an uncomfortable fact that the *Life of Basil* at 24/247–248 attempts to minimize.

3 Framing the Brotherhoods of Emperor Basil I

Four of the historiographies discussed in the previous chapter, the *Life of Basil*, both editions of Symeon the Logothete's *Chronographia*, and Pseudo-Symeon's *Chronographia* show Basil becoming a ritual brother to other men (see Figure 2.2). With mild variations in terminology, they all speak of Basil contracting a brotherhood, which usually has the adjective "spiritual" (*pneumatikos*/πνευματικός) or the phrase "in church" (*en tei ekklesiai*/ἐν τῇ ἐκκλησίᾳ) associated with it.[1] While *adelphopoiesis* does not have a necessary relationship to carnal intimacy, it is being used by a young man whose beauty was surrounded by an aura of same-sex sexual erotics. Indeed, some of the accounts feature strong implication of carnality between the brothers, so it is distinct possibility for all brothers, as the historiographers are not interested in fabulation untethered from reality.

The story here is a tenth-century one. What do the historiographers, in their moment, regard as plausible about these brotherhoods from the previous century? What don't they say but assume their audience will understand and know about? The historiographers don't describe the rite but there is an illustration in the eleventh-century manuscript, the *Madrid Skylitzes*.[2] But the audience for the historiographies would not have needed the illustration, as the rite of ritual brotherhood was common throughout the empire in these centuries.[3]

Adelphopoiesis was part of the broader panorama of male homosociality. It existed in a milieu that featured, to take some examples, need for protection, ambition, *hetaireiai*, competition, masculine beauty, and same-sex desire. Contracting a brotherhood could have been for any number of reasons, including fear, ambition, affection, desire for intimacy, or some combination of these.[4] The rite probably had an origin in monastic practice in the fourth century CE,[5] and was performed in a church. And while this rite, which was common among the laity at this time, had importance as a moment of positive religious sanction, it was only an articulation point in the lives of the men it made brothers. The brothers-to-be came to the church with a relation and purpose(s) already.[6] But this is not to minimize the importance of *adelphopoiesis*, especially in developing an

DOI: 10.4324/9781351135238-4

understanding of Byzantine masculine homosociality. As this ritual intersected with so many things that were, well, not sacred, a vision of the complicated terrain of men's intimate relations that recalls the collocation of things carnal and religious in Nikephoros Ouranos' *Letter 26*, or in the letters that passed between Constantine VII and Theodoros of Kyzikos comes into sight again.

At the intersection of so many things, *adelphopoiesis* has posed challenges to interpretation,[7] as it seems to be at cross-purposes with the church at times. But explicit controversy about ritual brotherhood dates to later centuries,[8] and it was being practiced in an unregulated fashion during 800s and 900s. The ritual and resulting enhanced connection are a site of unresolved energies and significations: sensuality and desire and the refusal of them occupy and jockey for position within the same space. And as will be shown below, the space of the church with bodily contact and the texts of the prayers themselves show that neat resolution of these tensions was not a concern, any more than it is in Nikephoros Ouranos' *Letter 26*. As directives from the church went out the door to discipline carnal exuberance on the outside, so carnal exuberance came into church. There was a semantic ebb and flow that contained both stricture and carnality; reality was messy.[9]

Basil's Brotherhoods in the Historiographies

Nicholas

The story of Nicholas, who discovered a young and bedraggled Basil at the church of St. Diomedes just after he arrived in Constantinople and who contracted a spiritual brotherhood with him, appears in both editions of Symeon the Logothete's *Chronographia* and in Pseudo-Symeon's. These sources are divided on the status of Nicholas. In some he is an overseer (*prosmonarios*/προσμονάριος) of the church,[10] while others make him a lowly worker, or even a slave (*neokoros*/νεωκόρος).[11] The connection Basil forged with Nicholas was arguably the one that enabled his glorious career to come. It is through his brotherhood with Nicholas that he came to the attention of Nicholas' brother, who then brought Basil to Theophilitzes' attention, which then led, eventually, to the imperial court.

In all the narratives that feature Nicholas as his ritual brother, Basil was making his way to Constantinople because he had not found the advantages he hoped for from the general Tzantzes.[12] Exhausted after his journey, the young man Basil laid down to sleep on the steps of the church of St. Diomedes. Awakened from his rest, Nicholas heard a heavenly voice that told him to go out and lead the emperor into the church. He got up twice to take a look and saw only an apparently no-account young man asleep outside. Each time he went back to bed. Then the same voice returned, this time with

Framing the Brotherhoods 123

a sword, a *rhomphaia* (ῥομφαία), to poke him in the side, while it repeated the order that Nicholas bring the emperor in:

> And immediately someone gave a him a poke with a sword in his side, saying, "going outside, lead the one you see lying outside the gate in: he is the emperor."
> (Symeon the Logothete, *Chronographia* [first edition] 131.14)[13]

Nicholas then went out and finally bundled Basil in. The next day he took him to the baths, cleaning him up, and becoming brothers with him in church, a turn of events that delighted the both of them. Symeon the Logothete puts it this way in his first edition:

> And so, going out, trembling with purpose, and finding Basil with his pouch and staff, he led him into the church. And on the next day, having gone out with him to the baths, he transformed him, and, having gone to the church, made [with him] a ritual brotherhood (*adelphopoiesin*/ἀδελφοποίησιν), and they were rejoicing together in one another.
> (131.14)[14]

Having seen Basil, Nicholas noticed that Basil had a pouch (*pera*/πήρα) and staff (*rhabdos*/ῥάβδος). It has been suggested that a double-entendre is present with the pouch and staff standing in, for logical morphological reasons, for Basil's genitalia.[15] Pouch and staff are in the other versions of Symeon the Logothete's *Chronographia* and Pseudo-Symeon's too. In the case of two versions of the second edition of the Symeon the Logothete's *Chronographia*, the staff is provocatively in Basil's hand:

> He (Nicholas) led Basil, kitted out with a pouch and holding his rod in his hand, inside the church.
> (Istrin 5 and Featherstone 424/10)[16]

Morphology, especially given what is to come in Basil's life, makes pouch and staff a durable double-entendre all on its own. But intertextual analysis of *pera*/πήρα and *rhabdos*/ῥάβδος, suggesting what a devout and educated audience could sense about the pouch and staff, supports and facets the impression made by Basil's accoutrements.

A pouch and staff appear in the New Testament at Mt 10:10. In the lead-in to this moment, Jesus tells the disciples to go forth and preach:

> Going forth, spread the word, saying that the empire of celestial things has drawn near. Heal those who are sick. Raise the dead. Cure the lepers. Drive out demons…
> (Mt 10:7–8)[17]

124 *Framing the Brotherhoods*

Jesus then specifies that the disciples take no pay (Mt 10:9). They should also travel as light as possible and look to getting their needs met through working as they go, and not by bringing money along to pay for provisions:

> Don't have in your possession [monies]... nor pouch (*peran*/πήραν) for the way, nor two tunics, nor sandals, nor a staff/rod (*rhabdon*/ῥάβδον); for the workman is worthy of his provisions.
>
> (Mt 10:9–10)[18]

This passage arguably would have been one of the first to come to mind, as it is the words of Jesus in one of the synoptic gospels. And then immediately a thing to note is that Basil behaves precisely not as one of the twelve disciples would. He travels with pouch and rod and therefore is precisely *not* one of Jesus' godly disciples. Indeed, while the pouch may at the moment be empty, it will in time be filled with treasure that will come his way.

There is further intertextuality to consider. An epigram from Book 16 of the *Greek Anthology* features the pouch and rod. This epigram, by the second-century BCE poet and grammarian, Moschos, is called "To an Eros who Ploughs" (Εἰς Ἔρωτα ἀροτριῶντα):

> Having set aside his torches and arrows, cruel Eros took up an ox-tormenting rod/staff (*rhabdon*/ῥάβδον) and had a pouch (*peren*/πήρην) thrown over his shoulder. And having put under the yoke the labor-bearing necks of bulls, he was sowing the wheat-bearing furrow of Demeter. Looking up, he said to Zeus himself, "Fill the acres (*sc.* with rain), or I will put you, Europa's bull, up under the ploughs.
>
> (*Greek Anthology* 16.200)[19]

Giving up his usual erotic accoutrements of torches and arrows, Eros trades them in for pouch and rod. This is supposed to mark a change, a sort of disguise. But it does nothing of the kind, as the poem does not stray from the erotic subjects of desire and sex. Double-entendres proliferate in the poem. Eros is ploughing and sowing seed in a furrow[20]; Zeus' rain can also be semen; there are two references to yoking, which is yet another double-entendre. And the threat to yoke Zeus is worth a close look. If Zeus does not provide the "rain" to make the furrow fruitful, then he will be put under the ploughs, which reads as a sexual threat: "Zeus be a man, or I will be the man!" Is the young Basil, then, with his pouch and staff, an Eros come to town to spread his seed pretty much anywhere he likes, and even to the point of topping the top-dog? He is certainly not one of Jesus' disciples, in possession of the pouch and rod that Jesus told his disciples not to have.

A moment in a text attributed to the fourth-century BCE philosopher, Diogenes of Sinope (AKA the Cynic) provides a third intertext. Diogenes, famous for being socially inappropriate and wishing to expose the hypocrisies that civilization imposes on people, was known for his pouch and rod. Here, as example of this discourse, is an excerpt from a letter, probably from the opening centuries of the Roman empire, that was passed down under Diogenes' name:

> Don't be vexed, father, that I speak as a Cynic, wear the threadbare double cloak, carry the pouch (*peran*/πήραν) on my shoulders, and hold the rod (*rhabdon*/ῥάβδον) in my hand. It is not worthwhile to be vexed over these sorts of things, but instead to be delighted, because your son is satisfied with little, and is free of the [materialistic] belief [system], by which all the Greeks and barbarians are enslaved...
> (*Letters of Diogenes of Sinope* 7.1–6)[21]

Again, as is the case with Matthew, there is distance between Basil and the figure in the intertext. Basil will not be philosophical but acquisitive of possessions, and he will enthusiastically subscribe to the prevailing materialism. But there is also a similarity between Basil and Diogenes. This text, with its mention of rod in hand, is close to two of the versions of the second edition of Symeon the Logothete's *Chronographia*. Diogenes also is the philosopher who, notoriously, was liable to masturbate and do other things which were inappropriate to do in public.[22] The pouch and rod with this text in mind promise behavior liable to be sexually frank and that may be against at least some of the rules, say, in civil law.

And so there is support, in addition to the pervasive penumbra of same-sex sexual erotics seen in the various narratives of the life of Basil, to see pouch and rod in a sexual way. In possession of the things not to be carried, Basil's accoutrements simultaneously recall and repel the prescriptions of Jesus. There is instead a possible association with Eros who, desirable, has ambitions to dethrone Zeus. This rod and pouch also bring to mind Diogenes, who was shameless about sexual urges and exposing himself. In summation, the three intertexts just discussed, one religious the other two secular, push Basil away from religious morality, and instead underscore carnality and frank sexuality, which the historiographies underscore in their tale of his rise to power.

On the next day, Nicholas took Basil to baths to clean him up and get better clothes on him. In the first edition of Symeon the Logothete's *Chronographia*, it is a matter of going out to the baths and then a subsequent transformation (he clearly needed to be cleaned up): "having gone out with him to the baths, he transformed him."[23] The versions of the second edition have mild differences. Bekkerus has the addition "he washed him" *or* "he had him washed" (ἔλουσεν αὐτόν) and is otherwise identical to Symeon the Logothete's first edition.[24] The two versions of the second edition from Istrin and Featherstone don't mention the baths and, similar to Bekkerus, have him cleaning Basil up himself or perhaps having someone else do it,

126 *Framing the Brotherhoods*

and, instead of transforming him, these two versions, nearly identical to one another, speak of Nicholas clothing him. Here is Istrin:

> On the next day, having washed him/having had him washed and having put a cloak (on him)...
> (Symeon the Logothete, *Chronographia* [second edition], Istrin 5)[25]

Pseudo-Symeon does not mention the baths and provides the shortest statement of this moment of all: "having washed him (*or* having had him washed), he transformed him,"[26] which puts the onus on the reader to determine what transform can mean.

After this solicitous and intimate behavior are depictions of the ritual brotherhood. It is essential to note all the variations of language in these descriptions, especially variations in the usage of the verb "to rejoice together" *suneuphrainein*/συνευφραίνειν, which appears in two versions of Symeon the Logothete's *Chronographia* (the first edition and the Bekkerus version of the second edition) and in Pseudo-Symeon's. (Interestingly, two versions of Symeon the Logothete's second edition, Istrin and Featherstone, don't have this verb and instead speak of Nicholas and Basil living under the same roof for a time. But more about that below.) The varying usages of this verb, which is intertextual with scripture, and has a presence in epistolography, indicates a range of ideas about how two spiritual brothers can relate to one another.

In Symeon the Logothete's first edition, Nicholas took Basil to church to make an *adelphopoiesis*, which was a happy thing for both men:

> ...having gone to the church, he made (with him) a ritual brotherhood (*adelphopoiesin*/ἀδελφοποίησιν), and they were rejoicing together in/ within one another.
> (Symeon the Logothete, *Chronographia* [first edition], 131.14)[27]

First, there was a rite in a church that joined Nicholas and Basil together. Mutual happiness was in evidence ("they were rejoicing together") and each was the cause of this for the other, and, interestingly, they express their happiness "in" or "within one another" (*en allelois*/ἐν ἀλλήλοις). The double-entendre is strong here and memories of the *Life of Mary the Younger* come to mind.[28] This moment of rejoicing is intertextual with Proverbs 5:18,[29] and attention to the Septuagint at this moment pays dividends, as it speaks of connections between persons in which carnality is present.

Proverbs 5 takes a young man, i.e., "son"/"υἱέ," to task, counseling him against consorting with prostitutes. Made vulnerable through desire, he will give physical labor to people who will be happy to take from him until he is used up:

> Do not draw near to her (i.e., the prostitute's) houses' doors, lest you let your life and existence fall into the hands of people without mercy; lest others

take their fill of your strength, all your labors go to the houses of others, and you regret to the utmost, when the flesh of your body is worn down.
(Pr 5:8–11)[30]

But using up muscle and sinew is not the only expenditure mentioned in Proverbs 5. It is clear via metaphor that the son will be expending his semen to no good purpose too.

Shortly after the passage just quoted, the speaker launches into how to handle liquids properly. It seems vaguely a sexual metaphor, with drinking from one's own vessels a metaphor for sex, especially coming on the heels of how sex with a prostitute makes the son a laborer for others. But then a second metaphor, one of irrigating one's own land, arrives and becomes graphic, as it takes as its referent the young man's own capacity to produce liquid:

> Drink from your own vessels and from the spring of your wells. Don't let your waters overflow out of your spring and let your waters course into your own land. Let them be for you alone and let no other partake of them. Let your spring of water be your very own and rejoice together with the wife of your youth.
> (Pr 5:15–18)[31]

The metaphor says that the son should not expend his semen consorting with prostitutes. Just as he should only irrigate his own land, so the one who should receive his semen is his wife, the one together with whom he rejoices. So in the warm world of Byzantine elite homosociality, awareness of Proverbs 5 makes for a semantics of carnality. "They were rejoicing together in/within one another" is sexy.

As noted above, "rejoice together" also appears in one of the versions of Symeon the Logothete's second edition and in Pseudo-Symeon's *Chronographia*:

> And having gone to the church he made a ritual brotherhood (with him), and together they were making each other rejoice.
> (Symeon the Logothete, *Chronographia* [second edition], Bekkerus 820/9)[32]

> And having done a brother-making,[33] he was rejoicing[34] in/within/with/on account of him.
> (Pseudo-Symeon, *Chronographia* 656/11)[35]

The Bekkerus version of Symeon the Logothete's second edition is nearly identical to the first edition, only varying at the moment of rejoicing together, giving the verb an object, "each other": "together they were making each other rejoice." The Bekkerus version therefore seems to back away from double-entendre, not reproducing the spicy "in/within one another" of the first edition. But as the carnality imported by memory of Proverbs and the son's liquids remains, reflection suggests that it is only a minor change to mutuality (Mutual masturbation? Taking turns somehow?). In Pseudo-Symeon, the rejoicing is not mutual and more instrumentalizing. Represented by the pronoun *autoi*/αὐτῷ ("him"), Basil is the means that enables Nicholas' rejoicing. This pronoun in the dative case offers an imprecise adverbial qualification of the verb (*suneuphraineto*/συνευφραίνετο), an imprecision which can only be captured by refusing to translate it one way and instead offering four translations to capture the penumbra of meanings this dative calls up simultaneously: in, within, with, and on account of. Notably, parts of this penumbra include the feeling of "in" and "within," which recall the frankness of Symeon the Logothete's first edition.

In the other two versions of Symeon the Logothete's second edition, Istrin and Featherstone, the intertextuality with Proverbs 5 is not present, and, besides differing editorial decisions about punctuation of the Greek, they are identical:

> Having made a spiritual brother for himself, he was having (*eiche*/εἶχε) him as one who shared the same house and meals with him.
> (Symeon the Logothete, *Chronographia* (second edition), Istrin 5; Featherstone 424/10)[36]

Instead of rejoicing together, Basil and Nicholas lived together for at least a time, as the imperfect *eiche*/εἶχε suggests. While intimacy between Nicholas and Basil is definitely indicated, it would be rash all the same to assume some kind of household that two men in the modern West might set up, a situation which might lead to assumptions about desire and sexual behavior in modern times.[37] And so this detail does not necessarily support a narrative of sexual desire, but these two more chaste versions included the rod, in hand!, and pouch and a trip to the baths. Carnality is therefore not hard to find.

John

The *Life of Basil* presents another brotherhood Basil contracted, this one with John, the son of Danelis, a powerful woman in the Peloponnesos. This brotherhood is illustrated in the *Madrid Skylitzes* (see Figure 3.1). This *adelphopoiesis* was not made in the environs of the church of St. Diomedes, when Basil was freshly arrived to Constantinople, but when Basil was already associated with Theophilitzes and on a trip with him to southern Greece. This brotherhood, designated by the mildly different term *adelphotes*, lacks the overt erotic overtones perceptible around his brotherhood with Nicholas. Indeed, it was John's mother Danelis who prevailed upon Basil to become a brother to her son. The relationship, therefore, had a different quality to it, and this difference attests to the varying nature of ritual brotherhoods and their dependence on a relation that preexists the ritual and the possibility that motivations can vary. This *adelphopoiesis* was all the same, though, the creation of an enduring connection featuring intimacy over time.

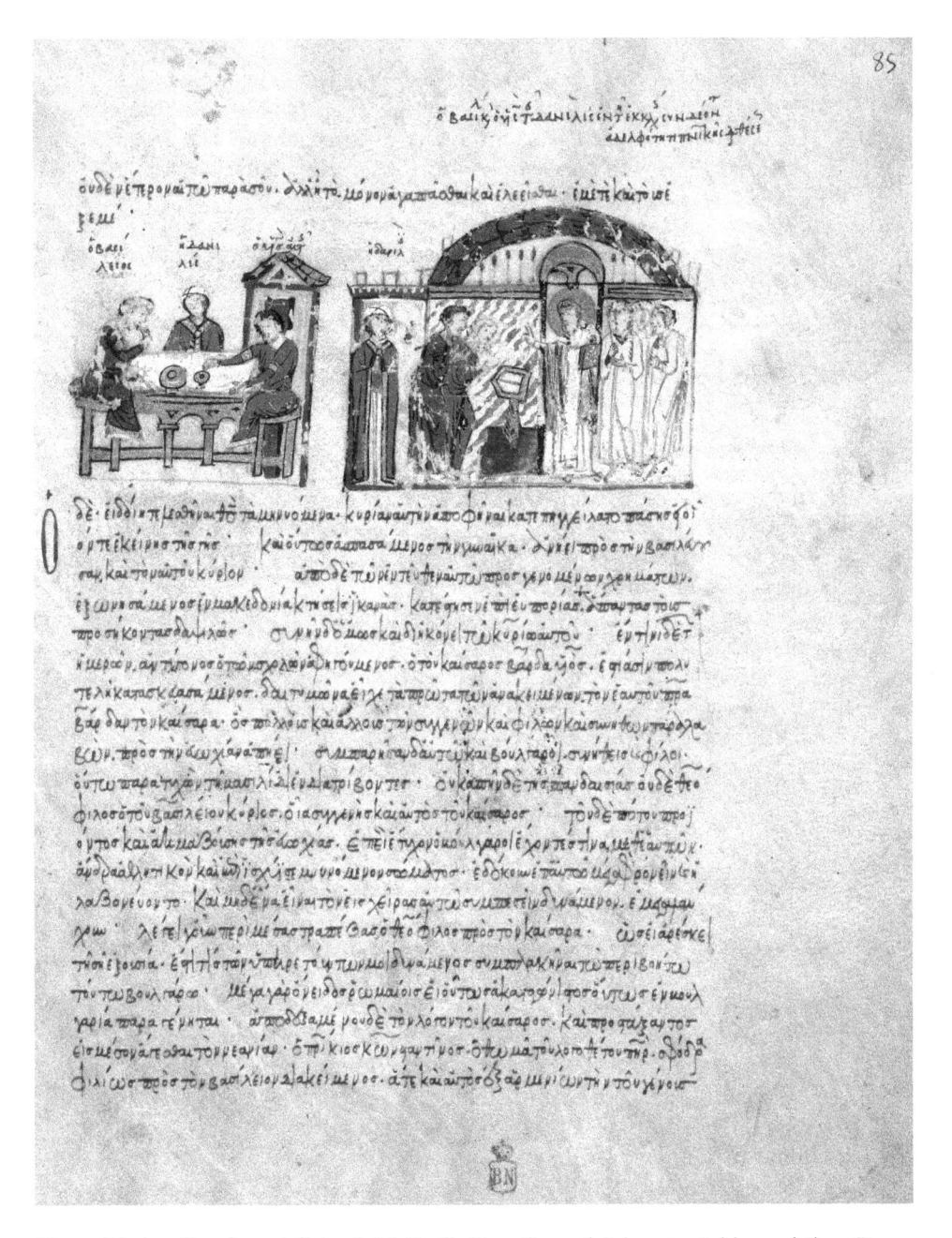

Figure 3.1 (reading from left to right) Basil, Danelis, and John at a table, and then Danelis witnessing the *adelphopoiesis* ceremony of Basil and John in church (Skylitzes Manuscript fo. 82r. Biblioteca Nacional, Madrid).

130 *Framing the Brotherhoods*

Basil accompanied Theophilitzes to the Peloponnesos:

> It happened during that time that Basil's master Theophilos [*sc.* Theophilitzes] was sent to the Peloponnesos on account of some duties related to the public treasury by Emperor Michael and *Kaisar* Bardas. And Basil was with him, performing the service required of him.
>
> (*Life of Basil* 11/226)[38]

While there, Basil visited a church and caused a stir. There was a monk there and, when Theophilitzes visited the church on prior occasion, this monk had ignored him.[39] But it was different when he saw Basil:

> ...when Basil was entering, he (the monk) arose as for someone from the greater ones and offered an acclamation of the kind fit for emperors.
>
> (*Life of Basil* 11/226)[40]

The monk's salutation, whatever it was, recalls the heavenly voice that kept waking Nicholas and telling him to go out and bring the emperor inside. Word got around the Peloponnesos that Basil had been accorded an honor that a relative of the emperor himself, i.e., Theophilitzes, had not. A rich and powerful widow, Danelis, found the monk, whom she addressed as a spiritual father,[41] and asked why when had never risen for her, her son, or her grandson, he accorded this honor to Basil.[42] He answered that he felt that he was gazing upon the emperor and was merely showing the respect due the anointed of God.[43]

Danelis took this to heart. Later, when Basil had stayed behind in the Peloponnesos because of a transient illness after Theophilos left, and when he was preparing to return to Constantinople, she summoned him:

> Danelis, the aforementioned woman, having summoned him, welcomed him with many great favors, entirely wisely and intelligently as though sowing some seed in good land (Mk 4:24), so she might reap things multiplied many times (Lk 18:30) at an appropriate time (Ps 31/32). She gave to him sufficient gold, thirty slaves for his retinue, much treasure in clothing and in yet other forms, having asked for nothing else beforehand than that he make a tie of spiritual brotherhood (σύνδεσμος πνευματικῆς ἀδελφότητος) to John, her son. He was refusing this connection, as being very much above his station, as there was, on the one hand, the reputed brilliant position of the woman, and, on the other, the paltry estate, to all appearances, of himself. All the same, having received more...[*text is troubled in a minor way here*[44]]...and exhortation from her, he did it. And at that moment as though heartened all the more, she said openly to him, "God believes you to be a great man and is about to raise you to great honor. I request or beg for nothing other than that you love and take pity on us."
>
> (*Life of Basil* 11/227–228)[45]

Danelis decided Basil was going places and so there were gifts, gold, slaves, rich clothing, and other unspecified items to make him beholden to her. In return, she asked for one thing: that he contract a ritual brotherhood with her son. At first Basil was reluctant as she was an important person in southern Greece with enviable resources and position. He felt unworthy. Ultimately, she prevailed and the brotherhood happened. Her confidence increased, she expressed the hope that he would remain kindly disposed to her and her son in the future.

There is significant intertextuality in this passage. When Danelis' favors and gifts are compared to "sowing some seed in good land, so she might reap things multiplied many times at an appropriate time," a number of moments from scripture are present: Mark 4:24, Luke 18:30, and Psalms 31/32.

Mark 4 as a whole has a prominent concern with the spreading of the gospel and expectations one may have about how well it will be understood and taken up. Jesus speaks only in parables to the *ochlos*, or mob of common people,[46] but explains things in more detail to his disciples.[47] Before speaking of sowing to his disciples, Jesus tells of the revelation of hidden things and follows with an injunction that they listen carefully: level of effort at sorting out the meaning of his parables is directly related to eventual benefit obtained. And lack of effort can even deepen confusion. Then Jesus speaks of sowing, drawing a picture of seed sprouting hidden from prying eyes, then the increasingly visible evidence of a crop, and at last the harvest:

> "For there is no hidden thing, but that it may be revealed. It was not hidden away, but so that it might come out into evidence. If someone has ears to hear, let them listen." And he said to them, "Pay attention to what you hear. By what measure you take the measure [of the content of what you are hearing], it will be measured out to you, and more in addition will be given to you. For the one who has, it will be given to him and the one who does not have, even what he has will be taken from him." And he added, "Thus is the Empire of God, that a man will sow seed (*balei ton sporon*/βάλη τὸν σπόρον, cf. *Life of Basil* 11/228: *sporon...kataballomene*/σπόρον... καταβαλλομένη) in the land, sleep and arise night and day, and the seed sprouts and grows great in such a way as he does not know. For the self-moving earth bears fruit, first the stalk, then the ear, then mature grain in the ear. When the fruit allows it, he dispatches the sickle straightaway, for the harvest has arrived."
>
> (Mk 4:22–29)[48]

Both the *Life of Basil* and Mark feature thematization of hidden things coming to visible fulfillment over time and an idea of profit realized through effort. Danelis cultivated Basil, planted the seed, and after a time, there was profit. The sowing of the word in Mark is similar. The word is spread and happy results will come in time but the process is hard to see in the meantime. But this is not all. When Jesus tells the disciples to pay close attention to what they read, that profit comes to the ones who work hard to understand what they hear, this suggests to a reader of the *Life of Basil* that they be of a similar determined nature. To the extent a reader had this section of Mark in mind, then to that extent the call to be a disciple who reads carefully became audible. This has an effect of bringing carnalities to the surface and knitting this section of the *Life of Basil* to sections of the life that depict Basil's rise amid the warm homosocialities of the court. The other intertextualities, Luke 18 and Psalms 31/32, show how this works. Danelis sowed seed "so she might reap *things multiplied many times* (cf. Lk 18:30: *pollaplasiona*/πολλαπλασίονα) *at an appropriate time*" (cf. Ps 31/32:6: *en euthetoi kairoi*/ἐν εὐθέτῳ καιρῷ). As with the reference to Mark, the reader was likely to know these contexts and would have seen that these intertexts highlight discontinuities between the situation with Danelis and what appears in scripture. These discontinuities connect this moment in the *Life of Basil* with other worldly and carnal moments in it.

In the broader context of Luke (18:22–30), Jesus tells his disciples to let go of attachments. Wealth, of course, for famously, the rich man has as much chance getting into heaven as a camel has of going through the eye of a needle.[49] And at 18:29–30, Jesus' advice expands to leaving behind household, wife, brothers and sisters, parents and children. The ones who makes themselves free will enjoy "things multiplied many times" in this life and in the eternal life to come:

> And he (Jesus) said to them: "Amen I say to you, and that there is no one who has let go of house, wife, siblings, parents, and children on account of the Empire of God who will not enjoy things multiplied many times (*pollaplasiona*/πολλαπλασίονα) in that moment and in the eternity that is the coming eternal life."
>
> (Lk 18:29–30)[50]

If one follows this asceticizing advice about despising wealth and letting go of attachments to other people, good things will happen. Accordingly, the discontinuity between the materialistic ambitions of Danelis, the exchange of goods, and the forming of a brotherhood connection, on the one hand, and Luke, on the other, is sharp. And there is also a discontinuity in the case of Ps 31/32. King David speaks there about how "each holy man will pray to you (*sc.* God) at an appropriate time,"[51] confessing his sins.[52] In contrast to this moment in the Septuagint, there is no confession in the *Life of Basil* and holiness is not an emphasis.

So, what would a reader make of these diverging intertextualities? While the reference to Mark has at least one straightforward aspect, i.e., investing now for a return later, the Luke and Psalms intertextualities, instead of fitting neatly into a groove with Danelis' elite strategizing, pose questions about it. Danelis was fantastically wealthy and the opposite of the kind of person Jesus idealizes in Luke. And there was neither soul searching nor the confession of sins that the psalm speaks of. A discontinuity between scripture and Byzantine reality appears and it renders the scriptural glosses brittle. Reality acquires a spotlight. What is visible in this reality?

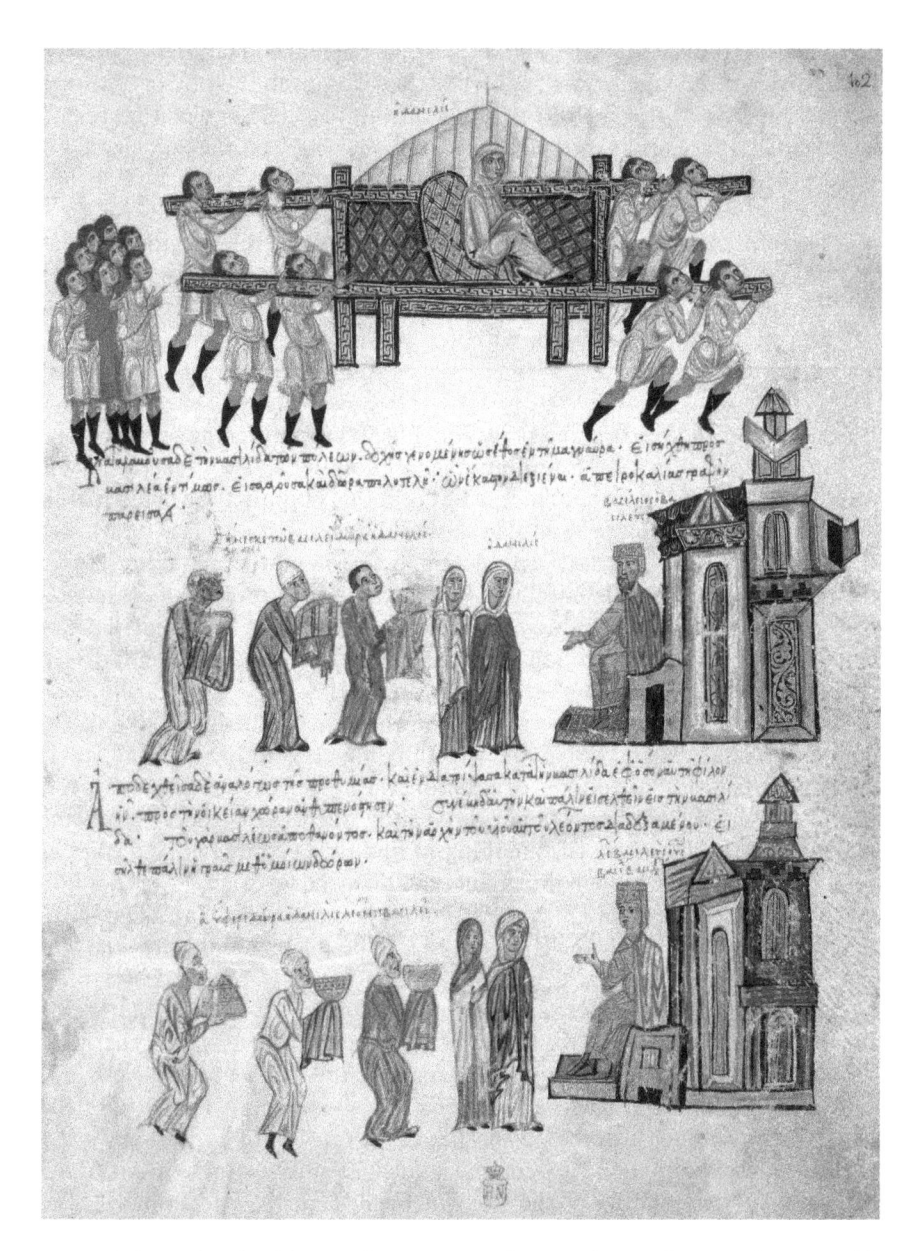

Figure 3.2 Top bank of figures features Danelis traveling to Constantinople. Middle bank of figures features Danelis giving gifts to (now) Emperor Basil I. The bottom bank shows her giving gifts to Basil's son, Leo VI. (Skylitzes Manuscript fo. 102r. Biblioteca Nacional, Madrid).

When Basil was emperor, John was made *protospatharios* and had privileged access to Basil himself.[53] And the flow of favors and honors continued both ways where Danelis was concerned. She was given the title of "Mother of the Emperor"[54] and made a trip to Constantinople later (see Figure 3.2) and deeded a large part of the Peloponnesos to "her son the emperor," for the brotherhood with John made Basil her son in a way:

> Therefore she magnanimously added still more to the previously mentioned gifts, a not insignificant part of the Peloponnesos, which, as it happened to be her property, she at that moment, happily gifting, graced her son the emperor with it...
>
> (*Life of Basil* 75/319)[55]

It is clear that the seeds planted have yielded a crop different from the one in Mark 4 for all involved, and another discontinuity between Byzantine present and biblical past has emerged. It is at this point that one who has an ear to hear reads with the careful attention that Jesus counsels at Mark 4.[56]

The planting of seed in a well-ploughed furrow, the gradual sprouting, then rising up of the stalk, swelling of the ear, and the revelation of the mature grain are images that always tremble on the point of becoming double-entendres for sexual penetration and male tumescence. And a reader is driven in this direction, in the first place, by the journey they have been on with Basil in the *Life of Basil*: his membership in the *hetaireia* of Theophilitzes, his encounters with eagle and horse, the wrestling match, and the uncomfortable confrontation over Basilikinos. In addition, the misfit between salient aspects of the story and scripture (Danelis is wealthy; there is no confession being made) suggests that there is something to find that's concealed, as Mk 4:22 says: "For there is no hidden thing, but that it may be revealed. It was not hidden away, but so that it might come out into evidence." The ear to hear[57] will perceive an usettling of Danelis' cast seed into double-entendre, especially as she is joining her son up with Basil, whose backstory is one of desire, male beauty, and the rest. All these aspects in Basil's biography provide the "measure" to "take the measure" of the content of the making of his brotherhood with John, a way to understand the semantics this story could have had.[58] Indeed, there is much that recalls the brothers, Baanes and Theodoros, who who plough virtue in/within one another in the *Life of Mary the Younger*.[59]

But even without such ears to hear and the ability or inclination to develop this understanding of the story of Basil, Danelis, and John via similarity and difference from scripture, a reader will still note that Danelis has bought for her son a brother who was in the *hetaireia* of Theophiltzes, a group that Basil remained associated with after leaving the Peloponnesos.[60] Its members, chosen for their manliness and attractiveness, would have been a stylish and cosmopolitan bunch looking good in silks, and there is no reason to imagine that homoerotics already seen in the *Life of Basil* are no longer present. A route to power and riches is through homosocial connections and a seed may be planted in the darkness. Things may happen over time such that are not visible, but it is possible that riches and even the office of, say, *protospatharios* will be the eventual result.

Other Brothers

Besides the two ritual brothers, Nicholas and John, who receive extended treatment in the tenth-century historiographies, there is evidence of three additional men with whom Basil contracted brotherhoods. He treated these men well. The first edition of Symeon the Logothete's *Chronographia* shows Basil, now emperor, rewarding his brothers, starting with Nicholas, with positions of eminence, which recalls the benefits that John enjoyed in the *Life of Basil*:

> Basil honored the aforementioned Nicholas, surnamed Androsalites (the *prosmonarios* of the church of St. Diomedes, to whom the martyr [*sc.* in the form of the heavenly voice] appeared concerning the emperor, as was said above) as *oikonomos* and *sunkellos*. And another brother of his, John, (he honored) as *droungarios of the bigle*.[61] Another brother of his, Paulos (he honored with) a position of financial administration, and, another brother, Constantine (he put) in charge of taxation.
> (Symeon the Logothete, *Chronographia* [first edition], 132.11)[62]

This passage, which is more or less repeated in two versions of the second edition of Symeon the Logothete's *Chronographia*[63] and in Pseudo-Symeon's,[64] shows that Basil had at least three additional ritual brothers to add to Nicholas and Danelis' son John. They included another John, a Paulos, and a Constantine. Now while it cannot be ruled out that there are some natural brothers among these men, the most natural reading of the above passage is that all have been made brothers with Basil in church.

Liturgies for the *Adelphopoiesis* Ritual

When Basil became brothers with Nicholas, John, or any of the others, what happened in the church in the ninth century, or, better, what might have tenth-century readers and writers imagined happened? What would get said and done in an *adelphopoiesis* ceremony?

The rite of *adelphopoiesis*/ἀδελφοποίησις (and there are synonyms for this term to be seen, e.g., *adelphopoiia*/ἀδελφοποιία, *adelphotes*/ἀδελφότης or *adelphopoiesia*/ἀδελφοποιησία) itself consisted of actions and prayers, and was therefore a combination of movement of bodies through space and into contact, as well as texts read and heard. There were ritual prayers specific to joining brothers that appeared in *euchologia*, or guides to liturgy for church services, many of which still survive from medieval times. They have been the object of scholarly attention on and off for centuries. The *euchologia*, especially the later ones, contain directions for how the ritual should proceed, dictating not only the prayers to be said but also what the priest and brothers-to-be should do with their bodies in the course of the ritual. Analysis of both the *adelphopoiesis* ritual as a physical event and the prayers invites consideration of the embodied lives of these men inside and outside the church. It is also possible to build lexical connections between these prayers and contemporary historiographies and epistolography. All this enables informed suggestions about the semantics of the rite for these men who came to church bound by a preexisting tie, over which a brotherhood was laid.

Envisioning what went on physically in the church in Byzantine times during an *adelphopoiesis* ritual, especially in the ninth century (the actual time of Basil I) or in the tenth century (the time of the historiographers) poses challenges. While there are prayers surviving from this time and before, directions for the conduct of the rites are sparse in the *euchologia*, which usually print just the prayers, and it is in the later *euchologia* that more detailed descriptions of the ritual situation appear. While some of the textual evidence to be discussed presently, especially about the physical aspects of the rite, comes from after the tenth century, it may be assumed that rites described in these manuscripts from two or even four centuries later would not be radically different from what might have transpired according to tenth-century imaginations of a rite in the ninth century. The increase of directions in later *euchologia* attests to a wish to keep things going as they have been and to avoid innovation. But before proceeding further with discussion of the liturgies, it will be useful to make remarks about the situation in the secondary literature and how I am using it, as there are a lot of names.

First and foremost, I found Rapp's discussion from 2016 of ritual brotherhood, from its very beginnings in late antiquity all the way through the Byzantine period, to be invaluable. Particularly helpful is her careful explication of the situation with the manuscripts and relations among the prior secondary sources. I follow her numbering of the prayers. Writing in 2010, Panagou provides almost all the Greek texts of the prayers and rituals discovered to that date. The presence of the Greek texts in Panagou's book makes his work an essential supplement to Rapp's work, as she did not include the Greek texts. I also had occasion to consult the Greek in Dmitrievskij's collection of *euchologia* from 1901 (which was reissued in 1965) and in Goar's old, though still useful, presentation of *euchologia* from the eighteenth century. Where possible I have preferred Panagou's text, as his is the most complete and recent. I use others where needed and cross reference where relevant. On two occasions, I have printed others' Greek texts because they were more complete.

Here are directions for an *adelphopoiesis* ritual taken from a thirteenth-century manuscript[65]:

> A prayer for brother-making:
> "Lord, Our God, who has given graciously all things for salvation to us..." Goar page 707. He (the priest) makes an *ektene*, names them (i.e., the brothers-to-be), and [then] says the prayer. He dismisses them, and both of them (i.e., the brothers) kiss the holy bible and each other.
> (Dmitrievskij 1901/1965, 157)[66]

After the title of the ritual, "a prayer for brother-making,"[67] words in quotation appear, "Lord, Our God, who has given graciously all things for salvation to us...." These words are the beginning of a specific prayer for brotherhood, the one which Rapp calls Prayer B.[68] In *euchologia*, the opening words of a prayer are quoted and then priest knows which prayer he should be saying. Prayer B is first seen in the ninth century,[69] and it appears on page 707 of Goar in full text, as Dmitrievskij's text indicates. As do all the brotherhood prayers, Prayer B has a tripartite structure: invocation followed by request and concluding with doxology (these are marked in the translation[70]):

> [INVOCATION:] Lord, Our God, who has graciously given all things for salvation to us and laid the command on us that we love one another and forgive each other's sins, [REQUEST:] may you, as also a humanity-loving master, upon these your slaves who love each other with spiritual love and who have come into your holy church to be blessed by you—may you graciously give them faith unashamed, love genuine, and as you have made a gift to your disciples of your peace, may you make a gift to these men of all their requests for salvation and life eternal. [DOXOLOGY:] Because you, God, show mercy and are humanity-loving, we send glory up to you. This we ask of the Lord in the name of the Father, the Son, and the Holy Spirit.
>
> (Prayer B,[71] Goar 1730, 707)[72]

The invocation to God generally includes a reference to qualities he possesses and/or expectations he has for humanity. In the case of this prayer, God has made salvation possible, and he wants people to love each other and find forgiveness in their hearts. This is followed by the request, which in the case of these prayers, is some variation on the idea God will strengthen the brothers' bond. And so it is here: may God, right here and now in this church, make these two men's spiritual love genuine.[73] The request also asks for a strengthening of faith, as well as the peace of the disciples (which suggests a relation that will [continue to] be harmonious), salvation, and eternal life. The prayer concludes with a doxology, or glorification of God. In the case of this prayer, God is glorified because he is merciful and loves humanity. The prayer closes with reference to Father, Son, and Holy Spirit.

The description of the ritual itself is brief. There is, to start, an *ektene*, which consists of nine petitions from the priest, each answered by the choir with a three-fold *kyrie*, while the celebrants pray silently.[74] The priest will also single out the prospective brothers during the *ektene*. Here is an example of brothers being highlighted in the midst of responsal prayers:

> Let us pray to the Lord for the slaves of God to come forward to be blessed in him and for their love in God. Let us pray to the Lord that the knowledge of apostolic singleness of mind be bestowed upon them. Let us pray to the Lord that faith without shame and genuine love be

offered to them. Let us pray to the Lord that they are deemed worthy of glory in the cross of honor.

(Goar 1730, 707)[75]

And so, after the *ektene* is complete, the priest recites Prayer B over them, "Lord, Our God, who has given graciously all things for salvation to us..." that begins the description in Dmitrievskij. The rite then concludes with the brothers kissing the bible and each other. The rite is ecclesiastical endorsement of a relation via words and physical actions.

Other manuscripts give more information about what the *adelphopoiesis* ritual was like. "An office and form for brother-making" (ἀκολουθία καὶ τάξις εἰς ἀδελφοποίησιν) from the thirteenth or fourteenth century[76] contains not one prayer like the ritual just discussed, but five, and it begins in this way:

Those about to become brothers advance to the priest and he takes the bible to the heart of the altar. The first brother places his hand on the bible and the second [brother places] his hand on the hand of the first brother, and then, having made the sign of the cross over them, the priest proceeds with the service...

(Panagou 2010, 187–188)[77]

There follow abbreviated notes on liturgy, which is responsal and which, as in the previous ritual discussed, has occasion to mention the brothers. The priest then says the prayer that Rapp calls A.[78] Following are a wish for peace, a directive for all to bow their heads,[79] and four prayers in succession: the one from the previous discussion that Rapp calls B,[80] and then prayers K, C, and I.[81] When these prayers are concluded, as in the previous rite, the brothers kiss the bible and each other and the rite is finished.[82]

One last liturgy is worth attention. This one, from a twelfth-century manuscript,[83] has been chosen for the presence of Ps 132/133 in it.[84] Here is its beginning:

[Prayer] for *Adelphopoiia*:
When they are putting their hands on each other, the priest places a cross on them and says Ps 132[/133]: "Indeed look! What is beautiful, or what is pleasant, or, especially, when brothers live together...?" three times, all the way to the blessing and life. [And then] the priest says the prayer...

(Panagou 2010, 125)[85]

The rite begins with the men putting their hands on each other. The priest lays a cross on them, most likely with one hand, while he recites Ps 132/133 three times, reading from a text he holds in the other hand. Ps 132/133 is well suited to a brother-making ritual:

Indeed look! What is beautiful, or what is pleasant, or, especially, when brothers live together with the same thing in mind? Like myrrh from the head flowing down the beard, the beard of Aaron, flowing to the fringe of his cloak; like the dew of Aermon which falls upon the hills of Zion. For here the Lord gave his blessing, life even everlasting.

(Ps 132/133)[86]

The psalm praises a home in which brothers live together in harmony. It is beautiful and inspires pleasure. The psalm proposes a number of equivalencies to this beautiful and pleasant state of affairs. First, there is the myrrh on the head of Aaron that suffuses his beard down to his collar. The bearded and manly body of Aaron with fragrant oil on it is a thing of delectation and pleasure.[87] This comparison of concord between brothers to the body of Aaron gives way to another one of moisture that comes from above: dew that falls on the hills of the holy land. This leads to a further implicit comparison. This place where the dew falls is the place where life received a blessing of eternity that flowed down from God.[88] Repeated three times over the brothers who have their hands on each other and a cross laid upon them, Ps 132/133 offers a series of striking visions which three-fold repetition emphasizes: manly Aaron, a beard fetching in perfume, dew falling upon the holy land, and a blessing of everlasting life all mix together in a complexity of brotherly togetherness, masculinity, fluids, Septuagintal glamor, and both bodies and life made eternal.[89] This psalm, luxuriant, packs a punch in this setting: the sublimations of devotion coexist with somatic presence. Two prayers follow, Rapp's Prayers E and H,[90] the second of which is accompanied by the bowing of heads.[91] In this ritual, there is no mention of final kisses and the rest, but they may be assumed because the manuscript is on the earlier side; it shows the tendency of the earlier testimonia to include fewer details.

In summation, *adelphopoiesis*/ἀδελφοποίησις, or the making of men into *adelphoi pneumatikoi*/ἀδελφοὶ πνευματικοί had its own prayers and the broader liturgical context featured such things as responsal *ektenai*/ἐκτεναί, prayers to God and the trinity, and readings of scripture. The holy book was touched by the men and they could have a cross put on them. There was physical contact between the brothers: hands on one another and kisses. The priest touched the men also. *Adelphopoiesis* was not just words; it was also a physical experience. Lastly, this ritual blessed a preexisting relation: the brothers brought their connection into the church.[92] This moment in the church influenced life outside of the church, but it was also the case that the outside came in. Much as epistolography has both the things of scripture and of carnal life in it, such that it is hard to see where one ends and the other one begins, so even a prayer could seem to have its life both in the church and outside of it.

A Tenth-Century Prayer: "A Thing Flowery and Much-desired by Us, The Sweet Scent of Love"

An elaborate prayer, which only occurs once in the manuscripts,[93] survives in a manuscript that dates to the first half of the tenth century, the time of the historiographers of Basil I.[94] This prayer, "A thing flowery and much-desired by us, the sweet scent of love" is Rapp's prayer D.⁹⁵ It is lavish and benefits from consideration in relation to elite Byzantine homosocial culture.

The prayer is long, in excess of 600 words of Greek. It has ambitions to style, and so recalls a cosmopolitan and educated milieu. Ring composition is present, as it opens with "the sweet scent of love" (ἡ τῆς ἀγάπης εὐωδία) which then recurs toward the end of the prayer. There are other moments that point to careful composition of the prayer, so it may appeal to literary sensibilities. Love is "fulfilled" many times. The structure of invocation-request-doxology is blurred, since after the request for the brothers-to-be, the doxology seemingly has begun, but then a request for all the members of the congregation appears amid a brilliant haze of praises via the Septuagint and New Testament. This expansive adjustment to the usual structure, such that a hybrid of request and doxology is visible, creates an impression of masterful textual control and demonstrates an ability to address multiple audiences at the same time, i.e., those looking for practicalities will not be disappointed, and those, whom sophistication in language might please, will be gratified. Lastly, there is a series of comparisons between heaven and earth that provoke reflections on connections between heavenly love and love down here on earth:

Εὐχὴ ἄλλη εἰς ἀδελφοποιησίαν·

Ἀνθηρὸν ἡμῖν καὶ πολυπόθητον ἡ τῆς ἀγάπης εὐωδία ἄγει ταῖς πατρικαῖς ἀρχαῖς τεθεμελιωμένη καὶ προφητικαῖς φωναῖς ὁδηγουμένη καὶ ἀποστολικοῖς κηρύγμασιν ἡγιασμένη, ὅτι πάντων τῶν καλῶν τῶν ἐπὶ τῆς γῆς ὑπεράγει ἡ ἀγάπη· Ἀβραὰμ ὁ προπάτωρ ἡμῶν ὑπὸ τὴν δρῦν τὴν Μαμβρῆ τὴν ἀγάπην ἐτέλεσεν, καὶ λαβὼν ἀρχὴν τῆς ἀγάπης "ἐπίστευσεν τῷ Θεῷ καὶ ἐλογίσθη αὐτῷ εἰς δικαιοσύνην" καὶ κληρονόμον κέκτηται τῆς ἀγάπης τὸν πρωτότοκον Ἰσαὰκ ἐν εὐλογίαις, τὸν τῆς πίστεως ἀρραβῶνα, τὸν τῆς θυσίας θυμιατήν, τὸν τοῦ σωτῆρος προμηνυτήν, τὸν τῆς δικαιοσύνης διάδοχον, τὸν πατέρα πολλῶν ἐθνῶν καὶ θεμέλιον τῆς ἐκκλησίας·

Αὐτὸς οὖν, Δέσποτα Κύριε, δώρησαι καὶ τοῖς δούλοις σου Δ καὶ Δ τὴν ἀγάπην καὶ τὴν εἰρήνην τῶν ἁγίων σου μαθητῶν, ἣν ἐδωρήσω αὐτοῖς λέγων "εἰρήνην τὴν ἐμὴν δίδωμι ὑμῖν καὶ εἰρήνην τὴν ἐμὴν ἀφίημι ὑμῖν." Αὕτη οὖν ἡ ἀγάπη τοὺς ἁγίους ἀποστόλους διὰ τῆς φιλαδελφίας συνήγαγεν εἰς τὸν εὔδιον λιμένα τῆς ἐκκλησίας. Ἡ ἀγάπη τοὺς ἁγίους σου μάρτυρας τοὺς πόνους διὰ τῶν ἄθλων τὴν ὑπομονὴν ἐδίδαξεν, ἵνα τὸν ἀμαράντινον στέφανον τῆς αἰωνίου δόξης κληρονομήσουσιν. Ἡ ἀγάπη τοὺς προφήτας ὑπεδέξατο ἀγγελικὴν διακονίαν ἐκτελέσαι, ἡ ἀγάπη τοῦ σωτῆρος γέγονεν πρόδρομος ἐκτελοῦσα τὰς διακονίας πᾶσιν τοῖς ἁγίοις, ἡ ἀγάπη τὰ τέκνα αὐτῆς τῷ Θεῷ θυσίαν παρέστησεν τοὺς τὴν φιλαδελφίαν ἀγαπήσαντας καὶ τὴν φιλοξενίαν τῶν πενήτων τὴν πρὸς τὸν Θεὸν ποιήσαντας, ἣν παραλαμβάνουσιν παρὰ Χριστοῦ μυριονταπλασίονα.

Another Prayer for *Adelphopoiesia*:[96]

[INVOCATION:] A thing flowery and much-desired by us, the sweet scent of love—established in our forefathers' beginnings, led by the voices of the prophets, and then made holy through apostolic pronouncements—leads (us), because love surpasses all beautiful things on earth. Our forefather, Abraham, under the oak at Mamre (Gen 18:1) brought love to fulfillment, and taking a beginning from love, "he trusted in God and he relied on him for justice" (Gen 15:6) and he came to possess the heir of love, Isaac, the first-born in blessings: the pledge of faith, the censer in sacrifice, the one who foretells the savior, the successor of justice, the father of the many peoples, and foundation of the church.

[REQUEST:] And so, God, Our Master, may you yourself give to your slaves, x and y, the love and peace of your holy disciples, which you gave to them saying, "I give you my peace and leave you my peace" (cf. Jn 14:27). And so love itself led the holy apostles through brotherly affection to the calm harbor of the church. Love taught your holy martyrs the endurance of travails in trials, so they would be heir to the never-fading crown of eternal glory. Love enabled the prophets to bring their proclamatory service to utter fulfillment. Love, forerunner of the savior, became the bringing of the service of all the saints to utter fulfillment. Love has offered for sacrifice to God its children, those who have loved brotherly affection and those who have aided the poor in service to God, for which they receive from Christ [love] ten-thousand fold.

Ἡμεῖς δὲ διὰ τῆς ἀγάπης δοξάζομεν τὸν Θεὸν καὶ πατέρα τοῦ Κυρίου ἡμῶν Ἰησοῦ Χριστοῦ, τὸν συγκαλεσάμενον ἡμᾶς ἐκ τόπων διαφόρων ἐλθεῖν καὶ θεάσασθαι τὸν τῆς ἀγάπης θησαυρόν, ὃν πάντες οἱ ἅγιοι ποθήσαντες στέφανον ἀμαράντινον πλέξαντες ἄξια τῷ Θεῷ προσεκόμισαν δῶρα. Ταύτην τὴν ἀγάπην ποθήσας Ἄβελ τὸ πρωτότοκον ἀρνίον τῷ Θεῷ προσεκόμισεν· ταύτην τὴν ἀγάπην ποθήσας Ἐνὼχ ὁ γραμματεὺς τῇ δικαιοσύνῃ εὐηρέστησεν τῷ Θεῷ, ἡ ἀγάπη τὸν Ἀβραὰμ ἐπιστώσατο, ἵνα τοῖς ἀγγέλοις δοχὴν ἑτοιμάσῃ, ἡ ἀγάπη τὸν Λὼτ ἐκ Σωδόμων ἔσωσεν. Ταύτην τὴν ἀγάπην ποθήσας Ἀβραὰμ τὸν μονογενῆ αὐτοῦ υἱὸν τῷ Θεῷ θυσίαν προσεκόμισεν, ταύτην τὴν ἀγάπην ποθήσας Ἰακὼβ ὁ σοφώτατος τὴν εὐλογίαν τοῦ Ἡσαῦ ἐκληρονόμησεν. Ἡ ἀγάπη τὸν Δανιὴλ ἐκ στομάτων λεόντων ἐρρύσατο, ἡ ἀγάπη τὸν Ἠλίαν ἐν ἅρματι πυρίνῳ εἰς οὐρανοὺς ἀναληφθῆναι ἐποίησεν, ἡ ἀγάπη τὸν Ἐλισσαῖον ἐν τῷ ὄρει διέσωσεν. Ταύτην τὴν ἀγάπην ποθήσαντες οἱ ἅγιοι τρεῖς παῖδες ἐν τῇ καμίνῳ τοῦ πυρὸς ἀπεδύσαντο καὶ ὕμνον εὐωδίας τῷ Θεῷ προσεκόμισαν. Καὶ πάντες σὲ γινώσκομεν διὰ τῆς ἀγάπης τὸν ἐπὶ πάντων Θεόν, οἱ δοῦλοι τὸν δεσπότην, οἱ θνητοὶ τὸν ἀθάνατον, οἱ πρόσκαιροι τὸν αἰώνιον, οἱ ἐπίγειοι τὸν ἐπουράνιον. Οὐκ ἐπιτάσσομεν, ἀλλὰ παρακαλοῦμεν, αὐτῷ δεόμεθα καὶ δεομένων ἡμῶν ἐπάκουσον. Σὺ γὰρ εἶπας, Δέσποτα, "αἰτεῖτε καὶ δοθήσεται ὑμῖν· ζητεῖτε καὶ εὑρήσετε· κρούετε καὶ ἀνοιγήσεται ὑμῖν. Πᾶς γὰρ ὁ αἰτῶν λαμβάνει καὶ ζητῶν εὑρίσκει καὶ τῷ κρούοντι ἀνοιγήσεται."

Ἡμεῖς οὖν, Δέσποτα φιλάνθρωπε, μεμνημένοι τῶν ἁγίων σου ἐντολῶν τῆς φοβερᾶς καὶ ἐνδόξου σου διαθήκης, κρούομεν ἐπὶ γῆς, ἄνοιξον ἡμῖν ἐν οὐρανοῖς, δὸς ἡμῖν μέρος μετὰ πάντων τῶν ἁγίων σου ἀγγέλων πίστεως καὶ ἀγάπης, κατάστησον ἐφ' ἡμᾶς τοιοῦτον ἡμῖν ἄγγελον τὸν τοῦ Ἀβραὰμ ὁδηγόν, τὸν τοῦ Ἰσαὰκ στρατηγόν, τὸν τοῦ Ἰακὼβ συνοδοιπόρον, τὸν τοῦ Λαζάρου ἐξυπνιστήν, τὸν εἰσελθόντα εἰς τὸν οἶκον Ζακχαίου τοῦ ἀρχιτελώνου καὶ εἰπόντι αὐτῷ "σήμερον σωτηρία τῷ οἴκῳ τούτῳ ἐγένετο." Ὅπου γὰρ ἀγάπη γίνεται, ἐχθρὸς οὐ καταπονεῖ, δαίμων οὐ κυριεύει, ἁμαρτία οὐ γίνεται, τρία γάρ εἰσιν ταῦτα· πίστις, ἐλπίς, μείζων δὲ πάντων ἀγάπη. Θαυμαστὴ καὶ πολυπόθητος ἡ τῆς ἀγάπης εὐωδία ἐπὶ γῆς σπείρει τὸν σῖτον τῆς εὐσεβείας καὶ ἐν οὐρανοῖς συλλέγει τῆς δικαιοσύνης τὰ δράγματα "Ἐσκόρπισεν, ἔδωκεν τοῖς πένησιν, ἡ δικαιοσύνη αὐτοῦ μένει εἰς τὸν αἰῶνα τοῦ αἰῶνος." Καὶ ἡμεῖς διὰ τῆς ἀγάπης παρακαλοῦμεν τὴν σὴν φιλανθρωπίαν "κλῖνον τὸ οὖς σου" τὸ ἅγιον "εἰς τὴν δέησιν" ἡμῶν δεομένων σου.

Ὅτι σὺ εἶ ὁ χορηγὸς τῶν ἀγαθῶν καὶ σωτὴρ τῶν ψυχῶν ἡμῶν, καὶ σοὶ τὴν δόξαν ἀναπέμπομεν τῷ Πατρὶ καὶ τῷ Υἱῷ καὶ τῷ ἁγίῳ Πνεύματι.

[DOXOLOGY/ REQUEST:][97] Through love we glorify God and father of our Lord Christ who has summoned us to come from various places and see the treasure of love, which all the saints, desiring, having woven a never-fading crown, have offered as worthy gifts to God. Desiring this love, Abel offered his first-born lamb to God. Desiring this love, Enoch the scribe pleased God with his justice. Love convinced Abraham so he made ready a feast for angels. Love rescued Lot from Sodom. Desiring this love, Abraham offered his only-begotten son to God as a sacrifice. Desiring this love, the most wise Jakob inherited the blessing of Esau. Love rescued Daniel from lions' jaws. Love made it so Elijah was taken up to heaven in a fiery chariot. Love saved Elisha on the mountain. Desiring this love, the three holy children in the furnace of fire undressed and offered a hymn of sweet scent to God (Dan 3:91–94). And we, all of us, also know you to be God of all through love; slaves know their master (*sc.* through love); mortals know the immortal (*sc.* through love); those of the moment know the eternal (*sc.* through love); those who live on earth know the one in heaven (*sc.* through love). We do not order but call out. We pray to you yourself and please hear us as we pray. For you have said, Master, "Ask and it will be given to you. Seek and you will find. Knock and it will be opened for you. Everyone asking receives; everyone seeking finds, and for the one knocking, it will be opened" (Mt 7:7–8/Lk 11:9).

Remembering the holy commandments of your fearful and glorious covenant, Master who has affection for mankind, we knock while on earth, please open for us in heaven. Grant to us a share of faith and love with all your holy angels. Place over us an angel like the one who guided Abraham, the general of Isaac, the travel-companion of Jakob, the awakener of Lazarus, the one who went to the house of Zakchaios the chief tax-collector, and [said] to him after he had spoken, "today salvation has happened in this house" (Lk 19:9). For where there is love, the enemy does not oppress; the demon does not hold sway; there is no sin. For there are three things: faith, hope, and, greater than all, love (1 Cor 13:13). Wonderous and much-desired is the sweet scent of love. On earth it (*sc.* love) sows the grain of piety and in heaven it harvests the sheaves of justice. "He has provided for and given to the poor; his justice stays forever and ever" (Ps 111/112:9; 2 Cor 9:9). And on account of love, we call upon your affection for humanity. "Incline your ear" holy "to our prayer" as we pray to you (cf. Ps 87/88:3).

[DOXOLOGY:] Because you are the bestower of good things and savior of our souls, we send glory up to you, the Father, and to the Son and to the Holy Spirit. (Prayer D,[98] Panagou 2010, 339–342 [Εὐχὴ Δ'] is the text, altered slightly.[99])

144 Framing the Brotherhoods

In words that recall the luxuriousness of the epistolographers, the invocation commences in sensual fashion with flowers, desire, sweet scent, and beautiful things. Love (*agape*/ἀγάπη) is important, repeated five times and many more times later in the prayer. After this brief focus on the present, the prayer cuts to Genesis and speaks of the miraculous arrival of Isaac, son of Abraham and Sara, who had been regarded as too old to bear a child. Love is a prime mover through the story and Isaac crystallizes all the power of history in himself going forward. He foretold the arrival of Jesus, brought law, fathered peoples, and made the church possible.

With this historical prospect of the power of love in place, the prayer passes to the request for love *and* peace (peace appears here for the first time) of the disciples for the two brothers-to-be. There follows a (mildly inexact) quotation of the words of Jesus from John (Jn 14:27),[100] the broader context of which includes verb related to love (*agape*/ἀγάπη), *agapao*/ἀγαπάω.[101]

The prayer continues to emphasize the power of *agape*, as love appears seven times in the request prior to its hybridization with doxology.[102] Love lashed the apostles together and brought them to the "calm harbor of the church." Love helped the martyrs endure tortures. Love brought the work of prophets and saints to fulfillment, which echoes the prior mention of how Abraham brought love to fulfillment at Mamre. Love motivated those who loved both community ("brotherly affection" *philadelphian*/φιλαδελφίαν), and the poor to sacrifice themselves, actions which Christ lavishly rewarded with, it is understood, love.

Next, the hybridization of request and doxology begins. Love's marked presence continues, appearing 18 times. Love, called a treasure at one point, is explicitly a thing desired seven times,[103] an agent that makes things happen eight times,[104] and three times it is not easy to decide if love is object or agent, which means it may be both.[105] The saints weave a crown and figures from the Septuagint follow: Abel, Enoch, Abraham, Lot,[106] Abraham (again), Jakob, Esau, Daniel, Elijah, Elisha, and the three children (men) who hymned God, naked, in the furnace into which they had been thrown by Nabouchodonosor.[107] It is significant, too, that they sing a hymn of "sweet scent" (*euodias*/εὐωδίας) while in the furnace. Sweet scent recalls the opening of the prayer and will appear again toward the prayer's end.

As the prayer continues, love is the guarantee for structures and ideas important to Byzantine society: relations between man and God, slave and master, mortal and immortal, the contingent and the eternal. Following this, request language returns, this time to God on behalf of everyone in the church and perhaps the world. It is quotation of Mt 7:7–8/Lk 11:9 on the efficacy of prayer: those who pray are like those who knock on a door with someone attentive and loving on the other side. This leads to further reflections on the nature of the relationship between God and humankind. To the extent that humankind remembers the commandments, then this knocking on earth will yield results in heaven. Subsequent is a request for faith and love, such as the angels possess. Indeed, the priest makes a plea for an angel, of the kind that was there for Abraham, Isaac, and Jakob.

And then, as the list continues and passes over into the New Testament, this angel changes into Jesus with the awakening of Lazarus and the news of salvation brought about by the change of heart in Zakchaios to help the poor and return fourfold ill-gotten gains (Lk 19:8). The words Jesus said after announcing that salvation had come to Zakchaios' house are relevant to analysis of this prayer:

> And Jesus said to him (Zakchaios), "today salvation has happened in this house, because this very one is also son of Abraham."
>
> (Lk 19:9)[108]

The relation that Jesus asserts exists between Zakchaios and Abraham recalls the earlier part of the prayer where Abraham "brought love to fulfillment"[109] under the Oak of Mamre. Love worked overtly there in the prayer and, while hidden here, is nonetheless present and efficacious.

Love becomes overt again with a listing of powers that love has; love protects the people from enemies, the devil, and sin. There is reference to Paul's encomium of *agape* in 1 Corinthians, which makes love the greatest of the trinity of faith, hope and love (13:13). And then, there follows a sentence that recalls the opening of the prayer. Here is the opening phrase of the prayer followed by the sentence later in the prayer that echoes it:

> A thing flowery and much-desired by us, the sweet scent of love...
> (Ἀνθηρὸν ἡμῖν καὶ πολυπόθητον ἡ τῆς ἀγάπης εὐωδία...)
>
> Wonderous and much-desired is the sweet scent of love...
> (Θαυμαστὴ καὶ πολυπόθητος ἡ τῆς ἀγάπης εὐωδία...)

Wonder, which calls to mind the wonderment the young Basil I caused in historiographies surveyed earlier, replaces flowers in this later evocation of the sweet scent of love. This rewriting brings more of the outside in, as it were: wonder is now added to desire, flowers, love, and sweet scent. Indeed, sweet smells are important in this prayer. Sweet scent occurs three times and Isaac, early on, is called, among other things, "the censer in sacrifice." All of these appeals to the nose are something to keep in mind, as there are connections to scripture and to cultivated literature outside of church.

The prayer then concludes with one last look at the power of love. It sows on earth the crop that is harvested in heaven. Then there is quotation of Ps 111/112, which 2 Corinthians also quotes, speaking of God's solicitude for the poor and of his eternal justice. After one last plea that God listen to the prayers sent his way, the prayer ends with a moment of pure doxology. In words and sentiments that recall other brotherhood prayers, there is glorification of God's divine goodness, in this case God is the bestower of good things and savior of souls, followed by the sending of glory up to God, the Son, and the Holy Spirit.

Framing "A Thing Flowery and Much-desired by Us, The Sweet Scent of Love"

Here again is the opening sentence, which sets an agenda:

> A thing flowery and much-desired by us, the sweet scent of love—established in our forefathers' beginnings, led by the voices of the prophets, and then made holy through apostolic pronouncements—leads (us), because love surpasses all the beautiful things on earth.[110]

After leading sensually with flowers, desire, and "the sweet scent of love," the sentence makes a promise, which it keeps through the thicket of scriptural citations to come in the prayer, to consider love and to be led by it on a journey through the Septuagint and thence to the New Testament. The sentence concludes with a statement of the value of *agape*: it is greater than "all the beautiful things on earth" (πάντων τῶν καλῶν τῶν ἐπὶ τῆς γῆς). Whether this is a tribute to the power of love such that it has won a contest with other earthly things, or that *agape* ought to be considered above and beyond things called beautiful on earth, is and remains an open question. It also turns out, as will be seen below, that "sweet scent" (*euodia*/ εὐωδία) is both in the physical world and transcendent of it. The location of "sweet scent of love" in the world and beyond it addresses the fact that brothers-to-be, who live in this world with a connection that preexists this ritual, are orienting their connection to God and heaven. What one, say, brother-to-be might think at the beginning of the prayer about sweet scent and love, about earth and heaven, and, finally, how these relate to his life and the connection to his brother are things the prayer encourages him to return to: love is everywhere in the prayer and sweet scent appears three times.

So, what would have an educated brother-to-be or a member of the congregation thought when they heard these words: "a thing flowery and much-desired by us, the sweet scent of love?" Given this is a ritual in a church, scripture is a good place to start.

Scripture

In the Septuagint, *euodia*/εὐωδία ("sweet scent") occurs over 50 times to refer to sacrifice to God. It appears often with the noun "smell" (*osme*/ὀσμή), and these two words frequently accompany the preposition *eis*/εἰς to form a common phrase *eis osmen euodias*/εἰς ὀσμὴν εὐωδίας, which, while difficult to translate into English, might be rendered, awkwardly literal, as "for the purpose of the smell of sweet scent." This phrase refers to sacrifices of various kinds to God. They can be of animals ritually slaughtered and then cooked, which creates smoke to delight God:

> [Yaweh:] And you will take one ram, and Aaron and his sons will lay their hands on the ram's head. You will slaughter it and taking the blood pour it in a circle on the altar. You will dismember the ram and clean

the entrails and hooves with water and place them on the dismembered parts with the head. You will offer the whole ram back at the altar as a burnt offering to the Lord for the purpose of the smell of sweet scent. This is a mode of sacrifice to the Lord.

(Ex 29:15–18)[111]

Offerings of libations and fruits, also "for the purpose of the smell of sweet scent," can accompany animal sacrifice:

[Yaweh:] You will do [as sacrifice] one lamb in the morning and a second lamb in the afternoon; and a tenth [measure] of fine wheat flour mixed in a fourth of a *hin* of beaten oil and a libation of a fourth of a *hin* for the one lamb. And you will do [as sacrifice] the second lamb in the afternoon, like the morning sacrifice and like the libation for it, you will do [as sacrifice] an offering of fruit to the Lord for the purpose of the smell of sweet scent, a sacrifice persisting through your generations at the doors of the tabernacle of witness before the Lord, and through these acts I will be known to you there with the result that I speak to you.

(Ex 29:39–42)[112]

So anyone who had awareness of scripture, which would include everyone at a posited tenth-century *adelphopoiesis* ceremony, and who heard *euodia* in this prayer in church, was going to be thinking of sacrifice to the God of Israelites (and the Byzantines).

Occasionally, *euodia* appears separately from sacrifice in the Septuagint. "Sweet scent" is twice an attribute of the fragrant trees, "an entire of wood of sweet scent," that God makes grow up to shade the Israelites.[113] At Sir 24:15, wisdom or Sophia speaks of how nice she smells: "like cinnamon and aspalathus I have given off the smell (*osmen*/ὀσμήν) of perfumes, and as the best myrrh, I have given off sweet scent (*euodian*/εὐωδίαν)."[114] Given the presence of smell (*osme*/ὀσμή) nearby, the gravitational pull of sacrificial language is strong. But at the same time, this sweet scent belongs to an abstraction, and so pulls away from sacrifice's physicality. The move to abstraction prefigures the semantic drift of "smell of sweet scent" in the letters of Paul, as he uses the phrase to refer to things other than ritual sacrifice.

Paul twice uses the phrase "smell of sweet scent." It appears in Philippians where he calls the sustenance the people of Philippi have given him "the smell of sweet scent, an acceptable sacrifice, pleasing to God" (Phil 4:18).[115] The Septuagintal language aggrandizes the aid, probably money and/or food, he received, but it also, significantly, refers to things that are physical. His other use of the phrase occurs in the letter to the Ephesians:

Be therefore imitators of God, like beloved children, and walk in love, just as Christ loved us and gave himself on our behalf as an offering and sacrifice to God for the purpose of the smell of sweet scent (εἰς ὀσμὴν εὐωδίας).

(Eph 5:1–2)[116]

148 *Framing the Brotherhoods*

Paul refers to sacrifice here, but it is not of livestock, it is the prospective sacrifice the people will make of themselves in imitation of Christ, who gave up his body on the cross. Christ's sacrifice was physical but what is being asked of the people is something different than that. With the physical sacrifice of Christ in mind, the people, beloved (*agapeta*/ἀγαπητά) children whom Christ loved (*egapesen*/ἠγάπησεν), take the lesson and build community, i.e., "walk in love." Significant in the present circumstances is the arrival of love. It is reasonable to imagine someone hearing the brotherhood prayer's phrase "the sweet scent of love" was going to remember Paul's addition of love to the Septuagintal sacrifice language.

In the second letter to the Corinthians, Paul does not directly quote the Septuagint phrase, but smell and sweet scent are present and close to one another:

> There is thanks to God who leads us everywhere in triumph in Christ and makes manifest the *smell* of knowledge of him through us in every place, because we are the *sweet scent* of Christ to God among those being saved and among those being lost. For some we are the *smell* of death [that leads] to death and to others we are the *smell* of life [that leads] to life.
>
> (2 Cor 2:14–16)[117]

The notion of imitation of Christ emerges here also. The people are the sweet scent of Christ and manifestation of God's will on Earth, as was Christ. Furthermore, the people are both the smell of life and of death. This is a typically dense Pauline formulation. The scent of death can refer to mortal bodies, while souls, consecrate to God, give off a scent that promises life. Paul intertwines the disembodied/transcendent with the embodied/physical. Scent works at the metaphorical level to express things that are abstract and at the literal level to express things that are physical: soul, knowledge of God, and even his will, on the one hand, and, on the other, actual bodies, doing what they should and heading toward life, or what they should not and heading toward death. The ambiguity around scent, especially "sweet scent," does not dissipate. Indeed, the people are this sweet scent to God, and are sweet in both the physical and the disembodied registers, just as Christ was.

Court Ceremonial and Epistolography

There is more to consider than the tension interior to Paul and between Paul and the Septuagint where sweet scent is concerned. The brothers-to-be would have come into the church with a preexisting relation, forged in the cosmopolitan world of court culture, a world which the cultivated prayer "A thing flowery and much-desired by us, the sweet scent of love" likely addressed and was responsive to. It is possible to track sweet scent, flowers and love outside of the church in these environs. Meanings these terms acquire outside of the church are brought into the church with the brothers and their relation.

In Constantine VII's *De Ceremoniis* are protocols to be followed for when it was time to celebrate the Vintage Festival.[118] At this festival, notable personages in the court each would receive a bunch of grapes from the emperor and the demes (the people) were present to chant. The chant featured a collocation of flowers and sweet scent in a religious setting:

> When the bunch of grapes is handed by the emperor to the first *magistros*, the two factions[119] recite in unison an *apelatikos*,[120] mode 1: "Having gathered flowers (*anthe*/ἄνθη) of wisdom from our ruler's meadow of knowledge, let us, the sacred order of honored *patrikioi*, while offering a wealth of hymns, crown his head, home to thoughts of sweet scent (*euodias*/εὐωδίας), receiving in return his delightful favors. Immortal Emperor of all (i.e., God), may you grant to the world for a long time this festival of the power of the sovereign X, the divinely crowned and anointed emperor."
> (*De cer.*, Book 2.176.3–13 [Vogt 1939]; R374–375; Book 1, Chapter 78/87)[121]

Of particular interest here is the presence of flowers and sweet scent in the emperor's head. The abode of authority, characterized in this way in a festival that had religious facets to it, accordingly had aspects in common with the prayer for a brotherhood ceremony.

What can be learned from interpreting this collocation is that the power of the emperor and his lofty mind were characterized by terms, flowers and sweet scent, that softened him and made him as welcoming as a spring garden. Imperial authority wished to project something soft. "The flowery much-desired sweet scent of love" from the prayer, also soft, made these relations to be sanctified ones that were fetching and pleasurable. Byzantine male self-styling, when the matter of connection was at issue—in the case of the festival, communal *cohesion*, and in the case of the prayer, the *joining* of two men—thought in terms of aesthetic beauty that would please the eye and nose. Physical indulgence in what is sensual characterizes these rites that foster connection.

Going to another part of court life and leaving Constantine VII's *De Ceremoniis*, but staying with the emperor, examination of a number of letters written to him by Theodoros of Kyzikos discovers flowers and sweet scent, with the addition of love, which makes for a tight fit with the prayer. For example, Theodoros' *Letter B4*, analyzed in a previous chapter, contains relevant language. This letter features Theodoros correcting Constantine's friendly biting to desirous/erotic biting, followed by the turning over the

150 *Framing the Brotherhoods*

soul, which calls to mind manhandling and sexual activity. After these audacious images, Theodoros speaks of sweet scent and flowers (and rejoicing):

> I have received recompense many times over for yesterday's fruits, these fruits that have nothing brilliant about them other than the fact that they were chosen [for you by me], [recompense that is these] ripe and sweet words of yours, words that, through desirous/erotic biting and turning over my soul have a sweet scent (*euodiazousin*/εὐωδιάζουσιν), more than how the praised scent of flowers (*anthosmias*/ἀνθοσμίας) knows how to make the hearts of men rejoice (*euphrainein*/εὐφραίνειν) or even nectar itself, on which the blessed ones used to get drunk.
>
> (Theodoros of Kyzikos, *Letter B4*)[122]

The sweet scent[123] and the scent of flowers recall the prayer and the word rejoice brings to mind the rejoicing in the bride of one's youth from Proverbs 5 and therefore the rejoicing of Nicholas and Basil after their brotherhood ceremony in the historiographies and *Letter 111* of Symeon the Logothete. This letter from the milieu of the writing of the historiographies and contemporaneous with the manuscript appearance of the prayer argues that an understanding of the opening of "A thing flowery and much-desired by us, the sweet scent of love" could hold an erotic charge. But Theodoros' correspondence is a gift that keeps on giving.

Letter A2 of Theodoros,[124] also addressed to Constantine, brings sweet scent, flowers and love into evidence. This lengthy letter begins with these words:

> How will I describe to you the keen pleasure which, sweetest and desired (*pothoumene*/ποθούμενε) master, your all-wise and honey-dripping chain of words has dripped upon this heart of mine? For, in reality, drops fragrant, as it were, or ambrosial, or of manna from that primeval rain or springs of nard and balsamon were flowing upon this soul of mine, [flowings that were] flowery (*antheroi*/ἀνθηροί), possessing a sweet scent (*euodeis*/εὐώδεις[125]), and thick with the flowers (*anthesi*/ἄνθεσι) of your speech's wisdom...
>
> (Theodoros of Kyzikos, *Letter A2*)[126]

In a luxurious atmosphere of desire and bodily pleasure (*hedone*/ἡδονή), Theodorus emphasizes the senses: moisture to feel, perfume to smell, honey to taste, and flowers to see. Later in the letter, in a return to this sensuality, another passage features desire and sweet scent again, with the addition of love:

> And already ablaze and, as it were, aflame in my soul with desire (*pothoi*/πόθῳ) for you—Come on! What were you thinking at that moment?—I have been burned by the dew-shedding flame (*drosoboloi puri*/δροσοβόλῳ πυρί) and light of your love (*agapes*/ἀγάπης) coming out of this letter, of a kind sufficient to drag, summon and persuade, on account of affection

Framing the Brotherhoods 151

for you, the nature of rocks, trees and, furthermore, wild beasts to run after the myrrh of your friendly sweet scent (*euodias*/εὐωδίας), just as Orpheus' lyre, so the story goes, charming the inanimate objects compelled them to follow him.

(Theodoros of Kyzikos, *Letter A2*)[127]

Present in *Letter A2* is the complete constellation of items in the opening to "A thing flowery and much-desired by us, the sweet scent of love": flowers, desire, sweet scent, and love. Again, it is evident that the prayer leads with the sort of erotic language found in epistolography. And this passage has two other items worth attention.

In the first place, there is the paradoxical phrase "dew-shedding flame." It is a fire that does not cause harm, and does the opposite: it refreshes with gentle moisture and is attractive, as the talk of affection, sweet scent, and Orpheus shows. Harmless flames, found in the company of love and sweet scent, appear in the prayer with the mention of the three men who were thrown into the fiery furnace by Nabouchodonosor:

> Desiring this love, the three holy children in the furnace of fire undressed and offered a hymn of sweet scent to God.[128]

Like these men, Theodoros loves amid sweet scent and flames that don't actually burn. And resort to the *Suda*'s entry for "*puraphlektos*/πυράφλεκτος" ("unburnt by fire")[129] shows "dew-shedding" was associated with this story from Daniel:

> When the burning Chaldaean furnace is at issue, it is said to be "blazing with fire," as in that [passage that says], "the children demonstrated long ago that the furnace blazing with fire was shedding dew (*drosobolousan*/δροσοβολοῦσαν)."
>
> (*Suda*, Pi 3195)[130]

And so, when Theodoros makes reference to "dew-shedding flame,"[131] he presents an image that is at home in erotic and ecclesiastical contexts, as are the other items (desire, love, sweet scent) shared by his letters and the prayer.

There is another intertextuality between *Letter A2* and scripture: this time with Song of Songs. Here again from *LetterA2* is the end of the passage being discussed:

> ...this letter, of a kind sufficient <u>to drag</u>, summon and persuade, on account of affection for you, the nature of rocks, trees and, furthermore, wild beasts to <u>run after the myrrh of your</u> friendly sweet scent...
>
> ...τῆς τοιαύτης γραφῆς, ἣ καὶ λίθων φύσιν καὶ δένδρων προσέτι καὶ ἀγρίων θηρῶν ἱκανὴ ἦν πρὸς τὸ περὶ σὲ φίλτρον <u>ἑλκῦσαι</u> καὶ ἐκκαλέσασθαι καὶ πεῖσαι <u>ὀπίσω τρέχειν τοῦ μύρου</u> τῆς φιλικῆς εὐωδίας <u>σου</u>...

Theodoros' words are intertextual with the rapturous beginning of the Song of Songs:

> Let him kiss me with kisses from his mouth. Because your breasts are excellent beyond wine and the smell of your myrrh surpasses all aromas. Your name is myrrh poured out. The maidens therefore loved you, and <u>they have dragged</u> you, and <u>we will run after you</u>[132] toward the smell <u>of your myrrh</u>. The emperor[133] has led me into his closet. Let us luxuriate and rejoice in you, we will love your breasts surpassing wine: [my] uprightness loved you.
>
> (S of S 1:2–4)

> Φιλησάτω με ἀπὸ φιλημάτων στόματος αὐτοῦ, ὅτι ἀγαθοὶ μαστοί σου ὑπὲρ οἶνον, καὶ ὀσμὴ μύρων σου ὑπὲρ πάντα τὰ ἀρώματα, μύρον ἐκκενωθὲν ὄνομά σου. διὰ τοῦτο νεάνιδες ἠγάπησάν σε, <u>εἵλκυσάν</u> σε, <u>ὀπίσω</u> σου εἰς ὀσμὴν <u>μύρων σου δραμοῦμεν</u>. Εἰσήνεγκέν με ὁ βασιλεὺς εἰς τὸ ταμίειον αὐτοῦ. Ἀγαλλιασώμεθα καὶ εὐφρανθῶμεν ἐν σοί, ἀγαπήσομεν μαστούς σου ὑπὲρ οἶνον· εὐθύτης ἠγάπησέν σε.

The kaleidoscopic opening to Song of Songs features frequently changing gender in the speaking voice, and erotic investment in and display of, now, a woman's body and, now, a man's. There are kisses for the speaker from a man; breasts whose loveliness leaves fine wines in the shade; myrrh expressing the totality of the desired one's being; maidens pulling on the desired one; a speaker (joining up with the maidens? voicing the maidens?) running after the one who smells so good; an emperor taking the speaker aside into a private place; rejoicing that recalls Pr 5; a return of the breasts; and finally a double-entendre for an erection ("[my] uprightness [εὐθύτης] loved you").

There is something for everyone in this passage. The speaker can seem to be a man and, other times, a woman. And there is more than one way to read it, but it is unmistakable that the gender of the speaking voice is unstable. The desire in view is mostly that which men and women might feel for each other. But desire between women perhaps briefly registers at least once ("the maidens therefore loved you…"). And desire of man for man possibly registers with "we will run after you" and is eminently possible in the case of the emperor's closet. Lastly, the enticing and enduring ambiguity of reference of this passage is most evident when the journey the first person goes on is highlighted. At the beginning, he kisses *me* with his mouth; *we*, along with the maidens, will run after you; while at the end, *we* rejoice in you and love your breasts, and it is (*my*) uprightness, *sc.* erection, that has loved you. This reads as moving from passive to active and from woman to man, and, again, same-sex reference is possible at multiple spots.

It is clear that the dragging, running after, and myrrh in Theodoros' letter are meant to recall the Septuagint. The strong textual resemblances increase the eroticism of his letter, which is not surprising from Theodoros.

Furthermore, if Emperor Constantine had picked up on the references to the Septuagint and remembered a nearby verse, then the eroticism of the letter increased again; "the emperor has led me into his closet" possesses an erotic charge when addressed to an emperor (βασιλεύς), especially as mention of an erection is coming shortly.

Some degree of territory has been traversed from the opening of "A thing flowery and much-desired by us, the sweet scent of love" to *Letter A2* and thence into Song of Songs. But not that far, actually: it is but one degree of separation from the prayer to Song of Songs. And besides, another analysis could start from the prayer and be thinking already of Song of Songs on the basis of interpersonal connection and love, being in church, and an equivalence between "sweet scent" and, in Song of Songs, aromas (*ta aromata*/τὰ ἀρώματα) and repeated references to myrrh.

The coincidences of language in the prayer with both scripture and secular productions, as has been shown here with discussion of the letters between Constantine and Theodoros and other sources, can be duplicated. One could mention, for example, Nikephoros Ouranos' *Letter 50* in which he centers the perception of sweet scent in his warm letter to John Ostiarios.[134] And *Letter 26* of Nikephoros Ouranos, which was discussed in the introduction to this book, features talk of flowers, spring, religious feeling, and togetherness. In any case, these analyses have demonstrated the kind of mental associations that were eminently possible to occur to brothers-to-be or members of the congregation when they heard the words of "A thing flowery and much-desired by us, the sweet scent of love" in the church.

Conclusion

Interpretation of the intertextualities in the narrations of Basil I's brotherhoods and in the brotherhood rituals and prayers has suggested a range of thoughts that a reader of the historiographies and witnesses and participants in the ritual could have had. This reparative analysis has suggested that *adelphopoiesis* is an indicative site of conflicting energies in Byzantine society around masculine togetherness. A ritual brotherhood was the bringing together of men, who already had a connection, in a societal structure, the church, which had strong ideas about what was appropriate and not appropriate. The church took a hard line against corporealities of all kinds, so everyone who was going to be sexual had some or a lot of finessing to do. But there were ideas about and indulgences in masculine same-sex desire and sexual behavior in this society that conflicted with the church. These ideas and indulgences coexisted with ecclesiastical sanctions and the rite of *adelphopoiesis* showcases the fact that the empire was a place of competing discourses around the homosociality of its men. Nicholas saw a handsome lad destined for great things, as a divine voice said, so they went to a church to become brothers, and after that "rejoiced in one another." Basil I, beloved of God, proved his mettle provocatively, an illustrated manuscript reports, in a wrestling match. The evident and elaborate carnal intertextuality in "A thing flowery and much-desired by us, the sweet scent of love" needs no further elaboration.

Brothers-to-be brought their existing relation with them into the church prior to being made ritual brothers. There were a variety of reasons, e.g., ambition, fear, desire, for becoming ritual brothers, and these reasons depended on the existing relation. *Adelphopoiesis* did not address sex, but the physicality of the ritual and the words in the prayers could call it to mind, and the brothers might have already had some experience of sexual intimacy anyway. These facts make ritual brotherhood an aspect of Byzantine society that needs to be positioned carefully in relation to the sum total of Byzantine men's homosociality. Historians must resist the impulse to smooth out contradictions, and should, instead, cultivate a perspective that accepts that conflicting discourses were in play in the medieval empire, as the extended contextualization of "A thing flowery and much-desired by us, the sweet scent of love" has shown. Vocabulary and concepts were being shared across ecclesiastical and secular/erotic contexts. As church told society what must be, so society visibly brought desire and ideas back in, even in contravention of the church.[135] Opposing discourses shared the same spaces.

Appendix of Prayers

Note: The prayers are printed in the order that they are referred to in Chapter 3.

Prayer A (Rapp)/Prayer 1 (Panagou)

Text = Parenti and Velkovska (2011), section 211 (*TLG*).

(See Panagou 2010, 337 [Εὐχὴ Αʹ; the doxology is not printed by Panagou]; Rapp 2016, 293 [Prayer A]; cf. Goar 1730, 707; Dmitrievskij 1901/1965, 215; Boswell 1995, 313–314, 352.)

Prayer for *Adelphopoiesis*:

[INVOCATION:] Lord God, master of all, who made humanity according to your image and likeness and gave to it eternal life, who thought it right that your holy and wholly blessed apostles Peter, the utter leader, and Andrew, Jakob and John, the sons Zebedaios, and Philip and Bartholomew, become brothers of one another, not bound in the way of nature, but in the way of faith and the Holy Spirit, and also thought it worthy that your holy martyrs Sergios and Bacchos, Kosmas and Damianos, and Cyrus and John become brothers: [REQUEST:] also bless your slaves x and y, not bound in the way of nature but in the way of faith. Grant to them that they love one another, that their brotherhood be without hate and without offence and, for all the days of their life, be in the power of the Holy Spirit; with the intercession of the entirely holy and stainless mistress of us, the *theotokos* and always virgin Mary; [with the intercession] of Saint John, the forerunner and baptist; [with the intercession] of the holy and wholly blessed apostles; and [with the intercession] of all your holy martyrs. [DOXOLOGY:] Because you, Christ our Lord, are the oneness,[136] safety, and the binding of peace, we send up to you glory and thanks.

Εὐχὴ εἰς ἀδελφοποίησιν·

Κύριε ὁ θεὸς ὁ παντοκράτωρ, ὁ ποιήσας τὸν ἄνθρωπον κατ' εἰκόνα σὴν καὶ ὁμοίωσιν καὶ δοὺς αὐτῷ ζωὴν αἰώνιον, ὁ εὐδοκήσας τοὺς ἁγίους σου καὶ πανευφήμους ἀποστόλους Πέτρον τὸν κορυφαιότατον καὶ Ἀνδρέαν, καὶ Ἰάκωβον καὶ Ἰωάννην υἱοὺς Ζεβεδαίου, Φίλιππον καὶ Βαρθολομαῖον, ἀμφοτέρους αὐτῶν ἀδελφοὺς γενέσθαι, οὐ δεσμωμένους φύσεως, ἀλλὰ πίστεως καὶ πνεύματος ἁγίου τρόπῳ· ὁ καὶ τοὺς ἁγίους σου μάρτυρας Σέργιον καὶ Βάκχον, Κοσμᾶν τε καὶ Δαμιανόν, Κῦρον καὶ Ἰωάννην ἀδελφοὺς γενέσθαι καταξιώσας, εὐλόγησον καὶ τοὺς δούλους σου ὁ δεῖνα καὶ ὁ δεῖνα, οὐ δεσμωμένους φύσεως, ἀλλὰ <πίστεως> τρόπῳ· δὸς αὐτοῖς τοῦ ἀγαπᾶν ἀλλήλους, ἀμίσητον καὶ ἀσκανδάλιστον τὴν ἀδελφοσύνην αὐτῶν εἶναι πάσας τὰς ἡμέρας τῆς ζωῆς αὐτῶν ἐν τῇ δυνάμει τοῦ ἁγίου σου πνεύματος, πρεσβείαις τῆς παναγίας, ἀχράντου δεσποίνης ἡμῶν θεοτόκου καὶ ἀειπαρθένου Μαρίας καὶ τοῦ ἁγίου Ἰωάννου τοῦ προδρόμου καὶ βαπτιστοῦ, τῶν ἁγίων καὶ πανευφήμων ἀποστόλων καὶ πάντων <τῶν> ἁγίων σου μαρτύρων. Ὅτι σὺ εἶ ἡ ἕνωσις καὶ ἀσφάλεια καὶ δεσμὸς τῆς εἰρήνης, Χριστὲ ὁ Θεὸς ἡμῶν, καὶ σοὶ τὴν δόξαν καὶ εὐχαριστείαν ἀναπέμπομεν.

Prayer K (Rapp)/Prayer 13 (Panagou)

Text = Panagou 2010, 347 (Εὐχὴ ΙΓ΄).
(See Boswell 1995, 316, 355; Rapp 2016, 299 [Prayer K]; cf. Dmitrievskij 1901/1965, 215.)
[INVOCATION:] Lord our God, who, through your unspeakable *oikonomia*, have deemed it worthy to name (as) brothers the holy apostles and heirs to your kingdom—[REQUEST:] these men, your very slaves, x and y, proclaim them spiritual brothers and deem it worthy that they be without offence in their dealings with one another…[a copyist error]… free from the tricks of the devil and his evil spirits, so that, as they are advancing forward in virtue and justice and in pure love, [DOXOLOGY:] the holy name of the Father, the Son, and Holy Spirit may be extolled through both them and all of us…

Κύριε ὁ Θεὸς ἡμῶν, ὁ διὰ τῆς ἀφάτου σου οἰκονομίας καταξιώσας ἀδελφοὺς καλέσαι τοὺς ἁγίους ἀποστόλους καὶ κληρονόμους τῆς βασιλείας σου, αὐτοὺς τοὺς δούλους σου τόνδε καὶ τόνδε ἀδελφοὺς πνευματικοὺς αὐτοὺς ἀνάδειξον καὶ ἐν μέσῳ αὐτῶν γενέσθαι καταξίωσον ἀσκανδαλίστους…ἐκ τῶν μεθοδίων τοῦ διαβόλου καὶ τῶν πονηρῶν αὐτοῦ πνευμάτων, ὅπως, ἐν ἀρετῇ καὶ δικαιοσύνῃ προκόπτοντας καὶ ἐν ἀγάπῃ εἰλικρινεῖ, δοξάζηται δι᾽ αὐτῶν καὶ δι᾽ ἡμῶν πάντων τὸ πανάγιον ὄνομά σου τοῦ Πατρὸς καὶ τοῦ Υἱοῦ καὶ τοῦ ἁγίου Πνεύματος…

Prayer C (Rapp)/Prayer 3 (Panagou)

Text = Panagou 2010, 338 (Εὐχὴ Γ΄).
(See Passarelli 1982, 131 [#207]; Boswell 1995, 316, 355; Rapp 2016, 294 [Prayer C]; cf. Dmitrievskij 1901/1965, 215.)
[INVOCATION:] Lord our God, glorified in the council of the saints, the one who is great and causes awe among all those in a circle about him, [REQUEST:] bless your slaves, x and y, graciously give them knowledge of Your Holy Spirit. Guide them in holy awe of you. Make them rejoice, so that

they become spiritual brothers, greater than brothers in the flesh. [DOXOLOGY:] Because you are the one who blesses and sanctifies those who obey you, we send glory up to you.

Κύριε ὁ Θεὸς ἡμῶν, "ὁ ἐνδοξαζόμενος ἐν βουλῇ ἁγίων," ὁ "μέγας καὶ φοβερὸς" ὑπάρχων "ἐπὶ πάντας τοὺς περικύκλῳ αὐτοῦ,"[137] εὐλόγησον τοὺς δούλους τοὺς Δ, χάρισαι αὐτοῖς τὴν γνῶσιν τοῦ ἁγίου Σου Πνεύματος· ὁδήγησον αὐτοὺς ἐν τῷ φόβῳ σου τῷ ἁγίῳ, εὔφρανον αὐτούς, ἵνα γένωνται πνευματικοὶ ἀδελφοὶ ὑπὲρ τοὺς σαρκικούς· ὅτι σὺ εἶ ὁ εὐλογῶν καὶ ἁγιάζων τοὺς ἐπὶ σοὶ πεποιθότας καὶ σοὶ τὴν δόξαν ἀναπέμπομεν.

Prayer I (Rapp)/Prayer 8 (Panagou)

Text = Panagou 2010, 343-344 (Εὐχὴ Η΄).
(Boswell 1995, 316–317, 356; Rapp 2016, 298 [Prayer I]; cf. Dmitrievskij 1901/1965, 215)
[INVOCATION:] Lord, "our God, who lives in the high places and looks upon the lowly things,"[138] you who sent Your Only Begotten Son for the salvation of the human race,[139] our Lord Jesus Christ, the one who received Peter and Paul, Peter from Kaisareia Philippi and Paul from Kilikia, and made them his brothers according to the Holy Spirit: [REQUEST:] make these men, your slaves, like the two very apostles of Yours, preserving them blameless for all the days of their lives. [DOXOLOGY:] Because it has been made holy and glorified: the all-honorable and magnificent name of You, the Father, and of the Son, and of the Holy Spirit…

Κύριε, "ὁ Θεὸς ἡμῶν, ὁ ἐν ὑψηλοῖς κατοικῶν καὶ τὰ ταπεινὰ ἐφορῶν," ὁ διὰ τὴν σωτηρίαν τοῦ γένους τῶν ἀνθρώπων ἐξαποστείλας τὸν Μονογενῆ Σου Υἱόν, τὸν Κύριον ἡμῶν Ἰησοῦν Χριστόν, ὁ ὑποδεξάμενος Πέτρον καὶ Παῦλον, Πέτρον μὲν ἀπὸ Καισαρείας τῆς Φιλίππου, Παῦλον δὲ ἀπὸ τῆς Κιλικίας, ποιήσας αὐτοὺς κατὰ Πνεῦμα Ἅγιον ἀδελφούς, ποίησον καὶ τοὺς δούλους σου τούτους, ὡς αὐτοὺς τοὺς δύο ἀποστόλους Σου, ἀμέμπτους αὐτοὺς διατηρῶν πάσας ἡμέρας τῆς ζωῆς αὐτῶν. Ὅτι ἡγίασται καὶ δεδόξασται τὸ πάντιμον καὶ μεγαλοπρεπὲς ὄνομά Σου τοῦ Πατρὸς καὶ τοῦ Υἱοῦ καὶ τοῦ Ἁγίου Πνεύματος…

Prayer E (Rapp)/Prayer 12 (Panagou)

Text = Panagou 2010, 346 (Εὐχὴ ΙΒ΄).
(See Rapp 2016, 296–297 [Prayer E]; cf. Dmitrievskij 1901/1965, 122.)
[INVOCATION:] Lord, our God, who has graciously given all things for the benefit of human kind, and who has contrived spiritual brotherhood and put the desire for love (in our hearts), now you yourself (see that) your slaves—these ones, note it—wishing to enter into brotherhood, to agree before all to spiritual love with angels and men witnessing, to name each

other brother in the church with the martyrs witnessing, and to be made holy through your words from the priest. [REQUEST:] Lord, our God, graciously give them genuine[140] love, unashamed faith, a light of discernment so that they preserve the bonds of spiritual brotherhood, they forgive each others' trespasses, and not grow weary in their hearts as did Cain.[141] But graciously grant them, Lord, your love, which you have for humanity, make bright their oil lamps which are filled with the oil of their efforts and your earthly goods, and fill them with your heavenly (goods) too, and make them ready them for eternity, and grant them eternal life, peace, and brotherly affection. [DOXOLOGY:] For You alone have the power to forgive sins,[142] as you are merciful. Because you are the one who makes love grow (in hearts), Christ our God, and we send glory up to you...

Κύριε ὁ Θεὸς ἡμῶν, ὁ τὰ πάντα πρὸς τὸ συμφέρον χαρισάμενος τοῖς ἀνθρώποις, ὁ καὶ πνευματικὴν ἀδελφότητα συστησάμενος καὶ θήσας πόθον ἀγάπης, αὐτὸς καὶ νῦν τοὺς δούλους σου τούτους, τοὺς βουλομένους εἰς ἀδελφότητα ἐλθεῖν, καὶ ὁμολογῆσαι ἐπὶ πᾶσιν πνευματικὴν ἀγάπην ἐπὶ ἀγγέλων καὶ ἀνθρώπων, καὶ ἀδελφοὺς ἀλλήλους ἐν τῷ ναῷ ὀνομάζειν καὶ ἐπὶ μαρτύρων καὶ ἁγιασθῆναι διὰ τῶν σῶν λογίων ὑπὸ τοῦ ἱερέως. Κύριε ὁ Θεὸς ἡμῶν, χάρισαι αὐτοῖς ἀγάπην ἀνυπόκριτον, πίστιν ἀκαταίσχυντον, φωτισμὸν γνώσεως τοῦ φυλάξαι αὐτοὺς τὰς ἐπαγγελίας τῆς πνευματικῆς ἀδελφότητος, συγχωρεῖν ἀλλήλοις τὰ παραπτώματα αὐτῶν καὶ μὴ ἐκκακεῖν ὡς ὁ Κάιν ἐν ταῖς καρδίαις αὐτῶν, ἀλλὰ χάρισαι αὐτοῖς, Κύριε, τὴν ἀγάπην σου, ἣν ἔχεις πρὸς τοὺς ἀνθρώπους, καὶ τὰς λαμπάδας αὐτῶν φαίδρυνον, πεπιασμένας τῷ ἐλαίῳ τῶν ἑαυτῶν ἔργων καὶ τῶν ἐπιγείων σου ἀγαθῶν, ἔμπλησον αὐτοὺς καὶ τῶν ἐπουρανίων σου, ἑτοίμασον αὐτοὺς εἰς τοὺς ἀτελευτήτους αἰῶνας καὶ ζωὴν αἰώνιον καὶ τὴν εἰρήνην καὶ τὴν φιλαδελφίαν δώρησαι αὐτοῖς. Σὺ γὰρ μόνος ἔχεις ἐξουσίαν ἀφιέναι ἁμαρτίας, ὡς εὔσπλαγχνος. Ὅτι σὺ εἶ ὁ φυτουργὸς τῆς ἀγάπης, Χριστὲ ὁ Θεὸς ἡμῶν, καὶ σοὶ τὴν δόξαν ἀναπέμπομεν...

Prayer H (Rapp)/Prayer 6 (Panagou)

Text = Panagou 2010, 342 (Εὐχὴ ΣΤ΄).
  (See Rapp 2016, 298 [Prayer H]; cf. Dmitrievskij 1901/1965, 122–123.)
  [INVOCATION:] Lord, our God, with your swift hearing and your swift concern, listen to us as we pray to you. [REQUEST:] Dispatch the treasure of compassion from Yourself to these men, your slaves, for their spiritual brotherhood, for their thinking alike and loving each other, and send to them, as with your holy apostles and prophets, Your Holy Spirit which will preserve them in a beautiful association and manifest Your will for all the days of their life. [DOXOLOGY:] Because you are the consecration[143] especially to you (*sc.* we send up glory)...
  Κύριε ὁ Θεὸς ἡμῶν, ἡ ταχινὴ ἀκοή, τὰ ταχινὰ σπλάγχνα, ἐπάκουσαν ἡμῶν δεομένων σε. Κατάπεμψον τὸ παρὰ Σοῦ πλούσιον ἔλεος ἐπὶ τοὺς δούλους Σου τούτους εἰς ἀδελφότητα πνευματικήν, εἰς τὸ φρονεῖν αὐτοὺς καὶ ἀγαπᾶν

ἀλλήλους, καὶ κατάπεμψον αὐτοῖς τὸ Πνεῦμά Σου τὸ Ἅγιον, ὡς ἐπὶ τῶν ἁγίων Σου ἀποστόλων καὶ προφητῶν, τοῦ διαφυλάττειν αὐτοὺς ἐν καλῇ πολιτείᾳ καὶ ποιεῖν τὸ θέλημά Σου πάσας τὰς ἡμέρας τῆς ζωῆς αὐτῶν. Ὅτι σὺ εἶ ὁ ἁγιασμὸς καὶ Σοί...

Notes

1 *Life of Basil* 11/228 (τὸ ποιήσασθαι πνευματικῆς ἀδελφότητος σύνδεσμον) and 74/317 (κοινωνίαν τῆς πνευματικῆς ἀδελφότητος); Symeon the Logothete, *Chronographia* (first edition) 131.14 (ἐν τῇ ἐκκλησίᾳ ἐποίησεν ἀδελφοποίησιν); Symeon the Logothete, *Chronographia* (second edition) Bekkerus 820/9 (ἐν τῇ ἐκκλησίᾳ ἐποίησεν ἀδελφοποίησιν), Istrin 5 and Featherstone 10/424 (πνευματικὸν ἀδελφὸν ἐποιήσατο); Pseudo-Symeon, *Chronographia* 656/11 (ἀδελφοποιητὸν ποιήσας) has neither these designations, but this may be understood as an instance of his liking for abbreviation.
2 This illustration appears below as Figure 3.1 in the section on one of Basil's brothers, John.
3 Rapp (2016, 67, 200).
4 See, e.g., Bray (2003, 35–41); Messis (2008, 239, 40–41); Pitsakis (2006, 322–323); Rapp (2016, 86–87).
5 Rapp (2016, 88–179).
6 Pott (1996, 289): "l'Église n'institue pas un lien entre deux contractants, mais transforme le lien déjà existant entre deux de ses membres en implorant pour eux un surcroît de ce qu'ils ont en commun avec tous les baptisés: la foi et l'amour." ("The Church does not establish a connection between the two who are forming [the brotherhood], but transforms an already existing connection between two of its members by imploring for them a surplus of what they have in common with all the baptized: faith and love.")
7 For more on *adelphopoiesis*, a subject about which there has been contention and much written, see the following: Boswell (1995); Bray (2003); Brown (1997); Du Fresne (1688); Goar (1730); Koschaker (1974/1936); Kyriakidis (1926); Macrides (1990); Messis (2008); Michaelides-Nuaros (1952); Morris (2016); Nallino (1974/1936); Oschema (2006); Otto (1732); Panagou (2010, 2013); Patlagean (1982/1946); Pitsakis (2006); Pott (1996); Puchner (1994); Rapp (1997, 2016); Rhalle (1909); Shaw (1997); Shopland (2018); Sidéris (2008); Smythe (1999); Tamassia (1886); Tougher (1999).
8 Betancourt (2020, 123); Macrides (1990, 110n12); Pitsakis (2006, 320, 323); Rapp (2016, 234–236, 242); Rhalle (1909, 299).
9 Bray says that complicated evidence should be allowed speak in all its complexity (he speaks of friendship here but relevant to *adelphopoiesis*, a topic which he addresses in any case in his book):

> If the historian of friendship is ready to put aside the unavailing attempt to impose an order on the diversity of evidence about friendship in traditional society, and rather listens to what that diversity is saying, it tells its own story...
>
> (2003, 77)

10 Symeon the Logothete, *Chronographia* (first edition) 131.13; Symeon the Logothete, *Chronographia* (second edition) Bekkerus 9/819; Pseudo-Symeon, *Chronographia* 656/11.
11 Symeon the Logothete, *Chronographia* (second edition) Istrin 5, Featherstone 423/10.

160 Framing the Brotherhoods

12 Symeon the Logothete, *Chronographia* (first edition), 131.13; Symeon the Logothete, *Chronographia* (second edition), Bekkerus 819/9, Istrin 5, Featherstone 423/10; Pseudo-Symeon, *Chronographia* 655/11.
13 καὶ εὐθέως μετὰ ῥομφαίας τις δέδωκεν αὐτῷ εἰς τὴν πλευρὰν αὐτοῦ, λέγων "ἐξελθὼν εἰσάγαγε ὃν βλέπεις ἔξωθεν τοῦ πυλῶνος κείμενον· οὗτός ἐστιν ὁ βασιλεύς." As far as the whole story of Nicholas being compelled to bring Basil in is concerned, the versions of the second edition of Symeon the Logothete's *Chronographia* (Bekkerus 820/9, Istrin 5, Featherstone 423–424/10) and Pseudo-Symeon, *Chronographia* 656/11 are all broadly similar, though Pseudo-Symeon has, as usual, more abbreviation.
14 ἐξελθὼν οὖν μετὰ σπουδῆς σύντρομος καὶ εὑρὼν Βασίλειον μετὰ τῆς πήρας καὶ τῆς ῥάβδου εἰσήγαγεν ἔσωθεν τῆς ἐκκλησίας. καὶ τῇ δευτέρᾳ ἡμέρᾳ ἀπελθὼν μετ' αὐτοῦ εἰς τὸ λουτρὸν ἤλλαξεν αὐτόν. καὶ ἐλθὼν ἐν τῇ ἐκκλησίᾳ ἐποίησεν ἀδελφοποίησιν· καὶ συνηυφραίνοντο ἐν ἀλλήλοις.
15 Tougher (1999, 156). Tougher also notes that there is a perceptible "tone of sexual ambiguity" and desire provoked by "the sight of Basil's genitalia" (1999, 156).
16 τὸν Βασίλειον ἔνδον τῆς ἐκκλησίας εἰσήγαγε πήραν, ἐνημμένον καὶ ῥάβδον κατέχοντα τῇ χειρί.
17 πορευόμενοι δὲ κηρύσσετε λέγοντες ὅτι Ἤγγικεν ἡ βασιλεία τῶν οὐρανῶν. ἀσθενοῦντας θεραπεύετε, νεκροὺς ἐγείρετε, λεπροὺς καθαρίζετε, δαιμόνια ἐκβάλλετε....
18 Μὴ κτήσησθε...μὴ πήραν εἰς ὁδὸν μηδὲ δύο χιτῶνας μηδὲ ὑποδήματα μηδὲ ῥάβδον· ἄξιος γὰρ ὁ ἐργάτης τῆς τροφῆς αὐτοῦ.
19 Λαμπάδα θεὶς καὶ τόξα βοηλάτιν εἵλετο ῥάβδον
   οὖλος Ἔρως, πήρην δ' εἶχε κατωμαδίην,
  καὶ ζεύξας ταλαεργὸν ὑπὸ ζυγὸν αὐχένα ταύρων
   ἔσπειρεν Δηοῦς αὔλακα πυροφόρον·εἶπε
  δ' ἄνω βλέψας αὐτῷ Διί, "πλῆσον ἀρούρας
   μή σε τὸν Εὐρώπης βοῦν ὑπ' ἄροτρα βάλω."
20 When the Greek noun meaning plough, *arotron*/ἄροτρον, is in plural, and it is plural in Moschos' poem (ἄροτρα), it can be a metaphor for penis. When telling of this meaning, *LSJ* I.2 cites a line and a half in Nonnos' *Dionysiaka*, an epic poem from late antiquity that the Byzantines knew well, which features this meaning for *arotra* in remarks concerning Zeus's father and grandfather, who both were famous in the matter of *phalloi*, as the former castrated the latter: "As many things as old man Kronos accomplished, when, cutting the masculine ploughs of his father, he ploughed the ocean that produces offspring..." (*Dionysiaka* 12.45–46: ...ὅσσα τέλεσσε γέρων Κρόνος, ὁππότε τέμνων / ἄρσενα πατρὸς ἄροτρα λεχώιον ἤροσεν ὕδωρ...).
21 Μὴ ἀνιῶ, ὦ πάτερ, ὅτι κύων λέγομαι καὶ ἀμπέχομαι τρίβωνα διπλοῦν καὶ πήραν φέρω κατ' ὤμων καὶ ῥάβδον ἔχω διὰ χειρός· οὐ γὰρ ἄξιον ἐπὶ τοῖς τοιούτοις ἀνιᾶσθαι, μᾶλλον δὲ ἥδεσθαι, ὅτι ὀλίγοις ἀρκεῖται ὁ παῖς σου, ἐλεύθερος δέ ἐστι δόξης, ᾗ πάντες δουλεύουσιν Ἕλληνές τε καὶ βάρβαροι....
22 See, e.g., Diogenes Laertios 6.46 and 69 for reference to Diogenes' public masturbation.
23 Symeon the Logothete, *Chronographia* (first edition), 131.14: ἀπελθὼν μετ' αὐτοῦ εἰς τὸ λουτρὸν ἤλλαξεν αὐτόν.
24 Symeon the Logothete, *Chronographia* (second edition), Bekkerus 820/9: ἀπελθὼν μετ' αὐτοῦ εἰς τὸ λουτρὸν ἔλουσεν αὐτὸν καὶ ἤλλαξε.
25 τῇ δὲ ἐπαύριον λούσας αὐτὸν καὶ ἱμάτιον περιβαλών...; Featherstone 424/10 has a plural (ἱμάτια) where Istrin has a singular (ἱμάτιον): "On the next day, having washed him/having had him washed and having put cloaks (on him)..." (τῇ δὲ ἐπαύριον λούσας αὐτὸν καὶ ἱμάτια περιβαλών...).

26 *Chronographia* 656/11: λούσας ἤλλαξεν αὐτόν.
27 ...ἐλθὼν ἐν τῇ ἐκκλησίᾳ ἐποίησεν ἀδελφοποίησιν· καὶ συνηυφραίνοντο ἐν ἀλλήλοις.
28 30/704: "they were ploughing *in/within one another*" (*erotrion* en heautois/ ἠροτρίων ἐν ἑαυτοῖς).
29 This moment of contextuality has been noted before (Boswell 1995, 232; Tougher 1999, 155) but not discussed in detail.
30 μὴ ἐγγίσῃς πρὸς θύραις οἴκων αὐτῆς, ἵνα μὴ πρόῃ ἄλλοις ζωήν σου καὶ σὸν βίον ἀνελεήμοσιν, ἵνα μὴ πλησθῶσιν ἀλλότριοι σῆς ἰσχύος, οἱ δὲ σοὶ πόνοι εἰς οἴκους ἀλλοτρίων εἰσέλθωσιν, καὶ μεταμεληθήσῃ ἐπ' ἐσχάτων, ἡνίκα ἂν κατατριβῶσιν σάρκες σώματός σου.
31 πῖνε ὕδατα ἀπὸ σῶν ἀγγείων καὶ ἀπὸ σῶν φρεάτων πηγῆς. μὴ ὑπερεκχείσθω σοι τὰ ὕδατα ἐκ τῆς σῆς πηγῆς, εἰς δὲ σὰς πλατείας διαπορευέσθω τὰ σὰ ὕδατα· ἔστω σοι μόνῳ ὑπάρχοντα, καὶ μηδεὶς ἀλλότριος μετασχέτω σοι· ἡ πηγή σου τοῦ ὕδατος ἔστω σοι ἰδία, καὶ συνευφραίνου μετὰ γυναικὸς τῆς ἐκ νεότητός σου.
32 καὶ ἐλθὼν ἐν τῇ ἐκκλησίᾳ ἐποίησεν ἀδελφοποίησιν, καὶ συνευφραίνοντο ἀλλήλους.
33 Pseudo-Symeon's *adelphopoieton*/ἀδελφοποιητόν is more generic than the *adelphopoiesis*/ἀδελφοποίησις that has so far been in Symeon the Logothete. The slacker translation reflects this aspect of the Greek.
34 Note that it is not possible to get the English "together," which reflects the *sun/* συν in *suneuphraineto*/συνευφραίνετο, into the translation while representing the dative *autoi*/αὐτῷ in the translation.
35 καὶ ἀδελφοποιητὸν ποιήσας συνευφραίνετο αὐτῷ.
36 Istrin: πνευματικὸν ἀδελφὸν ἐποιήσατο καὶ ὁμώροφον εἶχε καὶ ὁμοδίαιτον; Featherstone: πνευματικὸν ἀδελφὸν ἐποιήσατο, καὶ ὁμώροφον εἶχε καὶ ὁμοδίαιτον.
37 A conclusion to which Boswell precipitously jumped in 1995, 233:

> Taken with the statement by Harmartolos [for which read Symeon the Logothete, *Chronographia* (second edition, Istrin)—Boswell did not have the advantage of later scholarship which has assigned authorship to Symeon the Logothete, much less the appearance of Featherstone, which only makes the case stronger that this is a version of Symeon the Logothete's *Chronographia*—] that the union led to a sharing of home and hearth, it strongly evokes a wedding, followed by jubilation and a shared life.

38 Συνέβη δὲ κατ' ἐκεῖνον τὸν χρόνον τὸν κύριον τοῦ Βασιλείου Θεόφιλον διά τινας τοῦ δημοσίου δουλείας παρὰ τοῦ βασιλεύοντος Μιχαὴλ καὶ Βάρδα τοῦ Καίσαρος ἀποσταλῆναι εἰς Πελοπόννησον. συνῆν δὲ αὐτῷ καὶ ὁ Βασίλειος, εἰς τὴν ἀφορισθεῖσαν αὐτῷ δουλείαν καθυπουργῶν.
39 *Life of Basil* 11/226.
40 ...τοῦ Βασιλείου εἰσερχομένου ὑπεξανέστη τε ὥς τινι τῶν κρειττόνων καὶ τὴν ἐξ ἔθους τοῖς βασιλεῦσιν εὐφημίαν προσήνεγκεν.
41 *Life of Basil* 11/227: πάτερ πνευματικέ.
42 *Life of Basil* 11/227.
43 *Life of Basil* 11/227:

> The pious monk answered her, "I did not see, as you say, a man who was one of those who just happen to be around, but a great Emperor of the Romans who has been anointed by Christ, and I rose and acclaimed (him). To those honored by God honor from men is in every case especially owed."
>
> (ὁ δὲ εὐλαβὴς ἐκεῖνος μοναχὸς πρὸς αὐτὴν ἀπεκρίνατο, ὅτι· "οὐχ, ὡς σὺ λέγεις, ἕνα τῶν τυχόντων εἶδον τὸν ἄνδρα ἐγώ, ἀλλ' ὡς μέγαν βασιλέα τῶν Ῥωμαίων ὑπὸ Χριστοῦ κεχρισμένον ἰδών, καὶ ἐξανέστην καὶ ἐπευφήμησα· τοῖς γὰρ ὑπὸ θεοῦ τετιμημένοις ὀφειλομένη πάντως ἐστὶν καὶ ἡ ἐξ ἀνθρώπων τιμή.").

44 See Ševčenko (2011, 44).
45 Μετακαλεσαμένη δὲ αὐτὸν ἡ προρρηθεῖσα γυνὴ Δανηλὶς πολλοῖς καὶ μεγάλοις δεξιοῦται χαρίσμασιν, ἐμφρόνως πάνυ καὶ συνετῶς ὥσπερ τινὰ σπόρον εἰς ἀγαθὴν αὐτὰ καταβαλλομένη χώραν, ἵνα ἀμήσηται πολλαπλασίονα ἐν εὐθέτῳ καιρῷ· δέδωκεν γὰρ αὐτῷ καὶ χρυσὸν ἱκανὸν καὶ ἀνδράποδα πρὸς ὑπηρεσίαν τριάκοντα καὶ ἐν ἱματισμῷ καὶ διαφόροις εἴδεσι πλοῦτον πολύν, μηδὲν ἕτερον ἐπιζητήσασα τὸ πρότερον παρ' αὐτοῦ, ἢ τὸ ποιήσασθαι πνευματικῆς ἀδελφότητος σύνδεσμον πρὸς Ἰωάννην τὸν ταύτης υἱόν. ὁ δὲ ὡς ὑπὲρ αὐτὸν μᾶλλον οὖσαν διωθεῖτο τὴν ἔντευξιν, διὰ τὸ δοκοῦν τῆς γυναικὸς περιφανὲς καὶ τὸ αὐτοῦ κατὰ τὸ ὁρώμενον εὐτελές. ὅμως πλείονα *** καὶ παράκλησιν δεξάμενος ὑπ' αὐτῆς, τοῦτο πεποίηκεν. Καὶ τότε οἱονεὶ ἐπὶ πλέον θαρρήσασα εἶπεν φανερῶς πρὸς αὐτόν, ὅτι· "σε ὁ θεὸς μέγαν ἄνθρωπον ἔχει καὶ ἐπὶ μεγάλης μέλλει τιμῆς ἀνυψοῦν, καὶ οὐδὲν ἕτερον ἐπιζητῶ ἢ ἀπαιτῶ παρὰ σοῦ, πλὴν ἵνα ἀγαπᾷς καὶ ἐλεῇς ἡμᾶς."
46 Mk 4.1: ὄχλος.
47 Mk 4.10–34.
48 "οὐ γάρ ἐστιν κρυπτὸν ἐὰν μὴ ἵνα φανερωθῇ, οὐδὲ ἐγένετο ἀπόκρυφον ἀλλ' ἵνα ἔλθῃ εἰς φανερόν. εἴ τις ἔχει ὦτα ἀκούειν ἀκουέτω." Καὶ ἔλεγεν αὐτοῖς, "Βλέπετε τί ἀκούετε. ἐν ᾧ μέτρῳ μετρεῖτε μετρηθήσεται ὑμῖν καὶ προστεθήσεται ὑμῖν. ὃς γὰρ ἔχει, δοθήσεται αὐτῷ· καὶ ὃς οὐκ ἔχει, καὶ ὃ ἔχει ἀρθήσεται ἀπ' αὐτοῦ." Καὶ ἔλεγεν, "Οὕτως ἐστὶν ἡ βασιλεία τοῦ θεοῦ ὡς ἄνθρωπος βάλῃ τὸν σπόρον ἐπὶ τῆς γῆς καὶ καθεύδῃ καὶ ἐγείρηται νύκτα καὶ ἡμέραν, καὶ ὁ σπόρος βλαστᾷ καὶ μηκύνηται ὡς οὐκ οἶδεν αὐτός. αὐτομάτη ἡ γῆ καρποφορεῖ, πρῶτον χόρτον, εἶτεν στάχυν, εἶτεν πλήρη σῖτον ἐν τῷ στάχυϊ. ὅταν δὲ παραδοῖ ὁ καρπός, εὐθὺς ἀποστέλλει τὸ δρέπανον, ὅτι παρέστηκεν ὁ θερισμός."
49 Lk 18:24–25:

> With what difficulty will those who have wealth make their way to the Empire of God. A camel is more able to go through the eye of needle than the rich man will make his way to the Empire of God.

> (Πῶς δυσκόλως οἱ τὰ χρήματα ἔχοντες εἰς τὴν βασιλείαν τοῦ θεοῦ εἰσπορεύονται· εὐκοπώτερον γάρ ἐστιν κάμηλον διὰ τρήματος βελόνης διελθεῖν ἢ πλούσιον εἰς τὴν βασιλείαν τοῦ θεοῦ εἰσελθεῖν).

50 ὁ δὲ εἶπεν αὐτοῖς, "Ἀμὴν λέγω ὑμῖν ὅτι οὐδείς ἐστιν ὃς ἀφῆκεν οἰκίαν ἢ γυναῖκα ἢ ἀδελφοὺς ἢ γονεῖς ἢ τέκνα ἕνεκεν τῆς βασιλείας τοῦ θεοῦ, ὃς οὐχὶ μὴ ἀπολάβῃ πολλαπλασίονα ἐν τῷ καιρῷ τούτῳ καὶ ἐν τῷ αἰῶνι τῷ ἐρχομένῳ ζωὴν αἰώνιον."
51 Ps 31/32:6: προσεύξεται πᾶς ὅσιος πρὸς σὲ ἐν καιρῷ εὐθέτῳ.
52 Ps 31/32:5.
53 *Life of Basil* 74/317:

> When in possession of the imperial throne, he (*sc*. Basil) summoned the son of Danelis, honored him with the office of *protospatharios*, and granted him the right of freedom of access/frank speech (*parrhesia*/παρρησία), on account of their prior connection of spiritual brotherhood.

> (τὸν δὲ τῆς Δανηλίδος υἱὸν ἅμα τῷ γενέσθαι τῆς ἀρχῆς ἐγκρατὴς μεταπεμψάμενος, τῷ τοῦ πρωτοσπαθαρίου ἐτίμησεν ἀξιώματι καὶ τῆς πρὸς αὐτὸν παρρησίας μετέδωκεν διὰ τὴν φθάσασαν κοινωνίαν τῆς πνευματικῆς ἀδελφότητος).

54 *Life of Basil* 75/318: μήτηρ...βασιλέως.
55 Διὸ δὴ καὶ προσέθηκεν ἔτι μεγαλοψύχως ἐπὶ τοῖς εἰρημένοις δώροις οὐ μικρὸν καὶ τῆς Πελοποννήσου μέρος, ὅπερ ὡς ἴδιον κτῆμα τυγχάνον αὐτῆς φιλοδώρως τότε τῷ υἱῷ καὶ βασιλεῖ ἐχαρίζετο....
56 Mk 4:23–24: "...if someone has ears to hear, let them listen." And he said to them, "Pay attention to what you hear. By what measure you take the measure [of the content of what you are hearing], it will be measured out to you, and

more in addition will be given to you" ("...εἴ τις ἔχει ὦτα ἀκούειν ἀκουέτω." Καὶ ἔλεγεν αὐτοῖς, "Βλέπετε τί ἀκούετε. ἐν ᾧ μέτρῳ μετρεῖτε μετρηθήσεται ὑμῖν καὶ προστεθήσεται ὑμῖν").
57 Mk 4.23.
58 Mk 4.24.
59 As was discussed in the introduction to this book: "Yoked to him, like a bull of good lineage and strong, they were ploughing in/within one another as though into rich farmland, and they were sowing the seeds of excellences, as though the best of farmers" (*Life of Mary the Younger* 30/704) (ᾧ δὴ συζευχθείς, οἷα μόσχος εὐγενής τε καὶ ἰσχυρός, ὡς εἰς πίονα γῆν ἠροτρίων ἐν ἑαυτοῖς καὶ τῶν ἀρετῶν τὰ σπέρματα ὡς ἄριστοι γεωργοὶ κατεβάλλοντο).
60 *Life of Basil* 11/228.
61 This office was the leader of the men who guarded the emperor.
62 Τὸν δὲ προειρημένον Νικόλαον, τὸν Ἀνδροσαλίτην, τὸν καὶ προσμονάριον τοῦ ἁγίου Διομήδους, ᾧτινι ὁ μάρτυς ἐπεφάνη, ὡς προείρηται, περὶ τοῦ βασιλέως, ἐτίμησεν αὐτὸν οἰκονόμον καὶ σύγκελλον, τὸν δὲ ἕτερον αὐτοῦ ἀδελφὸν Ἰωάννην δρουγγάριον τῆς βίγλης, καὶ τὸν δὲ ἕτερον ἀδελφὸν αὐτοῦ Παῦλον τοῦ σακελλίου, τὸν δὲ ἕτερον Κωνσταντῖνον γενικὸν λογοθέτην.
63 Bekkerus 842–843/10; Istrin 21.
64 691/10.
65 The Patmos 104 manuscript, dated to 1234, from Greece (Rapp 2016, 269 [no. 29b, the "bis"]).
66 Εὐχὴ εἰς ἀδελφοποίησιν· "Κύριε ὁ Θεὸς ἡμῶν, ὁ πάντα πρὸς σωτηρίαν ἡμῖν χαρισάμενος..." Goar p. 707. Καὶ ποιεῖ ἐκτενὴν καὶ μνημονεύει αὐτῶν καὶ λέγει τὴν εὐχήν, καὶ ἀπολύει, καὶ ἀσπάζονται ἀμφότεροι τὸ ἅγιον εὐαγγέλιον καὶ αὐτοὶ ἀλλήλους (punctuation altered slightly).
67 It is mildly confusing that this ritual is called a prayer, for it is the case that the prayers appear within rituals.
68 Rapp (2016, 294).
69 Rapp (2016, 284).
70 For the tripartite structure of the brotherhood prayers, see Rapp (2016, 82).
71 Rapp (2016, 294).
72 Κύριε ὁ Θεὸς ἡμῶν, ὁ πάντα πρὸς σωτηρίαν ἡμῖν χαρισάμενος, καὶ ἐντειλάμενος ἡμῖν ἀγαπᾶν ἀλλήλους, καὶ συγχωρεῖν ἀλλήλων τὰ παραπτώματα· αὐτός, καὶ νῦν δέσποτα φιλάνθρωπε, τοὺς δούλους σου τούτους τοὺς πνευματικῇ ἀγάπῃ ἑαυτοὺς ἀγαπήσαντας, προσελθόντας τῷ ναῷ σου τῷ ἁγίῳ ὑπό σου εὐλογηθῆναι, χάρισαι αὐτοῖς πίστιν ἀκαταίσχυντον, ἀγάπην ἀνυπόκριτον. καὶ ὡς ἐδωρήσω τοῖς ἁγίοις σου μαθηταῖς τὴν σὴν εἰρήνην, δώρησαι καὶ τούτοις πάντα τὰ πρὸς σωτηρίαν αἰτήματα, καὶ ζωὴν τὴν αἰώνιον. Ὅτι ἐλεήμων, καὶ φιλάνθρωπος Θεὸς ὑπάρχεις, καὶ σοὶ τὴν δόξαν ἀναπέμπομεν· τῷ Πατρί, καὶ τῷ Υἱῷ, καὶ τῷ ἁγίῳ Πνεύματι Τοῦ Κυρίου δεηθῶμεν (*TLG*=48.37–50).

A mildly incomplete text of this prayer can be found in Panagou (2010, 338) (Εὐχὴ Β') and, with minor differences, in Boswell (1995, 354–355).
73 καὶ νῦν δέσποτα φιλάνθρωπε...πνευματικῇ ἀγάπῃ ἑαυτοὺς ἀγαπήσαντας... χάρισαι αὐτοῖς...ἀγάπην ἀνυπόκριτον.
74 See *Lampe*, ἐκτενή and ἐκτενής 2. For examples of this kind of responsal activity, see Goar (1730, 707) (*TLG*=48.15–36) or Boswell (1995, 358).
75 Ὑπὲρ τῶν δούλων τοῦ Θεοῦ τῶν προσελθόντων εὐλογηθῆναι ἐν αὐτῷ, καὶ τῆς ἐν Θεῷ αὐτῶν ἀγαπήσεως, τοῦ Κυρίου δεηθῶμεν. Ὑπὲρ τοῦ δωρηθῆναι αὐτοῖς τῆς ἀποστολικῆς ὁμονοίας τὴν ἐπίγνωσιν, τοῦ Κυρίου δεηθῶμεν. Ὑπὲρ τοῦ παρασχεθῆναι αὐτοῖς πίστιν ἀκαταίσχυντον, ἀγάπην ἀνυπόκριτον, τοῦ Κυρίου δεηθῶμεν. Ὑπὲρ τοῦ καταξιωθῆναι αὐτοὺς ἐγκαυχᾶσθαι ἐν τῷ τιμίῳ σταυρῷ, τοῦ Κυρίου δεηθῶμεν (*TLG*=48.23–30).

164 *Framing the Brotherhoods*

76 The Sinai gr. 966 manuscript, dated to the thirteenth or fourteenth centuries, is from Southern Italy (Rapp 2016, 271 [no. 41]). This ritual appears in its entirety in text (353–356) and in translation (314–317) in Boswell (1995). See Panagou (2010, 187–188) for text and 196–198 for discussion.
77 Προσέρχονται οἱ μέλλοντες ἀδελφοὶ γενέσθαι τῷ ἱερεῖ καὶ ἀποτίθησι τὸ Εὐαγγέλιον εἰς τὸ στῆθος τοῦ θυσιαστηρίου καὶ ὁ πρῶτος ἀδελφὸς τίθησιν τὴν χεῖρα αὐτοῦ ἐπάνω τοῦ Εὐαγγελίου καὶ ὁ δεύτερος ἐπάνω εἰς τὴν χεῖρα τοῦ α΄ ἀδελφοῦ καὶ εἶθ' οὕτως σφραγίσας αὐτοὺς ὁ ἱερεὺς λέγει τὴν Συνάπτην... (cf. Dmitrievskij 1901/1965, 215).
78 Rapp (2016, 293); Panagou (2010, 188); Dmitrievskij (1901/1965, 215) refers readers to Goar (1730, 708) for the Greek text, it is actually on 707. This prayer and a translation of it are printed in the appendix to this chapter.
79 Panagou (2010, 188)/Dmitrievskij (1901/1965, 215): Εἰρήνη ὑμῖν. Τὰς Κεφαλάς.
80 Rapp 2016, 294.
81 Rapp (2016, 299 [K], 294 [C], and 298 [I]). These prayers and translations of them are printed in the appendix to this chapter.
82 Panagou (2010, 188)/Dmitrievskij (1901/1965, 215): Καὶ ἀσπασάμενοι τὸ ἅγιον Εὐαγγέλιον καὶ εἶθ' οὕτως ἀλλήλους, καὶ ἀπολύει.
83 The Sinai gr. 973 manuscript, is dated to 1153 (Rapp 2016, 266 [no. 14]), cf. Dmitrievskij (1901/1965, 122). See Panagou (2010, 125, 152–157) for discussion.
84 This rite is not the only one from Dmitrievskij's collection that refers to Ps 132/133; two others do so too. See Dmitrievskij (1901/1965, 466–467) (=Rapp 2016, 273–274 [no. 53] *Note*: Rapp does not include notice of the psalm in her summary; Dmitrievskij may have made an error, which she has corrected) and 854–855 (=Rapp 2016, 275 [no. 63]). Relatedly, Stephen Morris' book of historically informed advocacy from 2016, *"When Brothers Dwell in Unity": Byzantine Christianity and Homosexuality,"* quotes this psalm appropriately in its title.
85 Ἐπὶ Ἀδελφοποιΐας· Ἐπιτιθέντων ἐπ' ἀλλήλων τῶν χειρῶν αὐτῶν, τιθεῖ ἐπάνω Σταυρὸν, καὶ ὁ ἱερεὺς ψαλμὸν ρλβ΄. "Ἰδοὺ δὴ τί καλὸν ἢ τί τερπνόν ἀλλ' ἢ τὸ κατοικεῖν ἀδελφοὺς" λέγει γ΄ (τρίς). ἕως τὴν εὐλο(γίαν καὶ) ζωήν. Ὁ ἱερεύς λέγει τὴν εὐχήν...
86 Ἰδοὺ δὴ τί καλὸν ἢ τί τερπνὸν ἀλλ' ἢ τὸ κατοικεῖν ἀδελφοὺς ἐπὶ τὸ αὐτό; ὡς μύρον ἐπὶ κεφαλῆς τὸ καταβαῖνον ἐπὶ πώγονα, τὸν πώγονα τὸν Ααρων, τὸ καταβαῖνον ἐπὶ τὴν ᾤαν τοῦ ἐνδύματος αὐτοῦ· ὡς δρόσος Αερμων ἡ καταβαίνουσα ἐπὶ τὰ ὄρη Σιων· ὅτι ἐκεῖ ἐνετείλατο κύριος τὴν εὐλογίαν καὶ ζωὴν ἕως τοῦ αἰῶνος.
87 The beard in the psalm, and by extension the ritual too, makes psalm and prayer challenging if one or both of the brothers is a beardless eunuch, i.e., made one before puberty. But no matter that, as masculinity in this milieu is more an ascribed quality than one strictly about the body. The conclusion to this book revisits this point.
88 And one will note that the directions to the priest remind him of the end of the psalm: "all the way to the blessing and life" (ἕως τὴν εὐλο[γίαν καὶ] ζωήν) is a clear reference to the psalm's "his blessing, life even everlasting" (τὴν εὐλογίαν καὶ ζωὴν ἕως τοῦ αἰῶνος).
89 Due to constraints of space, discussion of John Chrysostom's exegesis of Ps 132/133 (*PG* 55 384–386) could not be included in this book. This work of late antiquity certainly could have come to mind during the ritual from Sinai gr. 973, or when the lengthy prayer analyzed at the end of this chapter, "A thing flowery and much-desired by us, the sweet scent of love," was heard.
90 Rapp (2016, 296–297) (Prayer E), 298 (Prayer H). These prayers and translations of them are printed in the appendix to this chapter.
91 Panagou (2010, 125)/Dmitrievskij (1901/1965, 122): Εὐχὴ τῆς κεφαλοκλισίας.
92 Pott (1996, 289).

93 Rapp (2016, 294).
94 The Grottaferrata Gamma beta (Γ. β.) VII manuscript, dated to the first half of the tenth century, from Calabria (Rapp 2016, 264 [no. 3]); See Panagou (2010, 121, 143–150) for discussion. See Passarelli (1982) for the entire manuscript.
95 Rapp (2016, 294–296); Prayer D only appears once in the manuscripts.
96 This title does not appear with the full text in Panagou (2010, 339) but on the listing of its contents on p. 121. The title is with the full text in Passarelli (1982, 131).
97 This is the point where doxological features appear in combination with continuing requests. I mark the start of the doxology here because of these words: "through love we glorify God and father of our Lord Christ" (ἡμεῖς δὲ διὰ τῆς ἀγάπης δοξάζομεν τὸν Θεὸν καὶ πατέρα τοῦ Κυρίου ἡμῶν Ἰησοῦ Χριστοῦ). What makes this boundary unclear is that the notion of a request appears repeatedly below: (1) requesting God to listen to prayers; (2) quotation from Mt 7:7-8/Lk 11:9; (3) requesting God for faith and love; (4) requesting God for angels such as the ones who helped Abraham and the rest; (5) a pair of final requests for God to show his love for humanity and to listen to this very prayer. It is best to look at this section that begins just past the one-third mark of the prayer as an hybridization of request and doxology that extends nearly to the end of the prayer, until a short and clear doxology, similar to ones seen in other prayers, emerges.
98 Rapp (2016, 294–296); Boswell (1995, 292–294) also translates this prayer, too freely at times.
99 Passarelli (1982, 131–133) (#208) also has this prayer.
100 At Jn 14:27 Jesus says, "I leave peace to you, I give you my peace" (εἰρήνην ἀφίημι ὑμῖν, εἰρήνην τὴν ἐμὴν δίδωμι ὑμῖν), whereas the prayer offers these words (to be understood as the words of Jesus): "I give you my peace and leave you my peace" (εἰρήνην τὴν ἐμὴν δίδωμι ὑμῖν καὶ εἰρήνην τὴν ἐμὴν ἀφίημι ὑμῖν).
101 Jesus speaks about which apostles love him and which ones do not, words that would have been in the minds those who heard this prayer:

> Jesus answered and said to him, "If someone *loves* me, he will keep my word safe and my father will *love* him, and we will come to him and make a home with him. The one not *loving* me does not keep my words safe....
> (Jn 14:23–24)

> ἀπεκρίθη Ἰησοῦς καὶ εἶπεν αὐτῷ, Ἐάν τις *ἀγαπᾷ* με τὸν λόγον μου τηρήσει, καὶ ὁ πατήρ μου *ἀγαπήσει* αὐτόν, καὶ πρὸς αὐτὸν ἐλευσόμεθα καὶ μονὴν παρ' αὐτῷ ποιησόμεθα. ὁ μὴ *ἀγαπῶν* με τοὺς λόγους μου οὐ τηρεῖ....

102 The noun (*agape*/ἀγάπη) appears six times and one occurrence of the verb, *agapao*/ἀγαπάω, makes seven.
103 Love is treasure desired by saints; object of the desires of Abel, Enoch, Abraham, Jakob, and the three children in the furnace; a thing requested along with faith; its sweet scent is "wonderous and much-desired" (θαυμαστὴ καὶ πολυπόθητος).
104 The people glorify God through their love. Love convinced Abraham, rescued Lot and Daniel, carried Elijah to heaven, and saved Elisha. Love keeps an enemy, demons, and sin at bay. Love sows religious feeling on earth and brings about justice in heaven.
105 Through love the people know God, slaves their masters, mortals the immortals, contingent the eternal, and earthly the celestial, and this seems to envision the people and all the lower entities as both active and passive, and so it is with love. As a correlate to faith and hope, in reference to the quotation of Mt 7:7–8/Lk 11:9, love can be seen as object and/or agent; spurred on by love, the people

166 *Framing the Brotherhoods*

call on God, whether it is viewed as something the people possess or something acting on them is unclear.

106 Lot being saved from Sodom might suggest a prohibition on same-sex desire between the brothers. But the reference here is on Lot being saved and not on the sins of the town. In any case, the discourse of sodomy is not well developed in the textual record in Byzantium in these centuries. Talk of *aresenokoitia* and *aselgeia* is more prevalent. At this time, the association of Sodom with male same-sex desire and behavior seems mostly a western idea. That said, there is reference to sodomy to be found in the *Life of Andrew the Fool* (17.1057, 1097 [Rydén 1995]) (which is roughly contemporary with the source material in this book), and Symeon the New Theologian says he was a sodomite (see Chapter 4 of this book), so it can be found. Be it also said that this topic needs more research.

107 It is well to note that it is three Jewish *men* (Dan 3:91), who sing in the fiery furnace. Furthermore, the spectacle of nakedness referred to in the prayer is lacking in Daniel. When the men emerge from the furnace, their clothes have not been burned (Dan 3:94: "their trousers were not altered and the smell of fire was not on them" [τὰ σαράβαρα αὐτῶν οὐκ ἠλλοιώθη, καὶ ὀσμὴ πυρὸς οὐκ ἦν ἐν αὐτοῖς]). The brotherhood prayer, in contrast, wants naked men.

108 εἶπεν δὲ πρὸς αὐτὸν ὁ Ἰησοῦς ὅτι Σήμερον σωτηρία τῷ οἴκῳ τούτῳ ἐγένετο, καθότι καὶ αὐτὸς υἱὸς Ἀβραάμ ἐστιν.

109 τὴν ἀγάπην ἐτέλεσεν.

110 Ἄνθηρὸν ἡμῖν καὶ πολυπόθητον ἡ τῆς ἀγάπης εὐωδία ἄγει ταῖς πατρικαῖς ἀρχαῖς τε θεμελιωμένη καὶ προφητικαῖς φωναῖς ὁδηγουμένη καὶ ἀποστολικοῖς κηρύγμασιν ἡγιασμένη, ὅτι πάντων τῶν καλῶν τῶν ἐπὶ τῆς γῆς ὑπεράγει ἡ ἀγάπη.

111 καὶ τὸν κριὸν λήμψῃ τὸν ἕνα, καὶ ἐπιθήσουσιν Ααρων καὶ οἱ υἱοὶ αὐτοῦ τὰς χεῖρας αὐτῶν ἐπὶ τὴν κεφαλὴν τοῦ κριοῦ· καὶ σφάξεις αὐτὸν καὶ λαβὼν τὸ αἷμα προσχεεῖς πρὸς τὸ θυσιαστήριον κύκλῳ. καὶ τὸν κριὸν διχοτομήσεις κατὰ μέλη καὶ πλυνεῖς τὰ ἐνδόσθια καὶ τοὺς πόδας ὕδατι καὶ ἐπιθήσεις ἐπὶ τὰ διχοτομήματα σὺν τῇ κεφαλῇ. καὶ ἀνοίσεις ὅλον τὸν κριὸν ἐπὶ τὸ θυσιαστήριον ὁλοκαύτωμα κυρίῳ εἰς ὀσμὴν εὐωδίας· θυσίασμα κυρίῳ ἐστίν.

112 τὸν ἀμνὸν τὸν ἕνα ποιήσεις τὸ πρωὶ καὶ τὸν ἀμνὸν τὸν δεύτερον ποιήσεις τὸ δειλινόν· καὶ δέκατον σεμιδάλεως πεφυραμένης ἐν ἐλαίῳ κεκομμένῳ τῷ τετάρτῳ τοῦ ιν καὶ σπονδὴν τὸ τέταρτον τοῦ ιν οἴνου τῷ ἀμνῷ τῷ ἑνί· καὶ τὸν ἀμνὸν τὸν δεύτερον ποιήσεις τὸ δειλινόν, κατὰ τὴν θυσίαν τὴν πρωινὴν καὶ κατὰ τὴν σπονδὴν αὐτοῦ ποιήσεις εἰς ὀσμὴν εὐωδίας κάρπωμα κυρίῳ, θυσίαν ἐνδελεχισμοῦ εἰς γενεὰς ὑμῶν ἐπὶ θύρας τῆς σκηνῆς τοῦ μαρτυρίου ἔναντι κυρίου, ἐν οἷς γνωσθήσομαί σοι ἐκεῖθεν ὥστε λαλῆσαί σοι.

113 PsSol 11:5 and Bar 5:8: *pan xulon euodias*/πᾶν ξύλον εὐωδίας.

114 ὡς κιννάμωμον καὶ ἀσπάλαθος ἀρωμάτων δέδωκα ὀσμὴν καὶ ὡς σμύρνα ἐκλεκτὴ διέδωκα εὐωδίαν.

115 ὀσμὴν εὐωδίας, θυσίαν δεκτήν, εὐάρεστον τῷ θεῷ.

116 γίνεσθε οὖν μιμηταὶ τοῦ θεοῦ, ὡς τέκνα ἀγαπητά, καὶ περιπατεῖτε ἐν ἀγάπῃ, καθὼς καὶ ὁ Χριστὸς ἠγάπησεν ἡμᾶς καὶ παρέδωκεν ἑαυτὸν ὑπὲρ ἡμῶν προσφορὰν καὶ θυσίαν τῷ θεῷ εἰς ὀσμὴν εὐωδίας.

117 Τῷ δὲ θεῷ χάρις τῷ πάντοτε θριαμβεύοντι ἡμᾶς ἐν τῷ Χριστῷ καὶ τὴν ὀσμὴν τῆς γνώσεως αὐτοῦ φανεροῦντι δι' ἡμῶν ἐν παντὶ τόπῳ· ὅτι Χριστοῦ εὐωδία ἐσμὲν τῷ θεῷ ἐν τοῖς σῳζομένοις καὶ ἐν τοῖς ἀπολλυμένοις, οἷς μὲν ὀσμὴ ἐκ θανάτου εἰς θάνατον, οἷς δὲ ὀσμὴ ἐκ ζωῆς εἰς ζωήν.

118 "What it is necessary to observe on the day of the Vintage Festival in a procession to Hiereia." (Ὅσα δεῖ παραφυλάττειν ἐν τῇ ἡμέρᾳ τοῦ τρυγητοῦ ἐν προκένσῳ τῆς Ἱερείας.) (Book 2.175.1–2 [Vogt. 1939]; R373; Book 1, Chapter 78/87) Translation by Moffatt and Tall (2012, Vol. 1, 373). Moffatt and Tall, *ad loc.*, also note that Hiereia was across the water from Constantinople and south of Chalcedon.

119 Demes are meant here; "demes of the two factions" (οἱ τῶν δύο μερῶν δῆμοι) appears earlier in this section (Book 2.175.8 [Vogt. 1939]; R 374; Book 1, Chapter 78/87; Moffatt and Tall 2012, Vol. 1, 374). See Moffatt and Tall's discussion of the demes and their connection to Blue (and White) and Green (and Red) factions (2012, Vol. 2, 828).
120 An *apelatikos* is a "hymn-like" acclamation (Moffatt and Tall 2012, Vol. 2, 826).
121 Ὅτε δὲ τῷ πρώτῳ μαγίστρῳ ἐπιδοθῇ παρὰ τοῦ βασιλέως ἡ σταφυλή, λέγουσιν τὰ δύο μέρη ἡνωμένοι ἀπελατικὸν ἦχος α΄· "Ἐκ τοῦ λειμῶνος τῆς γνώσεως τοῦ Δεσπότου τῆς σοφίας τρυγήσαντες ἄνθη, ἱερὰ τάξις τῶν ἐντίμων πατρικίων, ἐν τῷ προσφέρειν τῶν ᾀσμάτων τὰ πλήθη, κεφαλὴν καταστέψωμεν, ὡς οἶκον τῆς εὐωδίας τῶν νοημάτων, ἀντιλαμβάνοντες τῶν ἐκείνου τερπνῶν χαρίτων. Ἀλλά, ἀθάνατε Βασιλεῦ τῶν ἁπάντων, σὺ δίδου ἐπὶ πολὺ ταύτην τὴν ἑορτὴν τῷ κόσμῳ τῆς αὐτοκράτορος ἐξουσίας, ὁ δεῖνα, τοῦ θεοστέπτου χρισθέντος βασιλέως."
   The translation of this passage is Moffatt and Tall's (2012, Vol. 1, 374–375), modified slightly.
122 Τῶν δὲ χθίζων ὀπωρῶν, οὐδὲν ἐχουσῶν λαμπρὸν ἢ μόνην τὴν προαίρεσιν, πολλαπλασίαν ἐδεξάμην τὴν ἀμοιβήν, τοὺς ὡραίους σου λόγους καὶ γλυκερούς, οἵπερ ἐν τῷ δάκνειν ἐρωτικῶς καὶ στρέφειν μου τὴν ψυχὴν πλέον εὐωδιάζουσιν ἤπερ ὁ ἐπαινεθεὶς ἀνθοσμίας οἶδεν εὐφραίνειν καρδίαν ἀνθρώπων ἢ καὶ τὸ νέκταρ αὐτό, ᾧπερ οἱ μάκαρες ἐμεθύσκοντο [Text=Tziatzi-Papagianni 2012, 89–90].
123 The verb *euodiazo*/εὐωδιάζω and the noun *euodia*/εὐωδία are as closely related as can be imagined, and for all intents and purposes, they indicate the same semantic content.
124 Tziatzi-Papagianni (2012, 8–12).
125 The adjective *euodes*/εὐώδης and the noun *euodia*/εὐωδία are as closely related as can be imagined, and for all intents and purposes, they indicate the same semantic content.
126 Πῶς σοι παραστήσω τὴν ἡδονήν, γλυκύτατε καὶ ποθούμενε δέσποτα, ἥν μου πρὸς τὴν καρδίαν κατέσταξεν ἡ πάνσοφός σου καὶ μελισταγὴς τῶν λόγων σειρή; Τῷ ὄντι γὰρ οἷον ἀρωματώδεις ἢ οἷον ἀμβρόσιοι σταγόνες ἢ τοῦ μάννα ἐκείνου τοῦ παλαιοῦ ὑετοῦ καὶ νάρδου καὶ βαλσάμου κρουνοὶ κατέρρεόν μου πρὸς τὴν ψυχὴν οἱ ἀνθηροὶ καὶ εὐώδεις καὶ τοῖς τῆς σοφίας πυκαζόμενοι ἄνθεσι λόγου σου... [Text= Tziatzi-Papagianni 2012, 8–9].
127 Ἐγὼ δέ, καὶ πρότερον πυρπολούμενος καὶ οἷον ἐμπυριζόμενος τὴν ψυχὴν τῷ περὶ σὲ πόθῳ, πῶς οἴει νῦν ἐξεκαύθην τῷ δροσοβόλῳ πυρὶ καὶ φωτὶ τῆς ἀγάπης σου ἐκ τῆς τοιαύτης γραφῆς, ἣ καὶ λίθων φύσιν καὶ δένδρων προσέτι καὶ ἀγρίων θηρῶν ἱκανὴ ἦν πρὸς τὸ περὶ σὲ φίλτρον ἑλκῦσαι καὶ ἐκκαλέσασθαι καὶ πεῖσαι ὀπίσω τρέχειν τοῦ μύρου τῆς φιλικῆς εὐωδίας σου, ἤπερ ἡ τοῦ Ὀρφέως, ὡς ὁ λόγος, λύρα τὰ ἄψυχα θέλγουσα ἀκολουθεῖν αὐτῷ κατηνάγκαζεν [Text=Tziatzi-Papagianni 2012, 11].
128 Ταύτην τὴν ἀγάπην ποθήσαντες οἱ ἅγιοι τρεῖς παῖδες ἐν τῇ καμίνῳ τοῦ πυρὸς ἀπεδύσαντο καὶ ὕμνον εὐωδίας τῷ Θεῷ προσεκόμισαν [Text= Panagou 2010, 340].
129 This *Suda* entry defines πυράφλεκτος ("unburnt by fire") and then, in the excerpt to be discussed distinguishes it from *puriphlektos*/πυρίφλεκτος, which means "blazing with fire."
130 ὅτε δὲ τὴν ἐξαφθεῖσαν Χαλδαϊκὴν κάμινον, λέγεται πυρίφλεκτος· ὡς ἐν τῷ, κάμινον παῖδες πυρίφλεκτον πάλαι δροσοβολοῦσαν ἀπέδειξαν.
131 The adjective used by Theodoros, *drosobolos*/δροσοβόλος ("dew-shedding"), and the verb *drosoboleo*/δροσοβολέω ("to shed dew"), read in the *Suda*, are as closely related as can be imagined. For all intents and purposes, they indicate the same semantic content.
132 The second principal part of τρέχω is δραμοῦμαι. They look different but they are related through well over 1,500 years of sedimented use by the time of the tenth century.

168 *Framing the Brotherhoods*

133 I translate βασιλεύς as "emperor" here because I am thinking through a Byzantine reception of this passage, i.e., a highly favored word for emperor in the medieval empire was *basileus*/βασιλεύς.
134 Darrouzès (1960, 247–248).
135 And if it was the case that church and society were substantially the same thing, as I have read here and there now and again, well, the case is more easily made in a way.
136 It is worth comparing the end of this prayer to the end of *Letter 26* of Nikephoros Ouranos: "Let us, each other, together spend a spring prior to the season with our *unifying* God" (κοινῇ πρὸ τῆς ὥρας ἑκάτεροι τῷ ἑνοποιῷ Θεῷ καὶ ἀλλήλους ἐνεαρίσωμεν).
137 Ps 88/89:8.
138 Ps 112/113:5–6.
139 Gal 4:4.
140 Rom 12:9.
141 Gen 4:1–16.
142 Mt 9:6; Mk 2:10; Lk 5:24.
143 ἁγιασμός: JgAl 17:3, 1 Th 4:7.

4 Revisiting the Bachelorhood of Emperor Basil II

Introduction

Basil II was the most accomplished emperor of the Macedonian dynasty that started with Basil I in 867 and concluded with his niece Theodora in 1056.[1] Emblem of Byzantine success in the Middle Ages, he receives glowing press in historical accounts. Military triumph and consolidation of imperial power were hallmarks of a lengthy reign, effectively as sole emperor,[2] that stretched from 976 to 1025. Probably born in 958, he was associated with his father Romanos II as emperor from an early age. When Romanos died in 963, he was subordinate first to his mother Theophano, who was regent (963), then to Emperor Nikephoros II Phokas (963–969), and finally to Emperor John I Tzimiskes (969–976). And even after Tzimiskes was no longer on the throne, all authority was not his: unofficially, but in a real way, he shared the rule with his powerful great-uncle, the eunuch Basil the *Parakoimomenos*, until the mid-980s.[3] Among his accomplishments, once he was sole emperor, were the bloody suppression of the Bulgarian state, significant land legislation against the interests of the major families, and a full treasury by the end of his reign.[4] Basil also faced significant revolts early on: those of Bardas Skleros (976–979 and 987–989) and Bardas Phokas (987–989). Great-great-grandson of Basil I, Basil II traced his Macedonian lineage down from him through Leo VI and Constantine VII Porphyrogennetos, to his father, Romanos II. He also counted another emperor, Romanos I Lekapenos, as a great-grandfather. Lineage and marriage were important in this dynasty and in Byzantine society as a whole. Basil had been betrothed along with his brother, Constantine, to Bulgarian princesses when he was young.[5] Given the importance of lineage which would keep members of the dynasty on the throne in the eleventh century past Basil's death, it was remarkable that he did not take a wife at some point over the course of his long reign. Basil has been called an "elusive figure," due to the lack of personal details known about him.[6] His bachelorhood is the most elusive thing about him. There is, however, evidence to work with.

A parable from Symeon the New Theologian's *Oratio Ethica 10*, in which an emperor takes a rebel to bed, makes a statement about same-sex desires

DOI: 10.4324/9781351135238-5

in Basil II. Seen in relation to attitudes toward same-sex sexual behavior between men in Byzantium, the political situation in Basil's reign, Symeon's position as an ecclesiastical leader both apart from the secular world and in it, and the depiction of emperor and his court in Symeon's writings, this work from the early 1000s gives evidence for a stream of thought about the bachelorhood of the current emperor. Symeon's text suggests that Basil's compatriots felt comfortable attributing same-sex desire to their emperor. Indeed, while certainty is elusive, a narrative that attributes this to him and appreciates the presence of same-sex desire between men in these rarified court circles is more persuasive than what has been a *communis opinio* on Basil's bachelorhood.

Taking the portrait of Basil as a generally grim man by the eleventh-century intellectual and historiographer, Michael Psellos, as a starting point, scholarly accounts have often explained Basil's demurral to wed by making him a monk manqué whose asceticism has a vague religious basis. At other times, it is considered possible that Basil wished to avoid meddling in-laws. While Psellos reports that Basil did affect a spare demeanor and the prospect of a wife's relatives plausibly might have given him pause, these things do not conclusively answer the question of why he remained a bachelor, especially as there is evidence of another conversation in Symeon the New Theologian. But before proceeding to this discussion, though, it is necessary first to reveal the problems with the *communis opinio* so that the ground is clear and the actual evidence, which gains in persuasiveness to the extent the nature of Byzantine educated elite masculine homosociality is kept in mind, can be made to speak.

The State of the Question of Basil's Bachelorhood

Most of the time, scholars explain the bachelorhood of Basil with evidence from Psellos and, at times, Ademarus Cabannensis (Adémar de Chabannes), about whom more below. Psellos provides a grim and ascetic demeanor and Ademarus a vow that Basil supposedly made to become a monk. Asceticism and (sometimes) a vow explain imperial bachelorhood. Concern about in-laws sometimes supplements this explanation, or is offered by itself. But the question of his bachelorhood is not as settled as it sometimes is implied, or is said to be.[7] But first, as the aim is to trouble the combination of Psellos and Ademarus as a basis for approaching Basil's bachelorhood, what is the evidence from these two medieval authors and how has it been deployed by scholars?

Psellos' portrait of Basil in Book One of the *Chronographia*, a masterpiece of Byzantine historiography, is an overwhelming presence in scholarly commentary on Basil's unmarried state. Of particular importance is the austere manner Psellos says Basil assumed after he put down the revolts of Bardas Skleros and Bardas Phokas. Psellos says that he was different prior to the revolts: "he used to feast openly and frequently made love."[8] After these revolts, Basil was "carried away from luxury by full sails, and he held himself to endeavor with all his soul,"[9] and once Bardas Phokas' head had been presented to him,[10]

> the emperor became someone else, and the changed state of affairs was gladdening him no more than had the terror of events vexed him. Subsequently, he was seen to be suspicious of all, haughty in his bearing, hiding his thoughts, quick to anger and heavy in his wrath with those who made mistakes.
> (*Chronographia* 1.18)[11]

Grim affect was correlated by sober dress,[12] possible asceticism,[13] and a court that was, in Psellos' opinion, insufficiently brilliant.[14] It is probable, too, that Psellos addresses Basil's unmarried state in the advice he says Bardas Skleros gave him, when Basil and he met after his second revolt ended:

> He [Bardas Skleros] did not offer military counsel but gave cunning advice instead ... [a point in this advice was the following:] don't bring (*eisagagein*/εἰσαγαγεῖν) a wife (*gunaika*/γυναῖκα) into the palace (*ta basileia*/τὰ βασίλεια).
> (*Chronographia* 1.28)[15]

While there is scope in how to read *eisagagein, gynaika,* and *ta basileia*, the most natural interpretation of this passage is that Bardas is telling Basil not to marry.[16]

In recent decades, scholars have shown awareness of the constructed nature of Psellos' account and of complexities in it that militate against viewing his Basil as only dour.[17] Crostini has underscored how Psellos speaks to his eleventh-century audience about an imperial court proper to the empire and Basil's court provides an example not to be followed. Psellos' narrative is tendentious at times, for, as Crostini points out, a number of Basil's associates were estimable intellects[18] and cultivated letters from them have survived.[19] Garland notes that Psellos has often been read in ways that are reductive of the complexity of his portrait of Basil: not grim all the time, Basil joked.[20] Crostini counsels that Psellos is not that reliable and Garland suggests that he be read with greater care. Taking a different tack, Holmes calls less and more directly for decreased reliance on Psellos to understand Basil's reign.[21] She has presented a case for putting John Skylitzes' *Sunopsis Historion* into a commanding position.[22] She also offers nuanced understandings of the varied relationships Basil had with leading families in the empire and the essential role the military played in the maintenance of his power.[23]

Still, though, this nuancing of Psellos and addition of Skylitzes has had no effect on understandings of Basil's bachelorhood. One reason for this is the fact that neither Psellos nor Skylitzes discusses it, though, as noted above, Psellos at least mentions it when he speaks of not bringing a wife into the palace. In any case, when addressing his demurral to wed, scholars to a person do not see same-sex desire as a possible driver in Basil's unmarried state. The *Chronographia*'s proffered grim affect leading into asceticism[24] sets most of the agenda, along with occasional speculation that he did not want troublesome in-laws. Basil did not marry because he had embraced "an ascetic way of life early in his reign."[25] He, now "cruel and austere" in 989 after the revolts of Skleros and Phokas and "[having spent] his bachelorhood in various love affairs"[26] (a characterization that places much weight on Psellos' *thama era*/θαμὰ ἤρα,[27] and indeed, assumes too much about both the Greek verb and the matter at hand), did not take a wife because he wanted "to avoid meddling by a wife or her relatives."[28] Tougher does not think "sexual preference" was at issue and finds it "likely that his decision [not to wed] was taken on religious grounds."[29] Still others think there was a religious vow.[30] Religiously motivated asceticism is possible, but the vow, as Crostini points out, is not supported by Psellos' text.[31] Indeed, Psellos doesn't connect Basil's moods and affect to his bachelorhood, and bachelorhood is addressed only by Bardas Skleros in his advice.

And so, a vow confirming Basil in his bachelorhood is not present in Psellos. This vow that leads Basil full sail away from marriage is found in another text, the *Chronicon* of Ademarus Cabannensis. This work, penned in France in the early years of the eleventh century,[32] is the unreliable centerpiece of Arbagi's 1975 article "The Celibacy of Basil II." This article, which is cited often and even relatively recently,[33] is problematic and should no longer be the go-to on the subject of Basil's celibacy. What makes the prize piece of evidence, Ademarus' *Chronicon*, so unreliable?

In the third book of the *Chronicon* (a work concerned mostly with the history of France and the Franks), Ademarus relates how Basil swore to become a monk if he defeated the Bulgarians. Ademarus' narrative in general has problems, chief among them mistakes about what happened during Basil's lengthy conflict with the Bulgarians.[34] But Ademarus' handling of the chronology of the vow and its fulfillment particularly diminishes his persuasiveness as a source on Basil:

> [E]nraged at them (*sc.* the Bulgarians), Emperor Basil bound himself with a vow to God that he would become a monk, if he could subdue the Bulgarian people for the Greeks...[and once success was achieved]... just as he had promised with his vow, he assumed the monastic way of life in the Greek style for the rest of his life [from 1018 going forward; though perhaps from 1014], abstaining from sexual pleasure and meat, while he was surrounded on the outside by imperial regalia.
>
> (*Chronicon* 3.32)[35]

With defeat of the Bulgarians achieved once and for all in 1018, though it is possible to regard the vow as acted on in 1014 with the Bulgarians' disastrous defeat at the Battle of Kleidion (an important event *not* mentioned in Ademarus' account), this means that Basil finally keeps his promise to God when he is around 60 years old (1018), or perhaps around his 56th birthday (1014). So, according to Ademarus, Basil's determination to bring the dangerous Bulgarian state to heel was the reason for his bachelorhood. But a vow to become a monk fulfilled so late in life, while providing an answer, raises questions: what, for example, happened in the years before? In any case, Arbagi finds Ademarus useful because his depiction of Basil's character is "uncannily accurate," by which he means it corroborates what Psellos says.[36] This then means that other things are to be believed, including the vow.

In an article concerned with Ademarus himself that takes the position that Basil did not make a vow but was just inclined to asceticism,[37] Wolff discusses Ademarus' tastes for forgery and delusion which are relevant here. In addition to his demonstrable ignorance of the realities of Basil's reign, Ademarus shows himself to be untrustworthy in general: he tried his utmost to make St. Martial the 13th apostle, even forging documents to bolster his case.[38] In any case, to the extent that Wolff speaks of Basil's asceticism, he replicates a simplified version of Psellos' viewpoint. Wolff also vaporizes Ademarus as testimony to Basil's bachelorhood, and we, now having no vow, lean hard on Psellos' characterization of grim Basil's sense of purpose in performing his duties and a suite of mostly unmotivated actions in Ademarus.

In considering the general effect of scholarship that uses Psellos and Ademarus, sometimes via Arbagi and sometimes not, to understand Basil's character and bachelorhood, one notes that Psellos is used to validate Ademarus who only, it is to be believed, exaggerated things. The question of Basil's celibacy, which is of great interest from the standpoint of gender and sexuality studies and should attract careful attention because of its nearly unprecedented nature,[39] is not well explained by placing overwhelming emphasis on Basil's deportment as observed in one source that advertises its literary constructedness, on the one hand, and, on the other, by using a source from an author known to be mendacious and who clearly has only the vaguest idea of what was going on in the Byzantine Empire.

While it cannot be said for sure why this yoking of cultivated Byzantine man of letters with shifty Frankish chronicler has not received the hard questioning it deserves, it seems anxiety about possible sexual "irregularity" in the great military emperor has disabled critical faculties. Leaving Basil unmarried amid his exceedingly homosocial court, into which no wife was to enter, leads to questions about same-sex desire. And so unconscious or not so unconscious nervousness among scholars about same-sex desire and sexual relations has kept this unlikely team yoked and pulling the wagon, as it were, of Basil's bachelorhood (when the question has been broached at all). But this unsatisfactory place need not be home. There is other evidence, probably ignored because of reasons just stated and because of its metaphorical nature, which is contemporary and situated in Basil's milieu: a parable from Symeon the New Theologian's *Oratio Ethica 10*.

Symeon the New Theologian's Evidence

Symeon the New Theologian was a monk, *hegoumenos* (abbot) of a monastery, possessor of a chapel, and important ecclesiastical writer who was a little older than Basil and a eunuch.[40] His dates were probably 949–1022. Before becoming a monk, he held a position, *spatharokoubikoularios*,[41] in the imperial court.[42] If, as seems likely, one of his works, the *Catecheses*,[43] features a moment of autobiography,[44] Symeon was well informed about the ways and means of same-sex desire at this point of his life,[45] though he later embraced restraint. He probably wrote the tenth *Oratio Ethica*, as part of a set of 15 orations, during the first decade of the 1000s, which was a time when he was at odds with Basil II and the imperial government. Darrouzès thought the tenth oration and the others in the collection bear the marks of struggle.[46] In this difficult decade, he lost control of the St. Mamas monastery in Constantinople,[47] after having been tried in ecclesiastic court for allegedly fostering improper reverence for his recently deceased mentor, Symeon Eulabes.[48] In the middle of the decade, he was also tried for heresy,[49] and at the decade's end, he went into exile across the Bosporus to Chrysopolis.[50] There, one of Symeon's lay supporters, Christopher Phagoura, bought him the chapel dedicated to St. Marina at Paloukiton.[51] He resided there until his death.[52]

The tenth *Oratio Ethica* contains a parable of an emperor who forgives a rebel. This parable is drenched in same-sex eroticism. Arguments to come will suggest that a Byzantine audience would have had reason to think of Basil II when hearing/reading the parable and that Symeon would have wanted this.[53] First, though, what is this oration and its parable?

The prevailing theme of Symeon's tenth *Oratio Ethica*, called *On the Fearful Day of the Lord and On the Judgement to Come*,[54] is that life should be lived as though the Final Judgement were already present. Living this way is not hard to do.[55] The light speaks in the here and now.[56] Living in accordance with God's commandments is to have it as easy as a rebel does in a parable Symeon offers as an illustrative example (10.234: *paradeigma*/παραδεῖγμα). In this lengthy parable,[57] Symeon tells the story of a rebel who was in the service of an opponent of the Emperor of the Christians.[58] The emperor tries to persuade the rebel to defect and, rewarded, join him on the throne:

> He was given secret messages through various means by the Emperor of the Christians that he should come to him, be with him,[59] receive great gifts, and rule with him.
>
> (*Oratio Ethica* 10.239–241)[60]

Revisiting the Bachelorhood 175

This man initially is not persuaded and even redoubles his hostility.[61] Ultimately, he surrenders, showing much stagey regret: "going to the emperor and embracing his feet, he begged with wailing for pardon" (*Oratio Ethica* 10.252–253).[62] The emperor accepts, and his acceptance is quite demonstrative:

> [The emperor] "fell upon his neck and kissed him"[63] all over and [kissed too] those eyes of him [i.e., the rebel] which were shedding tears for many hours. Then, having ordered that a crown, robe, and shoes similar to those he was wearing be brought, he himself personally clothed his erstwhile enemy and opponent, in all ways avoiding any verbal abuse of him. And not only this, but as he was making merry and rejoicing together (*suneuphrainomenos*/συνευφραινόμενος)[64] with him all day and all night, holding him tight and kissing him mouth to mouth, to so great extent did he "over-love" (*huperegapesen*/ὑπερηγάπησεν) him that he did not separate himself from him in sleep, lying down with him, holding him tight on the bed, covering him completely with his *paludamentum*,[65] and putting his face on all his members.
> (*Oratio Ethica* 10.261–273)[66]

This is an astonishing passage, erotic and carnal. It could be a description of the night after an *adelphopoiesis* ceremony: the rebel and emperor are "rejoicing together" (*suneuphrainomenos*/συνευφραινόμενος). The presence of this verb recalls the eroticism perceptible in the description of Basil I's brotherhood with Nicholas in Symeon and Pseudo-Symeon's *Chronographiai* through the connection they have to Proverbs.[67] Indeed, Proverbs 5 would have been a primary intertext for Symeon the New Theologian's Byzantine audience. Another aspect of the parable, the bestowal of imperial raiment, also recalls the story of Basilikinos, who briefly threatened to supplant Basil I.[68] This passage from *Oratio Ethica 10* has struck some readers over the years as excessive.[69] Symeon signals that it is excessive by saying that the emperor did not merely love the rebel, he "over-loved" (*huperegapesen*/ὑπερηγάπησεν) him. This verb with its prepositional prefix *huper*/ὑπέρ pushes the reader or listener to the conclusion that something is too much. *Huper* is an invitation to interpretation.

A first approach to this "excessive" carnal content might regard the sheer inappropriateness of the imagery as a fitting depiction of the singularity that is the fearful day of Final Judgement. As the Final Judgement is the end of all things, there is nothing to which it is comparable. The worldly ways and means of sex between men hardly fit this incomparable celestial event. The metaphor stages the inevitable failure of representation and the event's incomparability. The passage as a whole is ironic and gestural on this reading.

A second approach to the "excessive" carnality thinks in terms of continuities things of this world have with things celestial. Seeing the parable in relation to Symeon's frequent embrace of the corporeal, Krueger "argue[s] that Symeon employs same-sex desires in order to emphasize the male monastic body as a locus of *theōsis*, the deification of humanity."[70] Indeed, Symeon's embrace of the bodily leads him, in the context of making a point about the Incarnation, to say that even as his finger is Christ, so also is his penis, which he calls his *balanos*/βάλανος.[71] And so this passage speaks to the nature of the Incarnation[72] and only "over-love," the word and not the entire passage, is the locus of an irony. Another way to put this is that *huper* brings to a reader's or listener's notice the understanding of someone who is skeptical about the nature of the Incarnation and connections between this world and the next.

But there is more to note. "Over-love," advertising excess as it does, counsels the listener/reader to think about how this instance of forgiveness has discontinuities with other portrayals of forgiveness. This is emphatically a direction to go in, for there is a portrayal ready to hand. Symeon quotes Lk 15:20, a text that all in his audience would have known. The carnal approach to forgiveness on display in Symeon's parable far outpaces Luke (from the tale of the prodigal son):

> While he [the prodigal son] was still keeping himself a fair ways away, his father saw him. He felt compassion, and, running, he fell upon his neck and kissed him.
>
> (Lk 15:20)[73]

The demonstrativeness in Luke is more chaste: none of the togetherness day and night, covering *paludamentum*, or face on all the members. The parable, therefore, is no moment of scriptural exegesis but a registering of distance, and the emperor's distance from the paradigm offered in the New Testament is an implicit criticism of the emperor.

Luke is not the only text that can underscore via comparison the parable's excessiveness, the semantics of which again is disapproval. The fact that Symeon was also the currently embattled, or recently dispossessed, leader of the monastery of St. Mamas could have called to mind another scene of imperial forgiveness: that by Emperor Maurice (582–602). The monastery of St. Mamas was founded by Maurice,[74] and this emperor features in a parable concerning him and a bandit in Anastasios of Sinai's oration (c. 700) on Ps 6/7.[75] In this parable of imperial forgiveness, Anastasios relates how an arch bandit (*archileistes*), who had been laying waste to Thrace, was made good through the forgiving excellence of the emperor. The bandit meets Maurice, and like a sheep falls to the emperor's feet, embraces them, and begs forgiveness. Maurice grants it. The bandit falls mortally ill shortly thereafter. While the bandit was breathing his last, his doctor saw a vision of the weighing of the sins of the *archileistes*. Things did not look good for the bandit, whose misdeeds were weighty. But two angels discovered the bandit's tears on his tunic and these outweighed the sins. Awakening from his

Revisiting the Bachelorhood 177

dream, the doctor rushed to find the body of the *archileistes* still warm. The doctor then told the emperor everything, remarking that the bandit helped himself through his confessions to authorities celestial and terrestrial:

> I have heard that the bandit was saved through confession to the cross of the heavenly emperor, and I know that the bandit was [also] saved through confession to your imperiality (*basileias*/βασιλείας).
> (Anastasios of Sinai, *Oratio in Psalmum VI* [*PG* 89: 1116A])[76]

In comparison, Symeon's Emperor of the Christians (which is what Anastasios calls Maurice too: *PG* 89: 1112A) is excessive and, as in the case of comparison with the scene in Luke, surely "over-loving" his rebel, if the reader has Maurice in mind; an embrace of his feet is the extent of Maurice's bodily contact with the bandit. Nor does Maurice put the bandit in a position of authority or dress him in imperial costume. Symeon's over-loving emperor shows excess at the level of the body (bed) and excess in giving up authority (this man becomes co-emperor). Luke says that Symeon's emperor's behavior is out of step with the New Testament, and memory of Maurice's *archileistes* makes the parable legible as commentary on the current holder of the throne, Basil II, as a rebel is getting very much a sweeter deal in the case of the later text. This homoerotic behavior, excessive, is quite the semantic vehicle. But how serious a thing would it be to say that Basil, obstinately unmarried, had tastes in the direction of other men? Before formulating the answer to this question, some of the elements of which are anticipatable for readers of the earlier chapters of this book, how does Symeon handle same-sex desire between men elsewhere in his works?

The parable is not the only place in his works where Symeon speaks of desire and sex between men.[77] In *Hymns 24*, amid continually asserting that since all are sinners, sin need not be a barrier to eventual communion with Christ, Symeon admits to being a sodomite: "I became, alas, an adulterer in my heart and a sodomite in reality and by disposition."[78] Later, he gives the impression that he, when young and handsome (*kath' horan*/καθ' ὥραν), was sexually penetrated:

> How was I able to bear in silence those things happening during my desirable young manhood, and, O my God, those things being done in / within wretched me?
> (*Hymns* 24, 175–177)[79]

This hymn also features confession of many sins. He admits, for example, to being a male prostitute, a magician, and a pederast, all in line 76.[80] The scale of misbehavior poses the question as to whether some of his admissions are less than real and are, instead, exaggerations meant to teach.[81] Adjudication of the question of rhetoric versus reality postpones a necessary discussion, though, for a different question, "Why this didactic rhetoric?," is the one

178   Revisiting the Bachelorhood

that demands consideration. For Symeon says, to the discomfort of some scholars,[82] that adultery was merely aspirational, and that sodomy, suited to his desires, happened.[83] This sin seems more real, and the greater degree of reality shows this desire to be less remarkable within Symeon's milieu than perhaps anticipated by scholars. In any case, the words that introduce the parable of rebel and emperor cast the coming corporeality as but an image Symeon had to hand:

> Our master and God has commanded nothing severe, nothing burdensome, but, instead, things, all of them, easy and simple, just as – believe me – I myself know the command of God and the obtaining of him and his kingdom to be a simple thing. But I will show you this through an example...
>
> (*Oratio Ethica* 10.229–234)[84]

After finishing the parable, Symeon brings home its offhand nature in words that soon follow. Getting right with God is approaching him without pretension and running naked:

> Therefore, my beloved brothers, leaving everything behind, let us run naked and, coming to Christ, our master, let us fall down and wail in the face of his goodness, so that he, having seen our faith and humility, in similar fashion and even to a greater degree, may receive us, hold us in honor, and bestow on us his robe and diadem, and make us guests worthy of the celestial bridal chamber.
>
> (*Oratio Ethica* 10.304–311)[85]

Being right with God is as easy and true as corporeal intimacy; this pleasure functions as a vivid and effective metaphor. While Symeon's move is hardly unprecedented—the carnal had often provided metaphors since Plato—the reader of the *Oratio Ethica 10* and other works of Symeon has learned about the "erotic imaginary available to a middle-Byzantine monastic theologian"[86] and about "sexuality" in monastic settings in the late tenth to early eleventh century. It is well to remember Symeon's admission of same-sex sexual acts and the ease with which they pass into usable metaphor. A conclusion to draw is that this desire was not productive of shame that utterly disabled speech. Indeed, the relative ease with same-sex desire is to be found outside of Symeon's writings, as the previous chapters of this book attest, also shows this.

Basil II as Symeon's Referent

An understanding that same-sex desire and behavior were likely and things not that weighty for Symeon to discuss is only a precondition for seeing Basil in the parable's emperor. This referentiality must be argued. The bases for this argument are the fact of Basil's bachelorhood, the political situation in his reign, and Symeon's milieu which featured diffusion of his influence and writings among monks and laymen in the capital.

Basil's decision not to wed and play a direct part in the continuation of the Macedonian line was momentous one. Much attested among the politically powerful,[87] marriage was important, to say the least, in the empire at the time.[88] Not exempt, an emperor was expected to take a wife. The second book of *Theophanes Continuatus* has an episode from the reign of Michael II (820–829) in which this expectation is articulated directly. Michael compelled the senate to beg him to remarry after his first wife had died:

> [The senate, prompted by Michael] was saying, "it is not possible for the emperor to live without a wife or for our wives to be deprived of their mistress and empress."
>
> (*Theophanes Continuatus* 2.24/78)[89]

And so, his hand, as it were, forced,[90] Michael married Euphrosyne, daughter of Constantine VI (780–797): an emperor must be married.[91]

From marriage come children of the blood. Possession of Macedonian blood drove political calculations. This blood kept Basil II and his brother safe during their minorities when Nikephoros II Phokas and John I Tzimiskes reigned. Blood similarly safeguarded Constantine VII and made him marriageable, as his marriage to Helene Lekapene, daughter of Romanos I Lekapenos shows. The extension of the Macedonian dynasty through the marriages of Basil's niece Zoe Porphyrogennete in the eleventh century also argues for the blood's importance. One can only imagine the pressure to marry that Basil, star of the fifth generation of the dynasty, resisted.

Not only securing the continuation of the line, marriage could be a powerful bargaining chip. Basil could have married a woman from a powerful family to create an alliance, as his grandfather did when he married Helene Lekapene. Older scholarship generally saw Basil as opposed to the aristocracy as a whole, and so such a move seemed unlikely on these terms.[92] Recent scholarship has suggested Basil's opposition to the major families was selective.[93] Hence, marriage to a woman from one of the families he favored, say, the Skleroi, is conceivable. However, choosing a wife from one family would have created disappointment among the others. But Basil could have blunted disappointment by not playing a favorite. He could have married a woman of low status. His father, for example, married a comparative nobody, Anastaso in 955 or 956, who took the name Theophano.[94] In the previous century, Basil I's wife, Eudokia Ingerina, was also not lofty.[95] In this way, Basil also could have avoided entanglements with powerful in-laws.[96] But neither a strategic marriage nor one to a nobody occurred, and neither is there report of illegitimate issue, which had also been heard of, most famously in the person of Basil's own great-uncle, Basil the *Parakoimomenos*, who was the illegitimate son of Romanos I Lekapenos.

There is a final and important consideration bearing on Basil's refusal to wed: marriage between man and woman is a place of desire and sex.[97] It was well known, of course, that marriages, especially imperial ones, were about continuation of the line and alliance, but we also read that a beautiful empress attracted desire. Eudokia Ingerina entranced Michael III before he had to give her up and hand her over to Basil I.[98] Basil II's great grandmother, Zoe Karbonopsina (Zoe 'of the coal-black eyes') had a name which advertised her bewitching qualities. Basil's mother, the beautiful Theophano,[99] was said, in some of the sources, to have awakened strong desire in her second husband, Nikephoros II Phokas.[100] The corporeal rewards to being married were known.

Basil's bachelorhood in and of itself, then, creates a number of visibilities which predispose a reader now and a reader in the early eleventh century to see him in Symeon's emperor. Basil was manifestly bucking the expectation that an emperor wed and continue the imperial line through begetting sons. He also refused a salient connection with another family that would have occurred through marriage to and the bedding of one of their women. Finally, to the extent that marriage was seen as the site of enjoyable sexual activity with a woman, he was visibly refusing that also. Given that it was possible for him to wed "low" and avoid entanglements that, say, lofty in-laws might bring, the full-on force of these visibilities generates a question about the nature of his sexual desires. In summation, the decision not to wed, not only political and strategic, addresses sexuality and desire. Clearly sensitive to this, previous scholarship provided the answer of asceticism, but this is not a water-tight case and actually does not answer the question. If it is assumed that he was refusing sex, what kind of sex was he refusing? At this moment, the parable of Symeon becomes interesting. It provides a reading of the desire of the emperor: he is at least some of the time, if not more than that, interested in homoerotic encounters: he is not bedding a wife, he is bedding military men like himself. This reading becomes more convincing when the political situation in Basil's reign is considered.

Basil struggled with rebels early in his reign. He forgave some and punished others. The emperor in the parable "over-loved" a rebel. Did the parable provide a likely metaphor, given Basil's unmarried state, for this favoring that came to some, and not to others—others who would have found imperial forgiveness excessive? For example, Basil was surprisingly mild to one rebel, Bardas Skleros,[101] and his son, Romanos, took a place in Basil's inner circle. Skylitzes reports that after the fall of his uncle, Basil the *Parakoimomenos*, Basil needed new advisors, and he found one in Romanos Skleros:

> After he had received him with exceedingly friendly intention and great joy, he [Basil] straightaway honored this one [Romanos] as *magistros* and he was using him as an advisor in every aspect of his warring...he [Basil] deprived of the counsel of him [Basil the *Parakoimomenos*] and

needing friends and allies in his struggles, at the time truly welcomed Romanos, knowing him to be a man quick-witted, energetic, and just the one for the things of war.

(Skylitzes, *Sunopsis Historion*, *Basil II and Constantine VIII* 16/335)[102]

The Phokades, and others in a similar position, may have felt the emperor "over-loved" some rebels. The head of Bardas Phokas, torn from his dismembered body,[103] took a trip to Constantinople and then around Asia Minor after his revolt ended.[104] And just prior, Basil had Kalokyres Delphinas[105] either "hanged on wood"[106] or impaled.[107] His legislation against aristocratic interests, e.g. the law against the "powerful" (*dunatoi*) from 996,[108] would not have been perceived as showing love, much less "over-love." But what is to be noted, and which is supported by recent scholarship on Basil's reign, is that his opposition to the major families was a sometime thing.[109] From the point of view of someone not favored, it could be said Basil played favorites. The extravagant forgiveness of some in the eyes of those not so honored would have been galling. Symeon's emperor's carnal forgiveness is an allegory of the favor Basil showed to some of his former enemies.

But this argument that Basil could be perceived as the referent in the parable depends additionally on seeing Symeon commenting on current politics in his oration. This case is plausible for a number of reasons. In the first place, Basil had been the emperor for a long time by the time the *Orationes Ethicae* were written in the first decade of 1000s. Any reference to an emperor will encourage a reader or listener to compare and contrast Basil to the emperor appearing in the text. Second, Symeon had been struggling with Basil and his representatives, and the marks of struggle have been seen in the *Orationes Ethicae*. Darrouzès remarks that the *Orationes Ethicae* "sont en grande partie une oeuvre de controverse ou du moins composée durant une période de controverses."[110] The struggles, as noted above, were these: Symeon lost his monastery, St. Mamas[111]; he got in trouble for fostering what was seen as inappropriate rites to the memory of his mentor, Symeon Eulabes[112]; he even stood trial for heresy.[113] All this happened in the decade or so prior to the writing of *Oratio Ethica 10*. A critical perspective on the emperor becoming visible in Symeon's works would not have been and is not surprising. Furthermore, the parable of forgiveness of the rebel is not a singular event in Symeon's works. Emperor and imperial court appear elsewhere in his works.

Ambivalence and complexity characterize Symeon's metaphoric use of the emperor and his court. On the one hand, the magnificence and power of the emperor made imperial favor an apt metaphor for desirable divine interventions, such as God's grace, as seen in the parable from *Oratio Ethica 10*. On the other hand, Symeon shows an interest in bringing emperors down to earth.[114] The carnality of the parable is an illustration of this. Reading

182   *Revisiting the Bachelorhood*

other references by Symeon to the emperor together with the parable, we see that he finds emperor and court useful metaphors for divinity and heaven but also all too human and of this earth at the same time. Indeed, the image of the emperor in Symeon's thought is ambivalent, exhibiting idealizing and critical perspectives simultaneously. What this means is that the emperor in the parable with the rebel is a figure that embodies both God and an actual emperor, the latter of whom will be human and fallible, indeed the latter predominates in other examples from Symeon's works.

At *Catecheses* 2.107–109,[115] Symeon critically observes that the earthly emperor has no time for the poor, cannot bear to look at them, and is no better than arrogant rich men are.[116] *Catecheses* 4.470–472 is also critical: "the emperor separate from his army becomes weak and vulnerable to all and sundry and no longer appears to be emperor."[117] Making reference to 2 Sam 12, Symeon counsels in another *catechesis* that emperors (and other leaders) would do well to keep in mind that King David admitted his fault to Nathan and fell to the ground before him (the implication being that this advice from the Septuagint is not followed as often as it should be).[118] A final and significant example from Symeon's works features not only ambivalence about the emperor (and his court) but also employs the verb "over-love," which is the same word used in the parable from *Oratio Ethica 10*.

Symeon wrote the *Capita Theologica*, a work of practical instruction on virtues and vices, after he was removed as *hegoumenos* of St. Mamas.[119] In the eighth section of the second book of this work, he compares the pious elation a monk feels when "called aloft to the height of contemplation of the Holy Spirit"[120] to the pleasure the emperor can give when he bestows earthly position and riches. At the end of the comparison, Symeon compares donning Christ to being clothed in imperial purple:

> For he [the monk who has truly withdrawn from the world and its affairs[121]] looks always upon the grace of the Spirit shining around him, this grace which is called a raiment and imperial purple, or rather it is Christ himself, if [we care to say, and of course we do, that] those who have faith in him are clothed in him.
>
> (*Capita Theologica* 2.8.13–16)[122]

But this is not the entirety of the comparison. Symeon earlier describes the promotion in detail. Characteristically for Symeon, his comparison overshoots the mark by describing a scene whose corporealities make it an imperfect metaphor, and, hence, a text that additionally has criticism of the earthly emperor on its mind:

> Just as the one who has been raised from the most extreme poverty by the emperor, who has been clothed by him in brilliant office and a shining robe, who has been ordered to stand in his presence, just as this one looks upon the emperor with desire (*meta pothou*/μετὰ πόθου), over-loves

(*huperagapai*/ὑπεραγαπᾷ) him as his benefactor, studies intently the robe in which he has been clothed, knows well his office, and thinks about the wealth that has been given to him.

(*Capita Theologica* 2.8.1–7)[123]

The emperor can raise up a man who is a nobody and clothe him in office and robes. This benefaction awakens regard (desire [*pothos*/πόθος]) in the one so honored and he even "over-loves" the emperor in return. As in the parable from the *Oratio Ethica 10*, though not in as graphic a manner, Symeon calls to mind erotic desire through the use of the noun *pothos*. Even closer to the parable is the appearance of the verb "over-love" (ὑπεραγαπάω). In contrast to the passage from *Oratio Ethica 10*, however, "over-loving" does not rain down from above, but rises up from below. Reading this passage from the *Capita Theologica* together with the parable to come to an understanding of Symeon's ideas about desire and promotion in the imperial court enables two points. First, "over-loving" is something that does not belong solely to superior or inferior but can be expressed by either. Second, the imperial court is a place of excess, for, as with the parable, the picture of relations in the court has a surfeit of things of this world that make it a metaphor that does not quite fit. "Over-loves" conveys some disapproval. The one, whom the emperor has promoted, loves his royal highness, the gorgeous clothing, office and wealth to come more than is right, hence the "over" (*huper*/ὑπέρ). Is Basil's court, missing an empress and therefore heavily skewed to homo-sociality, visible here?

Ambivalence, accordingly, is present, or perhaps it is better to say that Symeon has his cake and eats it too. Preferment by the emperor provides a choice earthly metaphor for the celestial boons of the grace of the Spirit and being clothed in Christ, on the one hand, while, on the other hand, a critical stance to these marks of worldly advancement is also visible. The courtier has reached a summit of earthly ambition and so the metaphor is effective. But the courtier so honored does not merely love, he "over-loves." He places too great a value on the things of this world. Same-sex desire with its worldly corporealities and metaphoric possibilities presents a picture similarly complicated, especially for those who live in Symeon's thought world and/or may know the parable from *Oratio Ethica 10*.

Lastly, it is all well and good to demonstrate that Symeon was capable of twice constructing metaphors of imperial favor—metaphors containing same-sex desire and "over-love"—that both gesture in the direction of God and divine grace, and, yet, venture criticism of the emperor at the same time. In the absence of an audience, such a thing would be but a dead letter. But Symeon's writings were not solipsistic and removed from life. His thought world was not limited to him or to a small circle of readers or listeners. Symeon was almost never far away from action in the capital. Indeed, he was within the city walls for all those years at St. Mamas, and later was just across the Bosporus at Paloukiton at St. Marina's. Furthermore, the secondary literature discusses much interaction between monks and laymen.[124] As an estimable ecclesiastical leader, Symeon was spiritual father not only to monks in his own establishment, but also maintained pastoral connections to men in the world.[125] As noted above, Christopher Phagoura, a layman with whom he was connected, set him up in his chapel at Paloukiton.[126] Politics did not cease at the monastery door, indeed the door was open to traffic coming in and going out.[127] Lastly, it seems quite likely that the *Orationes Ethicae* were addressed to an audience both monastic and secular.[128] This was a broad audience for whom Basil would have been the only emperor in living memory: any parable about an emperor would have been measured against Basil for similarities and differences. It is logical in light of the facts about Basil, the political situation, and the context within which Symeon was writing to assume that the parable from *Oratio Ethica 10* would have been read as commentary on the current emperor's policies and sexual life.

Conclusion

Symeon's emperor was not only an idealized figure. He was both an idealizing metaphor and, at the same time, liable to criticism for being too much of this world. When Symeon criticized an emperor, at that moment, the current holder of the throne, Basil II, came into view. And so Symeon provided a reading of Basil's bachelorhood. Symeon would have had reason to wish to render some criticism, and his excessive portrayal in the parable from *Oratio Ethica 10* in a variety of ways encouraged the reader to form a question about bachelor Basil's desire: did he spend the time he saved by not being married with other men?

The old idea that Basil was a bachelor because of dedication to God has weaker support. Ademarus is not persuasive due to demonstrated ignorance and mendacity. Also, far away and from another milieu altogether, he was not capable of understanding the intense homosociality and attitudes toward same-sex desire among Byzantine elite men during these centuries. Psellos speaks of Basil's grimness and rather more than that, if he is read carefully with Crostini and Garland. Psellos likely addressed Basil's unmarried state in the advice he reports Bardas Skleros gave to Basil. But that is all. In contrast, Symeon's parable has a possible referent in Basil because of the question about desire his bachelorhood posed, his differential treatment of rebels, and the milieu in which Symeon wrote. A taste for women on Basil's part is possible, but there is no evidence for that and there is indication, via Symeon, that he had same-sex interests. Symeon had an axe to grind and it is plausible that he might have liked to deliver a chop—a chop, it must be understood, that would not be devastating, but rather to point out a carnal failing. The imperial court, of which he had experience earlier in his life,[129] was too materialistic in its practices and should hardly be telling him what to do. Exclusively homosocial, with no wife in sight, the court was liable to "over-loving" excesses. Symeon's critique should be viewed as something of a throwaway, and it illuminates the place of same-sex desire among men in Byzantium at this time.

Notes

1 A version of this chapter appeared in 2019, see Masterson (2019b).
2 His brother, Constantine VIII (1025–1028), was also emperor throughout this time, but all sources agree that he was side-lined until Basil's death: see for instance Tougher (2013, 316–318). Be it noted that Constantine married.
3 Psellos, *Chronographia* 1.19–21, narrates the fall of Basil the *Parakoimomenos*. At 1.3, he tells of happier days for the two Basils, great-uncle and grandnephew. For more on Basil the *Parakoimomenos*, see Brokkaar (1972); Tougher (2008, 138). For discussion focusing on his interactions with Basil II, see Crostini (1996, 59–64); Garland (1999a, 326, 326n20); Holmes (2003, 58–61; 2005, 469–474; 2006, 331–333).
4 For a classic statement of Basil's success, see Ostrogorsky (1968). Others, e.g. Angold (1997) and Holmes (2005), are skeptical to varying degrees, wondering if the success of the empire under Basil was as solid as it has often been made out to be. See Holmes (2005, 448–543), for narration of his reign, including the major campaigns. For legal enactments, see Svoronos (1994, 185–217). I should note here too that Holmes (2003) and (2005) and Sifonas (1994) have provided welcome nuance to overly schematized accounts of Basil's reign that see him as relentlessly attacking the aristocracy as a whole, for he opposed some families and not others.
5 Leo the Deacon, *Historia* 5.3; Shepard (2003, 15); Tougher (2013, 307).
6 Holmes (2005), v. In similar fashion, Garland (1999a, 321), calls Basil "something of an enigma."
7 E.g. Garland (1999a, 321), states that the question of Basil's non-marriage has been a non-issue since 1975: "A study by Arbagi (1975) has helped resolve the problem of why Basil never married...."
8 *Chronographia* 1.4: ἀπαρακαλύπτως ἐκώμαζε καὶ θαμὰ ἤρα.
9 *Chronographia* 1.4: ὅλοις ἱστίοις ἀπενεχθεὶς τῆς τρυφῆς, ὅλῳ πνεύματι ἀντείχετο τῆς σπουδῆς.
10 *Chronographia* 1.17: τὴν κεφαλὴν ἐκτεμόντες τῷ Βασιλείῳ προσάγουσιν.
11 Ἐντεῦθεν ἕτερος ἀνθ' ἑτέρου ὁ βασιλεὺς γίνεται, καὶ οὐ μᾶλλον αὐτὸν τὸ γεγονὸς εὔφρανεν, ἢ ἡ τῶν πραγμάτων δεινότης ἠνίασεν· ὕποπτος οὖν εἰς πάντας ὦπτο καὶ σοβαρὸς τὴν ὀφρὺν, τάς τε φρένας ὑποκαθημένος καὶ τοῖς ἁμαρτάνουσι δύσοργος καὶ βαρύμηνις.
12 *Chronographia* 1.22.
13 *Chronographia* 1.32.
14 *Chronographia* 1.29; Crostini (1996) shows that Psellos is being particularly tendentious here.
15 ὁ δὲ ἄρα οὐ στρατηγικὴν βουλήν, ἀλλὰ πανοῦργον εἰσηγεῖται γνώμην ... γυναῖκά τε εἰς τὰ βασίλεια μὴ εἰσαγαγεῖν.
16 It is possible to think that Skleros merely counsels against having a woman at imperial strategy sessions, as Sewter in his translation from 1953 seems to believe. This, however, is to understand the passage in an unnecessarily labored way. The passage's probable reference to advice to Basil to persist in his bachelorhood is strongly supported by reference to *LSJ*, which has the following, and which is as close to conclusive as can be imagined, at εἰσάγω: "ἐσαγαγεῖν or ἐσαγαγέσθαι γυναῖκα to lead a wife into one's house, Hdt. 5.40, 6.63." The

reference to Herodotus seals the deal, as Psellos' audience was cultivated. Furthermore, *ta basileia* was a favored term for "palace" from early times in Greek, and again this meaning would be a predominant one if we allow the fact of Psellos' audience's cultivation its proper weight. Lastly, this passage has not been mentioned in any scholarship that I have seen that addresses Basil's bachelorhood.

17 Crostini (1996); Holmes (2003, 61–62; 2005, 31–35, 516–517); Garland (1999a, 339–342), brings to light ways in which Psellos presents Basil as a comparandum to the eleventh-century Emperor Isaac I Komnenos (1057–1059).
18 Crostini (1996, 66–71).
19 Crostini (1996, 70) (cf. Van Opstall 2008, 26). Estimable intellects are to be found among Basil's associates. The reader of this book will be well acquainted now with the cultivated Nikephoros Ouranos and Symeon the Logothete. Leo of Synada provides another example. See Vinson's (1985) edition of Leo's letters.
20 Garland (1999a). *Chronographia* 1.20, 27, and 33.
21 Holmes (2003, 61), is the less direct; Holmes (2005, 34), is the more direct.
22 Holmes (2005).
23 Holmes (2005, 463–470), argues persuasively that understanding Basil as opposed to all the aristocratic families, full-stop, is incorrect. It was rather the case that he was against some families and a key issue in the maintenance of his authority was not so much land and revenue as control of the army (cf. Sifonas 1994 and Holmes 2003, 48–51).
24 Note that Psellos offers elsewhere a brief sketch of Basil's grim character: *Historia Syntomos* 106 (Aerts 1990).
25 Angold (1997, 5); cf. Wolff (1978, 144), "[Basil's] personal asceticism is historic fact."
26 Treadgold (1997, 513).
27 *Chronographia* 1.4.
28 Treadgold (1997, 519); cf. Holmes (2006, 336).
29 Tougher (2013, 307), "It seems likely that his decision was taken on religious grounds, rather than because of sexual preference, but the fact remains that this was a highly unusual act for a ruler…'; cf. Crostini (1996, 76–77).
30 Arbagi (1975); Garland (1999a, 321); Holmes twice reports that others have seen a vow by Basil as an explanation for his failure to wed (Holmes 2005, 45n60; 2006, 336). Magdalino (2003, 263–265), suggests that Basil's bachelorhood and religious interests be associated with general feelings in the empire that the millennium was going to bring with it the end of the world; he was unmarried because the end of days was nigh.
31 Crostini (1996, 74–75) (speaking of *Chronographia* 1.18): "[at this point in the *Chronographia*, Psellos only means to speak of] the emperor's zealous undertaking of duty, his business of governing of the state. No fanciful dedication to a religious lifestyle is here implied." However, Crostini (1996, 76–77), also believes that Psellos elsewhere (at *Chronographia* 1.32) implies that Basil was acting according to religious scruples when his behavior changed from fun-loving to grim. She even calls it a "religious conversion" (76). The situation at 1.32 on my reading is more about philosophical and martial self-denial (the latter especially), but the narrative of Psellos is complex, and unambiguous positions on many things in this work that has much on its mind are hard to find (see Kaldellis 1999).
32 For background on Ademarus, see Wolff (1978), *passim*, but 139.
33 See for example Tougher (2013, 307); Holmes (2006, 336, 339); Holmes (2005, 19, 45); Stephenson (2003, 73); Garland (1999a, 321).

34 Among the errors are the omission of the Battle of Kleidion, misconceptions about the personnel of the Bulgarian leadership, and the belief that Basil's struggles with the Bulgarians began around the year 1000 (they began in the 980s). For discussion of Ademarus' mistakes, see Arbagi (1975, 43–44) and Wolff (1978, 143–144).
35 [B]asilius imperator super eos nimis irritatus, voto se obligavit Deo monachum fieri, si Grecis gentem Bulgarorum subderet ... sicut voto promiserat, habitum monasticum greca figura subterindutus in reliquum est omni vitae suae tempore, a voluptate et carnibus abstinens, et imperiali scemate extrinsecus circumdabatur.
36 Arbagi (1975, 44).
37 Wolff (1978, 144).
38 Wolff (1978, 156–158).
39 Tougher (2013, 307), remarks that there was one other emperor who did not wed: Constans I (337–350), one of the sons of Constantine I. It is interesting to note in the context of the present investigation that there was discussion in the sources about Constans' interest in same-sex encounters. See my discussion, with bibliography: Masterson (2014, 24n53).
40 For more on Symeon's life, see Messis (2014a, 144–148), McGuckin (2005, 1996), and Turner (1990, 16–36), whose narratives in turn depend on Niketas Stethatos' life of Symeon (written in the decades following Symeon's death in 1022), as rationalized by Hausherr and Horn (1928). For a strong statement of the fact of Symeon's eunuch status, see Messis (2014a, 144–148).
41 *Spatharokoubikoularios* is a combined title: *spatharios* (a dignity, but lit. "swordbearer") with *koubikoularios*, i.e., a eunuch who waits upon the emperor and who may fulfill other administrative roles in the court.
42 Niketas Stethatos, *Vita Symeonis* 3; Turner (1990, 18); McGuckin (1996, 19).
43 A *catachesis* is a work of religious instruction.
44 *Catecheses* 22.24–28:

> [He (=I) had] a young man's beauty and possessed frame, personality, and gait that were like a vision, so that from these [aspects] some men even had raunchy suspicions about him, and others were only looking at his outer aspects and were judging him basely as regards other things...
>
> (ὡραῖος τῷ εἴδει καὶ φαντασιῶδες τό τε σχῆμα καὶ τὸ ἦθος καὶ τὸ βάδισμα κεκτημένος, ὡς ἐκ τούτων καὶ ὑπολήψεις πονηρὰς ἔχειν τινὰς εἰς αὐτόν, τοὺς τὸ ἔξωθεν μόνον βλέποντας περικάλυμμα καὶ κακῶς κρίνοντας τὰ ἀλλότρια...)

45 See comment by McGuckin (1996, 19), "a successful and somewhat rakish youth."
46 Darrouzès (1966, 8–13), provides a tidy presentation of the contentious atmosphere that likely surrounded Symeon when he wrote the *Orationes Ethicae*.
47 Niketas Stethatos, *Vita Symeonis* 59. Note that Niketas depicts Symeon as resigning from his leadership role voluntarily on account of his love of quiet (ὁ ἔρως τῆς ἡσυχίας). To see this incident (and others from Niketas' life) as suggesting him losing the monastery involves reading through panegyrical content (a necessary if precarious operation). At the moment I follow Turner (1990, 34).
48 Niketas Stethatos, *Vita Symeonis* 72.
49 Niketas Stethatos, *Vita Symeonis* 75–77.
50 Niketas Stethatos, *Vita Symeonis* 95.
51 Niketas Stethatos, *Vita Symeonis* 100.
52 See Messis (2014a, 145–146), for a chronology that places Symeon's travails a decade or so earlier.

53 Krueger's suggestion (2006, 100) that the parable might recall the political situation in Basil's reign was an important inspiration for this chapter. Krueger's goal diverges from mine. Krueger argues that the carnality between emperor and rebel be seen in the context of Symeon's interest in guiding the ascetic practices of his monks with lively and likely imagery; the evocation of homoerotic desire "is a powerful tool in the making of his monks" (Krueger 2006, 118). My analysis is to be seen as complementary to his.
54 Περὶ τῆς φοβερᾶς τοῦ Κυρίου ἡμέρας καὶ τῆς μελλούσης κρίσεως.
55 *Oratio Ethica 10*.229–231.
56 *Oratio Ethica 10*.646.
57 *Oratio Ethica 10*.235–273.
58 *Oratio Ethica 10*.235–236: δουλεύων τινὶ ἀντιδίκῳ καὶ τοῦ βασιλέως τῶν Χριστιανῶν ἐχθρῷ.
59 The perception a reader of this book may have that this "be with him" (*sun autoi einai*/σὺν αὐτῷ εἶναι) is a double-entendre is justified.
60 ἐμηνύθη παρὰ τοῦ βασιλέως τῶν Χριστιανῶν διαφόρως τοῦ προσελθεῖν καὶ σὺν αὐτῷ εἶναι καὶ ἀξιωθῆναι μεγάλων δωρεῶν καὶ συμβασιλεύειν αὐτῷ.
61 *Oratio Ethica 10*.241–243.
62 προσελθὼν τῷ βασιλεῖ καὶ τοὺς πόδας κρατήσας αὐτοῦ, συγχώρησιν μετὰ κλαυθμοῦ ἐξῃτήσατο.
63 Lk 15:20.
64 Pr 5:18.
65 Χλανίδιον is a Greek translation of *paludamentum*, which is the emperor's cloak (*LSJ*, χλανίδιον).
66 "ἐπέπεσεν ἐπὶ τὸν τράχηλον αὐτοῦ καὶ κατεφίλησεν αὐτόν" [Lk 15:20] τε ὅλον καὶ τοὺς δακρύοντας αὐτοῦ ὀφθαλμοὺς ἐπὶ ὥρας πολλάς. Εἶτα στέφος καὶ στολὴν καὶ ὑποδήματα ὅμοια ὧν αὐτὸς ἐφόρει ἐνεχθῆναι κελεύσας, αὐτὸς δι' ἑαυτοῦ τὸν πρώην ἐχθρὸν καὶ ἀντίδικον περιέβαλε, μηδὲν ὅλως προσονειδίσας αὐτόν· καὶ οὐ τοῦτο μόνον, ἀλλὰ νυκτὸς καὶ ἡμέρας συγχαίρων αὐτῷ καὶ συνευφραινόμενος, περιλαμβάνων τε καὶ κατασπαζόμενος στόμα πρὸς στόμα αὐτόν, τοσοῦτον "ὑπερηγάπησεν" αὐτὸν ὅτι οὐδὲ ἐν τῷ ὑπνοῦν αὐτοῦ ἐχωρίζετο, συνανακλινόμενος αὐτῷ καὶ περιλαμβάνων ἐπὶ τῆς κλίνης καὶ πάντοθεν τῷ ἑαυτοῦ χλανιδίῳ περισκέπων καὶ ἐπιτιθεὶς τὸ ἑαυτοῦ πρόσωπον ἐπὶ πᾶσι τοῖς αὐτοῦ μέλεσιν.
67 See Chapter 3 of this book.
68 See Chapter 2 of this book.
69 See Krueger (2006, 101), on the anxiety this passage has awakened in some of Symeon's modern commentators.
70 Krueger (2006, 99).
71 Krueger (2006, 109); *Hymns* 15.161–162.
72 Krueger (2006, 108–109).
73 ἔτι δὲ αὐτοῦ μακρὰν ἀπέχοντος εἶδεν αὐτὸν ὁ πατὴρ αὐτοῦ καὶ ἐσπλαγχνίσθη καὶ δραμὼν ἐπέπεσεν ἐπὶ τὸν τράχηλον αὐτοῦ καὶ κατεφίλησεν αὐτόν.
74 Niketas Stethatos, *Vita Symeonis* 34, mentions that St. Mamas was founded by Emperor Maurice when he discusses Symeon's renovations to the monastery.
75 *PG* 89: 1112–1116. This work exists in two nearly identical versions. The parable can also be found at *PG* 89: 1140–1142. I limit my discussion to the first version. Darrouzès (1967, 279), drew my attention to this parable from Anastasios in a note appended to Symeon's parable at lines 229–234.
76 Ἠκούσαμεν λῃστὴν σωθέντα δι' ἐξομολογήσεως ἐπὶ τοῦ σταυροῦ τοῦ οὐρανίου βασιλέως, καὶ εἴδομεν λῃστὴν σωθέντα δι' ἐξομολογήσεως ἐπὶ τῆς σῆς βασιλείας.
77 The coming remarks on various *loci* in Symeon's works owe much to Krueger's discussion from 2006.
78 *Hymns* 24, 74–75: γέγονα, οἴμοι, καὶ μοιχὸς τῇ καρδίᾳ / καὶ σοδομίτης ἔργῳ καὶ προαιρέσει.

79 πῶς γὰρ δυναίμην σιωπῇ ὑποφέρειν / τὰ γινόμενα καθ' ὥραν, ὦ Θεέ μου, / καὶ πραττόμενα ἐν ἐμοὶ τῷ ἀθλίῳ.
80 *Hymns 24*, 76: γέγονα πόρνος, μάγος καὶ παιδοφθόρος.
81 What is rhetoric and what is reality when Symeon confesses to so much are difficult questions. See Krueger (2006, 116); Golitzin (1997, 26–27); Turner (1990, 27–29).
82 E.g. Turner (1990, 28–29).
83 In the broad range of sources surveyed in this book, this is one of the rare appearances of sodomite to refer to a man who has sex, probably anal, with other men. As noted earlier, *aselges/aselgeia* and *arsenokoites/arsenokoitia* are more common when critique is involved. In moments of happy affect, which is the goal of reparative analysis, euphemism and words of love and desire (e.g., *agape/agape, eros/eramai, pothos, suneuphraino*, etc.) are employed instead.
84 οὐδὲν γὰρ φορτικόν, οὐδὲν ἐπαχθὲς ὁ Δεσπότης ἡμῶν καὶ Θεὸς ἐνετείλατο, μᾶλλον μὲν οὖν ῥᾴδιά τε ὁμοῦ πάντα καὶ εὔκολα, καθὰ—πιστεύσατέ μοι—καὶ αὐτὸς ἔγνων ἐγὼ εὔκολον εἶναι τὴν ἐντολὴν τοῦ Θεοῦ καὶ τὴν ἐπίτευξιν αὐτοῦ τε καὶ τῆς βασιλείας αὐτοῦ. Ἀλλὰ διὰ παραδείγματος τοῦτο ὑμῖν ὑποδείξω....
85 Τοιγαροῦν, ἀδελφοί μου ἀγαπητοί, πάντα ἀφέντες δράμωμεν γυμνοί, καὶ προσελθόντες τῷ δεσπότῃ Χριστῷ προσπέσωμεν καὶ προσκλαύσωμεν ἐνώπιον τῆς αὐτοῦ ἀγαθότητος, ἵνα καὶ αὐτός, θεασάμενος τὴν πίστιν καὶ τὴν ταπείνωσιν ἡμῶν, ὁμοίως ἡμᾶς, μᾶλλον δὲ μειζόνως, ἀποδέξηται καὶ τιμήσῃ, καὶ στολῇ καὶ διαδήματι τῷ ἑαυτοῦ κατακοσμήσῃ καὶ ἀξίους τοῦ ἐπουρανίου νυμφῶνος δαιτυμόνας ἐργάσηται. Cf. *Oratio Ethica* 10.274–278, and Krueger (2006, 107). Note that Krueger and I see the nudity differently: for Krueger the nudity describes the casting off of desire, for me the nudity is revelation and acceptance of the presence of desire.
86 Krueger (2006, 101).
87 There were marriages that built a man's authority within the empire, e.g. the marriage of Nikephoros II Phokas to Theophano, Romanos II's widow, is one. The second marriage of Michael II, to be discussed below, qualifies. John I Tzimiskes' marriage to the sister of Bardas Skleros, an important military commander who later revolted against Basil II, provides still another example (Leo the Deacon, *Historia* 5.5, 6.11, 7.3; Skylitzes, *Sunopsis Historion, John I Tzimiskes* 5/288). There also were marriages (or proposed marriages) of Byzantine notables to foreigners. Basil and his brother were betrothed to Bulgarian princesses (Leo the Deacon, *Historia* 5.3; Shepard 2003, 15; Tougher 2013, 307). In 1005–1006, Basil arranged the marriage of Maria Argyropoulina – sister of the later emperor, Romanos III Argyros (1028–1034) – to Giovanni Orseolo (the son of Peter II, Doge of Venice) for the purpose of alliance (Skylitzes, *Sunopsis Historion, Basil II and Constantine VIII* 25/343; Wortley 2010, 325n135). One need hardly mention Anna, Basil's sister, and her marriage to Vladimir of Kiev, or Theophano Skleraina's to Otto II (see, for example, Shepard 2003).
88 For discussion of the legislative background of marriage in Byzantine society, see Laiou (1992, 9–58) and Pitsakis (2000). For marriage among elite Byzantines, see Macrides (1992), Shepard (2003), and Schreiner (1991), *and* Tougher (2013) for a focus on the Macedonian dynasty. There also were moves toward having male members of the imperial house marrying foreign royalty in the tenth century. For example, Romanos II, Basil's father, was betrothed in 944 to Bertha, daughter of Hugh of Arles (Shepard 2003, 7). Basil II with some controversy married his sister Anna to Vladimir of Kiev: see discussion in Shepard (2003), and Tougher (2013). In any case, the importance of marriage for the formation of connections that would enable familial flourishing, political power, and even alliances with foreign powers is clear enough from the

190 *Revisiting the Bachelorhood*

histories of this time. Skylitzes' *Sunopsis Historion* positively coruscates with marriages: *Nikephoros II Phokas* 2; *John I Tzimiskes* 5, 7, 8; *Basil II and Constantine VIII* 2, 17, 24, 25, 44.

89 "οὐ γάρ ἐστιν οἷον ἄνευ γυναικός," φάσκειν, "βασιλέα τε ζῆν καὶ τὰς ἡμετέρας στερεῖσθαι γαμετὰς δεσποίνης καὶ βασιλίδος."

90 There is a further complexity to this story. The narrative, which is hostile to Michael, portrays Michael wanting it to look like he loved his deceased wife so much that he had to be compelled to remarry: "And so, when his wife had died and since he was wanting the opinion of the many to believe that inconsolable grief for her held [him]..." (*Theophanes Continuatus* 2.24/78) (τῆς γαμετῆς γοῦν τελευτησάσης αὐτοῦ, καὶ δόξαν θέλοντος κατασχεῖν τῶν πολλῶν ὡς πένθος ἄληστον ἔχει αὐτῆς...).

91 *Theophanes Continuatus* 2.24/78.

92 For bibliography and discussion, see Holmes (2005, 21–29), and Sifonas (1994, 118n1).

93 See Sifonas (1994) and Holmes (2005).

94 Skylitzes, *Sunopsis Historion, Constantine VII Palin* 7/240, reports that her name, prior to the assumption of the grand name Theophano, was Anastaso and that her background was not lofty; Wortley (2010, 232n32). It is possible that she was not as low as all that, see discussion in Garland (1999b, 126–127, 270n3). In any case, though, she was not as lofty as a Skleraina.

95 Symeon the Logothete, *Chronographia* 131.32 (first version); Eudokia Ingerina was at first mistress to Michael III. Empress Theodora (his mother) and the *logothete* Theoktistos thought her unsuitable for Michael, making him marry Eudokia Dekapolitissa instead. Notably though, Eudokia's modest background and the unpromising beginning of her involvement in imperial circles did not stop her from becoming mother to the Macedonian dynasty.

96 Treadgold (1997, 519).

97 Schreiner (1991, 189), points out that in the ninth and tenth centuries beauty in an empress was often more important than lineage and, hence, alliance. Desire was, therefore, a possible consideration.

98 The reader of this book will remember that both versions of Symeon the Logothete's *Chronographia* and the *Chronographia* of Pseudo-Symeon speak of the desire Michael felt for Eudokia.

99 Leo the Deacon, *Historia* 2.10.

100 Skylitzes, *Sunopsis Historion, Nikephoros II Phokas* 22/279, notes that Nikephoros and Theophano had sexual relations (*sunousia*). Zonaras 16.28 reports Nikephoros' strong sexual interest in Theophano: ἐρωτικῶς δὲ σφόδρα πρὶν διακείμενος. Cf. Garland (1999b, 271n36).

101 Psellos memorably relates the peaceable meeting Bardas Skleros and Basil had (*Chronographia* 1.28). Bardas Phokas died before he could have been forgiven by Basil (Psellos, *Chronographia* 1.16–17; Skylitzes, *Sunopsis Historion, Basil II and Constantine VIII* 18/337), but it does not seem likely that he would have fared as well as Skleros did.

102 ὃν οὗτος φιλοφρόνως ἄγαν δεξάμενος καὶ περιχαρῶς μάγιστρόν τε εὐθέως ἐτίμησε καὶ συμβούλῳ διὰ παντὸς ἐν τοῖς πολέμοις ἐχρῆτο...αὐτὸς δὲ τῆς ἐξ αὐτοῦ συμβουλῆς μονωθείς, καὶ φίλων δεόμενος καὶ συνεργῶν ἐν ταῖς περιστάσεσι, τότε γνησίως τὸν Ῥωμανὸν προσεδέξατο, ἄνδρα εἰδὼς ἐντρεχῆ καὶ δραστήριον καὶ τὰ πολεμικὰ ἱκανώτατον.

103 Psellos, *Chronographia* 1.17.

104 Leo the Deacon, *Historia* 10.9.

105 For more on Kalokyres Delphinas, see Talbot and Sullivan (2005, 216n87); Wortley (2010, 318n96).

106 Skylitzes, *Sunopsis Historion, Basil II and Constantine VIII* 17/336: ἐπὶ ξύλου κρεμᾷ.
107 Leo the Deacon, *Historia* 10.9: ἀνεσκολόπισε.
108 Holmes (2005, 461–462); Svoronos (1994, 190–217).
109 See Sifonas (1994) and Holmes (2005).
110 Darrouzès (1966, 8): "[the orations] are in large part a work of controversy, or at least composed during a period of controversies." The secondary literature has discussions of the evidence of struggle in these orations: Darrouzès (1966, 8–13); McGuckin (1996, 27–31, and 2005, 186–187). See also Turner's biographical sketch (1990, 16–36). Turner (1990, 11), believes the orations to be addressed to persons in and outside of the monastic context: "These, apparently written works from the outset, were addressed to a wider public than the monks of Symeon's monastery...." Darrouzès (1966, 8), remarks that Symeon "parle [in the *Orationes Ethicae*] en défenseur de la théologie mystique contre des adversaires indéterminés mais réels" ("[Symeon] speaks [in the *Orationes Ethicae*] in defense of a mystical theology against enemies indeterminate but real.")
111 Niketas Stethatos, *Vita Symeonis* 59.
112 Niketas Stethatos, *Vita Symeonis* 72.
113 Niketas Stethatos, *Vita Symeonis* 75–77.
114 Turner (1990, 21); Krivochéine and Paramelle (1963, 250–251n1 and 381n1); indeed, Krivochéine (252) says: "En général, quand il parle des 'rois terrestres,' c'est presque toujours sans sympathie, quelquefois avec ironie et hostilité" ("In general, when he speaks of earthly kings, it is almost always without sympathy, and sometimes with irony and hostility").
115 Precise dating of individual *Catecheses* is not possible. They were exhortations and advice to his monks and they date from the time when he was *hegoumenos* of St. Mamas, i.e., 980–1005 (Krivochéine and Paramelle 1963, 165).
116 *Catecheses* 2.107–109: Ἄνθρωποι μὲν γὰρ ἅπαντες σχεδὸν τοὺς ἀσθενεῖς καὶ πτωχοὺς ὥσπερ ἀποβδελύσσονται καὶ βασιλεὺς ἐπίγειος τούτους ὁρᾶν οὐκ ἀνέχεται....
117 *Catecheses* 4.470–472: Ὥσπερ γὰρ βασιλεὺς δίχα τοῦ ὑπ' αὐτὸν στρατεύματος ἀσθενὴς καὶ εὐχείρωτος τοῖς πᾶσι γίνεται καὶ οὐδὲ βασιλεὺς φαίνεται....
118 *Catecheses* 5.573–580.
119 The date of the *Capita Theologica* is late in the decade of the 1000s, or even later than that (Darrouzès and Neyrand 1996, 10).
120 *Capita Theologica* 2.8.10–11: πρὸς ὕψος πνευματικῆς θεωρίας ... ἀνενεχθείς.
121 *Capita Theologica* 2.8.7–9: μοναχὸς ὁ ἀληθῶς ἀπὸ τοῦ κόσμου καὶ τῶν ἐν αὐτῷ πραγμάτων ἀναχωρήσας.
122 βλέπει γὰρ ἀεὶ τὴν χάριν τοῦ Πνεύματος τὴν περιλάμπουσαν αὐτόν, ἥτις ἔνδυμα καλεῖται καὶ βασίλειος ἁλουργίς, μᾶλλον δ' ὅπερ αὐτός ἐστιν ὁ Χριστός, εἴπερ αὐτὸν οἱ εἰς αὐτὸν πιστεύοντες ἐπενδύονται.
123 Καθάπερ ὁ ἀπὸ πτωχείας ἐσχάτης ὑπὸ τοῦ βασιλέως εἰς πλοῦτον ἀνενεχθείς, καὶ περιφανὲς ἀξίωμα στολήν τε παρ' αὐτοῦ λαμπρὰν ἐνδυθεὶς καὶ πρὸ προσώπου αὐτοῦ ἵστασθαι κελευσθείς, αὐτόν τε τὸν βασιλέα μετὰ πόθου ὁρᾷ καὶ ὡς εὐεργέτην ὑπεραγαπᾷ, τὴν στολήν τε ἣν ἐνεδύσατο τρανῶς κατανοεῖ καὶ τὸ ἀξίωμα ἐπιγινώσκει καὶ τὸν δοθέντα αὐτῷ πλοῦτον ἐπίσταται....
124 Hussey (1967, 183); Turner (1990); Morris (1995).
125 For connections between monks and men in the world, see Turner (1990, 34, 55, 106, 119, 231, 234–241). Morris (1995) is dedicated to interactions between monks and laymen and is relevant frequently on this point. More specifically, Morris (1995, 76–80), delineates ways in which monks were often indistinguishable from their secular brothers in terms of education and family background. She also discusses a number of interactions between the secular and sacred milieux (Morris 1995, 84–87). Morris (1995, 106) sums up a dynamic that

she documents repeatedly throughout her study, referring here to relations of spiritual fatherhood:

> From members of the Byzantine administrative "middle management" as far up as the imperial families themselves, the clients [of the monks acting as spiritual fathers] represented a cross-section of the Byzantine ruling class. They consulted their spiritual fathers either in person or by letter, and it is very likely that they were well aware of others who also sought guidance from the same source.

Of interest too is the title of Symeon's fourth hymn, which is called "A teaching to the monks who have recently left the world and to those who are still in the world" (Διδασκαλία εἰς μοναχοὺς ἄρτι ἀποταξαμένους κόσμῳ καὶ τοῖς ἐνκόσμῳ). He addresses monks and those who, not living in a monastery, desired guidance. Relevant too are the comments of Rapp (2016, 168–169, 192–193, and 210), on relations between monks and laymen and the connections that Symeon maintained.

126 Niketas Stethatos, *Vita Symeonis* 100.
127 The reader of this book will be reminded of the gloss of the worldly things on the prayer "A thing flowery and much-desired by us, the sweet scent of love" that was analyzed at length in Chapter 3. As the church door is open to traffic going in and out, so the monastery door is also.
128 Turner (1990, 11).
129 Symeon the New Theologian, *Catecheses* 22.22–27; McGuckin (1996, 19–20).

Conclusion

Nikephoros Ouranos wrote *Letter 29* to Paulos *Krites*, who also received *Letter 44*, the letter with which this book opened. As with Nikephoros' other letters, *Letter 29* dates to the first decade of the 1000s. *Letter 29* makes for a good source to conclude this book, especially since the most important aspect of this letter is its probable reference to eight ritual brotherhoods. Discussion of this letter therefore is especially welcome as it has so far not appeared in any scholarly discussions of *adelphopoiesis*. Nikephoros' probable status as a eunuch makes *Letter 29* an interesting document in addition, because, since eunuchs could not wed, a ritual brotherhood was a way to join a eunuch man's family and for him to join someone else's. Lastly, reparative contemplation of this letter leads to general reflections on homosociality in elite Byzantine masculine culture and the place and purposes of same-sex desire in it.

Nikephoros begins *Letter 29* by referring, via nautical metaphor, to another letter, which does not survive, that "Lord Michael" wrote Paulos; this letter is a follow-up to that other letter:

> To Paulos *Krites*:
> The towed barges follow the great ships, those of Lord Michael: it's my letter! And it is directed toward what are his wants and it wishes for the same things as his. And this is the marvelous skill of mine, toward not ignoring my friends when they think something worthy, nor to come off tiresome to you by deeming many matters—great ones!—of little importance. This is my skill: to follow the wishes of our common friend and to write when he does (*sc.* Lord Michael). So when he, taking the lead, has decided someone [Mr. X] is worthy, so I too have dared this and deemed him worthy too. And emphatically do both of us also make a favorable judgment about a(nother) man [Mr. Y] whose friendship and handsome body/excellent disposition (*ten philian...ten euphuian*/ τὴν φιλίαν...τὴν εὐφυΐαν) you esteemed greatly. And I, having also felt wonder (*thaumasas*/θαυμάσας) at both of these things and numbering him [Mr. Y] not only among my friends but among my brothers, I was also joined [to him] in the Spirit! What matters to one, they say, are the

DOI: 10.4324/9781351135238-6

things that matter to both; if then both you and this man [Mr. X] are my brother, what is left to talk about, except that you be brothers of a brother to each other?

What other thing would at once be more affectionate, intimate, sweet, and beneficial? A brother will be at a man's side everywhere and always, whenever he is rejoicing (*euphrainomenoi*/εὐφραινομένῳ), pained, or in danger, so that, on the one hand, he might preserve his pleasures (*hedonas*/ἡδονάς), or so that he might, especially, make his life more pleasurable and glorious, and so that, on the other hand, he might help with, that is to say, bear along with or have a share in his [brother's] pains, reverses, or dangers. For he, on the one hand, consoles when there has been misfortune, and, on the other, lightens the soul, as he shares the weight (*sc.* of misfortune). Thus, as this very man is my brother [*sc.* Mr. X], you will also think brotherly thoughts about him for me. May you have a healthy body and soul, and good fortune, and may you always have your John in your thoughts, as indeed he has his Paulos. For this you are to me, even should you be raised over/beyond third heaven (cf. 2 Cor 12:2), even should you hear things more unspeakable—and thus you are named [*sc.* brother] and loved.

(Nikephoros Ouranos, *Letter 29*)[1]

Nikephoros begins with reference to a letter that "Lord Michael" had already sent to Paulos. This Lord Michael may be Nikephoros' natural or ritual brother when other mentions of Michael in the letters of Nikephoros are taken into account.[2] Nikephoros asserts that there will be a harmony of content between his letter and Lord Michael's, and that this harmony will be secured with panache and interpersonal sensitivity. He also says that this concord extends to his and Michael's opinions about other men's worthiness, and it appears there is some man whom they think is worthy (unnamed but, say, Mr. X). Nikephoros also adds that he and Lord Michael trust Paulos' judgment in such matters. And there is an example of this to hand: so much did Nikephoros trust the judgment of Paulos about one man's (unnamed but, say, Mr. Y) friendship and beauty/goodness, that he became friends with him and also his brother "in the Spirit," which is a reference to *adelphopoiesis*. Nikephoros then concludes, in highly elliptical language, with the suggestion that Paul and Mr. X, both already Nikephoros' brothers, become brothers themselves.

In the second paragraph, Nikephoros makes happy observations about the nature of brotherhood. There are advantages of affection, sweetness, benefit, rejoicing, consolation, help for reputation, and pleasures. Nikephoros then reiterates his encouragement to Paulos to become brothers with Mr. X. The letter ends with wishes for Paulos' health, a mention of Paulos' dear John, and a look at Nikephoros' warm relation and brotherhood with Paulos, complete with intertextuality with 2 Cor 12, about which more below.

Conclusion 195

While *Letter 29* is not as warm as some of the other letters discussed in this book, corporeality and affection are present all the same. When Nikephoros speaks of Michael's recommendation of Mr. Y, he notes that a key part of Mr. Y's worthiness is his *euphuia*/εὐφυΐα, "handsome body/ excellent disposition," encompassing beauty of body and character. This moment recalls the moment from *Life of Basil* where Emperor Michael truly loved what he saw and took Basil from Theophilitzes to enroll him among his grooms:

> When the emperor had seen (the feat) and conceived a love for Basil's handsome body/excellent disposition endowed with manliness (*ten met' andreias euphuian*/τὴν μετ' ἀνδρείας εὐφυΐαν) and his intelligence, he immediately took him away from Theophilitzes and enrolled him among the imperial *stratores*.
>
> (*Life of Basil* 13/231)[3]

Also present in the letter are affection, intimacy, sweetness, and the preservation of pleasures (*hedonas*/ἡδονάς), and this word, *hedone*, has a primary meaning of pleasures that are bodily.[4] Feelings of wonder (*thaumasas*/ θαυμάσας) and rejoicing (*euphrainomenoi*/εὐφραινομένῳ) have been associated with desire in many of the sources discussed throughout this book.[5] The conclusion is that desire and the body come into evidence with but the gentlest pressure.

As noted above, the abundance of brothers and the characterization of both brotherhood itself and circumstances surrounding it make *Letter 29* a text relevant for developing an understanding of *adelphopoiesis* in tenth and early eleventh-century Byzantium. There are perhaps eight spiritual brotherhoods, of varying degrees of certainty, in this letter:

1 Nikephoros and Lord Michael (probable)
2 Nikephoros and Mr. X (certain)
3 Mr. X and Lord Michael (probable)
4 Nikephoros and Mr. Y (certain)
5 Paulos and Mr. Y (probable)
6 Nikephoros and Paulos (certain)
7 Paulos and Mr. X (prospective)
8 John and Paulos (almost certain)

Three are explicitly named, one is almost certain, three are probable, and one is prospective.

First is the probable relation of brotherhood between Nikephoros and Lord Michael. It is not stated outright that they are brothers, but it would be odd if they were not, given how they confer and make recommendations to others about the suitability of this or that man for brotherhood. Then there is Mr. X, who is a man identified as worthy by Lord Michael and Nikephoros. Nikephoros states late in the letter that he is brother in the spirit to him and, given the context, it seems likely that Mr. X is brother to Lord Michael also. There is still another man to whom the name Mr. Y has been given in the translation. He is the man that Paulos approved of, who became Nikephoros' friend, and then his brother in the Spirit (οὐκ ἐν τοῖς φίλοις μόνον ἀλλὰ καὶ τοῖς ἀδελφοῖς ἀρι[θμῶν], καὶ ἡρμόσθην τῷ πνεύματι), which is about as direct a reference, without using the word, to *adelphopoiesis* as can be imagined. Because of context, it seems likely that Paulos and Mr. Y were brothers prior to Mr. Y becoming brothers with Nikephoros. After the general statement on how interests of men who are close to one another will align,[6] Nikephoros says, naming Paulos as his brother, that Paulos should become brothers with Mr. X. The letter concludes both with talk of John, who, given the context again, is probably Paulos' brother in the Spirit, and with a restatement of the relation of affection and brotherhood that Nikephoros and Paulos share.

With its surprising number of brotherhoods, this letter nonetheless is mostly not about the church. Nikephoros' mention of "in the Spirit" in regard to his connection to Mr. Y is the exception.[7] Similar to what was said in the last chapter, multiple relations preexisting the ritual are visible. These relations are brought into the church and their nature outside of the church remains the focus, as brotherhood is an affiliation in this letter that is all about interpersonal warmth. Furthermore, at least in these circles, a brotherhood is very much embodied. A brother helps a brother preserve his pleasures amid rejoicing after all.

The letter concludes with intertextuality with the New Testament. The final sentence includes the following words: "even should you be raised over/beyond third heaven, even should you hear things more unspeakable."[8] The phrase "third heaven" and the comparative adverb, "more unspeakable" call to mind Paul's second letter to the Corinthians:

> ...it does no good but I will proceed to visions and revelations of the Lord. I know of a man in Christ, who, fourteen years ago, was the sort to be seized up to third heaven (*tritou ouranou*/τρίτου οὐρανοῦ) – whether it was in body or outside his body, I don't know, but God knows – [I know] that he was the sort of man – whether in body or apart from his body, I don't know, but God knows – [I know] that he was seized up to paradise and he heard unspeakable (*arreta*/ἄρρητα) words which are impossible for a man to tell of.[9]
>
> (2 Cor 12:1–4)[10]

This reference to Paul comes on the heels of much talk about warm relations between politically powerful men. The semantics of this intertextuality need discussion for the letter rewrites Paul in little but significant ways and the intertextuality is polysemous in addition.

Conclusion 197

The intertextuality is close but there are differences. "Third heaven" is present in Paul and *Letter 29*. But instead of Paul's "seized", "raised" appears in the letter, and instead of Paul's *arretos*/ἄρρητος, "unspeakable," a comparative form of an adjective that is close in meaning, *aporretos*/ ἀπόρρητος, features in Nikephoros' letter. A third difference between Paul and Nikephoros' letter concerns heaven or *ouranos*. In Paul, the man he speaks of is raised "*to* third heaven" (ἕως τρίτου οὐρανοῦ) while *Letter 29* proposes a scenario in which Paulos is raised "*over/beyond* third heaven" (ὑπὲρ τρίτον οὐρανόν).

With the similarities and differences between the text of Paul's and Nikephoros' letters kept in mind, interpretation of this moment of intertextuality reveals two disjunctive meanings. One is of political allegory, and the other addresses issues of desire and embodiment in relations between men.

When interpreted as political allegory, the end of *Letter 29* is coded communication that has Nikephoros saying in hope that Paulos will remain loyal to him no matter how important he gets, no matter how privy to high matters of state he becomes. Nikephoros, whose second name is *Ouranos*, also engages in word-play based on his own name when he writes beyond third *heaven*: "*huper triton* ouranon/ὑπὲρ τρίτον οὐρανόν," which features his name. He says, "should you rise so high beyond *the third Ouranos*, I know you will still be true." He could be referring to himself here as grandson to either Basil Ouranos or Michael Ouranos. Discussed in Chapter 1, Basil Ouranos is the addressee of Theodoros Daphnopates' *Letter 31*, and sent *Letters 17* and *18* under his own name about 40 or so years earlier. Michael Ouranos, *patrikios*, is mentioned in the *De Ceremoniis* of Emperor Constantine VII Porphyrogennetos, which places this man in the mid-tenth century also.[11] These men are plausible forebears to the powerful Nikephoros. The preposition *huper*/ὑπέρ also repays further attention, as it can mean not only "over/beyond", and hence higher up in terms of authority but also "in transgression of,"[12] in this case adumbrating a narrative that assures Paulos that Nikephoros will still trust him even if they are, or appear to be at odds.

Once Nikephoros makes himself visible by use of his own name, this not only energizes the political allegory but it also makes his own person *and* body visible, and the bodies of his brothers and certainly Paulos', a situation that consideration of the broader passage from 2 Corinthians intensifies. Paul twice poses the question of whether the seizure up into third heaven is a bodily event or not: "...whether it was in body or outside his body, I don't know, but God knows... whether in body or apart from his body, I don't know, but God knows...." A central concern of Paul when he speaks of third heaven is the body. Nikephoros' letter is centrally concerned with brotherhood and emphasizes bodily life in relations brothers can have with one another. And this in spite of the fact that *adelphopoiesis* is in the first instance of the soul. "Spiritual," *penumatikos*/πνευματικός, is attributed to it, and it is in the letter ("I was joined [to him] in the Spirit."). But the letter pays more attention to the body, as the relations between brothers frequently

198 Conclusion

manifest in physicality. Present are affection, intimacy, sweetness, Mr. Y's physical (and moral) beauty. Mr. Y also occasions feelings of wonder, which recalls the wonder Basil I caused in the historiographies, and there is rejoicing, which has been seen in scripture, historiography, epistolography, and Symeon's parable. A brotherhood also has the power to preserve pleasures (*hedonas*/ἡδονάς), an observation that emphasizes the body yet again. Nikephoros even dichotomizes the body with the soul with varying degrees of directness:

> For [a brother], on the one hand, consoles when there has been misfortune (*tou pathous*/τοῦ πάθους), and, on the other, lightens the soul, as he shares the weight (*sc.* of misfortune)…May you have a healthy body and soul…
> (Nikephoros Ouranos, *Letter 29*)[13]

Pathos/πάθος can refer to misfortune that happens to the body,[14] and its relation to the verb *pascho*/πάσχω means that it can even cause the perception of being penetrated to register.[15] The fact that soul is mentioned in the balancing phrase in the first sentence strengthens these impressions. And in the second sentence of this passage, Nikephoros mentions both soul *and* body.

In this context, the change Nikephoros makes from *arretos*/ἄρρητος in Paul to the comparative form[16] of *aporretos*/ἀπόρρητος is significant. While *arretos* and *aporretos* are synonyms and frequently are interchangeable across length and breadth of Greek texts, they are not the same. While both words have similar semantics of unspeakability and secretness, *aporretos*/ἀπόρρητος is the one more likely to designate a sexual secret, and *ta aporreta*/τὰ ἀπόρρητα (the unspeakable things) can designate the genitals, *ta aidoia*/τὰ αἰδοῖα,[17] in earlier literature. Indeed the "not-to-be spoken (*aporreta*/ἀπόρρητα) mysteries of the goddess (*sc.* Aphrodite)" was seen in Theodoros Daphnopates' *Letter 17* in a sexual context. Lastly, does a reader briefly think of the Paulos being over Nikephoros when reading the change of Paul's "*seized up to* third heaven" (ἁρπαγέντα…ἕως τρίτου οὐρανοῦ) to Paulos being "*raised over/beyond* third heaven" (ὑπὲρ τρίτον οὐρανόν ἀρθῆς), or to being "on top of the third Ouranos"? Such a judgment is only for God to make, Paul would say. And this brief glimpse of something sexual is not outlandish, considering what Nikephoros wrote to Paulos in *Letter 44* (as was discussed in the introduction):

> For this voice (of yours) is longed for by me, just as assaults and blows are by lovers from their beloveds…whether you praise me, accuse me, or take hands to me to treat me roughly, only may you write, providing things pleasant and sufficient to comfort me…[18]

In summation, the intertextuality with Paul in *Letter 29*, and especially through its imprecision, intensifies the dichotomy perceptible in Paul—all the way up in heaven is there frank carnality present?—and this leads to perception of an answer in the letter. Brothers have a relation that expresses itself spiritually and physically, and the intertextuality at the end of the letter underscores that the separation of body and soul in these relations is not for people on earth to adjudicate. This letter is yet another instance of a Byzantine epistolographer exploring the possibilities, licit and illicit, in relations between men.[19]

To conclude with *Letter 29*, a return to politics and to what else a reparative accounting can draw out of it about elite homosociality in the world capital of Constantinople. This group of men differs markedly from groups of men who might be leading organizations now, to say nothing of a mix of women and men working together in positions of authority. There is the language of warm affect, of course, that has featured so often in this book, but there is another difference, discussion of which *Letter 29* particularly enables: bodily modification has occurred, i.e., there are men who are eunuchs and men who are not castrated (the "bearded") working together. This terrain of masculine sociability in the middle centuries had this difference to finesse in order for all the men to work together and relate on a human level.

While there was considerable social integration of eunuch men in the Byzantine empire of its middle centuries,[20] and eunuchs were not the socially dead outsiders known from late antiquity,[21] there were markers of difference resulting from castration. There was of course the survival of attitudes dating from late antiquity that were critical of eunuchs, which would emerge when there was anger against a eunuch.[22] The stigmatizing practice of not allowing eunuchs to marry was reiterated by Emperor Leo VI around 900, though he did allow eunuch men to adopt.[23] And while nearly all offices were open to eunuchs, a eunuch could not be *eparch* of Constantinople, *quaistor*,[24] or emperor.

But in spite of these things, there is ample evidence of harmony and relation. In the first place, eunuchs are men. They are part of the masculine gender. At least two of the major figures of this book were eunuchs: Nikephoros Ouranos and Symeon the New Theologian. And yet there is no talk, or very little talk of this fact about them in the historical record. There are good reasons for this. Eunuch status became a topic when there was frustration with a eunuch. If things were going well and relations were happy, this status was not something to mention, and this has led to them being underreported in the sources.[25] Nikephoros Ouranos in his *Letter 5* makes reference to Basil the *Parakoimomenos* as a man,[26] and Psellos in his *Chronographia* is complimentary of Basil the *Parakoimomenos* in a description that would do any *aner* proud:

> This man (*aner*/ἀνήρ) had the greatest degree of authority/greatest reputation in the Empire of the Romans, according to the loftiness of his intellect, the sheer mass of his body and a form suitable for a ruler...
> (Psellos, *Chronographia* 1.3)[27]

He was imposing in all ways, and this included his body. This absorption of eunuchs into the category of *aner* along with the bearded leads to a number of conclusions about Byzantine men's masculinity and homosociality at this time.

In the first place, manly authority did not require an intact body, and bearded and eunuch both embodied Byzantine masculinity. The vesting of authority in eunuchs and absence of a need to demonstrate virility sexually with women divorced manly authority from strict somatic requirements. A more important question about men/*andres*, if a reparative approach is pursued, was how difference between bearded and eunuch and indeed between men of different social statuses was finessed so masculine homosociality in these lofty circles could run smoothly.

The answer will frequently come back to the making of connections between of men of different statuses, whether these statuses are somatic (*sc.* eunuch or bearded?) or social, e.g., a young man from the provinces who associated himself with men in the capital on his way to becoming emperor. There were connections of warm affect and desire between men (as has been seen repeatedly in this book), there was marriage into another man's family (as was seen in the story of Bardas marrying his friend Nikephoros to his wife's sister in the *Life of Mary the Younger*), or there was *adelphopoiesis*, which was essential when eunuchs were involved or status asymmetries were too substantial. All of foregoing leveled the playing field: difference in status was replaced be an equality of, say, *agape* or *pothos*. And if equality were already present, let love knock on the door and it will likely be opened.

And so, same-sex desire and sexual behavior had a complicated relationship to elite masculine homosociality in medieval Byzantium. Homosocial warmth and expressions of desire were an important constituent part of a *persona* that would command the attention of other men. These things were not only features of tenth-century masculine homosociality, as can be seen in the epistolography. They were also understood to be visible in ninth-century history according to the historiographers of the tenth century. Furthermore, as brothers brought a preexisting relationship to an *adelphopoiesis* ceremony, ritual brotherhood was pulled into this warmly homosocial milieu that featured same-sex desire. Accordingly, approved performance of elite Byzantine masculinity courted conflict with ecclesiastical strictures and civil law, indulging in thoughts and visualizations that would be strictly against the rules of church and state, and these indulgences indicated the presence of actions. The sum-total of evidence attests to a complex and unresolved scene.

But resolution must not be forced. Multiple discourses existed in conflict with one another. In *Letter 26*, Nikephoros Ouranos speaks of togetherness with God for him and his friend, and, at the same time, calls up thoughts of same-sex eroticism. Epistolography, centrally concerned with connection, juggles both scriptural references and pagan erotic literature, offering visions of carnality between men. A young man's beauty and attractiveness to other men makes history happen in a context where there is civil and ecclesiastical sanction against sex between men. A prayer for brotherhood features an influx of erotic language from outside of the church. Symeon the New Theologian narrates a sexy story of an emperor and rebel in bed that is both political allegory and metaphor for easeful living according to the Commandments of God. In summation, the method of this book has not been positivistic, as it has tarried with speculation, but it has presented, rather, a collection of reparative accounts that embrace positive affect and prioritize desire and connection over condemnation and negative sanction. And this has been with the avowed aim of thinking through the uses of and the needs met by desire between Byzantine men.

Notes

1 Παύλῳ κριτῇ·

> Ἕπονται καὶ ταῖς μεγάλαις ναυσὶ τὰ ἐφόλκια, τοῖς τοῦ κῦρ Μιχαήλ, γράμματα τὰ ἐμά· καὶ γὰρ ἄγονται πρὸς ὅπερ ἐκεῖνα καὶ ταὐτὰ κακείνοις ταῦτα βούλονται. Καὶ τέχνη γὰρ αὕτη παρ' ἐμοὶ θαυμασία, πρὸς τὸ μήτε τῶν φίλων ἀξιούντων ὑπερορᾶν, μήτε σοι φορτικὸν εἶναι μετὰ περὶ πολλῶν καὶ μικρὸν ἀξιοῦντα περὶ μεγάλων, ἥδε ἐστίν, ἕπεσθαι τοῖς τοῦ κοινοῦ φίλου θελήμασι καὶ γράφειν ὅτε κἀκεῖνος. Ἐπεὶ γοῦν ἐκεῖνος προλαβὼν ἠξίωσεν, ἐτόλμησα τοῦτο κἀγὼ καὶ ἀξιῶ, μᾶλλον δὲ ἀξιοῦμεν ἄμφω καὶ περὶ ἀνδρός, οὗ καὶ σὺ τὴν φιλίαν περὶ πολλοῦ ποιεῖς καὶ τὴν εὐφυΐαν· ἃ κἀγὼ ἄμφω θαυμάσας, οὐκ ἐν τοῖς φίλοις μόνον ἀλλὰ καὶ τοῖς ἀδελφοῖς ἀρι[θμῶν], καὶ ἡρμόσθην τῷ πνεύματι. Τὰ δὲ τῷ αὐτῷ, φασί, τὰ αὐτὰ καὶ ἀλλήλοις εἰσὶ τὰ αὐτά· εἰ γοῦν καὶ σὺ καὶ οὗτος ἐμὸς ἀδελφός, τί λείπεται; Καὶ ὑμᾶς πρὸς ἀλλήλους οὖν πλὴν ἀδελφοὺς ἀδελφοῦ.
>
> Τί ἄλλο εἴη καὶ φίλτερον ὁμοῦ καὶ ἀναγκαιότερον καὶ ἡδύτερον καὶ ὀφελιμώτερον, ἀδελφὸς ἀνδρὶ παρείη καὶ πανταχοῦ καὶ ἀεὶ καὶ εὐφραινομένῳ καὶ λυπουμένῳ καὶ κινδυνεύοντι, τὸ μὲν ἵνα φυλάττῃ τὰς ἡδονάς, ἢ ζωᾶς μᾶλλον δὲ καὶ ἡδυτέρας ποιῇ καὶ ἐνδοξοτέρας, τὸ δ' ἵνα θεραπεύῃ ἤγουν συναποφέρῃ τὰς λύπας, ἢ τὰς ἥττας, ἢ τοὺς κινδύνους, ἢ συμμερίζηται· τὸ μὲν γὰρ παραμυθεῖται τοῦ πάθους, τὸ δὲ καὶ ἐπελαφρύνει μερίζων ὥσπερ βάρος τὴν ψυχήν. Οὕτω δὴ καὶ αὐτὸς ἀδελφὸς ὢν ἐμὸς ἀδελφὰ κἀμοὶ φρονήσεις περὶ αὐτόν. Εὖ ἔχοις καὶ τὸ σῶμα καὶ τὴν ψυχὴν καὶ τὴν τύχην καὶ διὰ μνήμης ἄγοις ἀεὶ τὸν σὸν Ἰωάννην, ὥσπερ δὴ καὶ αὐτὸς τὸν αὐτοῦ Παῦλον· τοῦτο γὰρ ἡμῖν σύ, κἂν ὑπὲρ τρίτον οὐρανὸν ἀρθῇς, κἂν ἀπορρητοτέρων ἀκούσῃς, οὕτω καὶ ὀνομαζόμενος καὶ φιλούμενος.

2 Lord Michael is not called brother in this letter. But elsewhere in the corpus there is a brother whom Nikephoros sometimes calls Michael. Brother Michael is the addressee of *Letter 37* and there is talk of a brother in *Letter 39* ("I will love the brother who's mine and gentle" [ἀγαπήσω...τὸν ἐμὸν ἀδελφόν καὶ πρᾷον]) and Michael, called handsome (*kalos*/καλός), and who may or may not be Nikephoros' gentle brother, went on campaign with the emperor, leaving Nikephoros alone and distressed at the end of the letter:

> ...and I will add further about my desolation, that when my remaining comfort, the handsome Michael I mean, was away on campaign with the emperor, both desertion and disheartedness alone at that moment were clearly mine.
> (Nikephoros Ouranos, *Letter* 39)

(...προσθήσω δ' ὅτι καὶ τῆς νῦν ἡμῶν ἐρημείας, ὁπότε καὶ ὁ λοιπὸς ἐμὸς ὀφθαλμός, ὁ καλὸς φημὶ Μιχαήλ, ᾤχετο συνεκστρατεύσων τῷ βασιλεῖ, καὶ ἐρημία καὶ ἀθυμία νῦν μόνη σαφῶς τὰ ἡμέτερα.)

202 Conclusion

Without Michael's name being said, a brother appears in *Letter 36*, and Lord Michael, as in *Letter 29*, appears, without reference to him as brother, as the addressee of *Letter 48*. Darrouzès (1960, 48) believed that Michael was Nikephoros' natural brother. That may be, but nothing rules out Michael being a ritual brother to Nikephoros, as a relation by blood is not demonstrated in the letters.

3 ὃ θεασάμενος ὁ βασιλεύς, καὶ ἀγαπήσας τὴν μετ' ἀνδρείας εὐφυΐαν αὐτοῦ καὶ σύνεσιν, εὐθέως ἀπὸ τοῦ Θεοφιλίτζι αὐτὸν ἀνέλαβέ τε καὶ εἰς τοὺς βασιλικοὺς κατέταξε στράτωρας.
4 In Chapter 1, Constantine VII uses *hedone*/ἡδονή to refer to both the bodily pleasures of kissing and a double-entendre for intercourse (*Letter B3*). Chapter 3 features a similarly carnal use of *hedone*/ἡδονή by Theodoros in *Letter A2*.
5 Most notably, Basil I caused wonder in the historiographies, and there was his rejoicing with Nicholas. And rejoicing, famous from Pr 5, is to be found often in the letters surveyed in Chapter 1. Lastly, *euphrainein*/εὐφραίνειν (so here and at times in the letters) and *suneuphrainein*/συνευφραίνειν (the historiographies and Proverbs) are to be seen as close in meaning.
6 "What matters to one, they say, are the things that matter to both..." (Τὰ δὲ τῷ αὐτῷ, φασί, τὰ αὐτὰ καὶ ἀλλήλοις εἰσὶ τὰ αὐτά...)
7 "...I was also joined [to him] in the Spirit!" (...καὶ ἡρμόσθην τῷ πνεύματι).
8 κἂν ὑπὲρ τρίτον οὐρανὸν ἀρθῇς, κἂν ἀπορρητοτέρων ἀκούσῃς.
9 Or: "he heard unspeakable (*arreta*/ἄρρητα) words which are impossible to tell to mankind."
10 ...οὐ συμφέρον μέν, ἐλεύσομαι δὲ εἰς ὀπτασίας καὶ ἀποκαλύψεις κυρίου. οἶδα ἄνθρωπον ἐν Χριστῷ πρὸ ἐτῶν δεκατεσσάρων – εἴτε ἐν σώματι οὐκ οἶδα, εἴτε ἐκτὸς τοῦ σώματος οὐκ οἶδα, ὁ θεὸς οἶδεν – ἁρπαγέντα τὸν τοιοῦτον ἕως τρίτου οὐρανοῦ. καὶ οἶδα τὸν τοιοῦτον ἄνθρωπον – εἴτε ἐν σώματι εἴτε χωρὶς τοῦ σώματος οὐκ οἶδα, ὁ θεὸς οἶδεν – ὅτι ἡρπάγη εἰς τὸν παράδεισον καὶ ἤκουσεν ἄρρητα ῥήματα ἃ οὐκ ἐξὸν ἀνθρώπῳ λαλῆσαι.
11 *De cer.* 668.14. See Cheynet (2003, 89); Guilland (1967, 2.192).
12 *LSJ ad loc.* B II.2.
13 τὸ μὲν γὰρ παραμυθεῖται τοῦ πάθους, τὸ δὲ καὶ ἐπελαφρύνει μερίζων ὥσπερ βάρος τὴν ψυχήν...Εὖ ἔχοις καὶ τὸ σῶμα καὶ τὴν ψυχήν...
14 *LSJ ad loc.* A. *Pathos* can also designate an emotion experienced as all but a physical thing.
15 One need only remember the use of *pascho*/πάσχω in civil law (e.g., *Prokheiros Nomos* 39.73: "The *aselgeis*, both the one doing it and the one *enduring it*, let them be punished by the sword" [Οἱ ἀσελγεῖς, ὅ τε ποιῶν καὶ ὁ πάσχων, ξίφει τιμωρείσθωσαν ...]), discussed in the introduction of this book.
16 *aporretoteron*/ἀπορρητοτέρων.
17 τὰ ἀπόρρητα, = τὰ αἰδοῖα, Plu.2.284a, cf. Ar.Ec.12, Longin. 43.5.
18 Ποθεινὴ γὰρ ἡμῖν καὶ αὕτη, καθάπερ καὶ τοῖς ἐρῶσι παρὰ τῶν ἐρωμένων ὕβρις τε καὶ πληγή... εἴτ' ἐπαινοίης, εἴτε κατηγοροίης καὶ διασύρειν ἐπιχειροίης, ἀρεστὰ ποιῶν καὶ ἀρκετὰ πρὸς παραμυθίαν, γράφοις μόνον...
19 Angelidi (2002, 228–229).
20 Ringrose (2003, 186–193); Tougher (2008, 60–66, 129).
21 See, e.g., Hopkins (1978), Long (1996), Kuefler (2001), or Patterson (1982).
22 There are many examples of negative talk against eunuchs to be found. Ringrose (2003) and Tougher (2008) have many, as does Messis (2014a).
23 At the end of the ninth century, *Novel 26* of Leo VI allowed eunuchs to adopt, while the same emperor's *Novel 98* reiterated that eunuchs were not allowed to wed (Noailles and Dain 1944, *ad loc.*; Macrides 1990, 111; Tougher 2008, 66; Messis 2014a, 100–104. Note: I believe Messis means *Novel 26* when he says *23*.).

24 A *quaistor* was a high official who would oversee legislation and, as judge, matters of family law and inheritance.
25 For more on calling eunuchs men/*andres* in the sources, which renders them hard to perceive, see Masterson (2019a, 397–400); Messis (2016, 199, 207).
26 Nikephoros Ouranos speaks of the soul "of the truly godly man, the *Parakoimomenos*" (τοῦ θείου ὡς ἀληθῶς ἀνδρὸς τοῦ παρακοιμωμένου). Messis (2014a, 210–212, cf. 2016, 202–203) also draws attention to a poem by John Geometres that treats Basil the *Parakoimomenos* in a fashion similar to the way Nikephoros does. Messis (2016, 203) sees a similar dynamic at work in the presentation of Ioseph Bringas in *Theophanes Continuatus*.
27 Ὁ δὲ ἀνὴρ οὗτος ἀξίωμα μέγιστον τῇ βασιλείᾳ Ῥωμαίων ἐτύγχανε γεγονὼς, κατά τε φρονήματος ὄγκον, καὶ σώματος μέγεθος, καὶ μορφὴν τυράννῳ προσήκουσαν...

Works Cited

Major Primary Sources

Ademarus Cabannensis. *Chronicon* (Bourgain et al. 1999)
Anastasios of Sinai, *Oratio in Psalmum VI* (*PG* 89)
Constantine VII Porphyrogennetos, *Letters* (Tziatzi-Papagianni 2012)
Eklogadion (Simon and Troianos 1977)
Ekloge (Burgmann 1983)
Epanagoge (Zepos and Zepos 1931)
Genesios, Ioseph, *On Imperial Reigns* (Lesmüller-Werner and Thurn 1978)
Greek Anthology (*TLG*)
Life of Mary the Younger (Delehaye and Peeters 1925, 692–705)
Life of Andrew the Fool (Rydén 1995)
Menander Rhetor (Race 2019)
New Testament (*TLG*)
Nikephoros Ouranos, *Letters* (Darrouzès 1960)
Niketas Stethatos, *Life of Saint Symeon the New Theologian/Vita Symeonis* (Greenfield 2013)
Philostratus the Elder, *Letter 10* (Benner and Fobes 1949)
Plato, *Symposium* (*TLG*)
Prayer D (Rapp 2016/Panagou 2010/Passarelli 1982)
Prokheiros Nomos (Zepos and Zepos 1931)
Psellos, *Chronographia* (Renauld 1967)
———. *Historia Syntomos* (Aerts 1990)
Pseudo-Symeon, *Chronographia/Chronicon* (Bekkerus 1838)
Septuagint (*TLG*)
Skylitzes, *Synopsis Historion* (*TLG*)
Skylitzes Manuscript ("*Madrid Skylitzes*"). Biblioteca Nacional, Madrid. http://bdh-rd.bne.es/viewer.vm?id=0000022766.
Suda (http://www.stoa.org/sol-entries and *TLG*)
Symeon the Logothete, *Chronographia/Chronicon*, first edition (Wahlgren 2006)
———. *Chronographia/Chronicon*, second edition (Istrin 1920, Bekkerus 1938, Featherstone 1998)
———. *Letters* (Darrouzès 1960)
Symeon the New Theologian, *Capita Theologica* (Darrouzès and Neyrand 1996)
———. *Catecheses* (Krivochéine and Paramelle 1963, 1964, 1965)
———. *Hymns* (Kambylis 1976)
———. *Orationes Ethicae* (Darrouzès 1967)

Theodoros Daphnopates, *Letters* (Darrouzès and Westerink 1978/*TLG*)
———. *Life of Basil* (Ševčenko 2011)
———. *Theophanes Continuatus* (Featherstone and Signes-Codoñer 2015)
Theodoros of Kyzikos, *Letters* (Tziatzi-Papagianni 2012)

Secondary Sources

Adontz, N. 1933. "L'âge et l'origine de l'empereur Basile I (867–86)." *Byzantion* 8: 475–500.
Aerts, W. J. 1990. *Michaelis Pselli Historia Syntomos*. Berlin.
Althaus-Reid, M. 2000. *Indecent Theology: Theological Perversions in Sex, Gender, and Politics*. London.
Amedroz, H. F., and D. S. Margoliouth. 1921. *The Eclipse of the Abbasid Caliphate: Original Chronicles of the Fourth Islamic Century*. Vol. IV. Oxford and London.
Angelidi, C. 2002. "Αισθήσεις, σεξουαλικότητα και οπτασίες." *Ανοχή και καταστολή στους Μέσους Χρόνους*. K. Nikolaou, ed. Athens. 221–229.
Angelova, D. 2019. "'Weaver of Tales': The Veroli Box and the Power of Eros in Byzantium." *Emotions and Gender in Byzantine Culture*. S. Constantinou and M. Meyer, eds. Cham, Switzerland. 191–244.
Angold, M. 1997. *The Byzantine Empire 1025–1204: A Political History*. New York, NY.
Arbagi, M. 1975. "The Celibacy of Basil II." *ByzSt* 2.1: 41–45.
Arranz, M. 1993. *I Penitenziali Bizantini: Il Protokanonarion o Kanonarion Primitivo di Giovanni Monaco e Diacono e il Deuterokanonarion o "Secondo Kanonarion" di Basilio Monaco*. Roma.
Bech, H. 1997. *When Men Meet: Homosexuality and Modernity*. T. Mesquit and T. Davies, trans. Chicago, IL.
Beck, H. -G. 1984. *Byzantinisches Erotikon: Orthodoxie, Literatur, Gesellschaft*. München.
———. 1965. "Byzantinisches Gefolgschaftswesen." *SBMünch* 5: 1–32.
Bekkerus, I. 1838. *Theophanes Continuatus: Ioannes Cameniata, Symeon Magister, Georgius Monachus*. Bonn.
Benner, A. R., and F. H. Fobes. 1949. *Alciphron, Aelian, and Philostratus: The Letters*. Cambridge, MA: Loeb Classical Library 383.
Betancourt, R. 2020. *Byzantine Intersectionality: Sexuality, Gender, and Race in the Middle Ages*. Princeton, NJ.
Boswell, J. 1995. *Same-Sex Unions in Premodern Europe*. New York.
Bourgain, P. et al., eds. 1999. *Ademarus Cabannensis (Adémar de Chabannes): Opera Omnia*. Turnhout.
Bray, A. 2003. *The Friend*. Chicago.
Brokkaar, W. G. 1972. "Basil Lacapenus. Byzantium in the 10th Century." *Studia Byzantina et Neohellenica Neerlandica*. W. F. Bakker et al., eds. Leiden. 199–234.
Brown, E. A. R. 1997. "Introduction." *Traditio* 52: 261–283.
Burgmann, L. 1983. *Ecloga: Das Gesetzbuch Leons III. und Constantine V*. Frankfurt am Main.
Caillet, J. -P. 1985. *L'Antiquité classique, le haut Moyen âge et Byzance au musée de Cluny*. Paris.
Cameron, A. 1993. *The Greek Anthology: From Meleager to Planudes*. New York, NY.
Cavallo, G. 2006. *Lire à Byzance*. Paris.
Chatterjee, P. 2013. "Vision, Transformation, and the Veroli Casket." *Oxford Art Journal* 36.3: 325–344.

Cheynet, J. -C. 2003. "Basil II and Asia Minor." *Byzantium in the Year 1000*. P. Magdalino, ed. Leiden. 71–108.

Conte, G. 1986. *The Rhetoric of Imitation: Genre and Poetic Memory in Virgil and Other Latin Poets*. Ithaca, NY.

Crostini, B. 1996. "The Emperor Basil II's Cultural Life." *Byzantion* 64: 55–80.

Cutler, A. 1997. "The Veroli Casket." *The Glory of Byzantium. Art and Culture of the Middle Byzantine Era A.D. 843–1261*. H. C. Evans and W. D. Wixom, eds. New York, NY. 230–231.

———. 1994. *The Hand of the Master: Craftsmanship, Ivory, and Society in Byzantium (9–11th centuries)*. Princeton, NJ.

———. 1984–1985. "On Byzantine Boxes." *JWalt* 42/43: 32–47.

Dain, A. 1937. *La "Tactique" de Nicéphore Ouranos*. Paris.

Darrouzès, J., ed. 1967. *Syméon le nouveau Théologien: Traités théologiques et éthiques*. Vol. 2. Paris.

———. 1966. *Syméon le nouveau Théologien: Traités théologiques et éthiques*. Vol. 1. Paris.

———. 1960. *Épistoliers byzantins du Xe siècle*. Paris.

Darrouzès, J., and L. Neyrand, eds. 1996. *Syméon le nouveau Théologien: Chapitres théologiques, gnostiques, et pratiques*. Paris.

Darrouzès, J., and L. G. Westerink. 1978. *Théodore Daphnopatès: Correspondance*. Paris.

Delehaye, H. and P. Peeters, eds. 1925. *Acta Sanctorum: Novembris, Tomus IV, Quo Dies nonus et decimus Continentur*. Bruxellis.

Demosthenous, A. 2004. Φιλία και ομοφυλοφυλία τον 11ο και 12ο αιώνα στο Βυζάντιο. Thessalonike.

Dinshaw, C. 1999. *Getting Medieval: Sexualities and Communities, Pre- and Postmodern*. Durham, NC.

Dmitrievskij, A. 1901/1965. *Opisanie liturgitseskich rukopisej*. Vol 2. Hildesheim.

Doan, L. 2013. *Disturbing Practices: History, Sexuality, and Women's Experience of Modern War*. Chicago, IL.

Duffy, J. 2018. "Authorship and the Letters of Theodore Daphnopates." *Reading in the Byzantine Empire and Beyond*. T. Shawcross and I. Toth, eds. Cambridge. 547–557.

Du Fresne, C., and S. Du Cange. 1688. *Glossarium ad scriptores mediae et infimae Graecitatis*. Lugduni. (http://ducange.enc.sorbonne.fr/)

Edmunds, L. 2001. *Intertextuality and the Reading of Roman Poetry*. Baltimore, MD.

Ermarth, E. D. 2007. "The Closed Space of Choice: A Manifesto on the Future of History." *Manifestos for History*. K. Jenkins et al., eds. London. 50–66.

Featherstone, J. M. 1998. "The Logothete Chronicle in Vat. gr. 163." *OCP* 64: 419–434.

Featherstone, M., and J. Signes-Codoñer. 2015. *Chronographiae quae Theophanis Continuati nomine fertur Libri I-IV (nuper repertis schedis Caroli de Boor adiuvantibus)*. Berlin.

Fowler, D. 2000. *Roman Constructions: Readings in Postmodern Latin*. Oxford.

Fradenburg, L. 1997. "'So that We May Speak of Them': Enjoying the Middle Ages." *New Literary History* 28.2: 205–230.

Fradenburg, L., and C. Freccero. 1996. "Preface" and "Caxton, Foucault, and the Pleasures of History." *Premodern Sexualities*. L. Fradenburg and C. Freccero, eds. New York. vii–xxiv.

Freccero, C. 2007. "Queer Spectrality: Haunting the Past." *A Companion to Lesbian, Gay, Bisexual, Transgender, and Queer Studies*. G. E. Haggerty and M. McGarry, eds. Malden, MA. 194–213.

Freeman, E. 2005. "Time Binds, or, Erotohistoriography." *Social Text* 23.3–4: 57–68.
Furley, W. D. 1996. *Andokides and the Herms: A Study of Crisis in Fifth-Century Athenian Religion*. London.
Garland, L. 1999a. "Basil II as Humorist." *Byzantion* 69.2: 321–343.
———. 1999b. *Byzantine Empresses: Women and Power in Byzantium, AD 527–1204*. New York.
Goar, J. 1730. *Euchologion, sive rituale Graecorum*. Venice.
Goldschmidt, A. and K. Weitzmann. 1930/1979. *Die byzantinischen Elfenbeinskulpturen des X.-XIII. Jahrhunderts*. Berlin.
Golitzin, A. 1997. *Symeon: On the Mystical Life: The Ethical Discourses*. Vol. 3. Crestwood, NY.
Greenfield, R. P. H. 2013. *Niketas Stethatos: The Life of Saint Symeon the New Theologian*. Cambridge, MA.
Grünbart, M. 2005. *Formen der Anrede im byzantinischen Brief vom 6. bis zum 12. Jahrhundert*. Vienna.
Guilland, R. 1967. *Recherches sur les institutions byzantines*. 2 vols. Berlin: Akademie-Verlag.
Hamel, D. 2012. *The Mutilation of the Herms: Unpacking an Ancient Mystery*. North Haven, CT.
Hanson, J. 1999. "Erotic Imagery on Byzantine Ivory Caskets." *Desire and Denial in Byzantium*. L. James, ed. Aldershot. 171–184.
Hatlie, P. 1996. "Redeeming Byzantine Epistolography." *BMGS* 20.1: 213–248.
Hausherr, I., and P. G. Horn. 1928. *Un grand mystique byzantin: Vie de Syméon le Nouveau Théologien (949–1022) par Nicétas Stéthatos*. Rome.
Hinds, S. 1998. *Allusion and Intertext: Dynamics of Appropriation in Roman Poetry*. Cambridge.
Høgel, C. 2002. *Symeon Metaphrastes: Rewriting and Canonization*. Copenhagen.
Holmes, C. 2006. "Constantinople in the Reign of Basil II." *Byzantine Style, Religion and Civilization: In Honour of Sir Steven Runciman*. E. Jeffreys, ed. Cambridge. 326–339.
———. 2005. *Basil II and the Governance of Empire (976–1025)*. Oxford.
———. 2003. "Political Elites in the Reign of Basil II." *Byzantium in the Year 1000*. P. Magdalino, ed. Leiden. 35–69.
Hopkins, K. 1978. *Conquerors and Slaves*. Cambridge.
Hunger, H. 1989. *Schreiben und Lesen in Byzanz: Die byzantinische Buchkultur*. München.
———. 1981. "The Classical Tradition in Byzantine Literature: The Importance of Rhetoric." *Byzantium and the Classical Tradition*. M. Mullett and R. Scott, eds. Birmingham. 35–47.
———. 1978. *Die Hochsprachliche Profane Literatur Der Byzantiner*. 2 vols. München.
———. 1969/1970. "On the Imitation (ΜΙΜΗΣΙΣ) of Antiquity in Byzantine Literature." *DOP* 23–24: 15–38.
Hussey, J. M. 1967. "Byzantine Monasticism." *CMH*. Vol. 4.2. Cambridge. 161–184.
Istrin, V. M. 1920. *Knigy Vremen'nyi͡a I Obraznyi͡a Geōrgii͡a Mnikha: Khronika Georgii͡a Amartola v Drevnem Slavii͡anorusskom Perevodii͡e: Tekst, Izslī́edovanīe I Slovar'*. Petrograd.
James, L. 2018. "Eros, Literature and the Veroli Casket." *Reading in the Byzantine Empire and Beyond*. T. Shawcross and I. Toth, eds. Cambridge. 397–413.

———. 2013. "'The World Turned Upside Down': Art and Subversion in Byzantium." *Power and Subversion in Byzantium*. D. Angelov and M. Saxby, eds. Burlington, VT. 105–119.
Jeffreys, M. 2008. "Literacy." *OHBS*. E. Jeffreys et al., eds. Oxford. 796–802.
Jenkins, R. J. H. 1963. "The Hellenistic Origins of Byzantine Literature." *DOP* 17: 37–52.
———. 1948. "Constantine VII's Portrait of Michael III." *Bulletin de la classe des lettres et des sciences morales et politiques. Académie Royale de Belgique*. Fifth ser. 34: 71–77.
Joannou, P. -P. 1963. *Discipline générale antique (IIe-IXe s.). Vol. II: Les canons des pères grecs*. Rome.
Kaldellis, A. 2021. "The Reception of Classical Literature and Ancient Myth." *The Oxford Handbook of Byzantine Literature*. S. Papaioannou, ed. Oxford. 62–179.
———. 1999. *The Argument of Psellos' Chronographia*. Leiden.
———, trans. and intr. 1998. *Genesios: On the Reigns of the Emperors (813–886)*. Canberra.
Kambylis, A. 1976. *Symeon Neos Theologos, Hymnen*. Berlin.
Karlin-Hayter, P. 1991. "L'enjeur d'une rumeur." *JÖB* 41: 85–111.
Karlsson, G. 1962. *Idéologie et cérémonial dans l'épistolographie byzantine*. Uppsala.
Kislinger, E. 1981. "Der junge Basileios I. und die Bulgaren." *JÖB* 30: 137–150.
Koschaker, P. 1974/1936. "Adoptio in Fratrem." *Studi in onore di Salvatore Riccobono nel XL anno del suo insegnamento*. G. Baviera et al., eds. Vol. 3. Palermo. 359–376.
Koukoules, P. 1955. "Τὰ οὐ Φωνητὰ τῶν Βυζαντινῶν." *Byzantinon Bios kai Politismos* 6: 505–539.
Krivochéine, B., and J. Paramelle, eds. and trans. 1965. *Syméon le nouveau Théologien: Catéchèses*. Vol. 3. Paris.
———. 1964. *Syméon le nouveau Théologien: Catéchèses*. Vol. 2. Paris.
———. 1963. *Syméon le nouveau Théologien: Catéchèses*. Vol. 1. Paris.
Krueger, D. 2011. "Between Monks: Tales of Monastic Companionship in Early Byzantium." *Journal of the History of Sexuality* 20.1: 28–61.
———. 2006. "Homoerotic Spectacle and the Monastic Body in Symeon the New Theologian." *Toward a Theology of Eros*. V. Burrus and C. Keller, eds. New York, NY. 99–118.
Kuefler, M. 2001. *The Manly Eunuch: Masculinity, Gender Ambiguity, and Christian Ideology in Late Antiquity*. Chicago, IL.
Kyriakidis, S. 1926. "Adelphopoiia." *Megalè Ellénikè Encyclopaideia*. Athènes. 569–570.
Laiou, A. E. 1992. *Mariage, Amour et parenté à Byzance aux XIe-XIIIe siècles*. Paris.
Laurent, V. 1962. "La chronologie des gouverneurs d'Antioche sous la seconde domination byzantine." *MUSJ* 38/10: 219–254.
Lemerle, P. 1986. *Byzantine Humanism: The First Phase*. H. Lindsay and A. Moffatt, trans. Canberra.
Lesmüller-Werner, A., and H. Thurn. 1978. *Iosephi Genesii Regum libri quattuor*. Berlin.
Levin, E. 1996. "Eastern Orthodox Christianity." *Handbook of Medieval Sexuality*. V. L. Bullough and J. A. Brundage, eds. New York, NY. 329–343.
Littlewood, A. R. 1988. "A Statistical Survey of the Incidence of Repeated Quotations in Selected Byzantine Letter Writers." *Gonimos, Neoplatonic and Byzantine*

Studies Presented to L. G. Westerink at 75. J. Duffy and J. Peradotto, eds. Buffalo, NY. 137–154.

———. 1976. "An 'Ikon of the Soul': The Byzantine Letter." *Visible Language* 10.3: 197–226.

Long, J. 1996. *Claudian's In Eutropium; Or How, When, and Why to Slander a Eunuch.* Chapel Hill, NC.

Macrides, R. J. 1992. "Dynastic Marriages and Political Kinship." *Byzantine Diplomacy.* J. Shepard and S. Franklin, eds. Aldershot. 263–280.

———. 1990. "Kinship by Arrangement: The Case of Adoption." *DOP* 44: 109–118.

Magdalino, P. 2003. 'The Year 1000 in Byzantium." *Byzantium in the Year 1000.* P. Magdalino, ed. Leiden. 233–270.

Maguire, H. 2004. "Other Icons: The Classical Nude in Byzantine Bone and Ivory Carvings." *JWalt* 62: 9–20.

———. 1999. "The Profane Aesthetic in Byzantine Art and Literature." *DOP* 53: 189–205.

Malherbe, A. 1988. *Ancient Epistolary Theorists.* Atlanta, GA.

Markopoulos, A. 2013. "Οι μεταμορφώσεις της 'μυθολογίας' του Βασιλείου Α΄." *Antecessor.* V. A. Leontaritou et al., eds. Athens. 945–970.

———. 2008. "Education." *OHBS.* E. Jeffreys et al., eds. Oxford. 785–795.

Masten, J. 2016. *Queer Philologies: Sex, Language, and Affect in Shakespeare's Time.* Philadelphia, PA.

Masterson, M. 2019a. "Nikephoros Ouranos, Eunuchism, and Masculinity during the Reign of Emperor Basil II." *Byzantion* 89: 397–419.

———. 2019b. "Revisiting the Bachelorhood of Basil II." *The Emperor in the Byzantine World.* S. Tougher, ed. London. 52–82.

———. 2018. "Dreams, Visions and Desire in the Letters of Emperor Konstantinos VII Porphyrogennetos and Theodoros of Kyzikos." *Dreams, Memory and Imagination in Byzantium.* B. Neil and E. Anagnostou-Laoutides, eds. Leiden. 136–159.

———. 2014. *Man to Man: Desire, Homosociality and Authority in Late-Roman Manhood.* Columbus.

McGeer, E. 1991. "Tradition and Reality in the 'Taktika' of Nikephoros Ouranos." *DOP* 45: 129–140.

McGeer, E., J. Nesbitt, and N. Oikonomides, eds. 2001. *DOCat.* Vol. 4. Washington, DC: Dumbarton Oaks Research Library and Collection.

McGuckin, J. 2005. "Symeon the New Theologian's Hymns of Divine Eros: A Neglected Masterpiece of the Christian Mystical Tradition." *Spiritus* 5.2: 182–202, 225.

———. 1996. "Symeon the New Theologian and Byzantine Monasticism." *Mount Athos and Byzantine Monasticism.* A. Bryer and M. Cunningham, eds. Aldershot. 17–35.

Mercati, S. G. 1950. "Versi di Niceforo Uranos in morte di Simeone Metafraste." *AB* 68: 126–134.

Messis, C. 2016. "Les voix littéraires des eunuques: Genre et identité du soi à Byzance." *DOP* 70: 191–207.

———. 2014a. *Les eunuques à Byzance, entre réalité et imaginaire.* Paris.

———. 2014b. "Fluid Dreams, Solid Consciences: Dreams in Byzantium." *Dreaming in Byzantium and Beyond.* C. Angelidi and G. Calofonos, eds. Burlington, VT: Ashgate. 187–205.

———. 2008. "Des amitiés intimes à l'institution d'un lien social: l' 'adelphopoiia' à Byzance." *Corrispondenza d'amorosi sensi: L'omoerotismo nella letteratura medievale.* P. Odorico and N. Pasero, eds. Alessandria. 31–64.

———. 2006. "La construction sociale, les "réalités" rhétoriques et les représentations de l'identité masculine à Byzance." Doctoral Dissertation: Centre d'études byzantines, néo-helléniques et sud-est européennes.
Messis, C., and S. Papaioannou. 2021. "Memory: Selection, Citation, Commonplace." *The Oxford Handbook of Byzantine Literature*. S. Papaioannou, ed. Oxford. 132–161.
Michaelides-Nuaros, G. 1952. "Περὶ τῆς ἀδελφοποιΐας ἐν τῇ ἀρχαίᾳ Ἑλλάδι καὶ ἐν τῷ Βυζαντίῳ." *Τόμος Κωνσταντίνου Ἁρμενοπούλου*. Thessalonike 251–313.
Mills, R. 2006. "Queer Is Here? Lesbian, Gay, Bisexual and Transgender Histories and Public Culture." *History Workshop Journal* 62: 253–263.
Moffatt, A., and M. Tall. 2012. *Constantine Porphyrogennetos: The Book of Ceremonies*. 2 vols. Canberra.
Moravcsik, G. 1961. "Sagen und Legenden über Kaiser Basileios I." *DOP* 15: 59–126.
Morris, R. 1995. *Monks and Laymen in Byzantium, 843–1118*. Cambridge.
Morris, S. 2016. *"When Brothers Dwell in Unity": Byzantine Christianity and Homosexuality*. Jefferson, NC.
Mullett, M. 2008. "Epistolography." *OHBS*. E. Jeffreys et al., eds. Oxford. 882–893.
———. 2003. "The Detection of Relationship in Middle Byzantine Texts: The Case of Letters and Letter Networks." *L'épistolographie et la poésie épigrammatique: Projets actuels et questions de méthodologie*. W. Hörandner and M. Grünbart, eds. Paris. 63–74.
———. 1999. "From Byzantium, with Love." *Desire and Denial in Byzantium*. L. James, ed. Aldershot. 3–22.
———. 1997. *Theophylacht of Ochrid: Reading the Letters of a Byzantine Archbishop*. Aldershot.
———. 1995. "Originality in the Byzantine Letter: The Case of Exile." *Originality in Byzantine Literature, Art and Music*. A. R. Littlewood, ed. Oxford. 39–58.
———. 1988. "Byzantium: A Friendly Society?" *Past and Present* 118: 3–24.
———. 1981. "The Classical Tradition in the Byzantine Letter." *Byzantium and the Classical Tradition*. M. Mullett and R. Scott, eds. Oxford. 75–93.
Nallino, C. A. 1974/1936. "Intorno al divieto romano imperiale dell'affratellamento e ad alcuni paralleli arabi." *Studi in onore di Salvatore Riccobono nel XL anno del suo insegnamento*. Vol. 3. G. Baviera et al., eds. Palermo. 321–357.
Nesbitt, J., and N. Oikonomidès, eds. 1996. *DOSeals*. Vol. 3. Washington DC.
Nilsson, I. 2006. "To Narrate the Events of the Past: On Byzantine Historians, and Historians on Byzantium." *Byzantine Narrative: Papers in honour of Roger Scott*. J. Burke et al., eds. Melbourne. 47–58.
Noailles, P., and A. Dain. 1944. *Les novelles de Léon VI le Sage*. Paris.
Odorico, P. 1995. "L'indicible transgression." *Ordnung und Aufruhr im Mittelalter*. M. T. Fögen, ed. Frankfurt am Main. 301–312.
Oikonomidès, N. 1972. *Les listes de préséance byzantines des IXe et Xe siècles*. Paris.
Oschema, K. 2006. "Blood-Brothers: A Ritual of Friendship and the Construction of the Imagined Barbarian in the Middle Ages." *JMedHist* 32.3: 275–301.
Ostrogorsky, G. 1968. *History of the Byzantine state*. trans. J. Hussey. Oxford.
Otto, E. 1732. *De Jurisprudentia symbolica exercitationum trias*. Utrecht.
Panagou, C. 2013. "The Rite of Adelphopoeia: A Fresh Look at the Evidence." *Eastern Christian Studies* 18: 1–9.
———. 2010. *Η αδελφοποίηση· Ακολουθία ευχολογίου*. Athens.
Papaioannou, S. 2021. "Authors (With an Excursus on Symeon Metaphrastes)." *The Oxford Handbook of Byzantine Literature*. S. Papaioannou, ed. Oxford. 483–524.

212 Works Cited

———. ed. 2021. *The Oxford Handbook of Byzantine Literature*. Oxford.

———. 2012. "Fragile Literature: Byzantine Letter-Collections and the Case of Michael Psellos." *La face cachée de la littérature byzantine*. P. Odorico, ed. Paris. 289–328.

——— 2010a. "The Aesthetics of History: From Theophanes to Eustathios." *History as Literature in Byzantium*. R. J. Macrides, ed. Burlington, VT. 3–21.

———. 2010b. "Letter-Writing." *The Byzantine World*. P. Stephenson, ed. London. 188–199.

Parenti, S., and E. Velkovska. 2011. *L'Eucologio Barberini gr. 336*. Omsk.

Passarelli, G. 1982. *L'Eucologio Cryptense Γ. β. VII*. Thessalonika.

Patterson, O. 1982. *Slavery and Social Death*. Cambridge, MA.

Patlagean, E. 1985. "Byzance Xe-XIe." *Histoire de la vie privée. 1. De l'empire romain à l'an mil*. P. Ariès and G. Duby, eds. Paris. 547–627.

———. 1982 (1946). "Christianization and Ritual Kinship in the Byzantine Area." *Ritual, Religion, and the Sacred*. R. Forster and O. A. Ranum, eds. E. Forster and P. M. Ranum, trans. Baltimore, MD. 81–94.

Paverd, F. 2006. *The Kanonarion by John, Monk and Deacon and Didascalia Patrum*. Rome.

Pitsakis, K. 2008. "L'homoérotisme dans la culture byzantine: le cadre normatif et ses reflets littéraires." *Corrispondenza d'amorosi sensi: L'omoerotismo nella letteratura medievale*. P. Odorico and N. Pasero, eds. Alessandria. 1–29.

———. 2006. "Parentés en dehors de la parenté: Formes de parenté d'origine extra-législative en droit byzantin et post-byzantin." *Parenté et societé dans le monde grec de l'antiquité à l'âge moderne*. A. Bresson et al., eds. Paris. 297–325.

———. 2000. "Législation et stratégies matrimoniales: Parenté et empêchements de mariage dans le droit byzantin." *L'Homme* 154/155: 677–696.

———. 1993. "'Η Θέση των Ομοφυλοφίλων στη Βυζαντινή Κοινωνία." *Οι Περιθωριακοί στο Βυζάντιο*. C. Maltezou, ed. Athens. 171–269.

Poliakoff, M. B. 1981. "Studies in the Terminology of the Greek Combat Sports." Doctoral Dissertation: The University of Michigan.

Pott, T. 1996. "La 'Prière pour faire des frères' de l'Euchologe slave du Sinai (Xe siècle): Essai d'approche théologique." *Studia Monastica* 38.2: 269–289.

Puchner, W. 1994. "Griechisches zur *adoptio in fratrem*." *Südost-Forschungen* 53: 187–224.

Race, W. H. 2019. *Menander Rhetor, Dionysius of Halicarnassus: Menander Rhetor. Dionysius of Halicarnassus, Ars Rhetorica*. Cambridge, MA.

Rapp, C. 2016. *Brother-Making in Late Antiquity and Byzantium: Monks, Laymen and Christian Ritual*. New York, NY.

———. 1997. "Ritual Brotherhood in Byzantium." *Traditio* 52: 285–326.

Renauld, É. 1967. *Michel Psellos: Chronographie ou histoire d'un siècle de Byzance (976–1077)*. Vol. 1. Paris.

Rhalle, G. A. and M. Potle. 1854. *Syntagma tōn theōn kai hierōn kanonōn tōn te hagiōn kai paneuphēmōn Apostolōn, kai tōn hierōn oikoumenikōn kai topikōn Synodōn, kai tōn kata meros hagiōn Paterōn*. Volume 4. Athens.

Rhalle, K. 1909. "Περὶ Ἀδελφοποιίας." *Ἐπιστημονικὴ Ἐπετηρίς Γ (1906–1907)*. Athens. 293–306.

Richlin, A. 1992. *The Garden of Priapus: Sexuality and Aggression in Roman Humor*. New York.

Ringrose, K. M. 2003. *The Perfect Servant: Eunuchs and the Social Construction of Gender in Byzantium*. Chicago, IL.
Rohy, V. 2006. "Ahistorical." *GLQ: A Journal of Lesbian and Gay Studies* 12.1: 61–83.
Rydén, L. 1995. *The Life of Saint Andrew the Fool*. Uppsala.
Schneider, J. 2008. "L'Expression hyperbolique de l'amitié dans les lettres d'un moine byzantin." *Queer: Ecritures de la différence? Volume 1: Autres temps, autres lieux*. P. Zoberman, ed. Paris, France. 79–101.
Schreiner, P. 1991. "Réflexions sur la famille impériale à Byzance (VIIIe-Xe siècles)." *Byzantion* 61: 181–193.
Scott, J. W. 2007. "History-Writing as Critique." *Manifestos for History*. K. Jenkins et al., eds. London. 19–38.
Sedgwick, E. K. 2003. "Paranoid Reading and Reparative Reading, or, You're So Paranoid, You Probably Think this Essay is about You." *Touching Feeling: Affect, Pedagogy, Performativity*. Durham, NC. 123–151.
———. 1990. *Epistemology of the Closet*. Berkeley, CA.
Ševčenko, I. 2011. *Chronographiae quae Theophanis continuati nomine fertur liber quo Vita Basilii Imperatoris amplectitur (Vita Basilii)*. Berlin.
Ševčenko, I., and C. Mango, eds. 1975. *Byzantine Books and Bookmen*. Washington, DC.
Sewter, E. R. A., trans. 1953. *Fourteen Byzantine Rulers: The Chronographia of Michael Psellus*. New York, NY.
Shaw, B. D. 1997. "Ritual Brotherhood in Roman and Post-Roman Societies." *Traditio* 52: 327–355.
Shepard, J. 2003. "Marriages towards the Millenium." *Byzantium in the Year 1000*. P. Magdalino, ed. Leiden. 1–33.
Shopland, N. 2018. "Belated Vindication for John Boswell." *Gay & Lesbian Review Worldwide* 25.3: 26–28.
Sidéris, G. 2008. "L'*adelphopoièsis* aux VIIe-Xe siècles à Byzance: Une forme de fraternité jurée." *Oralité et lien social au Moyen Âge (Occident, Byzance, Islam)*. M.-F Auzépy and G. Saint-Guillain, eds. Paris. 281–292.
Sifonas, C. S. 1994. "Basile II et l'aristocratie byzantine." *Byzantion* 64: 118–133.
Simon, D., and S. N. Troianos, 1977. "Eklogadion und Ecloga privata aucta." *FM II*: 45–86.
Simon, E. 1964. "Nonnos und das Elfenbeinkätschen aus Veroli." *JDAI* 79: 279–336.
Smythe, D. C. 1999. "In Denial: Same-Sex Desire in Byzantium." *Desire and Denial in Byzantium*. L. James, ed. Aldershot. 139–148.
Spiegel, G. 1990. "History, Historicism, and the Social Logic of the Text in the Middle Ages." *Speculum* 65.1: 59–86.
Steckel, S. et al., eds. 2014. *Networks of Learning: Perspectives on Scholars in Byzantine East and Latin West, c. 1000–1200*. Berlin.
Stephenson, P. 2003. *The Legend of Basil the Bulgar-slayer*. Cambridge.
Stockton, W. 2011. *Playing Dirty: Sexuality and Waste in Early Modern Comedy*. Minneapolis, MN.
Svoronos, N., ed. and trans. 1994. *Les novelles des empereurs macédoniens concernant la terre et les stratiotes*. Athens.
Talbot, A. -M. 1996. *Holy Women of Byzantium: Ten Saints' Lives in English Translation*. Washington, DC.

Works Cited

Talbot, A. -M., and D. F. Sullivan. 2005. *The History of Leo the Deacon: Byzantine Military Expansion in the Tenth Century.* Washington, DC.

Tamassia, G. 1886. *L'Affratellamento (ΑΔΕΛΦΟΠΟΙΙΑ) Studio storico-giuridico.* Torino.

Tobias, N. 1969. "Basil I (867–886), the Founder of the Macedonian Dynasty: A Study of the Political and Military History of the Byzantine Empire in the Ninth Century." Dissertation. New Brunswick: Rutgers.

Tomadakis, N. 1969/1993. *Βυζαντινή Επιστολογραφία.* Thessalonica.

Tougher, S. 2013. "Imperial Families: The Case of the Macedonians (867–1056)." *Approaches to the Byzantine Family.* L. Brubaker and S. Tougher, eds. Burlington, VT. 303–326.

———. 2010a. "*Cherchez l'Homme*! Byzantine Men: A Eunuch Perspective." *The Byzantine World.* P. Stephenson, ed. London. 83–91.

———. 2010b. "Having Fun in Byzantium." *A Companion to Byzantium.* L. James, ed. Malden, MA. 135–145.

———. 2008. *The Eunuch in Byzantine History and Society.* New York.

———. 1999. "Michael III and Basil the Macedonian." *Desire and Denial in Byzantium.* L. James, ed. Aldershot. 149–158.

Treadgold, W. 2013. *The Middle Byzantine Historians.* New York.

———. 1997. *A History of the Byzantine State and Society.* Stanford, CA.

Troianos, S. 1997. "Έρως και νόμος στο Βυζάντιο." *Έγκλημα και τιμωρία στο Βυζάντιο.* S. Troianos, ed. Athens. 173–201.

———. 1993. "Τύποι ερωτικής 'επικοινωνίας' στις Βυζαντινές νομικές πηγές." *Η επικοινωνία στο Βυζάντιο.* N. G. Moschonas, ed. Athens. 237–273.

———. 1989. "Kirchliche und weltliche Rechtsquellen zur Homosexualität in Byzanz." *JÖB* 39: 29–48.

———. 1980. *Ὁ «Ποινάλιος» τοῦ Ἐκλογαδίου (Συμβολὴ εἰς τὴν ἱστορίαν τῆς ἐξελίξεως τοῦ ποινικοῦ δικαίου ἀπὸ τοῦ Corpus Iuris Civilis μέχρι τῶν Βασιλικῶν).* Frankfurt am Main.

Turner, H. J. M. 1990. *St. Symeon: The New Theologian and Spiritual Fatherhood.* Leiden.

Tziatzi-Papagianni, M. 2012. *Theodori Metropolitae Cyzici Epistulae: Accedunt Epistulae Mutuae Constantini Porphyrogeniti.* Berlin.

Van Opstall, E. M. 2008. *Jean Géomètre: Poèmes en hexamètres et en distiques élégiaques.* Leiden.

Vinson, M. P. 1985. *The Correspondence of Leo, Metropolitan of Synada and Syncellus.* Washington, DC.

Vogt, A. 1935–1939. *Constantin VII Porphyrogénète: Le Livre Des Cérémonies.* Paris.

Wahlgren, S. 2006. *Symeonis Magistri et Logothetae Chronicon.* Berlin.

Webb, R. 1999a. "The Aesthetics of Sacred Space: Narrative, Metaphor, and Motion in 'Ekphraseis' of Church Buildings." *DOP* 53: 59–74.

———. 1999b. "Ekphrasis Ancient and Modern: The Invention of a Genre." *Word & Image* 15.1: 7–18.

Weitzmann, K. 1951. *Greek Mythology in Byzantine Art.* Princeton, NJ.

Weller, A. 2014. "Imagining Pre-Modern Imperialism: The Letters of Byzantine Imperial Agents outside the Metropole." Doctoral Dissertation. Rutgers.

Williamson, P. 2010. *Medieval Ivory Carvings: Early Christian to Romanesque.* London.

Wolff, R. L. 1978. "How the News Was Brought from Byzantium to Angoulême; or, the Pursuit of the Hare in an Ox Cart." *BMGS* 4: 139–189.

Wortley, J., comm. and trans. 2010. *John Skylitizes: A Synopsis of Byzantine History, 811–1057.* New York.

Zeikowitz, R. 2003. *Homoeroticism and Chivalry: Discourses of Male Same-Sex Desire in the Fourteenth Century.* New York.

Zepos, I. D., and P. I. Zepos. 1931. *Jus Graecoromanum II. Leges Imperatorum Isaurorum et Macedonum.* Athens.

Index

Note: *Italic* page numbers refer to figures and page numbers followed by "n" denote endnotes.

Achilles 93, 98
adelphopoiesis 9, 16, 17, 67, 71, 108, Chapter 3 *passim*, 193–199, 200; hand on hand at ritual 138, *139*; kissing 138, *139*; liturgies for 135–139; Prayers A 138, 155–156; B 137, 138; C 138, 156–157; D 139–153; E 139, 157–158; H 139, 158–159; I 138, 157; K 138, 156
Ademarus Cabannensis (Adémar de Chabannes) 170, 172–173, 184
agape 14, 27, 29, 73–74, 83, 144, 145, 146, 148, 150–151, 200; *agape vs. eros vs.* 74; *see also* love; "over-love" (*huperagapao*)
Althaus-Reid, M. 9–11
anal sex 11–12, 13, 14, 49, 78–79, 81, *82*, 88, 102, 103
Anastasios of Sinai 176–177
Aphrodite 3, 8, 28, 29, 30, 31, 33, 34, 37, 96, 198
Apocalypse (NT) 44–45
aporretalos 37, 197, 198
Arbagi, M. 172, 173
Aristophanes 36–37, 51–52, 80
arrenomania 13
arsenokoitia 13
asceticism 170, 172
asekretis 26, 50
aselges/aselgeia 11–12, 88, 89, 101, 102, 103, 104
Asstown (Koloneia) 103

Baanes (*Life of Mary the Younger*) 13–14, 134
backsides, male 42, *72*, 96, 100, 101–107
Bardanes Tourkos 75

Bardas Bratzes (*Life of Mary the Younger*) 14, 29
Bardas Phokas 169, 170–171, 181
Bardas Skleros 169, 180; advice to Basil II not to marry 171, 172, 184
Basil I (Emperor) 15–16, 24, 25, 50, Chapter 2 *passim*, 70, *82*, 86, *91*, *129*, 150, 153–154, 175
Basil II (Emperor) 1, 6, 15, 16–17, 50, Chapter 4 *passim*
Basil of Caesarea 12–13
Basil Ouranos 24, *25*, 26, 27, 28, 32, 197
Basil the *Parakoimomenos* 169, 179, 180, 199–200
Basilikinos 71, *72*, 75, 85–89, *86*, 175
Basiliskianos *see* Basilikinos
baths 123, 125, 126, 128
beard 8, 35, 36, 105, 139, 199, 200
beauty 2–4, 14, 16, 27, 29, 49, 69, 73, 74, 75–76, 83, 85, 87–89, 93, 107, 121, 134, 138–139, 141, 144, 146, 149, 180, 194, 195, 198, 200–201
bestiality 78–79, 96, *96*, 98
biting 41–42, 44, 46, 47, 48, 149–150
brotherly affection (*philadelphia*) 144

canon law 4, 5, 5–6, 12–13, 32, 122, 200-201
children, three in the furnace 143, 144, 151
Chiron 93, 98
civil law (Byzantine) 11–12, 15, 32, 88, 102, 104, 125, 200-201
Constantine, a ritual brother to Basil I 135
Constantine Kephalas 7

218 Index

Constantine VII Porphyrogennetos (Emperor) 15, 24, *25*, 38–39, 67, 68, 149, 153, 179; *Letter B3* (collection of Theodoros of Kyzikos) *25*, 41–46, 53, 122
Corinthians, 1 (NT) 143, 145
Corinthians, 2 (NT) 143, 145, 148, 194, 196–199
Cornutus 36
Crostini, B. 171–172, 184

Danelis 71, 128–135; "Mother of the Emperor" 71, 134
Daniel 143
Daniel (Septuagint) 143
Darrouzès, J. 174, 181
De Ceremoniis 39, 149, 197
Dejanira 98
Diogenes of Sinope 124–125
Diogenes Laertius 36
Dmitrievskij, A. 136, 137, 138
Double-entendre (sexual) 7, 8–9, 46, 47, 48, 52, 75, 79, 80, 103, 123, 124, 126, 134, 152
doux 1
doxology 137, 140, 144, 145

eagle 69, *72*, 90–101
Eklogadion 12
Ekloge 11–12
ektene 136, 137–138, 139
enupnion 39–40
Epanagoge 12
eparch(os) 26, 30, 199
Ephesians (NT) 147–148
epistolography 24, 25–26, 32–33
eramai 74, 76
erastes (erastai) 2, 41, 42
eromenos (eromenoi) 1–2, 41, 42–43, 45
eros/Eros/Erotes 2, 4, 8, 28, 29, 30, 31, 33, 34, 37, 41, 42, 43, 45–46, 74, 87–88, 93, 96, 98, 100, 102–103, 104, 124, 125; *eros vs. agape* 74
euchologia see adelphopoiesis, liturgies for
Eudokia Ingerina 69, 71, 74, 77, 87, 89, 179, 180
eunuch 1, 15, 17, 32, 105, 169, 174, 193, 199–200
euphuia (handsomeness/good disposition) 193, 195
Europa 96, 98, 124
Exodus (Septuagint) 146–147

Father Mario 10–11
flame, dew-shedding 150, 151
flatulence *72*, 101–107
flowers 3, 6, 7, 8, 28, 33, 41, 47, 48, 93, 98, 139, 141, 144, 145, 146, 148, 149, 150, 151, 153, 154

Ganymede 73, 93–101
Garland, L. 171, 184
Genesios, Ioseph 67, 68, 69; *On Imperial Reigns* Chapter 2 *passim*, *72*
Genesis (Septuagint) 141, 144
Goar, J. 136, 137, 138
Graces 7, 28, 29, 33, 51, 52
Greek Anthology 7–8, 42–43, 47–48, 48–49, 100, 124
Gregory Nazianzenus 5
Gregory of Nyssa 5, 12–13
Grullos 102, 103, 105, 106

hedone 46, 150, 194, 195, 198
Herakles 28, 31, 33, 98, 104
Herm *35*, 35–38
Hermes, "Laborer of the Night" 30, 31, 34–35; "whispering" 37–38, 53
Hesiod 27
hetaireia 71, 73, 74–76, 77, 89, 102, 104, 107, 121, 134
Himerios 103–104
Holmes, C. 171
Homer 8–9, 39–40
homosociality 7, 9, 15, 16, 17, 24, 27, 32, 33, 50, 67, 69, 75, 76, 102, 104, 106, 107, 108, 121–122, 127, 132, 134, 140, 153, 154, 170, 173, 183, 184, 193, 199, 200; *see also hetaireia*; *phatria*
horse, to be tamed 71, *72*, 77–79
Hupar (waking vision) 39, 40–41, 46, 51, 52–53
hupnos (slumber) 38

Ignatios, Patriarch 103, 105
indeterminacy 5, 6, 15
intertextuality 3, 4–5, 6, 7–8, 9, 15, 24, 25, 29, 33, 42, 43, 50, 52, 78–79, 81, 104, 106–107, 123–125, 126, 128, 131–135, 146–153, 154, 175, 196–199
invocation 137, 140, 144
ivory caskets, Byzantine 93

John (NT) 141, 144
John the Faster 12–13

Index 219

John, a ritual brother to Basil I (not son of Danelis) 135
John, friend/brother to Paulos *Krites* 194, 195, 196
John, son of Danelis and ritual brother to Basil I 71, *72*, 128–135
Julian, Emperor 40–41

Kalokyres Delphinas 181
keeper of the imperial inkstand 68, 108n6
kiss(ing) 41, 42, 46, 93, 136, 138, 139, 152, 175, 176
Koloneia *see* Asstown
kourator 1
Krites 1
Krueger, D. 176

Laiou, A. 12
Leo VI, Emperor 100, 133, 199
Leviticus (Septuagint) 78–79
Life of Basil 24, *25*, 26, Chapter 2 passim, 68, 69, *72*, 101, 128–135, 195
Life of Mary the Younger 13–15, 29, 126, 134, 200
Logothete 26, 53n3
love (*agape*) 139–153
Luke (NT) 131, 132, 143, 144, 145, 176

Madrid Skylitzes 70, 79, 81, *82*, 85, *86*, *91*, 121, 128, *129*, *133*
magistros 50, 77, 149, 180
Marcian, Emperor 92
Mark (NT) 131–132, 134
marriage, importance of 179–180
masturbation 13, 31, 48, 125, 128
Matthew (NT) 123–124, 143, 144
Maurice, Emperor and Bandit 176–177
Meleager 8
men, three in the furnace 143, 144, 151
Menander Rhetor 29–30, 33–34
Michael, Lord 193–196
Michael II, Emperor 179
Michael III, Emperor 15, 67, 68, 69, 71, 85–90, 101–107
Michael Ouranos 197
Mr. X 193–196
Mr. Y 193–196
Musée Cluny casket 98–99, *99*
mutilation of the herms 37
myrrh 8, 138–139, 147, 151, 152, 153

Nero 87–88
Nessus 98
Nicholas, Metropolitan of Neokaisareia 6–7
Nicholas, ritual brother to Basil I 71, *72*, 74–75, 122–128, 135, 150, 153, 175
Nikephoros (*Life of Mary the Younger*) 14, 29
Nikephoros Ouranos 1, 24, *25*, 26, 50; *Letter 5* 199; *Letter 26* 6–9, *25*, 122, 153, 200; *Letter 29* 17, *25*, 193–199; *Letter 44* 1–4, *25*; *Letter 50* 153

Odorico, P. 32–33
oikonomos 71, 135
oneiron/oneiros (dream) 39–40, 41, 46, 47, 48, 51
over-love (*huperagapao*) 175–177, 180–181, 182–183, 184–185

paideia 2, 4–5, 7, 9, 39, 51, 76
Panagou, C. 136, 138, 143
Pathos 31–32, 34, 198
patrikios 26, 30, 68, 77, 85, 103, 149, 197
Paul, the Apostle 37
Paulos, a ritual brother to Basil I (not son of Danelis) 135
Paulos (*Krites*), friend/brother to Nikephoros Ouranos 1–2, 4, 193–199
pederasty 1–3, 42–43, 45, 47, 93, 100–101, 177
penitentials 12–13; *see also* canon law
Phagoura, Christopher 174, 184
phatria 73, 75, 102, 103, 104, 105, 107
philia/friendship 28, 41, 42, 43, 45–46, 48, 193
Philippians (NT) 7, 147
Philostratus the Elder, *Letter 10* 3–4
philtron 2, 73
Photios 100
ploughing 14, 124, 134
Plutarch 34
podreza 83
pothos 2, 73, 150, 182–183, 200
pouch and staff 123–125, 128
Prokheiros Nomos 12
Prokopios 92
prostitute 10, 103, 104, 126, 127, 177
protoasekretis 26, 50
protospatharios 1, 26, 27, 30, 71, 134, 135
protostates see protostrator
protostrator 73, 76, 78, 79

Index

Proverbs (Septuagint) 7, 52, 126–127, 150, 152, 175
Psalms (Septuagint) 7, 42, 43, 131, 132, 138–139, 143, 145, 176
Psellos 170; depiction of Basil II 170–172, 173, 184, 199–200
Pseudo-Symeon 67, 68, 69; *Chronographia* Chapter 2 *passim*, 68, 69, *72*, 122–128, 135

Rapp, C. 136, 137, 138, 139, 140
rebel and emperor of Christians *see* Symeon the New Theologian at "carnal parable"
rejoicing 7, 40, 41, 42, 46, 47, 48, 51, 52, 123, 126, 127–128, 150, 152, 153, 156, 175, 194, 195, 196, 198
reparative reading 4, 5–6, 9, 15, 17, 24, 26, 53, 67, 153, 193, 199–200, 201
request 137, 140, 144
Romanos I Lekapenos, Emperor 38, 69, 169, 179
Romanos Skleros 180–181
Romans (NT) 73, 102, 104, 106–107
rose and thorn(s) 41, 42–43, 45

St. Mamas monastery 174, 176, 181, 182, 183
same-sex desire 2–4, 4, 5, 6, 7, 9, 11, 12, 13–14, 15, 16, 24, 26, 27, 33, 53, 67, 69, 73, 75, 76, 79, 85, 89, 101, 103, 104, 107–108, 121, 152, 153, 169–170, 172, 173, 174, 176, 177, 178, 183, 184–185, 193, 198, 200–201
Samuel, 2 (Septuagint) 182
Sicilian Expedition 37
Sirach (Septuagint) 44, 147
Skleroi, the 179
Skylitzes, John 81, 171, 180–181
smell (*osme*) 146–152
Sodom 143
sodomite 177
sodomy 178
Song of Songs (Septuagint) 151–153
spatharokoubikoularios 174
Strato 7–8
Suda 36, 37, 38–39, 39–41, 46, 92, 100–101, 151
sumpleko 80–81
sunetheia 14, 28–29
sunkellos 71, 135
sweet scent (*euodia*) 47, 48, 139, 140, 141, 143, 144, 145, 146–151, 153, 154
sword, two-edged 41, 43–45
Symeon Eulabes 174, 181

Symeon the Logothete 15, 24, *25*, 49–50, 67, 68; *Chronographia* 24–25, *25*, 50, 52, Chapter 2 *passim*, 68, 69, *72*, 122–128, 135; *Letter 96 25*, 50; *Letter 110* 25; *Letter 111* 25, *25*, 50–53, 80, 150; Metaphrastes 49–50
Symeon the New Theologian 16–17, 169–170, 174, 183–184, 199; carnal parable 174–177, 201; *Capita Theologica* 182–183; *Catecheses* 174, 182; *Hymns* 177–178; *Oratio Ethica* 10 174–177, 178, 181–182, 184
Symposium (Plato) 3, 51–52, 80–81, 83

Thaumazo see wonder
Theodora, Empress 90, 102, 105, 106
Theodoros (*Life of Mary the Younger*) 13–14, 134
Theodoros Daphnopates 15, *25*, 26, 67, 68, *72*, 76; *Letter 17* 24, *25*, 30–38, 52, 53, 197, 198; *Letter 18* 24, *25*, 27–30, 197; *Letter 31* 24, *25*, 27, 197
Theodoros of Kyzikos 24, *25*, 38, 39; *Letter A2 25*, 150–151; *Letter A30 25* (discussion cut in late draft); *Letter B3* (by Constantine VII) *25*, 41–46, 53, 122; *Letter B4 25*, 46–49, 53, 122, 149–150; *Letter 109* (in Symeon the Logothete's collection) 25
Theodoros the Studite 12, 13
Theophanes Continuatus 24, *25*, 26, 68, 69, *72*, 85, 87, 88, 89, 90, 102, 104–105, 179
Theophanes the Confessor 68, 92
Theophano 169, 179, 180
Theophilidion *see* Theophilitzes
Theophiliskos *see* Theophilitzes
Theophilitzes 71, *72*, 73, 74–76, 77, 78, 79, 89, 100, 128, 130, 134, 195
third heaven 196–199
Thucydides 37
Tougher, S. 172
tumescence 7, 8, 31, 34, 49, 134, 152
tzangia 87, 88

Veroli Casket 93–98, *94*, *95*, *96*, *97*

whipping/scourging, ritual 71, *72*, 84
Wolff, R. L. 173
wonder (in forms related to *thaumazo*) 27, 73, 76, 77, 90, 104, 143, 145, 193, 195, 198
wrestling (grappling) 71, *72*, 79–84

Zeus 73, 93–101